Social research methodology

Also by Roger Gomm

Evaluating Research in Health and Social Care (co-edited with G. Needham and
A. Bullman)
Case Study Research: Key Issues, Key Texts (co-edited with M. Hammersley and
P. Woods)

Social research methodology

a critical introduction

Roger Gomm

palgrave
macmillan

First published 2004 by
PALGRAVE MACMILLAN
Houndmills, Basingstoke, Hampshire RG21 6XS and
175 Fifth Avenue, New York, N.Y. 10010
Companies and representatives throughout the world

PALGRAVE MACMILLAN is the global academic imprint of Palgrave
Macmillan division of St. Martin's Press LLC and of Palgrave Macmillan Ltd.
Macmillan® is a registered trademark in the United States, United Kingdom
and other countries. Palgrave is a registered trademark in the European
Union and other countries

ISBN 0–333–63728–3

This book is printed on paper suitable for recycling and made from fully
managed and sustained forest sources.

A catalogue record for this book is available from the British Library.

Library of Congress Cataloging-in-Publication Data
Gomm, Roger.
    Social research methodology : a critical introduction / Roger Gomm.
        p. cm.
Includes bibliographical references and index.
    ISBN 0–333–63728–3 (pbk.)
    1. Social sciences—Research—Methodology.   2. Social
sciences—Methodology.   3. Social surveys—Methodology.   I. Title.
    H61 .G593 2003
    300'.7'2—dc21   20030449830

10   9   8   7   6   5   4   3   2   1
13   12   11   10   09   08   07   06   05   04

Typeset by Footnote Graphics Ltd, Warminster, Wilts

Printed in China

Contents

List of Figures

List of Tables

List of Boxes

List of Transcripts

Acknowledgements

The author and publishers wish to thank the following for permission to use copyright material:

American Association for the Advancement of Science, for material from Rosenhan, 'On being sane in insane places', *Science*, 1971 (1973) p. 255 © American Association for the Advancement of Science.

British Journal of Psychiatry, for material from Atkinson, Kessel and Dalgaard, 'The comparability of suicide rates', *British Journal of Psychiatry* 127 (1975) table 1, p. 251 © Royal College of Psychiatrists.

Cambridge University Press, for material from Oakley, Rajan and Robertson, 'A comparison of different sources of information about pregnancy and smoking', *Journal of Biosocial Science* 22 (1990), table 9, p. 483 © Cambridge University Press.

Office for National Statistics, for material from Drever, Whitehead and Roden, 'Current patterns and trends in male morality by social class (based on occupation)', *Population Trends*, no. 86 (1996) figure 1, p. 16 © Office for National Statistics.

School of Education, University of Leicester, for material from Boydell and Jasmin, *The Pupil and Teacher Record: A Manual for Observers* (1987), p. 10 © University of Leicester.

John Gray, co-author, for material from Jesson, Gray and Tranmer, *GCSE Performance in Nottinghamshire 1991: Pupil and School Factors* (1992), table 3, p. 28, and figure 13, p. 29 © University of Sheffield.

Every effort has been made to contact all the copyright-holders, but if any have been inadvertently omitted the publishers will be pleased to make the necessary arrangement at the earliest opportunity.

1 | Overview of the Book

By the end of this chapter you should have some idea of the contents of this book and of the major themes which run through it:

- The difference between an interest in causality and an interest in meaning
- The trade-off between control and naturalism
- The trade-off between finding out a great deal about a few people or a little about a lot of them
- The importance of representativeness
- The difficulties of making generalisations on the basis of research
- The difference between value-neutral and value-led research
- Accountability to research subjects as opposed to accountability to readers
- Research as the production of accountable knowledge.

You will encounter these ideas on and off throughout the book.

1.1 Introduction

Social scientists differ greatly in what they think they are studying, and the purpose of doing this. But, despite this diversity, there is only a limited tool kit for research. Different social scientists choose different tools from the kit, use them in different ways, and interpret the results of using them differently. Nonetheless, there is much which can be learned about social science in general from learning about the tools themselves. The more important tools and the methods of using them are the topic of this book.

1.2 Looking for causes and looking for meanings

Two necessary assumptions for research are that there is something real to study, and that while we might never be sure about the truth, at least we can be fairly sure when we are wrong. This rules out the currently fashionable philosophies of **post-modernism** (Docherty 1993) as a basis for doing anything which can be called 'research'. Since post-modernist philosophies deny the possibility of there being any means for judging knowledge as being more or less true, they at the same time make research a senseless activity.

These ideas are intellectually interesting, but there is no place for them in a book on research methods.

Among social scientists who do think that research is a sensible activity there are radically different assumptions about what there is which exists to be investigated. They take very different positions about the nature of reality and about the possibilities of knowing about this. The former topic is often called **ontology**; the latter **epistemology**. However, the term epistemology (the theory of knowledge) is often used to describe both. Nearly all social scientists, and most natural scientists too, take a **phenomenological** position, recognising that we can never get in touch with raw reality *(noumena)* and can study only **phenomena** which are our perceptions of this (Thines 1987). Confusingly, the term **phenomenology** is usually used in a more limited sense in the social sciences to refer to the study of consciousness, and may carry the assumption that the most important matter to study is how people experience their lives and make sense of them.

If our perceptions are only a partial glimpse of reality, then the task of the social researcher is to manage perception so as to be able to see reality more clearly. I don't mean anything different in principle here from the example of using a microscope – and using it properly, on the assumption that what is important is very small. There is widespread agreement about the policy of improving perception in order to learn about reality. But pursuing it means making prior assumptions as to what reality is like. Without knowing what you are looking for, you can't devise appropriate means for finding it, and without having appropriate means for finding it, you can't find out what there is to look for. Social scientists differ in what they think is the reality they are trying to capture. So managing perceptions to improve the angle of view on reality means different things to different researchers.

This book is not the place for an extensive epistemological debate. Instead I will make a simple distinction between those researchers who think of the social reality to be captured as one of *cause and effect*, and those who think of it as a complex of *interpretations and meanings*. Some researchers think of these as mutually exclusive; others as different aspects of the same underlying reality.

1.3 Causal analysis

Causal models

Chapters 2–6 deal mainly with experiments, social surveys and some similar investigative strategies which are used by researchers whose basic question is 'What usually causes what to happen?' The 'usually' is important. Many historians are interested in documenting a unique set of circumstances leading to a unique event. But most social scientists, and some historians are interested in what often, or generally, causes what. The model which lies behinds these approaches is one of a network of **variables** connected together in cause–effect relationships: an electrical circuit or a plumbing system are not bad physical analogies for this. The term 'variable' means something which can vary: male *or* female, working class *or* middle class *or* upper class, percentages of people unemployed. The cause–effect relationship is such that if one variable changes, then other variables will change too. A change in the variable 'unemployment level' will produce changes in the variables, 'family income', 'consumer expenditure', 'average life expectancy' and so on. What is of interest is exactly which down-stream variables do change, and by how much, when an up-stream one changes. For example, what are the 'knock-on effects' of unemployment, or how much change in life expectancy can be attributed to changes in the labour market, including rates of unemployment?

The complexity of causation

Causal investigation like this throws into sharp relief a set of researcher problems associated with the complexity of causation. First, anything previous might be among the causes of anything that comes later. Second, whatever happens is likely to have multiple causes. Third, under normal circumstances, a very large number of things are going on at the same time. All in all, it simply is very difficult to see what is causing what, or which among past events are among the causes of some current state of affairs.

Experimental control and the study of cause and effect

Experimentation is one approach to these problems. A **controlled experiment**, as discussed in Chapter 2, is a simplified working model of reality, designed so that most cause–effect relationships are either insulated off, or are standardised, and only variables of interest are allowed to vary. If you wanted to see whether the gender of an examination candidate was among the causes of the different marks given to candidates by examiners, you might design an experiment where the *only thing* which could cause differences in the marks given would be the responses of the examiners to the gender of the candidates. That would mean excluding all other possibilities.

The term **control** is usually used for such exclusionary strategies. Sometimes people think that control has a sinister implication when applied to human affairs. It might at times, but usually in experiments it means something similar to controlling camera-shake by using a tripod; it means screening out whatever is irrelevant to the question being asked. In the research on gender-bias in exam marking, you might control for the effects of differences in the quality of the scripts, by arranging that for every examiner who got a script with a male name on it there would be another getting *the same* script with a female name on it. You might control for differences between examiners by making sure that there were two groups of them closely matched for age, gender and whatever other characteristics might be relevant, each group receiving the same permutations of scripts and genders. As Chapter 2 discusses, the design of a controlled experiment is one which attempts to exclude from influencing the results anything except that cause–effect relationship which the researcher is interested in investigating.

In the past sociologists have rarely conducted controlled experiments of this kind, although they are stock-in-trade for psychologists. But today there is a strong demand for research to determine whether nursing, or social work, educational or criminal justice practices are effective or not. The most convincing evidence for this comes from controlled experiments. Chapter 3 includes sections on effectiveness research.

More naturalism in experiments

For many topics in the social sciences, controlled experiments are either impracticable, or unethical, or both. Even when they might be conducted, they are vulnerable to the criticism that in producing a simplified environment in which to study cause and effect, experimenters create a situation which is so artificial that, whatever the results, they will have little bearing on what happens under ordinary circumstances. This is sometimes expressed by suggesting that controlled experiments have a low level of **external validity**. This is discussed at the end of Chapter 2.

Experimenters may attempt to meet this criticism by making their experiments more like real life: for example, by conducting them in settings such as schools or railway stations. Chapter 3 considers more naturalistic experiments. But the more naturalistic an experiment is, the less control the experimenter has over the situation, and the more possibilities there are for the results to be influenced by other factors in a way that might mislead the researcher as to what caused what. This is the first of two important **trade-offs** which you will encounter in this book. The *trade-off between control and naturalism* is between, on the one hand, being able to control the situation so as be able to draw confident conclusions about cause and effects, but at the cost of producing a result which might not apply outside the experimental situation and, on the other hand, researching naturally occurring situations, but being less able to draw confident conclusions as to what causes what.

Natural experiments

It is important not to confuse **experimentalism** with **experiments**. 'Experimentalism' or 'experimental design' refers to controlling variables, and this may be done for social surveys and other kinds of research as well as in experiments *per se*. The reason why controlled experiments are the topic of the first substantive chapter of this book is because they illustrate the logic of control so well. Other researchers either have to find alternative means to achieve the controls achieved in a controlled experiment or, if they don't, their results may be impossible to interpret with any confidence at all if the topic is a causal one.

If researchers cannot set up the right conditions by mounting a controlled experiment, they may look around for some circumstances where the right conditions crop up naturally, and conduct a **natural experiment**. When astronomers say they are doing an experiment, this means they are either making some strategically planned observations, or adding a twist to their latest computer model. In a natural experiment the kind of control exerted is **statistical control** rather than experimental control. This means analysing data to see what stays the same and what changes when the same data are classified in different ways. Chapter 5 illustrates some natural experiments including twin studies to investigate the relative contribution of heredity and environment and the investigation of what differences it makes for children to go to one school or another. Chapter 6 deals with the use of surveys in natural experiment approaches.

Surveys and representativeness

Many of the data for natural experiments come from social surveys. Censuses are social surveys which attempt to collect information from everyone. But most surveys are **sample surveys,** where data are collected from some people who are selected to be **representative** of much larger numbers of people. The topic of **representativeness** is an important one for most research, since it is often an issue as to how far what is true for the people studied will be true of other people too. Chapter 4 looks in detail at the means used by sample survey researchers to ensure that the sample selected is *representative of some wider population,* such that the results of the survey can be grossed up and treated as a reasonably accurate estimate of the state of affairs in the larger population.

Chapter 4 also draws attention to the difficulties of making such generalisations where the sample has been small and/or unrepresentative. Small and unrepresentative samples are often characteristic of controlled experiments and are among the reasons why it may be difficult to base generalisations on their results (Chapter 2). Small and unrepresentative samples are also characteristic of much **qualitative research** (see p. 13 below), and again there are difficulties in generalisation. There is another trade-off here. This is between collecting a small amount of information each from a large number of people, as is in a social survey, and being to make confident generalisations because of the large size of the sample, but at the cost of not gaining any detailed understanding of these people's lives, as against collecting a large amount of information from a small number of people with the chance of gaining a good understanding of them, but at the cost of being uncertain as to how far they represent anyone but themselves. For the same quantum of effort researchers can only do one or the other.

Prospective data

One of the few certainties in research is that something which happened later cannot have caused something which happens earlier. Thus in studying cause and effect it is important to be able to *assign events in time.* In controlled experiments this means that the state of affairs prior to the experiment needs to be investigated and compared with the state of affairs at the end. The chronology of events is rarely a problem in controlled experiments. However, many social surveys give only a snapshot of the state of affairs at one point in time. Then it will not be clear whether, for example, the people who are unemployed were in a worse state of health than others before they became unemployed, or whether becoming unemployed undermined their health. To a point this problem can be managed by collecting **retrospective data**: for example, asking people what happened to them at times earlier than the survey date. But retrospective data are notoriously unreliable. Human memories are very bad at storing accurate records of the past. Thus, for explaining cause and effect adequately, surveys and similar strategies need to be **longitudinal**, collecting data at various points in time so that what came before what can be clearly established. Taking a longitudinal approach in research is dealt with in Chapter 6.

Bureaucratic data

Social scientists often have to use data collected for bureaucratic purposes – for example, medical records, death certificates, examination results, or police data on arrests. Such information is generated from the routine working practices of doctors, examiners, or police officers. It often tells us more about the way they think and work than about whatever it is that is being classified and counted. If researchers use such data without recognising this, their results may be very misleading. The use of bureaucratic data for research purposes is discussed in Chapter 7.

Control and naturalism

The route from Chapter 2 to Chapter 7 is the route of the trade-off between control and naturalism (see above). Chapter 2 represents the highly controlled world of the controlled experiment which excludes nearly everything else in the quest for simplicity but at the risk of creating an entirely artificial picture. By the time we get to Chapters 5 and 6 researchers are faced again with the bewildering complexity of the real world over which they can exert no direct control. They have to rely on what conceptual control they can exercise through making strategic decisions about what data to collect and what potential data to ignore (which is most of them), how to collect data and how to analyse them. While necessary in the pursuit of naturalism, this loss of control is something which is very worrying for researchers concerned with issues of cause and effect. It is much less worrying for those who believe that the kind of reality which social science should be investigating is about meanings.

1.4 Research in pursuit of meaning

Qualitative and quantitative

The language of 'quantitative' and 'qualitative' has always been distinctly unhelpful as a technical guide to research methods and we would be better off without it.

(Oakley 2000:303)

It would be fortunate to be able to say that the distinctions 'cause' as against 'meaning' and 'quantitative' as against 'qualitative' mapped onto each other neatly. Unfortunately they do not. If 'quantitative' refers to research which counts things, analyses data statistically and quotes its results in numerical forms then, in psychology in particular, there are many researchers who both consider that their topic is how people make sense of their experience, and who do their research in numbers. Similarly, there are researchers who say that they are studying cause and effect and who never count anything – for example, many who observe classrooms in order to explain what causes differences in educational achievement between, for example, boys and girls (see Chapter 12, section 12.4). And, although the idea of cause and effect may be pushed into the background when the central interest is meaning, there is still an issue as to what causes people to make sense of the world in the way they do, and an issue as to what are the effects of their interpreting things this way rather than that way.

There are interesting discussions about where to draw the line between quantitative and qualitative research which come to different conclusions (compare, for example, Hammersley 1990:1-2 with Silverman 1993:23-28 or Bryman 1988:61-69). Most people who call themselves qualitative researchers are primarily interested in investigating how people experience the world and or how they make sense of it. This is often indicated by terms such as 'phenomenology', 'interpretivism', 'symbolic interactionism', 'interactionism', 'hermeneutics' and 'ethnomethodology'. Sometimes all of these are grouped together as **interpretive** approaches. Adding in selected elements from psychodynamic psychologies such as Freudian psychoanalytic theory or from socially critical sociology such as Marxism or feminism adds to the diversity. Philosophically speaking, qualitative researchers are much more diverse than quantitative researchers and the diversity is often expressed in arcane philosophical discussions. For this book I will draw a distinction between, on the one hand, the dramaturgical approach of Erving Goffman (Burns 1992) and ethnomethodological approaches and, on the other hand, all other qualitative approaches (Chapter 9). This marks a gap within qualitative approaches which is at least as large as that between qualitative and quantitative approaches.

Questions in surveys and questions in qualitative interviews

Much of the information in both quantitative and qualitative research comes from asking people questions and recording the results. But asking questions to produce numerical data is different from asking questions to produce the kind of data that the researcher will handle as words. Chapter 8 draws a contrast between questioning and answering in experimental and social survey research, on the one hand, and questioning and answering in qualitative interviews, on the other. The former is likely to involve forced choice questions because a major preoccupation will be to make precise point-by-point comparisons between respondents. Treating all the respondents in a similar way will also be an aim. Otherwise differences between their responses might not relate to differences between them, but to differences in the behaviour of the interviewer. In this, and in other ways, interviewing for social surveys shows many similarities with experimental procedures. This is described in Chapter 8, as are the problems which arise when survey researchers depart from these rules.

Just as experiments can be critiqued as artificial and unnatural, so also can the rather formal, structured and impersonal circumstances of a survey research interview. Such a critique backs the policy adopted by qualitative interviewers, who attempt to make the interview more like an ordinary conversation. Instead of adopting the impersonal stance of the survey interviewer they attempt to make more intimate relationships with the respondent. This is on the grounds that only through making such relationships will the researcher learn the important truths about the respondent. In Chapter 8 again we meet the trade-off between control and naturalism, since the qualitative interview is highly vulnerable to criticism that the results may tell us more about the interview*er* than about the interview*ees*

Two meanings of 'meaning'

The term 'meaning' is a difficult one. I shall suggest two different meanings for 'meaning' here. One of these is that the meaning of what people say or do is what is in their mind when they do so. The other is that the meaning of what people say or do is in whatever it is that they say or do which allows it to be seen as meaningful. The two renderings take analysis in two different directions (Table 1.1).

Suppose that we are trying to find the meaning of something someone said. Then the first approach takes us inwards to a private place which is very difficult to know about: the mind of the person who said it. But the second takes us outwards to the public realm, which is much easier to know about. The public question here is 'what is it about that utterance that allows it to be meaningful to the person who uttered it and to the people who hear it?' This must be a public matter because if it were not, communication between people would be impossible. We do not have to do research to know that communication between people is not impossible, though it can be problematic from time to time.

Mind-reading research

The first, 'mind-reading', approach to meaning is the more traditional and more commonsensical. It entails creating a picture of the mind that had to be there to have the experience the researcher says this person had and to contain the reasons which gave rise to the actions or the speech. All versions of this approach have in common that they involve constructing a picture of the mind behind the action, using as evidence for this the things that people say or do. But apart from this there is an enormous variety among exponents in their ideas as to what people's minds can be like. In psychology, for example, pictures of people's minds are drawn containing, perhaps some

TABLE 1.1	Two approaches to the meaning of what people say, or otherwise communicate	
	The mind-reading approach	Dramaturgical and ethnomethodological approaches
What people say is:	Evidence of what people think, feel, experience, how they make sense of and interpret the world	Evidence of how words (gestures and so on) are used to construct a situation at the time when they were used
Behind the words:	There are minds with knowledge, motives, ways of understanding, cognitive structures, interpretive schemes or some such (see the main text) which are in turn the product of past experiences	There is nothing researchable, the words represent a repertoire these people have for structuring situations.
The analysis of meaning is:	Modelling minds from the evidence of speech (gestures and so on)	Mapping utterances to the situations in which they were spoken

of, but rarely all of, conscious and unconscious sectors, defence mechanisms, self-serving biases, self-images, motivational sets, representational structures and other components. Sociology and psychology tend to merge into each other in the enterprise of modelling minds, but between them they select from a huge vocabulary of terms for the structure of minds, including: actor-theories, attribution sets, folk-theories, sub-cultural ideas, ideologies, perspectives, social theories, interpretive repertoires, typification schemes, schemes of relevance, world views, discourses and more. All of these express much the same idea, which is that people have ways of understanding the world. The object of research then is to produce descriptions of what that understanding is – what is in people's minds. The research usually goes on to explain how people got their minds made up that way, and what are the consequences of people having the minds they do.

There are mind-modellers who believe that minds can be known about by using precisely designed instruments such as attitude scales or various other kinds of questionnaires, or from laboratory experiments generating numerical data for statistical analysis. But those who take the qualitative line would claim that this is a hopeless path to follow. Indeed, they would argue that the kind of questions asked in social survey research not only fail to capture any sense of what it is like to be people going about their daily lives but also grievously misrepresents this. The forced choice questions of the typical questionnaire used in an experiment or a survey are seen to force respondents to answer questions which may be irrelevant to their lives, in words they wouldn't use themselves. On this basis then, if the qualitative researcher is going to use interviews, he or she prefers them to be discursive and only loosely structured, as described in Chapters 8 and 9.

Thematic analysis

The qualitative interview generates a large amount of verbal data. The mind-reading qualitative researcher then has to analyse all this to find the structure of the mind behind it: the actor theory, the actor perspective, the typification scheme, the world view, or what have you. The usual way in which the data from qualitative interviews are analysed for this purpose is by **thematic analysis**. The researcher looks for what comes up in the data commonly and interestingly, calls these 'themes' (or sometimes 'codes') and then uses these as headings for writing up the research report. In some way or other the themes stand for the way ideas are organised in the minds of the people studied. Thematic analysis is illustrated in Chapter 9 with a transcript from a qualitative interview. Just as qualitative interviews are vulnerable to the criticism that they tell us more about the interviewer than about the interviewee, so thematic analysis, based already on the qualitative interview, is vulnerable to the criticism that it tells us more about what was in the mind of the analyst than about what was in the mind of the interviewee.

Ethnomethodological and similar approaches to meaning

The other approach to meaning in qualitative research (Table 1.1) derives from ethnomethodology and linguistics, and or from the inspiration of Erving Goffman (Burns 1992). If the data are derived from an interview, then they are not taken to stand for what is in the mind of the respondent, but for what is going on in the interview. What is interesting is how the way people speak makes it clear that this was an interview, and not a chat, or a row, a valedictory oration, a seduction or a lecture. What the people were doing was producing an interview. To do that they must have known how to do 'interview talk'. They must each have known how to produce speech and other communicative action which was meaningful to the other as a contribution to an interview, and not a chat, a row, and so on. From this viewpoint there is no need to delve into minds in order to study meanings, since meaning is out in the open for any competent member of a culture to see, including the sociological observer. Thus most British adults know how to recognise a queue when they see one, and know how to do queuing, and hence know how to co-operate with others in order to organise themselves as a queue. Meaning is social organisation and social organisation is meaning. Moreover, who someone is (for that moment), and how they are appraised by others, depends on what kind of social organising is taken to be going on. Queues are also moral orders, and have their own forms of deviance; queue-jumping for example. When queuing, people know that they are likely to be judged by others in terms of abiding by whatever it is that people like them should do in a queue.

Ethnomethodologists are not keen on the idea of rules, but here it will do no harm to say that a meaningful act or utterance is one which complies with some rules which people can follow in producing it, and in inter preting it. This includes finding the meaning of a frown by one person, in another person's queue-jumping. Meaning, of course, is in the minds of people, but equally it is out in the open in their observable doings and hearable sayings. That's where ethnomethodologists, and others of similar ilk, look for meaning.

Conversation Analysis (CA)

These considerations suggest a way of analysing speech which is radically different from that of thematic analysis. Chapter 9, which demonstrates thematic analysis, also subjects the same transcript to the kind of analysis which would be carried out by a **conversation analyst**. Conversation analysis has its roots partly in ethnomethodology and partly in pragmatic linguistics. Analysing the same data thematically and by the methods of CA leads to two very different sets of conclusions.

From an ethnomethodological point of view, if you conduct interviews you will produce data which tell you about interviews, and perhaps about some more general features of communication and interaction. This is in contradistinction to other researchers who use interviews in order to find out about people's activities and thoughts as they are in circumstances **beyond the interview** situation. Ethnomethodologists take the earlier criticism of experiments or social survey research as being artificial one step further. Any attempt to find out about one kind of situation by interviewing people in an entirely different kind of situation makes no sense. Ethnomethodologists, however, would not use terms such as 'artificial'. Reasonably enough, they would say that any experiment is a real experiment; any interview is a real interview. They are as much part of social life as lying in bed in the morning, or making love in the back of a car. Everything is natural, all research is 'naturalistic' but it is not necessarily in the nature of an interview situation to generate the kinds of thoughts, feelings and interactions that are generated in some other situation which is being discussed as a topic of the interview.

Chapter 11 is on the analysis of written documents. Again it draws a distinction between mind-reading approaches and approaches where what is of interest is how a communication is put together. For writing, the former is an interest in what the writing tells us about the understandings and experiences of the writer, while the latter is an interest in the way pieces of writing are structured. Some of the techniques for analysing writing can be used for analysing speech, but analysis should always take account of the way the data are produced. Speaking and writing are very different kinds of activity and generate data of different kinds (Chapter 11, section 11.1).

Naturalistic observation

What makes it sensible to conduct interviews for researchers of the mind-reading kind is the idea that people carry around the same mind from situation to situation. Thus the person being interviewed is the same person who does whatever it is elsewhere that the researcher asks about, and can 'bring to mind' that other situation. This begs many questions as to how much people actually know about what they do and whether they are able to give accurate accounts of their own doings. And it raises concerns among mind-reading researchers as to whether people give honest accounts. Thus there is an attraction among such researchers for observing people going about their everyday activities. That is a preference for **naturalistic observation,** either as **participant observers,** to some extent acting like an ordinary member of the setting, or by **non-participant observation** – just observing.

Combining naturalistic observation with qualitative interviewing may look like the best of both worlds. The observation shows the researcher what people *actually do*. The interviews are designed to find out what those doings meant to the person concerned, since it would be disruptive of ordinary life for researchers to keep on asking 'what did you mean by that?' or 'what does that mean to you?'. But this pairing of interviews with observation still assumes that what the person says in the interview about what he or she did at some other time was the meaning at the earlier time. For obvious reasons ethnomethodologists also favour observation studies – though, of course, for them an interview is an observation study: an observation of an interview. Chapter 10 deals with naturalistic observation, its problems and its potentials, and some of the differences between naturalistic observers of different kinds.

1.5 Generalisation

Just as some historians do not seek to produce generalisable knowledge, some qualitative researchers make only limited claims that what they describe in their research will apply elsewhere. But most researchers do make some claims as to the general currency of their ideas. Three kinds of generalisation can be distinguished.

Empirical or statistical generalisation

Empirical or **statistical generalisation** refers to the kind of generalisability aimed for by survey researchers. Here the generalisation is the claim that what is true of the *sample* is true of the *population* from which the sample was drawn, in some designated ways, and for some limited period of time. Making it possible to make such generalisations safely is what survey design is all about, as described in Chapter 4.

Theoretical generalisation

Theoretical generalisation refers to the applicability to other times, places and people of some theoretical idea which seemed to explain what happened in the research. This is easier to understand if you think of researchers looking for cause – effect **mechanisms**: things that make things happen. The important mechanisms are the robust ones which make things happen in a wide range of circumstances. Natural science has many examples such as gravity, electricity, natural selection, or genes. The social sciences are less blessed in this regard. The same mechanism may not have the same effects in different contexts. For example, the mechanism which makes heroin an effective pain killer under one set of circumstances may lead to addiction under another; or, teacher expressions of disapproval might under some circumstances depress educational performance and under others to encourage pupils to strive harder.

Generalisations along these lines claim that the same mechanism has an effect in a large number of different circumstances, but the effects may be different according to the context. The task here is to specify also the *contextual factors* which make a mechanism have a particular effect. The law-like statements characteristic of the natural sciences both say what does what, and specify the circumstances under which it will do it: water will freeze at 0 degrees Celsius only if it is of a specified purity, and at a certain barometric pressure. Social phenomena hardly ever allow for specifications of such precision. Specification is discussed in Chapter 3.

Qualitative researchers have particular problems in deriving generalisations from their research. Given the way they use small and unrepresentative samples they cannot make empirical generalisations with any confidence at all. But in practice they actually do make such generalisations, as when they imply that the six teachers they studied in the school stand for, or represent, another thirty in the same school, or that the one school class they observed intensely represents other classes as well. More usually qualitative researchers claim to be making theoretical generalisations, of a weak kind termed 'sensitising concepts'. These are the kinds of concepts which direct attention to interesting similarities between different aspects of life. For example Goffman's term 'total institution' (Goffman 1968) gathers together under the same heading mental hospitals, boarding schools, military units, monasteries, merchant ships and so on. Looking at these all in the same way does throw interesting commonalities (and differences) into relief. Another concept which does similar work is the idea of a 'career' (Goffman 1968), when applied to criminals, mental patients, school pupils and so on. This implies that the trajectory taken by someone's life is shaped by the assumptions people make about what normally, naturally, ought to be true of someone at that 'stage in their career'. Although ideas like this lack the rigour of the kinds of mechanisms identified in natural science, they nonetheless point us in the direction of interesting features of social life which seem general in that they can be applied to a wide range of settings.

Naturalistic generalisation

Some qualitative researchers claim that it is not the purpose of their research to produce generalisations. Rather their purpose is to produce rich, or 'thick' descriptions of social life, so that readers can understand what it would be like to be someone else and experience the world from their point of view (Geertz 1973). This is often the purpose stated for participant observation research as described in Chapter 10. This idea of doing research to provide readers with vicarious experience of other people's lives is often associated with the idea of *naturalistic* generalisation (Stake 1994). Here it is not the researcher who does the generalising, but the readers. The research is presented as a resource for readers to extend their understanding of themselves and other people in the same way as they draw on and learn from direct experience, from plays, films, television documentaries and so on.

1.6 Ethics and values

Chapter 12 is about evaluation and evaluation studies, and Chapter 13 is about ethics in research. Both deal with questions about the proper purpose of research, the proper relationships which should obtain between researcher and researched and between researchers and the various audiences for research, and the extent to which the values of the researcher should influence the research.

Value-relevant, value-neutral research

Researchers are pleased if their research has some beneficial outcome. Most would allow that there are no great problems arising from researchers choosing their research topics according to their moral, political or career interests. It is legitimate then, for research to be **value relevant**. This is Max Weber's term and he is widely quoted in this context (Bruun 1972; Hammersley 2000b:18–19). Where matters become more controversial is over the issue of **value neutrality**. In Weber's terms, value-neutral research means that, while the topic might be chosen according to the values of the researcher, thereafter the values of the researcher should be excluded from the conduct of the research, except the value of getting at the truth and the values grounding the humane treatment of the people involved in and affected by the research. Value neutrality means not only preventing the personal preferences of the researcher influencing the result, but giving researchers significant freedom from those who employ them or who fund their research. Otherwise these might also exert an influence distorting the research away from the truth.

Chapter 2 describes how the controlled experiment is designed to exclude the influence of both the researchers' and the subjects' hopes, fears, desires and so on from producing misleading results. It draws attention to a large literature showing that people, including researchers, are very likely to see what they want to see. The most obvious way in which this potential for bias is managed in an experiment is through **blinding**. That is, depriving researchers and or subjects of knowledge which, if they had it, would allow their preferences to influence the results. This blinding is only a version of the widespread use of blind decision-making in other fields – for example, anonymising examination scripts for marking, preventing a jury knowing about previous offences before reaching a verdict, or awarding prizes by lottery. Blinding is not the only device used, and is often impossible. In addition, various means are used to ensure that each subject for the experiment is treated the same. In a similar way, most surveys are conducted so that the researchers' prejudices do not influence who gets selected as a respondent, and efforts are made to ensure that the questions are not written in such a way as to tilt the survey towards producing the results the researcher wanted to get (Chapters 4 and 8).

Pressure groups do conduct 'surveys' which are in effect 'petitions', going out of their way to find the people and record the opinions favourable to their cause. And similarly, charities and other agencies will conduct surveys, and other kinds of research, designed precisely to produce campaign ammunition. This is value-led, rather than value-neutral research. This raises an important issue, and a point of divergence between researchers, and gives two different meanings to the term 'bias' (Hammersley and Gomm 2000).

The more orthodox, mainstream position in the social, as in the natural, sciences, is the Weberian prescription for value-relevant/value-neutral research. Here 'bias' means a deviation from the truth. A particularly powerful source of bias would be the uncontrolled values of politics or commerce impacting on the researcher and his or her own personal values as well. Value neutrality refers to an intention to avoid such bias. This very frequently fails, but failure is taken as a case for trying harder, rather than for abandoning the attempt. It is also part of the Weberian argument that researchers' values, political preferences and so on should be excluded because being a researcher doesn't give anyone any particular expertise in making moral and political judgements.

The working out of this position is illustrated by the kinds of evaluation studies illustrated in the first half of Chapter 12. For example, experimental designs are frequently used to investigate the **effectiveness** of a medical, social work or educational intervention. Whether a treatment is effective or not is a causal issue and the experimental design is the most powerful way of investigating causality (Chapter 2, Chapter 3, section 3.4). The experimental design sets up a no-go area for values. If matters are arranged properly, a commercial company piloting the treatment is excluded from influencing the results. Even if it is the researchers themselves who have originated the treatment, the effects of their enthusiasm for it should be controlled through the devices such as random allocation, blinding and independent scrutiny described in Chapter 2. The researcher's role as researcher is to decide on the effectiveness of the treatment. It is not to act as advocate for it or to decide whether the treatment should pass into general use. Either that is a decision to be taken by others mandated to make such decisions, or if the researcher is involved in this, it will be on the basis of a position as a doctor, or a social services administrator or some other role which gives someone a mandate for making ethical and political decisions affecting other people. Putting matters around the other way it would be a breach of trust for researchers, as researchers, to allow their desires to change the world, or their personal values or career interests to influence the outcome of the research.

These kinds of considerations raise another criticism of qualitative research: that it has insufficient safeguards for preventing the biases of the researcher influencing the results and that pressures towards bias are likely to arise from the more personal involvement with research subjects that qualitative researchers prefer.

Value-led or partisan research

However, there is another meaning of the term 'bias'. That is of some ideas or some state of affairs being against, or favouring, the *interests* of someone. Social scientists operate in a world in which it is very obvious that social arrangements favour some people and disadvantage others. It can, and is, argued that this bias extends to the state of knowledge in society, such that current knowledge is biased against women, against poor people, or against members of minority ethnic groups and in favour of white middle-class men and big business and so on. If this is the case it can be argued that what is needed is not 'value-neutral' research, but 'value-led' research where the object is to produce knowledge which redresses the bias.

As Chapter 12 points out, a great deal of social science is socially critical in this way. Varieties of **critical research** include the various marxisms, the various feminisms, anti-racist research, disability research and queer theory, and various right-wing doctrines too. Researchers of such persuasions regard it as quite proper to 'take sides' and to do research in such a way as to produce knowledge which is favourable to the interests of disadvantaged groups. To do this researchers must assume that they have a superior expertise in judging what is morally right and what is morally wrong, in discerning who deserves what and what would be to the benefit of which people. Value-neutral researchers do not feel that being a researcher gives them the right or the expertise to decide such matters.

Research ethics

The two positions also predicate different kinds of ethical relationships with the subjects of research, as described in Chapter 13. Researchers who follow the policy of value neutrality largely restrict ethical considerations with regard to research subjects to avoiding doing them any harm. And they balance violations of privacy or of subjects' rights to make decisions for themselves, against the value of the research findings. Researchers who subscribe to a value-led approach usually believe that research is unethical if it does not do research subjects of selected categories some tangible good. This leads to research programmes which are designed less to produce knowledge and more to produce change. This might be change in the public reputation of some group where, as it were, researchers act as their public relations consultants. Or it might be change in the way research subjects think and feel about themselves, or tangible changes in their life circumstances. It is often part of such programmes that research subjects are co-opted as partners in research, although the extent of the partnership may vary from one in which they are consulted to one in which they operate as fully fledged researchers themselves. Research of this kind often looks very much more like social work, or counselling or political activism. 'Research methods' which consist of social work skills or the techniques of political mobilisation cannot be described in this book.

As discussed in Chapter 13 co-opting vulnerable people as co-researchers leads to another ethical problem, which has to do with the welfare of people encouraged to engage in a programme to change their lives. What are the ethics of researchers encouraging people to take risks with their own lives? What if it all goes horribly wrong?

Stake holders for research

There are various groups towards which researchers might be said to be accountable. As noted already, value-neutral researchers try to truncate their accountability towards those who employ them or fund their research. They are willing to take responsibility for doing the research properly but not for producing the results their paymasters would most like to see. Value-led researchers are inclined to say that their prime accountability is towards the subjects of the research. This is potentially in conflict with their accountability towards those who read the research. Readers may feel they have a right to receive an unbiased account. But the subjects of the research may feel that they have a right to determine what other people read about them and to make sure that this depicts them as they would wish to be depicted. In value-led research, subjects often are allowed to vet the research report prior to publication. From a readers' point of view this looks like a conspiracy between researchers and subjects against readers. However, not too much should be made of this. First, the kinds of people who choose to read critical social research are usually those who are pre-disposed to believe it anyway. Second, it is usually abundantly clear as to the partisan nature of such research, and therefore readers can read it with this in mind, just as they do with the output of political spin doctors. The employment title of many people who are called 'spin doctors' is usually 'researcher'.

1.7 Research as producing accountable knowledge

Research is about producing knowledge. We usually think of 'knowledge' as something which is stored in the head, in books or on floppy disks. And so it is. But a more useful way of thinking about knowledge is as a kind of claim. If I say I know something, I might be claiming that I can do something, such as ride a bike, or translate from Greek to English. Making such a claim I can be called out and asked to demonstrate that I can indeed do what I claimed. Or alternatively, saying 'I know' might be saying that I will vouch for the truth of this. For example, if I claim that 'Jesus loves me, this I know', I might vouch for this by saying I know 'because the Bible tells me so'. This would be quite appropriate since religious claims need to be vouched for in religious terms.

One of the ways of vouching for the verity of knowledge is to say: 'It is known to be so, because research has demonstrated it to be so.' Phrases of this ilk litter social science texts, and you will find them on and off throughout this one too. Saying that 'research has shown that ...' vouches for some claim, but how does research vouch for itself?

Objectivity

Research can claim to produce knowledge which is superior to other kinds because, and insofar as, and only insofar as, its credentials can be checked. This puts the emphasis on accountability in its traditional place, with the way that researchers make themselves accountable to their readers. This is another way of talking about **objectivity**. Objectivity has various meanings, and various opposites. I am inclined to use it in the ways in which it was used at the birth of modern science in the seventeenth century (Daston 1992), not as the opposite of subjectivity meaning emotionality. This is sometimes referred to as **procedural objectivity**. Here objective knowledge primarily means knowledge which is public, open to scrutiny and discussion, auditable or accountable, as opposed to knowledge which is secret, private, and requiring to be accepted on trust or having to be accepted on pain of punishment. The historical circumstance in which this meaning was shaped was one in which scientists – or rather 'natural philosophers' at the time, saw themselves as emancipating people from an irrational reliance on blind faith and from coercion and manipulation by religious dogmatists. Science, it seemed, allowed for a more 'democratic' way of producing knowledge as well as a more efficient way of getting at the truth: democratic in the sense that knowledge claims were based on evidence which, in principle, anyone could see, and arguments, which, in principle, anyone could follow and disagree with, though at that time 'anyone' was confined to a small male elite. At that time, then, the usual opposite of 'objective' was 'dogmatic'. In addition, however, objectivity also carried the implication that the person making the knowledge claim 'had no axe to grind': that the knowledge was disinterested, personal interests and emotional involvements being seen to bias perception and to be a reason for trying to deceive other people. Researchers are rarely entirely disinterested. But again it is the accountability of the knowledge claim which is supposed to protect people from being misled by the personal interests of others. If the evidence is available to all and the argument followable by all, the influence of such distortions should be easy to detect. Both the various safeguards against bias built into experimental designs (Chapter 2) and the policy of value-neutral research (Chapters 12 and 13) can be seen in this light.

When scientists claim that they produce objective knowledge they do not necessarily mean that the knowledge they produce is true – or at least they shouldn't mean this. What they should mean is that it is more likely that knowledge produced by research will be true because it is open to inspection so that any errors it contains are likely to be detected. Research knowledge is objective to the extent that the researcher says, honestly:

- Here are the assumptions I made about the nature of reality and how it can be known about
- Here is the question I asked
- Here are the methods I used to collect the data relevant to an answer
- Here are the data I collected
- Here is the way I analysed the data
- This is the answer I came up with
- I think I'm right, but I've given you enough to check all this to see if you come to the same conclusions.

It is relatively easy for quantitative researchers to give an objective account of their research because their procedures are protocol-driven and numerical data isn't particularly weighty. By contrast (Chapters 8 and 10) doing qualitative research is often a hand-to-mouth, flying-by-the-seat-of-your-pants activity, where at the end of the day the researcher may not be very clear what she has done herself. Such researchers will have to make large numbers of *intuitive* analytic decisions on the spot, and it will be difficult to keep track of these, let alone tell other people about them. The sheer bulk of the data from qualitative research means that it can be shared only selectively with readers. It may be difficult for a researcher to persuade readers that data standing against the researcher's interpretations hasn't been conveniently left hidden in the filing cabinet. This problem is discussed in Chapter 10.

Again, the idea of objective knowledge grew up with, and better fits with, the idea of value-neutral research. There are problems in using it where the aims of researchers include changing the moral values or political ideas of their readers, or where the results of the research are crafted to give a favourable impression of some category of person. Being objective about this would rather give the game away in the same way that it would give the game away for an advertiser to draw attention to the persuasive techniques used in an advert (Chapter 11, section 11.6). These problems are discussed in Chapter 12.

Many, if not most researchers, are careful to report their results objectively, drawing readers' attentions to underlying assumptions which have to be taken on trust, and to the shortcomings of the methods used. But these provisions get stripped away as research findings are quoted from source to source and prefaced with the confident phrase: 'research shows that ...'. Going back to the originals usually shows that research doesn't quite show that. Unpicking the originals and seeing how they were made usually shows that alternative interpretations are possible. Paying attention to the methodology of research studies gives the impression that the corpus of social research findings is based on a rather ramshackle foundation. This is not peculiar to social science, however. Go back twenty years in any field of science and, with the benefit of hindsight, you will find many truth claims which today are regarded as erroneous. The same will almost certainly be true twenty years hence. While most scientists would like to discover some eternal and absolute truths, the best any of them can do in practice is to offer up some possibilities for other people's consideration. As the philosopher Daniel Dennett (1995:380) says, what makes science distinctive, and what makes scientific knowledge superior to other kinds, is that science is a process of making mistakes in public so that they can be corrected.

Further reading

Reading appropriate for most of this chapter will be found at the end of chapters which deal with each issue in more detail. Any standard sociology text book for. AS/A2 level or under-graduate use will provide information about the diversity of theories held by social scientists which predispose them to use one investigative approach rather than another. Particularly lucid in this regard are Cuff, Sharrock and Francis (1990) and Jones (1993). Don't expect too close a match between theories and methods since the choice is often determined by what is possible rather than what is theoretically ideal.

An overview of causal thinking in social research is Hage and Meeker (1988), but this doesn't really get to grips with the revision of causal ideas in the natural sciences associated with chaos and complexity theories. For this in the social sciences see Bryne (1998). For an overview of qualitative research try Silverman (1985). Bryman (1988) is still probably the best discussion of the qualitative–quantitative distinction. For more on the differences between empirical and theoretical generalisation see the linked essays on this in Gomm, Hammersley and Foster (2000).

---

2   Controlled Experiments

By the end of this chapter, you will:

- Have an understanding of the way controlled experiments are designed to answer questions about cause and effect by attempting to exclude all those factors which might affect the results, except those of interest
- Be able to list and explain the various kinds of safeguards against confounding which can be built into the design of a controlled experiment, and explain the kinds of problems which might arise if these safeguards are absent or fail
- Know the dangers of bias on behalf of researchers or subjects affecting the results of research
- Understand the problem of external validity for controlled experiments.

And know the meaning of the following terms:
blinding ■ confounding ■ control ■ control group ■ expectancy effect (experimenter effect, Rosenthal effect) ■ experimental group ■ external validity ■ factorial design ■ generalisability ■ internal validity ■ inter-rater reliability ■ matched-pairs ■ placebo ■ precision-matching ■ pre-post test without controls ■ random allocation ■ replicability ■ significant and non-significant results ■ statistical control ■ subject reactivity or Hawthorne effect ■ test–re-test reliability.

At the end of the chapter there is an Activity which will test your understanding about the design of controlled experiments.

2.1 Introduction

Controlled experiments are often conducted by psychologists, but rarely by sociologists. But there is a very large demand these days for sociologists to conduct controlled experiments in evaluating the effectiveness of practice in fields such as medicine, nursing, education or criminal justice (see Chapter 3, section 3.4, Chapter 12, section 12.3). By carefully looking at the design of controlled experiments, sociologists can understand what it is necessary to achieve by other means when controlled experiments are impossible to conduct. The chapter title is a give-away. When studying causality researchers need to be able to achieve **control**. Throughout this book you will find examples of non-experimental ways of doing this, or of problems which arise when researchers fail adequately to control what they are studying.

The controlled experiment is the most powerful research design for investigating what can cause what to happen. This is because controlled experiments go a long way to solving a major problem in studying cause and effect. This is the problem that everything has a *multitude of causes*. The controlled experiment is a simplified working model of reality. It is designed as an attempt to fix most factors in place, to **control** them, while allowing just a few to vary. Figure 2.1 gives a picture of the basic structure of a controlled experiment of the similar subjects/different treatments kind. There is another basic format ; a different subjects/similar treatments kind. There are examples of this in Chapter 3, section 3.3 and Chapter 6, section 6.4.

Figure 2.1 shows the practical problems the experimenter has to solve. The experimenter has to:

- Create two or more comparison groups of people who are similar in all respects which might be relevant to the experiment
- Make sure that all the subjects are treated the same, except in the ways in which they are supposed to be treated differently
- Ensure that the same observations are made of each subject in the experiment in the same way, at least before (pre-) and after (post-).

This list hints at what can go wrong in a controlled experiment. Each of these topics is dealt with in detail in this chapter.

In all research designs, doing one thing well usually means doing something else badly. The well-designed controlled experiment is a splendid way of demonstrating clearly what caused what *under experimental conditions*. But experimental conditions are usually a gross over-simplification of what happens under real-life circumstances. This means that experimental results may not be very enlightening as to what actually happens in the real world. This problem of the **external validity** of experiments is dealt with in section 2.10 and again in Chapter 3.

2.2 Avoiding confounding

At the end of an experiment there will be a set of results. Imagine, for example, that the experiment involved giving a programme of anti-smoking education to one group of pupils (the experimental or treatment group) and no such programme to another (the control group). And imagine that two years later more pupils in the control group reported that they smoked. It would be tempting to conclude that the anti-smoking education had been successful. But that conclusion would be premature before making a careful check on the design and the execution of the experiment. Many other things might have caused the differences in the result, apart from having or not having experienced the anti-smoking education. In the vocabulary of

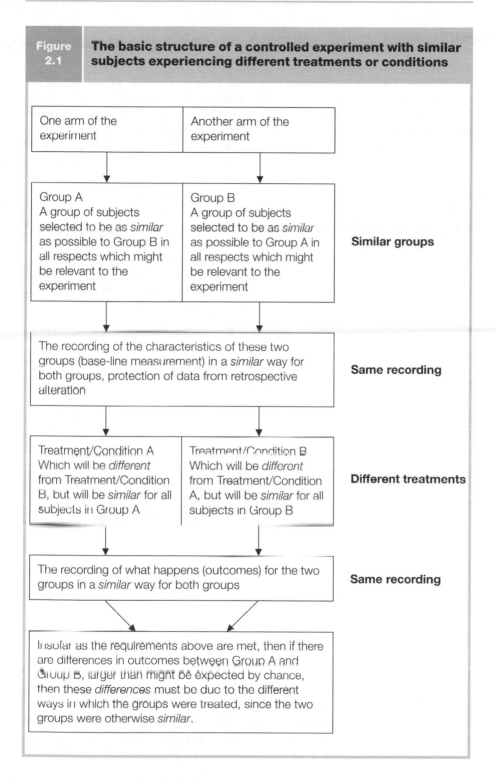

Figure 2.1 **The basic structure of a controlled experiment with similar subjects experiencing different treatments or conditions**

One arm of the experiment	Another arm of the experiment	
Group A A group of subjects selected to be as *similar* as possible to Group B in all respects which might be relevant to the experiment	**Group B** A group of subjects selected to be as *similar* as possible to Group A in all respects which might be relevant to the experiment	**Similar groups**
The recording of the characteristics of these two groups (base-line measurement) in a *similar* way for both groups, protection of data from retrospective alteration		**Same recording**
Treatment/Condition A Which will be *different* from Treatment/Condition B, but will be *similar* for all subjects in Group A	Treatment/Condition B Which will be *different* from Treatment/Condition A, but will be *similar* for all subjects in Group B	**Different treatments**
The recording of what happens (outcomes) for the two groups in a *similar* way for both groups		**Same recording**

Insofar as the requirements above are met, then if there are differences in outcomes between Group A and Group B, larger than might be expected by chance, then these *differences* must be due to the different ways in which the groups were treated, since the two groups were otherwise *similar*.

experiments the term **confounding** means drawing the wrong conclusion about the causes of experimental results. It might have been that the pupils who experienced the anti-smoking education were, at the outset, different in important ways from those who did not; less pre-disposed to smoke anyway. Or it might be that something which was happening at the same time as the anti-smoking education, or in the two years after it, influenced one group to smoke more than the other. If either were so then this would confound the results and it would be mistaken to attribute the difference in smoking habits two years later, to the differences in educational treatments.

Figure 2.2 shows the main ways in which the results of experiments can be confounded. In a perfectly conducted experiment the only differences in the results should be those created by treating the subjects differently in the way they should have been treated differently, plus some differences attributable to the play of chance. But no experiments are perfect. You can regard Figure 2.2 as a kind of fault-checker. If you were designing an experiment you should ask 'have I excluded the possibility of that kind of thing happening – 1, 2, 3, 4, 5 and 6?' And if you are reading about someone else's experiment you should ask 'Did they take adequate means to prevent confounding of these kinds?' The remainder of this chapter explains each of the items in Figure 2.2.

2.3 Creating comparison groups to control prior differences between subjects (Figure 2.2, Box 1)

It can sometimes appear that the experimental conditions or treatment have had an effect, when really what is being shown is that the people who received one treatment were already different from those who received another. Hence experimenters should arrange things so that people who are going to be treated differently in the experiment are otherwise as similar as possible to each other. This doesn't mean that everyone in an experiment has to be similar to everyone else. It does mean creating groups which *as groups* are similar to each other: for example, that, as groups, they have a similar age profile, ethnic mix, gender ratio, similar mix of educational backgrounds and such like. What is being referred to here is creating 'Group A' and 'Group B' in terms of Figure 2.1, or as many different groups (or 'arms') as the experiment requires. Creating comparison groups can be done in a number of different ways, as described below.

Random allocation to comparison groups

In psychology, and often in medicine, experiments using random allocation are called 'true experiments' and experiments using other means of creating comparison groups are called 'quasi-experiments' . The use of the term 'true' is a mark of how much randomisation is valued as a technique. Most experimental research used in testing medical treatments for their effectiveness takes the form of 'randomised controlled trials'. 'Trial' is just another word for an experiment. Putting everyone's name on a card, shuffling the

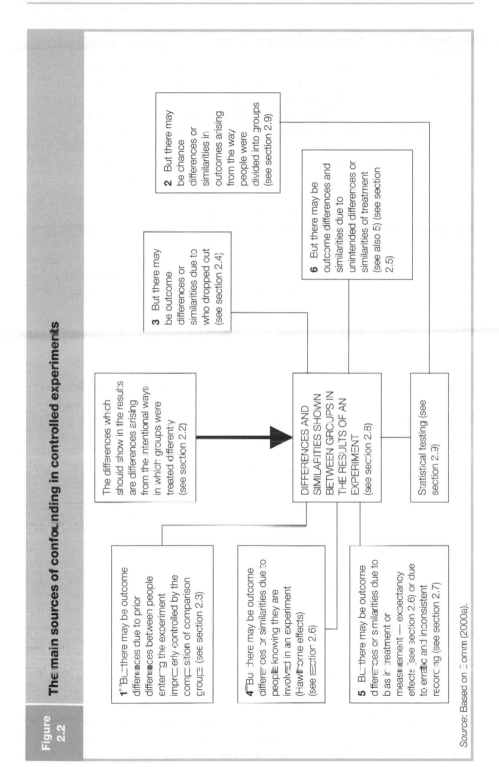

Figure 2.2 The main sources of confounding in controlled experiments

1 But there may be outcome differences due to prior differences between people entering the experiment improperly controlled by the composition of comparison groups (see section 2.3)

4 But there may be outcome differences or similarities due to people knowing they are involved in an experiment (Hawthorne effects) (see section 2.6)

5 But there may be outcome differences or similarities due to bias in treatment or measurement — expectancy effects (see section 2.6) or due to erratic and inconsistent recording (see section 2.7)

The differences which should show in the results are differences arising from the intentional ways in which groups were treated differently (see section 2.2)

DIFFERENCES AND SIMILARITIES SHOWN BETWEEN GROUPS IN THE RESULTS OF AN EXPERIMENT (see section 2.8)

Statistical testing (see section 2.9)

3 But there may be outcome differences or similarities due to who dropped out (see section 2.4)

2 But there may be chance differences or similarities in outcomes arising from the way people were divided into groups (see section 2.9)

6 But there may be outcome differences and similarities due to unintended differences or similarities of treatment (see also 5) (see section 2.5)

Source: Based on Gomm (2000a).

pack and then dealing into two piles is a common way of creating two groups at random.

It may appear odd to use chance as the means of dividing subjects for an experiment into two, or more, groups. Why not do it by using what is known about the people concerned? Creating groups on the basis of known characteristics is possible, as described later. But random allocation gives a better chance that the groups created will be similar for both known *and* unknown characteristics. It would be extremely easy to sort a deck of playing cards into two very similar piles on the basis of their suits and denominations – their known characteristics. But the resulting piles might still be very different in terms of the numbers of dog-eared cards in each, or in terms of the density of finger prints. In experiments with people it is often the case that the important characteristics are unknown, or at least difficult to find out about. For example, people respond differently to the situation of being involved in an experiment, and it is virtually impossible to know these differences in advance. Randomisation gives a good chance that for each person who will respond to being an experimental subject in a particular way in one group, there will be a matching person in the other group.

But randomisation will work to create similar groups only if the groups are large enough. An appropriate sample size for experiments is a complicated issue. It depends on, among other things, how many different characteristics there are which people can have, which might influence the results of the experiment, apart from the different treatments they receive. These are the factors which have to be distributed evenly between the groups. Think again of a pack of cards.

If you were interested only in creating two piles each with similar numbers of reds and blacks, then randomly dealing two piles of 10 would give you a good chance of achieving something close to this. But if you were interested in creating two piles with similar numbers of each denomination, then, since there are 13 denominations, two piles of 26 would be too small to do this reliably with a random deal. You will often read that two groups of 20 is around the minimum size for experiments with people. But people are enormously diverse, and some at least of this diversity is likely to be relevant to the experiment. Bald claims that two groups of 20 is enough should be regarded with suspicion.

The cost and effort of conducting an experiment is proportional to the number of subjects involved, so there are strong pressures to use small samples. And there is another way round the problem. If the diversity among people suggests that large and expensive samples are needed, then this can be dealt with by starting with a pool of subjects who are already very similar to each other; thus reducing the sample size needed. For example, bio-medical and psychological research with animals usually starts with animals bred to be genetically very similar to each other and raised in very similar conditions. Such researchers still randomise the animals to comparison groups, but the randomisation is just balancing out the groups for some rather small differences between animals. Again, in medical research with humans, it is typical to start the experiment with a pool of subjects who are already very similar – for example, of a single gender, with a limited age-range and excluding anyone who has complicating medical conditions. Restricting the diversity in this way solves one problem, but creates another. If the experiment has been conducted with a very narrow range of people, this raises a question about whether the results can be applied to a wider range of people. This just an aspect of the problem of drawing general conclusions from experimental results, which will be discussed further in section 2.10 and Chapter 3.

Apart from being an effective means for creating similar groups, randomisation has another advantage. Random allocation is automatically *blind* allocation. It means that neither the researcher nor the subjects can influence which subject belongs to which group. Blinding is discussed in section 2.6. The ethics of randomisation is discussed in Chapter 13, section 13.4.

Alternatives to randomisation in creating comparison groups

Intuitively, the most appealing way of creating comparison groups is a **matched-pairs** design. Here subjects for the experiment are sorted into pairs, each pair containing two people who are as alike as possible: same age, same gender, same ethnic group and so on. Then members of each pair would be assigned to a different comparison group: perhaps by tossing a coin. This would be called **quasi-randomisation**. A matched-pairs design takes a great deal of initial preparation, and attempting to match on many criteria usually turns out to be a rather messy business with many subjects not finding a match and having to be excluded from the experiment. This creates the same kind of problem as that created by starting with a rather homogeneous pool of subjects for randomisation (see above and section 2.10). In fact for most experiments it is not necessary to match individual by individual. It is usually enough to create two groups with similar profiles for the relevant factors, such as age, gender and so on. Compared with random allocation, matching on the basis of known characteristics, or **precision-matching** as it is sometimes called, can produce a better match between the two groups for the characteristics which were used as criteria for selection, but at the cost of producing a worse match between groups for other characteristics.

Sometimes experimenters depart from the simple structure shown in Figure 2.1, by using a **factorial design**. For example they might not only be interested in the differences caused by treating or not treating, but also particularly interested in gender differences. In this case a factorial design would mean four comparison groups at minimum: males treated, males untreated, females treated, females untreated. For this purpose it would be necessary to make sure that there were sufficient numbers in each gender. In practical terms all this means is running two experiments together on the Figure 2.1 design, one for males and one for females, using whatever technique is most appropriate or convenient for creating the four groups.

Thus the number of males and the number of females would be pre-decided and not left to chance.

There are circumstances in which experimenters cannot organise subjects into comparison groups, but have to use ready-made groups instead. Some-one doing experimental research on teaching programmes in schools is unlikely to be able to re-organise the system of school classes. Then the best which can be done will be to select two classes which seem to be composed of similar pupils, and give the educational programme to one of them, and not to the other. If the interest were in whole-school initiative – a multi-cultural programme, for example, then the experimenter would have to look for two different schools similar to each other, one to implement and the other not to implement the programme. Here we are sliding down a slope. At the top there are the very strong means of controlling the com-position of comparison groups via random allocation or matched-pairs designs. Here there is a good chance of creating groups of people similar in all respects relevant to the experiment, and hence of excluding prior differences between the groups from contaminating the experimental results. Selecting two pre-existing school classes for the experiment is a much weaker form of control because there are likely to be some very real prior differences even between school classes even which look very similar. There are likely to be even bigger uncontrolled differences between schools. An even weaker form of control is sometimes used by health education and mass media researchers where what are compared are the populations of geographical areas – for example, one area which has been targeted for a coronary health campaign (the experimental or campaign area) and another which has not been so targeted (the control area or the reference area) (Tudor Smith *et al.* 1998). Usually this kind of experiment involves a social survey to collect information about health attitudes and behaviours before and after the campaign (see Chapter 4) but the approach is experi-mental nonetheless. At the bottom of the slope are experiments without comparison groups at all, where something is done to everyone and any change is attributed to what was done to them: so-called **pre-post test studies without controls**.

There are very good practical reasons why experimental researchers sometimes have to use weaker forms of control at the subject level than those which would be ideal. The important point is that the weaker the form of control used, the more difficult it will be to be confident that differences in outcomes between groups were caused by the different ways in which the groups were treated. In the case of pre-post test studies without controls very little confidence can be had in claims that what was done to the subjects is what caused any changes recorded thereafter.

2.4 Refusals and drop-outs (Figure 2.2, Box 3)

An experimenter might be successful at the outset in selecting two or more groups of people similar in ways relevant to the experiment. But some of these may refuse to participate. Some may drop out before the experiment is completed. If people refused or dropped out at random, and in more or less equal numbers from each group, this would not be a problem until there were so few left that no sensible comments could be made about the results. But if the non-participants from one group are different types of people as compared with non-participants from the other, then two groups initially composed to be similar will cease to be so. Thus what look like differences in outcomes caused by differences in treatment may actually be differences caused by differences in the pattern of refusals and drop-outs as between comparison groups.

The problem of initial refusal can be managed to some extent by trying to make sure that people will participate *before* allocating them to groups. That has a downside. It has often been commented that most of the knowledge derived from experimental research relates to the kinds of people who are willing to co-operate with experimenters and leaves us bereft of knowledge about other kinds of people (Suls and Rostow 1988). There are also problems in using incentives to encourage people to participate. Both these latter problems are about the extent to which the results of an experiment can be generalised to other groups of people under non-experimental conditions (see section 2.10). For example, being paid to participate or being treated as a very important person in an experiment testing a medical treatment may be very different from receiving the same medical treatment in routine general practice.

Among other things, non-participation rates will depend on both the unpleasantness and inconvenience of participation and on the duration of the experiment. Many psychological experiments have durations of a few minutes and can be quite fun and have low drop-out rates. Some experiments designed to test the effectiveness of different forms of criminal rehabilitation can last for years, involve people whose life circumstances are very difficult and may have high drop-out rates. Where there is a reasonable expectation that the drop-out rate will be high, an experimenter will recruit a larger sample to start with. But this solves only the problem of numbers becoming too small, and not the problem of differential non-participation skewing the results.

Experimenters will usually do all they can to reduce refusal and drop-out rates, but they will usually have to fall back on **statistical control** rather than **experimental control**. Exerting experimental control means organising people and the environment so that some things are more likely to happen than others. By contrast, exerting statistical control entails making it possible to analyse the data in an attempt to work out what has happened. Statistical control is dealt with in more detail in Chapter 5. With regard to refusals and drop-outs it is important that there is as much detailed information as possible about each subject *before* the experiment starts and, if possible, data about each subject at various points as it proceeds. This is, first, a cross-check that the comparison groups were indeed similar at the outset, or warns of important ways in which they were not so.

And, second, should people refuse or drop out, what kinds of people they were will be known and this can be taken into consideration in interpreting the results of the experiment.

Non-participation is not all problem. Sometimes it can be regarded as an experimental **result**. If far more people drop out of the experimental than the control arm, then that is usually an indication that people find the experimental conditions unpleasant and that may be worth knowing. In some research in community mental health, the object of the research is to discover which kind of service is better at keeping clients 'engaged'. Here difference in drop-out rates between groups is an outcome measure rather than an experimental problem.

2.5 Controlling the experimental situation (Figure 2.2, Box 6)

The purpose of controlling the experimental situation is to attempt to ensure that the only differences experienced by the subjects of the experiment are the differences which have been planned for, or at least are differences which the experimenter knows about. Many psychological experiments are brief in duration and it is relatively easy to standardise the experience of subjects where it should be the same, and vary it only where it ought to be varied. Thus is it can be arranged that all subjects meet the same experimenter in the same room and that all those in the same comparison group are subjected to the same set of tasks and given the same standard instructions, perhaps on paper or on audio-tape to minimise differences. It might be worthwhile video-taping the experiment, and then viewing a sample to make sure that the experimenter didn't behave differently to people in different comparison groups in ways other than planned for. It can also be arranged that meetings between the experimenter and the subjects occur so that meetings for members of the two groups are time-tabled through the day in the same pattern, and both groups have appoint-ments spread throughout the week. The art of control here lies in drawing on other research, or in making informed guesses as to what might produce the kinds differences which the experimenter wants to exclude.

The limits of experimental control

Even in the kind of situation described above, the experimenter can't con-trol what happened to a subject the previous night or on the bus on the way to the laboratory. With many experiments running over a long period of time, most of the time what happens to subjects is outside of the control of the experimenter, but might still influence the results. If the composition of the comparison groups is similar, and the groups are large enough, then there is a good chance that what happens to someone in one group outside the experimenter's control will be matched by something with a similar effect happening to someone else in the other group – similar things tend to happen to similar people. But experimenters cannot put too much faith in this assumption. A particular difficulty arises where the experiment requires the subjects to do something themselves beyond the observation of the experimenter. Experiments involving diet, for example, rely on subjects sticking to their diets. Putting the results of many dietary experiments together shows that diets which are effective when dieting occurs in residential institutions are less so when dieting occurs at home (*Effective Health Care* 1998). The obvious interpretation of this is that many people living at home and involved in dietary experiments don't stick to their dietary regime, while those in residential institutions have less opportunity to cheat. One of the ways in which experimenters attempt to deal with matters which are outside their control is to collect data about such events. In long-running experiments it is common for subjects to complete questionnaires each time they meet the experimenter, detailing what has happened to them in the interim, or sometimes subjects are asked to keep diaries. Both, however, rely on the honesty of the subject. For the diet experiments, not only do many people cheat, many of them almost certainly lie as well.

In the paragraph above you will see something of a dilemma. Controlling people's behaviour and environment in a detailed way gives the experimenter a good chance of isolating causal mechanisms. But doing this creates very unusual circumstances. And each step towards more natural circumstances involves a loss of experimental control and a lowering of confidence in the experimental results. There is also a problem of whether it is wise to believe what people say. This is discussed in more detail in Chapters 5, 6, 9 and 11.

Simple and complex experimental treatments

There are some experimental treatments where it is easy for the experimenter to say 'this is exactly what we did and we did it in exactly the same way each time'. Perhaps the simplest example is where the experiment consists in giving one group of people an active pharmaceutical and another group a pill of an inert substance looking exactly the same – a **placebo**. Actually this isn't quite as simple as it looks since the effect of a medicine may depend on who gives it, how, in what location and when (Moerman 2002). Even the simplest experimental treatments are more complicated than they look at first sight. But there is no doubt that giving someone a medication is a much simpler matter than, say, giving someone a course of counselling, or teaching an educational programme, or setting up property marking projects (see Chapter 3, section 3.5).

There are two issues here. The first is about treating experimental subjects the same where they should be treated the same and differently where they should be treated differently. There are few inherent problems here with simple treatments. But consider a fairly common kind of experiment designed to test whether one kind of psychotherapy is more effective than another, or whether one kind of social work intervention has better results than another. It is in the nature of psychotherapy or social work that what is done is customised to the particularities of each client. Thus it is possible that some clients in the experiment receiving psychotherapy 'Type A' received something very like psychotherapy 'Type B' and vice versa: that there was, on the one hand, much diversity of treatment *within* arms of the experiment and, on the other hand, many similarities of treatment *between* arms of the experiment. In terms of Figure 2.1 this garbles the experiment because what should have been different was not different and what should have been the same was not the same. If this happens, whatever the results they will be impossible to interpret in terms of their being the effects of differences between treatment A and treatment B. In fact most of the experimental research on different kinds of psychotherapy, counselling or social work shows no difference in effectiveness between different kinds (Oakley and Fullerton 1996). This may be because in these experiments the subjects were not actually receiving distinctively different treatments. It might equally be that for these kinds of interventions what is important is not the technique used but something else, such as the demeanour of the practitioner or the rapport between practitioner and client, which isn't specific to an intervention with a particular name. Or it may be that none of the treatments has much greater effect than leaving people to their own devices. But the very complexity of these procedures, and their non-standardised nature, makes it very difficult to resolve this issue. This is a limitation of experimental method, but more so of research in general, because there really is no other kind of research design which would answer questions about the effectiveness of counselling or social work better than an experimental approach could do so (Oakley 2000).

The second issue about complex treatments relates to how an experimenter communicates results. In principle experimental research should be **replicable**. It should be possible for someone to read an experimental research report and repeat the experiment to see whether similar results can be obtained a second time. In practice experimental researchers do often repeat their own experiments many times. In medical research replication by others is required before a drug is given a licence, but outside this field exact replication is rare (Collins 1985). There are more career rewards in producing original work than in checking someone else's work by repeating it. Nonetheless, researchers reading each others' research reports do conduct a sort of replication as a thought experiment and, for this, it is important for them to know exactly what was done to produce the reported results. Where an experiment features a complex treatment, and especially one which is varied to take account of the differences between individual subjects, it is very difficult for researchers to convey precisely what was done. This becomes an additional problem where the research has a practical application. For example, an experiment showing that 'counselling' was an effective way of reducing criminal recidivism is of not much practical use if the researcher cannot describe of what 'counselling' consisted. Without this, it will be impossible for anyone to do 'the same thing' in order to produce the same results.

2.6 Expectations, bias and blinding

Expectancy effects (Figure 2.2, Box 5)

Much research is conducted under circumstances where there are career rewards for results coming out one way rather than another, and there is a general bias against inconclusive results. There is substantial research evidence that what experimenters expect to happen can influence the outcomes of experiments, and so also can what experimenters would prefer the results to be. The influence of experimenters' expectations on results is sometimes called an **expectancy effect**, sometimes an **experimenter effect** and sometimes a **Rosenthal effect**, after Robert Rosenthal who conducted pioneering research in this area (Rosenthal 1966; Rosenthal and Rosnow 1969; Rosenthal and Rubin 1978). All three terms mean the same. 'Expectancy effect' has the merits of saying what it means and of being applicable to any kind of research.

There are three main ways in which expectancy effects can confound the results of an experiment. The first is by fraud. Outright fraud is usually described as something different from an expectancy effect. But it is very difficult to make a sharp distinction between someone who sets out to mislead other people, and someone who so wants to produce results of a particular kind that they mislead themselves; self-delusion is certainly a basis for expectancy effects. Whether by intention or self-delusion, fraud is fairly common in scientific research (Broad and Wade 1982), including medical research (*British Medical Journal* 1998). Some researchers simply invent experiments they never conducted, or invent different results for experiments they have conducted. But without going to these lengths it is very easy for a researcher to produce the results he or she wants simply by 'losing' the data for the subjects which skew the results in the 'wrong' direction.

Most fraud reported comes from experimental research. But this gives a misleading picture. First, the areas where the rewards, and the temptations, are greatest are those where experimental research is the most common kind: in medicine, armaments and high-technology applications. Second, it is in experimental research that fraud is most easily detected. This brings us back to the idea of replication. Only if a piece of research is capable of being replicated is it easy to detect fraudulent work. For this reason, if the research is on an important topic, and experimental in kind, the fraud will usually be detected, sooner or later, or the research written off as being wrong for some other reason. Fraud may or may not be widespread in kinds of research other than experimental work but if it is, it is difficult to detect. In a paradoxical sense we should perhaps regard experimental research with more confidence than other kinds precisely because it gives rise to most of the scandals.

The second way in which an expectancy effect can operate is through experimenters inadvertently treating subjects in a way that influences subject responses to produce the results the experimenter expects or wants. One of

Rosenthal's best known experiments on experiments involved telling one group of postgraduate students that the rats they were to train were particularly intelligent, and telling another group that their rats were particularly stupid. In fact all the rats were randomly selected from the same batch (Rosenthal and Fode 1963). The result was that the allegedly intelligent rats, apparently, learned their tasks more quickly than the allegedly stupid ones. It appears that one of the ways that this expectancy effect operated was through the different ways in which the experimenters handled their rats: the 'clever' rats receiving more fondling and were spoken to more. It is not too difficult to imagine that in experiments involving human subjects experimenters' desires and expectations might lead them to treat people in one comparison group differently from those in another, provoking different responses, and thus influencing the results.

In their review of Rosenthal's work, Barber and Silver (1968) suggest that the most important route taken by expectancy effects is not through experimenters influencing the behaviour of experimental subjects, but through biased observation, interpretation and recording. In the experiment above, for example, the experimenters with the 'clever rats' were more likely to regard errors made by the rats as 'false starts', which they didn't record, while those with the 'stupid rats' were more likely to record such errors to stand as evidence of the rats' stupidity. And in other of Rosenthal's experiments there are many examples of experimenters using their discretion in what to record, or how to measure, what statistical test to use, and so on, and thus tilting the results one way or another. Table 3.4 in Chapter 3 lists the conditions under which expectancy effects are most likely to influence results.

Again it is worth drawing a comparison between highly structured research such as experiments (and here also, survey research using questionnaires), and the kinds of social research where researchers respond minute by minute in a flexible way to what the research situation throws up – for example, in loosely structured interviews where there are no pre-set questions (Chapter 8, section 8.5), or in naturalistic observation (Chapter 10) where the observer tries to observe and record what is going on, whatever that is. In the former kinds of research there is some hope of discovering how the researchers' behaviour influenced what the subjects did and said. In the latter kinds of research, without an audio or video recording it will be virtually impossible to know this. In these kinds of research expectancy effects are allowed free rein and will be very difficult to detect.

Subject reactivity, or Hawthorne effects (Figure 2.2, Box 4)

The story usually goes that research conducted in the Hawthorne works of the Bell Telephone Company (Roeslisberger and Dickson 1939) showed that if people know they are subjects of an experiment they will behave differently from normal in such a way as to produce results which would not occur under non-experimental conditions: hence the term **Hawthorne effect**. In fact subsequent re-analysis has demonstrated that the Hawthorne effect was not an important factor in producing the results of the Hawthorne experiments (Franke and Kaul 1978; Gillespie 1988). It is a tribute to the experimenters that their recording of these large-scale experiments was so thorough that it was possible for other researchers to re-analyse the results to show that the Hawthorne effect is a misnomer.

But misnomer or not, the Hawthorne effect certainly operates sometimes. Experimental subjects do get enthusiastic about being experimental subjects, and sometimes they would prefer the results to come out one way or another. For example, in experiments on para-psychology, complementary medicine, or gender differences it is to be expected that some subjects will be far from neutral. In experimental situations in health and social services, some of the subjects are practitioners who are pleased to be involved in piloting a new form of service. Their enthusiasm for being involved is likely to have an effect independent of whatever the treatment is. **Halo effect** is sometimes used as an alternative term where enthusiasm influences subjects' behaviour.

Hawthorne effects may sometimes operate equally across all comparison groups in the experiment. In this case any differences shown in the results will be 'net' of the Hawthorne effect and may really derive from the differences in the way the two groups were treated, just as the experimenter intended. Here there is only a problem of external generalisability. That is a problem that what happened in the experiment may not happen under non-experimental conditions, because under non-experimental conditions people won't feel important and involved (or afraid and alienated) as they did in the experiment (see section 2.10). But sometimes a Hawthorne effect might affect subjects in only one arm of the experiment. This is particularly likely when one group gets treated in a way that is new and interesting, and another group gets treated in the same boring old way as usual. In this case it is possible that any difference in results between the two groups will be caused by the novelty of one of the treatments, rather than by the treatment itself, and that any or a wide range of novelties would have had the same effect. Here there will be both a problem of external generalisability and a problem of confounding a Hawthorne effect with a treatment effect. Lopsided Hawthorne effects of this sort seem to be particularly common in experiments, and in other research, in the health, welfare, education and criminal justice fields (Chapter 3, section 3.4).

Blinding

Blinding is the main form of defence against the biases of researchers or of research subjects influencing results in an untoward way. This rather unfortunate term means depriving subjects and or researchers of knowledge which, if they had it, might allow them to influence the experiment to give misleading results. If Rosenthal's students had not been told their rats were intelligent or stupid, this knowledge could not have influenced the results. The term **double-blinded** means that both subjects and researchers are deprived of some knowledge. Further than this the term doesn't mean much because it doesn't say what knowledge is being hidden. Table 2.1 shows some forms of blinding and the problems which might arise if blinding is not practised.

The archetype of the double-blinded experiment is the randomised, double-blinded, placebo-controlled trial which is common in testing the effectiveness of pharmaceuticals. Here it is easy to hide to which group subjects have been allocated since a dummy pill – the placebo – can be made to look, taste and smell exactly like the active drug being tested. The random allocation of subjects to comparison groups is likely to be done by an independent agency so that no one in contact with the patients, nor the patients themselves, know who is getting the drug and who the placebo. This is disclosed only at the end of the experiment, or earlier if there are worries about a particular patient's health. The fact that an experiment is going on is likely to be kept secret from all those caring for the patient except for those who actually need to know. In addition, it is possible that data will be recorded by an independent observer, who not only doesn't know which patient is in which group, but doesn't know which drug is being tested. The ethics of blind allocation are discussed in Chapter 13, section 13.4.

Blinding to this extent is often impossible. For example, in an experiment about the effects of different styles of communication, the person doing the communicating has to know what kind of communication style to adopt with each subject. And each subject will know they are being communicated with – though since they probably won't know what it is like to be communicated with in the alternative way, they will be blind to this extent. It may be possible to use independent recorders and observers, but it may not be possible to blind them to which subject is experiencing which set of conditions.

Researcher expectancy effects and **subject reactive**, or 'Hawthorne' effects can be very powerful forces in influencing the results of experiments – or indeed of other research. Where and to the extent that blinding can be used, it will limit the opportunities for the play of these effects. Where blinding is impossible, as it often is, it will be important to consider how these effects might have influenced the results and to interpret the results cautiously in the light of this.

2.7 Reliable observation, recording and measurement (Figure 2.2, Box 5)

If different people are involved in collecting information they may interpret the task in different ways, so that for what is really the same situation, different recorders might record something different, or for what is a different situation, different recorders might record the same. Using well-designed data collection instruments leaving few opportunities for ambiguity, and training people to use them, is an important part of any experiment involving a number of different people collecting data. The same kind of data

TABLE 2.1	Kinds of blinding in experimental research	
Kinds of blinding	**Subjects**	**Researchers**
Blind to the fact of being involved in the experiment	It is usually considered unethical to involve people in experiments without their knowledge and consent (see Chapter 13), and this means that most experiments will be influenced by some degree of Hawthorne effect: people behaving differently because they know they are being researched	Researchers must know who is involved in an experiment
Blind to the purpose of the experiment	The more subjects know about the purpose of the experiment the more possible it will be for them deliberately or inadvertently to influence the results in untoward ways; many experiments in psychology depend on subjects being misled as to the purpose of the experiment: telling them this would often give the game away	Someone among researchers has to know the purpose of the experiment but sometimes the actual conduct of the research is left to someone who doesn't know what its purpose is: then it will be difficult for their expectancies to influence the results
Blind allocation to comparison groups (random allocation is one means of blind allocation: see section 2.3)	If people can influence which group they belong to this is likely to create important differences between groups; if people know which group they belong to it will be possible for them deliberately or inadvertently to influence the results though their behaviour	If the researcher can choose who is allocated to which group, this presents an opportunity to bias the results through selection, or through influencing drop-out
Blind treatment	Knowing to which comparison group they belong may influence their behaviour; for example, they may believe in the efficacy of some educational or psychotherapeutic treatment and this belief may influence what happens to them	If researchers (or collaborators) know which subject is in which group this knowledge may affect the way they interact with subjects in different groups over and beyond the planned for differences in treatment
Blind recording or measurement of data	Insofar as reports from subjects provide data, subjects knowing which group they are in may influence the responses given	If researchers know which group each subject belongs to this may influence the way they collect and interpret information; using 'blind' independent recorders or judges is common in experimental research

Source: Based on Gomm (2000a:53.)

collection instrument will also reduce the possibility of the same observer changing the way he or she interprets observations over a period of time, or from case to case. Many experimenters use data collection instruments which have widely used in the past, and extensively tested, or **validated**. On the one hand, this means that the instrument will have been de-bugged previously. On the other hand, if the same instrument is used in different research projects, the results will be directly comparable with each other. Most such instruments are questionnaires of one kind or another, either completed by subjects or by people observing them. One important test is for test–re-test reliability.

Test–re-test reliability

This refers to the capacity of an instrument to record what is the same in the same way every time it is used. Thus a thermometer which always shows 100 degrees Celsius when placed in water of this temperature is a reliable thermometer, and a question on a questionnaire which always gets the answer 'yes' from the same person is a reliable question, though since people are likely to get bored with being asked the same question several times this is rather unlikely. But the thermometer would also be reliable if it always showed 90 degrees when placed in water of 100 degrees: it would be reliable but wrong, just as consistently provoking a 'yes' answer when the person was lying would betoken a reliable question but an erroneous response. Reliability has to do with *consistency* rather than correctness, though often the two are the same (Gomm 2000b).

Inter-rater reliability

This refers to the degree of agreement between different judges about the same thing. An application of this idea is double-marking in scholastic examinations, ideally with each marker blind to the mark given by the other. There are special statistical tests for inter-rater reliability. It is quite common practice in experimental and other kinds of research to check the observations and measurements made, by having at least some of them recorded by two people independently, blind to each others' records, and then to measure the degree of agreement between them. The measurement for inter-rater reliability is a statistic which scores agreement above the level which might have been expected to have occurred just by chance. The statistic *kappa,* or simply *k,* is that most often used. A kappa score of 0.6 or above means that there is a good level of agreement, or better (Pett 1997:237–48). It is possible for several judges all to make the same *wrong* judgement as each other. So a high level of inter-rater reliability is not necessarily the same thing as accuracy of judgement. But a low level of inter-rater reliability must always suggest inaccuracy. If the judges disagree, then either one or more of them must be wrong, or the matter being considered is of the kind where right or wrong answers are not possible.

In addition to consistency of recording, it is also important that early recordings are not changed retrospectively. This is the same principle as with police or medical records, for the purpose of preventing later events influencing the record of earlier ones.

2.8 The internal validity of an experiment (Figure 2.2, Box 7)

At the end of an experiment there will be some results. Either these will show a difference between the groups, or no difference between them. The results might be in terms of, say, percentages of each group re-offending – in an experiment on the rehabilitation of offenders – or percentages of people expressing racially prejudiced attitudes – in an experiment on the influence of some mass media exposure on attitudes – or differences in smoking behaviour – in the experimental evaluation of a health education programme. The experimenter will have tried to design the experiment so that the only factors which *could* cause such similarities or differences were the different ways in which the comparison groups were treated. If this has been successful the results can be regarded as **internally valid**. The 'valid' means that it is true that any difference in the results were caused by, and only by, the intended differences in treatment, or that any absence of difference in the results was caused by, and only by, the fact that the different treatments had similar effects. The 'internal' means that this is true for this experiment, and would probably be true if it were repeated in the same format. But nothing is being claimed about whether similar results would be obtained under different conditions.

Most of the chapter so far has been about threats to internal validity because, as shown in Figure 2.2 ,while the results might be due to the intended differences in treatment they might also derive from, something about:

- Pre-existing differences between the comparison groups – Box 1
- Differences created by the patterns of refusals and drop-outs – Box 3
- Unintended differences of treatment – Box 6
- Biases on behalf of researchers – Box 5
- Subject reactions to being involved in an experiment, over and above their reactions to the experiences arranged for them – Box 4
- Unreliable or inaccurate data collection and analysis – Box 5.

Thus evaluating whether an experiment has achieved internal validity means judging whether the experimenter has taken adequate measures to avoid the five kinds of confounding listed above. Designing an experiment which will achieve internal validity means building in safeguards to minimise the chances of these kinds of confounding. These safeguards have been discussed above

2.9 Chance: significant and non-significant results (Figure 2.2, Box 2)

There is one more important factor which might influence the results of an experiment. That is chance. If the results of an experiment do show a difference, the question is whether the difference is bigger than might have reasonably been expected to have occurred by chance. This is usually settled by testing the results for their **statistical significance.**

Imagine an experiment consisting of one group of 11-year-old pupils receiving a drugs education programme, and another receiving the standard personal and social education (PSE) curriculum, with results such as those in Table 2.2

On the face of it, the drug education seems to have been successful insofar as at age 13/14 there are only half as many pupils reporting themselves as regular smokers in that group compared with the control group where pupils received the standard PSE curriculum. But could a difference of this size have occurred just by chance? That is what testing for statistical significance is designed to estimate.

A thought experiment might capture the logic of statistical testing. We will ignore the lost subjects for a moment and concentrate on those for

TABLE 2.2	Outcomes of experimental evaluation of drug education programme delivered at age 11/12. Outcomes in terms of smoking behaviour at age 13/14.			
	Number reporting themselves as regular smokers at age 13/14	Number reporting themselves as not regular smokers at age 13/14	Lost to the experiment owing to change of school or unavailability at date of data collection at age 13/14	Totals
Experimental group (Receiving drug education programme at age 11/12)	7	30	3	40
Control group (receiving standard PSE curriculum at age 11/12)	15	20	3	38
Totals	22	50	6	78

How to read this table:
The totals column (last column, first row) shows that 40 pupils aged 11/12 received a drug-education programme including anti-smoking education – the 'experimental group'. A year later an anonymous questionnaire was completed by 37 of them. The third column shows that 3 out of the 40 were unavailable for some reason. Of the 37, seven reported themselves as regular smokers, and 30 did not. The second row of the table gives the corresponding results for the 'controls': the 38 pupils who followed a standard Personal and Social Education (PSE) curriculum rather than the drug education programme.

Source: Invented data but see Hurry and Lloyd (1997).

whom data is available. In total there are 22 'regular smokers'. Imagine taking 22 blank cards and writing 'Smoker' on each. In total there are 50 pupils who are not 'regular smokers'. Imagine taking 50 blank cards and writing 'Non-smoker' on each. In your mind, shuffle all the cards together, and then think about dealing them into one deck of 35 and one deck of 37. Since this is a random deal the single most likely result of doing this would be that there would be 11 'Smokers' in each pile. But chance being what it is, you are rather unlikely to achieve 11 and 11 on a single try. If you did the dealing over and over again you might often achieve 11 and 11, 10 and 12, or 12 and 10: you wouldn't be surprised to get 9 and 13, or 13 and 9.

So these are all results which might have occurred by chance. The statistician argues that if a result *might* commonly occur by chance, then it would be unsafe to assume that it actually occurred for any other reason. What testing for statistical significance does is to give an estimate of how likely a particular set of results would occur by chance. So what about a result of 7 and 15: the actual result of the experiment? How commonly would a result like this occur by chance? If we repeated the card sorting exercise over and over again, then a result of 7 or less and 15 or more, or vice versa, would crop up a little less often than 5 times in one hundred: the so-called 5 *per cent level*. Using a statistical test would give us a similar estimate, though much more conveniently than spending hours dealing cards.

Conventionally, statisticians regard any results which might occur by chance more often than 5 times in a 100 as statistically **non-significant**, meaning that whatever caused the results to be as they are, it is the safest to regard them as the result of chance.

So the result 7 and 15 is *statistically significant at the 5 per cent level* and there are some grounds for regarding the result as being caused by something other than chance. Note that the test won't tell you what actually did cause the results. It won't tell you whether they are the results of differences in intended treatment or of unintentional or accidental difference, or of comparison groups which were dissimilar at the outset, or of researcher bias or subject enthusiasm or dislike of being subjects of an experiment. Given the difficulties of conducting experiments in school settings it seems likely that all the kinds of confounding shown on Figure 2.2 and listed in section 2.8, will have made some contribution to the results, even if only small ones, and even if largely balancing each other out. With this in mind it would be safest not to regard this experiment as showing the effectiveness of anti-smoking education, even though the results were statistically significant.

The result 7 and 15 is not statistically significant at the 1 per cent level, meaning that results like this might be expected to crop up by chance more often than once in a hundred times. The result is not *highly significant*. The results of statistical tests of significance are often expressed as values of *p*, which stands for probability, thus:

p = 0.10   There was a 10% chance of results like this occurring by chance

This is a non-significant result (any figure for p bigger than 0.05 is non-significant, in tables of results, non-significant results are often shown as 'NS').

p = 0.05   There was a 5% chance of results like this occurring by chance
This is a result significant at the 5% level.

p = 0.01   There was a 1% chance of results like this occurring by chance
This is a result significant at the 1% level. A highly significant result.

p = 0.001   There was a 1 in 1,000 chance of results like this occurring by chance
This is a very highly significant result.

The result 7 and 15 was significant, but not highly significant. In these circumstances it is worth looking again at an experiment to see if there are any kinds of confounding which might just be tipping the results in favour of being significant. Look, for example, at the lost subjects in Table 2.2. If in reality all the subjects lost to the experimental group were 'regular smokers' and all those lost to control group were 'non-smokers' then the overall result would cease to be statistically significant.

Statistical tests take the sample size into consideration. Thus a non-significant result might mean one of two things. First (confounding apart) it might mean that really in the experiment the two different treatments had much the same effect as each other. That would be useful information. But, second, it might mean that a real difference between the effects of the treatments was small, and that the size of the sample was too small for such a small difference to be distinguished from a chance effect.

2.10 External validity or generalisability

Section 2.8 dealt with internal validity; whether a piece of research is true in its own terms. *External validity* refers to the extent to which what happened in the experiment can be made to stand as an example for things which happen more widely. Of course, the external validity of any particular experiment is not something which the experiment itself can decide. Whether the results of a particular experiment have any relevance to anything else has to be decided by previous or further research.

It is often argued that experiments in the social sciences 'must' lack external validity because experimental conditions are so different from those of real life. There have been examples of such differences throughout this chapter. For example, the people who enter an experiment are only rarely a statistically representative sample of the people in some general population. Representativeness is dealt with in detail in Chapter 4. Those entering an experiment are more usually a 'grab' or a 'convenience' sample; the people who were around when the experimenter needed some research subjects. Co-operative people will be over-represented and unco-operative people under-represented. In the corpus of psychological experiments, university students are grossly over-represented as subjects (Suls and Rostow 1988). In medical research people with multiple illness conditions are usually excluded from experiments. In real life most sick people are sick with several conditions at once (Tudor Hart 1993). Again the experimental conditions are likely to vary from real life in the degree of influence that experimenters have in determining what happens. And under experimental conditions there are researchers – who know they are researchers and subjects who know they are subjects of an experiment, whereas in real life people play different roles.

It is hardly surprising that experimental circumstances are unlike those of 'real life'. Experiments are designed to overcome a feature of 'real life' which makes it difficult to discern what is causing what, which is that everything has a multitude of causes, and everything interacts with everything else. The way the controlled experiment attempts to solve this problem is to simplify things so that under experimental conditions most factors are controlled and only a few are allowed to vary. This is very unlike real life. But it is not the central purpose of experimental research to match real life point by point. What is necessary is to set up situations which allow interesting bits of reality to be investigated, screened off from all the 'noise' created by the multifarious number of things going on at the same time.

Thus, simply rejecting controlled experiments as 'artificial', first misses the point, because the point of an experiment is to be 'artificial'. And second, controlled experiments are artificial because they are trying to isolate a causal mechanism which while it might operate in a wide range of circumstances would not be expected to operate in the same way. For example, an experiment which demonstrated that knowledge of a candidate's gender influences the mark given to his or her examination script might be generalisable to some real examination systems and not to others. The next stage of the research would be work out which constellation of circumstances would allow this mechanism to operate and which would prevent it from doing so. So, third, whether or not experiments have any external validity is something to be *discovered not assumed*. For example, a convenient way of investigating gender stereotyping by teachers would be to construct a set of essays for them to mark, and then assign a male or female name to each essay, but differently for each teacher. In the past experiments like this did show teachers favouring the essays with the male names. This is obviously an artificial situation. Those who mark the work of people they don't know rarely know the gender, and teachers rarely mark the work of students they don't know personally. And the teachers would know that this was just an experiment and not for real. Whether the gender bias is specific to the experiment or could be generalised to more realistic situations is something to be discovered by studying more realistic situations. But if only the real situations were studied there would be so many differences between the essays, apart from the genders, that it would be difficult to know whether it was gender or something else determining differences in marking. The experimental structure allows this to be clearly seen and it does set up a reasonable presumption that what happened in the experiment will either happen in real life, or that in real life there will be some interesting factor counteracting the tendency shown in the experiment. And if the latter, it may be an important research question to find out what it is.

ACTIVITY 2.1 Designing a controlled experiment

This activity will test your understanding of much that is in the chapter. The activity asks you :

1. To design a controlled experiment to investigate whether knowing the gender of a student will influence the mark given to an essay by a marker. Use Figure 2.2 as a kind of check list to make sure that, as far as possible, your design avoids the kinds of problems it suggests.
2. Assuming that your experiment was conducted and gave results showing that there were *no* significant differences in the marks given by markers attributable to their knowing the gender of a candidate:
   (a) Which features of your research design would you pinpoint as being the most likely reason to regard this result with caution?
   (b) How would you compare the experiment and its results with marking for real, in order to estimate the external validity of your experiment? There is more about mapping experimental results against real life in Chapter 3, section 3.5.

2.11 Summary

This chapter dealt with controlled experiments in particular and experimentation in general. It has represented experimentation as a tidying up and simplifying practice conducted in order to lay bare what can cause what to happen. Even in a well-designed controlled experiment it is still possible to confuse the effects of one thing with the effects of another. Much about experimental design is to be understood as setting up safeguards to prevent confounding, including the confounding effects of bias on behalf of both researchers and subjects. The safeguards include the careful composition of comparison groups, the use of blinding where possible and the standardisation of experimental conditions and devices making for the reliable and accurate recording of data. The fact that confounding is still a strong possibility in the highly simplified environment of the controlled experiment, and with such safeguards in place, is itself a witness to the enormous possibilities for confounding in research designs of other kinds. There is no other research method which is better for demonstrating causality, and the absence of these safeguards in other research designs will make the problems worse.

However, the features which make the controlled experiment a strong design for avoiding attributing causality erroneously also make the controlled experiment very artificial when compared with 'real life'. This has led some researchers into rejecting controlled experiments entirely as being just too artificial to be relevant. But so long as there is an interest in causality, controlled experiments cannot be rejected out of hand. Other researchers have responded to the charge of artificiality by attempting to design experiments which are more naturalistic. This will be discussed in Chapter 3.

Controlled experiments were made the topic of this first substantive chapter of the book, not because they are the most frequently used method in the social sciences – indeed in sociology they are rarely used. Rather, the reason for an early introduction is that the controlled experiment represents the clearest example of a logic of research which you will encounter on and off throughout the book.

Further reading

Most standard psychology texts dealing with research methods give thorough accounts of experimental methods, for example Coolican (1994). A classic, and still excellent text is Campbell and Stanley (1996). Though entirely about experiments in medical research Shepperd, Doll and Jenkinson (1997) is a brief and very lucid account of randomised controlled trials. However the best way of learning more about experimental methods is to read, analyse and evaluate the results of experimental research. The topic of the research is relatively unimportant. What is important is getting to grips with the *logic of experimentation*. Gomm (2000c) gives advice on what to look for in evaluating experimental research.

For statistical testing Coolican (1994) is again a good choice. Most statistical testing these days is done using software packages such as SPSS. Dobbie and Halley (1994) is a combined disk and book kit which can be used as a primer in learning statistical methods supported by computer software. Though the examples concern the analysis of survey data, rather than data from experiments, the principles are the same.

3 More Naturalism in Experiments

By the end of this chapter, you will:

- Have considered the problems arising from relaxing control in order to make experimental situations more naturalistic as opposed to the problems of adopting rigorous control structures which may make experimental results difficult to generalise from
- Know the main factors to look for in a piece of research to judge the likelihood of its results being biased
- Understand more about the idea of generalisation and its relationship to specification
- Have practised analysing a piece of research to come to a considered judgement as to how far its results might have been an artefact of the research situation
- In the chapter Activity, have practised analysing a piece of research to come to a considered judgement as to the specific circumstances of the situations to which its results might be generalised.

And know the meaning of the following terms:
context-dependency ■ effectiveness ■ intuitive data processing
■ quasi-experiments as opposed to true experiments ■ specification.

3.1 Introduction

Chapter 2 identified a researchers' dilemma: the *trade-off between control and naturalism*. The shape of this dilemma is as follows. Controlled experiments are the best design for investigating causality. They attempt to exert experimental control over all the variables which might have a causal effect on whatever it is that is of interest. If this is done successfully, experiments can achieve a high degree of *internal validity*, which means that they can be successful in identifying what caused what to happen *in the circumstances of the experiment*. Achieving internal validity requires the experimenter to ensure that:

- The subjects for the experiment were really similar in the ways they should have been similar, and different in the ways they should have been different

46

- The treatments or experimental conditions were really different in the ways they should have been different and similar in the ways they should have been similar
- Any other factors which should have been excluded from influencing the out-turns were successfully excluded from having an influence, or their influence identified and this taken into consideration in interpreting the results.

The problem which arises from exerting strong experimental control is that this creates an artificial situation, so that what happened in the experiment may rarely, or never, happen under real-life conditions. Hence strong experimental control and high levels of internal validity can result in low levels of *external validity*. This means a difficulty in drawing conclusions which can be generalised beyond the experiment. Thus experimenters may be faced with a difficult choice between adopting designs with strong experimental controls and risking producing results which will not have much bearing on what usually happens, or of relaxing control to produce more naturalistic conditions but at the risk of being uncertain as to what actually did cause what to happen. Sometimes experimenters do not so much opt for more naturalism as have it thrust upon them since there may be practical and ethical reasons why experimental control cannot be imposed on some variables in an experiment (see Chapter 5).

This chapter looks first at two kinds of more naturalistic experiments, **field experiments** (section 3.2) and **decision-simulation experiments** (section 3.3) and considers the benefits of relaxing experimental control in pursuit of naturalism and the kinds of problems which arise when experimental control is relaxed. The experiments discussed here are controlled experiments, even though the controls are weak in some regards. They would be termed **quasi-experiments**, not because they are more naturalistic, but because **true experiments** always involve creating comparison groups by randomisation (chapter 2; section 2.3). The remainder of the chapter considers strategies which might be used to judge how naturalistic, or unnaturalistic an experimental situation was, in order to decide how far its results might apply more widely. In doing this the chapter will also look at a very important use of experimental designs; their use in applied social research in evaluating the *effectiveness* of medical, social work, educational or criminal justice interventions.

3.2 Field experiments

Sometimes the term 'field experiment' takes its meaning from the contrast with laboratory experiments', and means 'out in the field' and not 'inside the lab'. But as Oakley (2000 :174) notes the term 'laboratory method' is often used to mean any experimental approach, including what I shall call 'field experiments'. So there is no definitive meaning of the term 'field experiment'. When I use it I am thinking about the kind of experiment where the researcher injects some control into an otherwise naturally occurring situation – for example, those experiments where two actors playing the role of job applicants with identical CVs, but of different ethnicity apply for the same real jobs, and covertly record what happens (Brown and Gay 1985). As a major example I shall use part of a famous study by David Rosenhan (1973) which has been reprinted many times (for example, 1996). I have deliberately chosen this because it is a rather flimsy experiment and therefore offers a good illustration of what can go wrong in field experiments.

'I'm looking for a psychiatrist'

David Rosenhan is well known for his 'pseudo-patient experiment' which involved infiltrating 'sane' people into various American mental hospitals as patients, and their observations of what happened to them there. Despite behaving as sanely as possible they were treated as if they were genuine mental patients and in need of treatment. Since there were no controls, this properly shouldn't be called an experiment. 'Covert participant observation research' would be a more appropriate designation (see Chapter 10). As an adjunct and a follow-up to this, Rosenhan mounted a field experiment. A female assistant was sent to the University hospital precinct. Her task was to approach people who looked like medical staff and ask them for directions. After indicating that she wanted directions she provided the information either that she was 'looking for an internist' (an ordinary doctor), or 'looking for a psychiatrist'. She then went on to attempt to ask another five questions about the hospital. For a third group she just tried to ask the questions without saying she was looking for anyone in particular. Similar procedures were carried out on the University campus, where the same research assistant approached people who looked like University lecturers, asking directions to a non-existent part of the University, and five more questions, but without any reference to doctors or psychiatrists. The control structure here sets up comparisons in the hospital precinct between three groups according to how they were asked for directions, and between all of these and the people asked for directions on the University campus. The results are shown in Table 3.1.

For the hospital precinct the results seem to indicate that when the research assistant was perceived as looking for an ordinary medical doctor, people continued in conversation with her. But when she was perceived to be looking for a psychiatrist people were less likely to do so and overall people spent less time with her in her mental illness role. Rosenhan's interpretation of this was that a label of 'mental illness', here triggered by the reference to the psychiatrist, will intervene in a social relationship such that those who are labelled as 'mentally ill' will be treated differently from others. Although this could not be demonstrated by this experiment Rosenhan drew the further inference from the results that being treated differently from others in this way is likely to cause people who have been labelled as 'mentally ill' to experience themselves as being odd, and hence to contribute to their mental distress.

TABLE 3.1	Responses to requests for directions by researcher in different roles in a university hospital precinct, and on the university campus			
Responses	**University Campus**	**University Hospital precinct**		**No cues as to who was being looked for**
		'Looking for an internist'	**'Looking for a psychiatrist'**	
Moves on head averted (%)	0	0	0	0
Makes eye contact (but no more) (%)	0	0	11	0
Pauses and chats (but didn't stop to talk) (%)	0	0	11	10
Stops and talks (%)	100	100	78	90
Mean number of questions answered (out of 6, including the request for directions)	6	4.8	3.8	4.5
Number of Respondents	14	15	18	10

How to read this table

The columns of the table show what happened when the research assistant engaged with people in different places in slightly different ways. For the university campus she approached people who looked like lecturers and asked directions to a non-existent part of the university and five other questions, none of which carried any implications of mental illness. She asked 14 different people and all of them (100%) stopped, talked to her and answered all her enquires (mean number of questions answered = 6). For the hospital precinct she always asked directions of people who seemed to be staff, but to some (15) she indicated that she was looking for an 'internist' (any kind of doctor), for others (18) that she was looking for a psychiatrist, and with others (10) she gave no indication who she was looking for. In each case she also asked five other questions. The table shows that when she represented herself as looking for a psychiatrist she was less likely to have her request taken seriously. Only 78% stopped and talked, 11% made eye contact but then moved on, 11% paused but did not really stop to talk. When she was 'looking for a psychiatrist' on average the 18 people only answered 3.8 of her questions. The bottom row shows the number of respondents involved. From this you can work out that the difference in response between 'looking for an internist' and 'looking for a psychiatrist' is accounted for by the negative responses of only 4 people out of 18. Since 18 is the largest set of responses in the table there is a better chance that it will include rarer kinds of response than the smaller sets of responses. Usually, larger samples show more diversity than smaller ones.

Source: After Rosenhan (1973: 255).

The issue here is a causal one. The question is whether some intimation of mental illness causes people to be treated differently from others. As a causal question it is eminently suitable for experimental treatment. But since the issue is about whether *under ordinary conditions* this happens, it makes sense to conduct the research under as naturalistic conditions as possible. But the fact that these conditions are not under experimental control may give rise to difficulties in interpreting the results, as I discovered in attempting something like a replication of Rosenhan's experiment.

As an exercise for student social workers I conducted similar, though not identical experiments, two years running. The locale was a busy district general hospital with general medical and psychiatric facilities. The requests were; 'Excuse me, I've got an appointment with a consultant urologist', or 'Excuse me I've got an appointment with a psychiatrist' and in both cases 'and I don't know where to go'. The targets were anyone with a security badge. Student researchers alternated between the role of a urology patient and the role of a patient for psychiatry.

This wasn't arranged as an exercise in research methodology but as an experiential demonstration that 'mental illness' labels have very powerful effects on social relationships. Having read the research in this area I simply assumed they did. In this respect the results in the first year were very disappointing. Some students reported that there was no difference in how they were treated whichever kind of patient they represented themselves as being. Some did experience a difference but they 'couldn't put their finger' on what it was. None of the requests for assistance was ignored, even to the extent that a porter left a patient on a trolley to walk the requester part way to her destination (the psychiatric wing) including a journey in the lift. A doctor running across the car park nonetheless stopped and gave directions – to the department of genito-urinary medicine, in this case.

My first-year version of the experiment improved on Rosenhan's. I had 15 'research assistants' of both genders and various ethnic groups, and far more observations. His version was 'over-controlled' in the sense that there was only one female research assistant. That leaves his results vulnerable to the suggestion that they were produced by something special about her, which might not be true of someone else, and the number of observations in his experiment is perilously few (see Chapter 2, section 2.9).

In the second year I improved on the design. This time I sent students out in pairs: one to ask and one to observe and take notes. I provided an observation schedule saying what to look out for (Chapter 10). For some students it was agreed between requester and observer that there were no discernible differences in response whichever role was played. For some the observer recorded no differences, but the requester was sure there were some. But for some there were differences agreed between requester and observer in the same direction as in Rosenhan's results (Table 3.1). For these the observer often reported that the requester behaved differently according to the role he or she was playing. Requesters were often reluctant to accept this but according to observers, requesters who elicited a different response in their differing roles seemed to be 'acting out' a mental patient persona. Eye-contact was the most telling difference. In their mental illness roles these requesters did not make prolonged eye-contact with those they asked for assistance. There were also differences in tone of voice and their register was less assertive, or so observers claimed.

This was a rather ramshackle experiment and I certainly would not want to claim that the results of Rosenhan's experiment were created by his research assistant behaving differently in the different roles. Ten years and 6,000 miles separates the two so there are many other things which might be different between the two experiments. Nonetheless my experience does suggest that a number of uncontrolled variables might have been at play in both.

As with Rosenhan's experiment so mine also failed to control the selection of targets. Were requesters approaching different kinds of people in their different roles? It was also obvious in my experiment (probably not in Rosenhan's) that physical location was another uncontrolled variable with regard to the duration of encounters. Those offering assistance often walked the requester to a corner before pointing the way, but for some locations this was not necessary. Those in a position to point to a nearby reception desk often did so without giving further directions themselves. It also became apparent that there are two parties influencing how long an encounter lasts. The behaviour of the requesters had a definite influence on this. Sometimes requesters signalled that they were satisfied with a set of directions and thereby ended the encounter; sometimes they asked for further clarification or looked uncertain, and prolonged it. Lastly, my experiment added a problematic element which as not there in Rosenhan's: someone watching what was going on and making notes about it. I can claim that this greatly improved the recording of what happened, but if respondents were aware of being watched, this might have influenced their behaviour.

My version of the experiment, then, illustrates the way variables may be left uncontrolled in the attempt to experiment under more naturalistic circumstances. In summary there were:

- *Variables at the subject level*: no control over selection of targets for one treatment or the other (Chapter 2, section 2.3).
- *Variables at the treatment level*: differences in age, gender and ethnicity as between requesters, different behaviour by requesters in their different roles – an expectancy effect (Chapter 2, section 2.6). Different physical locations of those asked directions (Chapter 2, section 2.5). Some respondents perhaps realised that they were being observed; others not (maybe a lop-sided Hawthorne effect: Chapter 2, section 2.6).
- *Variables at the level of observation and recording* : no guarantee that different observers understood or used the observation schedule in the same way (Chapter 2, section 2.7). Possible expectancy effects among some observers (Chapter 2, section 2.6).

This wasn't a very well-designed experiment. Some of the problems above might have been ameliorated. But, apart from standardising the use of the observation schedule, going too far down the other routes of improving control themselves leads to problems. For example, controlling for location of request, by always making the requests in the same location, would lead to results which might be true for that location but no other. Controlling for location of request by selecting a number of different locations would then require an adequate sample of requests made in each location and an experiment on a much larger scale, a flooding of the hospital with researchers and perhaps an undermining of the whole enterprise.

Rosenhan's claim was that people suspected of being mentally ill are treated differently even when they behave *exactly the same* as everyone else. He added the results of his field experiment to other evidence about the power of labelling. Remember that this experiment followed research in which 'sane' people behaved 'normally' in mental hospitals, but were treated as if they were mad. One aspect of this was that often when they approached ward staff the pseudo-patients were simply ignored as if they were not there at all. His field experiment seems to cap this nicely since it is apparently another situation in which people who behave sanely are nonetheless treated differently even if, as here, there is only a smidgen of evidence about them that they may be mentally ill. Only when drawn onto a canvas including the way pseudo-patients were treated in mental hospitals do the very small differences shown in Rosenhan's experiment seem interesting. They are certainly not statistically significant (Chapter 2, section 2.9).

By contrast my results would bear only the commentary that people suspected of being mentally ill are treated differently when they themselves behave *a little bit differently* from others. And my results could also be read as evidence that asking some social work students to pretend to be mental patients causes them more embarrassment than asking them to pretend to be patients of the urology department. As with Rosenhan's interpretation, this one is still suggestive of the power of 'mental illness' labels to affect social interaction, but the causal mechanism suggested is different. In this regard it might have produced misleading rather than enlightening results to control the behaviour of the requesters so that each respondent was confronted with identical behaviour irrespective of the role played by the requester, apart from the destination mentioned. If the important mechanism is in the approach of the requester, then standardisation would have eliminated the most interesting feature of the phenomenon of interest. Looked at in this way it seems credible to argue that there was *so little* difference in response to requests made from different roles (Table 3.1), because Rosenhan's research assistant did usually behave in the same way irrespective of the role she was playing.

The experiment didn't disrupt normal goings on very much, and asking directions in a hospital seems an ordinary thing to do. Thus the experiment might be said to have achieved a high degree of naturalism. But because of all the uncontrolled variables it cannot be said with any confidence what it was about the way requests were made which caused differences and similarities of response. Because of its naturalism we might feel comfortable in generalising the results of the experiment to the normal interaction between requesters and respondents in a hospital. But because of the lack of control it is not at all clear what there is to generalise about.

Thus by comparison with the kind of control which can be achieved in laboratory experiments this one shows considerable shortcomings. But it is important also to make the comparison in another direction; between the field experiment and non-experimental approaches. Assuming the topic was the difference in interaction caused by intimations of mental illness then it might have been approached either through interviews or naturalistic observation. Interviews would tell us how people with some mental illness stigma experienced and interpreted their interaction with others, which would be interesting (for example, see Rogers, Pilgrim and Lacey, 1993). But such interviews could not tell us whether their experiences arose from their actually being treated differently from other people, rather than from their assumptions that they were. Observing the ordinary flux of life in the public areas of a hospital would first, give rise to the problem of actually finding and identifying the instances we wanted among the welter of other things going on. One of the reasons for doing experiments is to make something of interest happen frequently when we are around to observe it. Again, the field experiment, as an experiment, already suffered from there being too much diversity between encounters as to the permutations between requesters and respondents in terms of age, gender and ethnicity, in terms of busyness and status of the various responders, location of request and variation in requester behaviour. In the naturalistic observation such diversity would increase by a quantum leap, and it would be even more difficult to make confident statements as to what ingredients in encounters led to people being treated the same, or differently from each other.

3.3 Decision-simulation experiments

All experiments are 'simulations' because they set up simplified simulacra of what what might happen. But there are some kinds of experiments which quite explicitly simulate. These are particularly common in the study of the factors which influence decision-making. There are many naturally occurring situations which involve people sitting down at desks, reading and writing documents. These can be simulated with a high degree of naturalism. The activity at the end of Chapter 2 asked you to design just such an experiment to investigate the causal influence on examination grades of examiner knowledge of candidate gender.

Table 3.2 shows the results of a decision-simulation experiment to judge the extent to which it is sensible to draw conclusions about the causes of suicide from international comparisons of suicide statistics.

TABLE 3.2	Verdicts of five Danish Kredslaege and four English Coroners on the same 40 cases								
Verdicts	English Coroners				Danish Kredslaege				
	1	2	3	4	A	B	C	D	E
Suicide	23	21	17	16	32	31	28	27	27
Accident	9	8	10	13	6	5	8	12	6
Open	6	11	13	11	2	3	3	0	6
Natural									
Causes	2	0	0	0	0	1	1	1	1

English mean (average) for suicide verdicts = 19.25; Danish mean =29.00; the difference is highly statistically significant

How to read this table
The same 40 cases were presented to 4 English coroners (1–4) and 5 of their Danish counterparts (A–E). 4 verdicts were available. The numbers in the cells show the verdicts actually given by each decision-maker. Thus coroner 1 found for suicide in 23 cases, accidental death in 9 and so on. A statistical test was carried out comparing the average number of suicide verdicts for the English and the Danes respectively (Chapter 2, section 2.9). The test suggested that less than once in one thousand times would a difference of this size be expected to occur by chance and hence that this result was probably not due to chance and probably does reflect a real difference in the way English and Danish functionaries make decisions about cause of death.

Source: After Atkinson, Kessell and Dalgaard (1975).

In Chapter 2 we were dealing mainly with experiments of the similar subjects/different treatments design, used to investigate the causal effects of a particular treatment or set of experimental conditions (see Figure 2.1). The experiment here is an example of the other basic experimental design; a different subjects/similar treatments design, used to investigate the different responses of different kinds of people to the same treatment or set of conditions: see Figure 3.1.

Often this design is used without defining groups initially, identifying groups only at the end of the experiment. Essentially this is what happens with social surveys where everyone receives the same treatment: that is, the same set of questions administered in the same way, and in analysing the results the researcher identifies different groups according to their responses (see Chapters 5 and 6).

But in the coroner experiment the comparison groups are defined in advance and the 'same treatment' is the provision of the same sets of evidence about 40 deaths to two different groups of functionaries involved

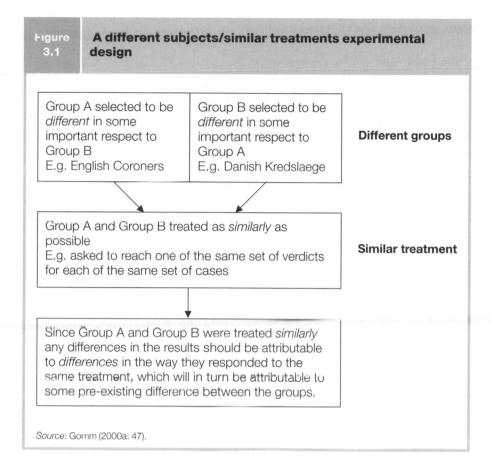

Figure 3.1 **A different subjects/similar treatments experimental design**

| Group A selected to be *different* in some important respect to Group B E.g. English Coroners | Group B selected to be *different* in some important respect to Group A E.g. Danish Kredslaege | **Different groups** |

Group A and Group B treated as *similarly* as possible
E.g. asked to reach one of the same set of verdicts for each of the same set of cases

Similar treatment

Since Group A and Group B were treated *similarly* any differences in the results should be attributable to *differences* in the way they responded to the same treatment, which will in turn be attributable to some pre-existing difference between the groups.

Source: Gomm (2000a: 47).

in classifying deaths, asking them to do what they would normally do, which is to reach a verdict on each. The simulation departs from reality in that normally only one functionary would decide on each case, the English coroners would have an option to enrol a jury and all would gather some of their evidence by questioning witnesses. There are excellent studies of coroners actually going about their business (for example, Atkinson 1978), but these cannot tell us clearly whether any differences in verdicts reached by different coroners arise from differences in the cases they dealt with, or from differences in the ways different coroners think and come to conclusions or, in this example, from differences built into different judicial systems. The experimental design here controls for the differences between cases and allows differences between decision-makers/decision-making systems to show up clearly.

As a group, the Danes were much more likely to reach a suicide verdict than were their English counterparts (Table 3.2). Each of the Danes reached more verdicts of suicide than any of the English. On this basis Atkinson and his colleagues suggest that the higher national suicide rate in Denmark compared with England may be due to differences in the way decisions on cause of death are made in the two legal systems. In England coroners have to find 'definite proof' of suicide in order to give a suicide verdict, whereas in Denmark it is necessary only to find that 'on balance of probabilities' a death was a suicide in order to apply that verdict. It's just much easier to reach a suicide verdict in Denmark. This explanation sounds credible. Whether it is valid or not, there is certainly evidence here that English and Danish suicide statistics are an unreliable basis for comparing the two countries in terms of how many people deliberately end their own lives.

What the figures in Table 3.2 do not show is that there is almost as much disagreement among individual functionaries *within* a national group as between the two groups. This is something for which an inter-rater reliability test is the best measure (Chapter 2, section 2.7). Following some analysis of differences in suicide rates emanating from different coroners' courts in London focusing only on poisonings, Atkinson and his colleagues concluded that differences in suicide rates may owe as much to the idiosyncrasies of individual coroners as to differences between the populations and the circumstances of the areas in which people do away with themselves. To this extent the problem is recognised in most modern analyses of suicide statistics by the analysis being done with the statistics of suicide and those of undetermined deaths combined. This is on the assumption that most disagreements between coroners would concern allocation between these two categories, and that combining them controls for much of coroner disagreement (Charlton *et al.* 1992). However, the research quoted here suggests greater room for disagreement than this. Undetermined deaths are the 'open verdicts' in Table 3.2. In this experiment the 'treatment', in the form of standard stimulus material, was well controlled, except for some problems in producing the same case materials in two different languages for two different legal systems. But control over subject characteristics looks less secure.

In a different subjects/similar treatments design, issues about controlling for subject characteristics depend on what the research is about. Here the research is about the difference between being an English Coroner and being a Danish Kredslaege. Hence the results might be confounded if, for example the English coroners in the experiment were younger on average than their Danish counterparts. If that were so then the differences between the two groups might be attributable to age differences rather than differences in the two legal systems. Generalising the results of this experiment to produce an explanation of differences in suicide rates between the two countries relies on the four English coroners being representative of all English coroners, and the five kredslaege being representative of all such Danish functionaries. Given that there are only four of one and five of the other there is a possibility that Atkinson and his colleagues may have been unlucky enough to have selected a set of English coroners more reluctant than their peers to reach suicide verdicts, and/or a set of Kredslaege more gung-ho about giving such verdicts than Kredslaege in general. Except by increasing the number of participants in the experiment it is difficult to think of ways in which experimental control over such differences might be exerted directly. If there were any information that decision-making behaviour in this field varied with some knowable characteristics such as age, rural or urban jurisdiction, or religion, then it might be possible to exert control by restricting all participants to those similar for that charac- teristic – similar in age for example, or only urban jurisdictions, or no catholics. However, there seems to be no such information available, and doing that would change the situation from one using participants of unknown representativeness to one using participants known to be unrepre- sentative but in a particular way. Possibly the best factor for control purposes would be track record, restricting entry to the experiment to those functionaries with a record of giving average-for-nation percentages of suicide verdicts per year.

But research is the art of the possible, and it was probably difficult enough for Atkinson and his colleagues to persuade nine people to co-operate, let alone being picky about who they should be. Remember also that in each country only a handful of functionaries account for all suicide verdicts nationally: four and five are quite large numbers in this regard.

In assessing such simulation research it must always be kept in mind that the subjects will know this is 'not for real' and may behave other than they would in natural conditions; a subject reactive or Hawthorne effect as discussed in Chapter 2, section 2.6. You probably thought of that in regard to your response to the activity in Chapter 2. However, in this case what is being simulated is decision-making which is normally conducted under highly accountable conditions. The difference between the experiment and the reality it is supposed to represent may not be very great here as compared with experiments which ask people to do under observation what they would normally do privately and/or informally (Bloor 1994; and see Chapter 7, section 7.3).

This was a fairly simple example of decision simulation experimentation. But it is possible to elaborate the stimulus material in order to build in variables of particular interest. For example, in researching social workers' decision-making about black children as opposed to white, Owusu-Bempah (1994) used a set of case notes where sometimes a black and some- times a white ethnicity was written into what were otherwise the same case notes, showing that, without further evidence, social workers interpreted the backgrounds and needs of the children differently according to their ethnicity.

3.4 Experimental designs and effectiveness research

In the latter half of the 1990s 'evidence-based practice' became a buzz word in health, social work, criminal justice and education. In simple terms, evidence-based practice means basing what is done on the best evidence available, usually meaning research evidence. This has given rise to a growth in applied social research in the form of *effectiveness studies*.

The key question is the 'does it work?' question: 'Is what you are doing effective; does it produce benign effects?' There are two issues here. One is about how it should be judged, and who should judge, whether an effect is worth achieving or not. This is a value decision and the issue of evaluation criteria is discussed further in Chapter 12, section 12.3. But before evaluation criteria are needed it is necessary to know whether practices have *any* effects, and if so what they are. This is a causal question and it suggests an experimental approach as the ideal. In medicine, in particular, experimental approaches to the question of effective practice have been regarded as almost the only credible sources of evidence and randomised control trials as the 'gold standard' of evidence among them. As Chapter 2 argues, there are good reasons for regarding well-conducted experiments as the best approach to investigating cause and effect, although there are often good reasons why an experimental approach cannot be used. But if the evidence derived from an experiment is to be the evidence on which routine practice is to be based it becomes particularly important that the results of the experiment will indeed be applicable to routine practice. Here differences between the artificial circumstances of an experiment and the real world of practice are likely to create serious problems, not just of interpretation but of patient or client welfare.

The bias towards success verdicts in effectiveness studies

A telling form of evidence for the need to take an experimental approach comes from comparing the results of effectiveness studies using experimental approaches of different levels of rigour. It began to become apparent in the 1970s that there was strong inverse relationship between the extent of experimental control in an evaluation study and the finding that the practice evaluated was effective. Table 3.3 shows the results of one of the earliest of these comparisons, that by Logan in 1972, concerning programmes to reduce crime and delinquency.

Since Logan, similar pictures have been given for other studies of effectiveness in criminology (Lipsey 1995) and in social work (Macdonald, Sheldon and Gillespie, 1992; Oakley and Fullerton 1996). In medicine the same picture had been discovered earlier (Cochrane 1972).This has led to the increasing use of experimental methods to replace knowledge based on poorly conducted research or other kinds of evidence based on the opinions of doctors or on the unsubstantiated claims of drug companies. Experiments have shown much such knowledge to be ill informed (Oakley 2000).

Studies of effectiveness without any control groups at all are very poorly designed to provide evidence to determine whether some intervention was the cause of any outcomes recorded. For example, if sick people are given a medical treatment and subsequently get better, without a control group there is no way of knowing whether they got better because of the treat-

TABLE 3.3	Experimental control and experimental results: research on programmes to reduce crime and delinquency		

	Number judged successful (%)	Number judged unsuccessful (%)
19 studies with randomised control groups	7 (37)	12 (63)
23 studies with non-randomised control groups	16 (70)	7 (30)
58 studies with no control groups	50 (86)	8 (14)

How to read this table

Logan reviewed 100 studies of programmes designed to reduce criminal behaviour; 58 of these had designs with no control groups – that is they only featured people receiving the programme, and not anyone receiving any alternative treatment or no treatment at all. The remainder had control groups, 23 with non-randomised control groups and 19 with randomised control groups (see Chapter 2, section 2.0). The table shows that where there were no control groups the researchers were very likely to judge the programme as a success, and that where there were randomised control groups they were much more likely to judge the programme as a failure.

Source: After Logan (1972: Table 1).

ment, or would have got better anyway. Similarly, there is no way of knowing whether they would have got better quicker without the treatment. Or again, the fact that some groups of people said they liked their experience of counselling provides no evidence as to whether they would have actually liked something other than counselling better, and no evidence that their morale was improved by counselling rather than simply improving with the passage of time, nor indeed whether their morale would have been better had they been left to their own devices. Thus these 'pre-post tests without control' studies cannot usually be used as a basis for declaring an intervention to be effective without some additional evidence of some kind. Yet as Table 3.3 shows these are precisely the kinds of studies where researchers have been most likely to declare an intervention effective. It seems likely that very strong expectancy effects are operating here (Chapter 2, section 2.6), with researchers being strongly influenced by the faith that practitioners have in favour of the effectiveness of their own practices, in a situation where the hard evidence provided by a control group design is lacking.

At a finer level of detail it seems also to be true that where randomisation is used to create control groups, findings of effectiveness are less likely than when control groups are created in other ways (Shultz *et al.*, 1995; Kunz and Oxman 1998). The reason for this is that control groups created at random control out more pre-existing differences between groups, while those not created at random let such differences filter through to create a spurious impression of effects caused by the intervention itself (see Figure 2.2).This continues the sequence above, so that the more rigorous the research design, the less likely a practice is to be found effective.

Table 3.4 gives a list of the conditions which would seem to offer the greatest opportunities for bias of this kind to play a part. The more of these characteristics a particular piece of research has, the more possible it is that any bias in favour of particular findings will have an influence. You will see that some of the items in the list are those which controlled experimental structures are designed to exclude (see Chapter 2). A particularly important item in the list is the one about 'ambiguous findings, difficult to interpret' for here a researcher's biases have room to allocate the benefit of the doubt in favour of the findings they would prefer. That probably explains a great deal about Logan's (1972) findings and others like them, because studies which claim to show cause and effect relationships, but do not include control groups within the design, always produce results which can be credibly interpreted in different ways, and hence are vulnerable to being interpreted in a biased way.

Sometimes a rigorous experimental approach will mistakenly designate an effective treatment or programme as an ineffective one and the scientific tradition of experimentation is a conservative one, setting high standards of proof before accepting that results are significant (see Chapter 2, section 2.9). But the overall picture given by studies such as Logan's is so stark that it forces the conclusion that there has been a distinct bias among researchers, many of them practitioners themselves, towards finding that health, social work, criminal justice or educational interventions are effective. It is important to remember that we are not dealing here with merely academic knowledge but with research findings which, if they are wrong, may result in people being poisoned, or being subjected to hundreds of hours of treatment or education which does them no good, or to investments in ineffectual patterns of service at the cost of non-investment in something else which might be more beneficial to more people.

Effectiveness under ordinary circumstances

But there is a problem in taking a rigorous experimental approach to evaluating effectiveness. It is a problem you are already familiar with. In using a rigorous research design in order to judge effectiveness, a researcher may well be creating a situation most unlike that which occurs in routine practice. Thus what proves effective in the research situation may not work when rolled out into more ordinary circumstances. And, to make matters worse, there is no one such thing as 'routine practice', but rather a wide range of different practice settings, each with its own characteristics which may alter the effectiveness of the intervention tested by the research.

Most effectiveness research is conducted in naturalistic settings: wards, schools, prisons and so on. If an experimental design is used these are 'field

TABLE 3.4	A recipe for bias

There is more room for bias to influence the results of research (experimental or otherwise) when:

- Those who sponsor the research have a considerable financial, emotional or political investment in the results coming out one way rather than another and where those who conduct the research are not independent of the sponsors; sponsors may be government departments, service agencies, commercial companies, political parties or pressure groups
- Those who are the subjects of the research have a strong preference for the results coming out one way or another and where those who conduct the research make close sympathetic relationships with the subjects or where the subjects are the sponsors as in participatory research (Chapter 12, section 12.5)
- For those who conduct the research, there are rewards for the results coming out one way rather than another; for example where one set of results would be taken as breaking exciting new ground
- Interested sponsors, and/or interested subjects and/or interested researchers can decide who is included in the research and can influence who drops out
- The research is broad-based and open-ended, such that preferred findings can be found (and dispreferred ones ignored) (see Chapter 10)
- Interested sponsors and/or interested subjects and/or interested researchers can determine what treatment different subjects get; particularly in an experiment where allocation to comparison groups is not blind and where researchers and subjects are not blinded to the treatment received (Chapter 2, Section 2.6)
- There are no control groups
- There are no accurate records of the state of affairs prior to the research and establishing a base line relies on memories (see Chapter 6, Box 6.1)
- Making records of what happens allows considerable discretion
- It is possible retrospectively to alter data collected at an earlier point in time, or where the situation at an earlier point in time is reconstructed from people's memories (see Chapter 6, Box 6.1)
- The results are ambiguous and difficult to interpret, allowing researchers to allocate the 'benefit of the doubt' in the preferred direction
- The results are not made available to other researchers and cannot be audited (for example, where they are regarded as commercially or politically sensitive)
- What gets published is vetted and amended by sponsors or subjects (see Chapter 13, section 13.6)
- What gets published is determined by publishers' preferences for novel findings, radical critiques or 'success stories' – *publication bias*

experiments' in my sense of the term (section 3.2). But for research purposes the settings and the procedures will be varied from normal practice. For example, in testing medical treatments it is common to select as subjects people who are similar to each other – same gender, similar age perhaps. By reducing the diversity among the subjects the experimenter can get away with using a smaller sample (see Chapter 2, section 2.3). But this means that the results may not be generalisable to people of a different gender or a different age group. Again in order to simplify the experiment, and to ensure the welfare of the subjects, people with medical complications may be excluded. But as Tudor Hart (1993) comments, this results in situations such as that where 90 per cent of the research on hypertension has been conducted with subjects who suffer from hypertension and nothing else, but 90 per cent of people with hypertension have at least one other medical condition as well. What was true for the subjects of experimental tests of hypertension treatments may not be true for the majority of people presenting to their doctor with hypertension.

Other differences may include that research is conducted where resources are more generous, and where staff are better trained than would be the case elsewhere. It is highly likely that doctors, nurses, teachers, counsellors, prison officers and so on who are involved in the research feel important and interested and behave in a different way from those of their counterparts in non-research situations. Knowing that they are subjects of research, subjects also may feel special and behave special. Where blinding is impossible this may affect the results (Chapter 2, section 2.6). All in all this suggests considerable difficulties in saying with any confidence that because something worked under the research conditions it will also work under more usual conditions. There is also the important issue of whether 'ordinary circumstances' should be, or could be, made more like those of the research setting, and in what regards, and what might have to be sacrificed in order to do so. In order to do one thing people usually have to give up doing something else.

The context-dependency of cause and effect

Faced with these problems of transferring findings from research into practice it is tempting to argue that effectiveness should therefore be investigated in an unobtrusive, non-disruptive way in ordinary circumstances. Some researchers have argued just this (Guba and Lincoln 1989). There are some merits in the suggestion. But this doesn't really solve the problem of transfer. If we studied, say, practice in a children's home by observing it as it usually was, without the research affecting it in any way, we might reach some conclusions as to what was most effective practice there in, say, improving the children's social skills. Given the problems of linking cause and effect under uncontrolled circumstances it would be, or it should be, difficult to be confident about such findings, but at least we might be sure that the findings were not an experimental artefact. But it would still be likely that what was effective practice in one children's home in its normal day-to-day practice would not be effective practice in another children's home in its different normal every-day practice.

The important point here is about the *context-dependency* of cause and effect relationships. Put simply, this means that doing something in one set of circumstances may have different effects from doing the self-same thing in another set of circumstances. And, what is the same point in other words, it means that doing something with regard to one set of people may have effects different from doing the same with another set (Pawson and Tilley 1997: Chapter 3) It is a reasonable presumption that some causal mechanisms are more *robust* than others, in the sense that the same mechanism will have the same effects in a wide range of circumstances. Thus the kinds of physiological mechanisms which are triggered by pharmaceuticals are probably more robust – more consistent in their effects – than the kinds of psycho-social mechanisms which are triggered in group dynamic situations or in consumer behaviour or organisational behaviour. In social science we are usually dealing with mechanisms which are highly context-dependent.

Specification: cross-mapping for generalisation

There are no sure-fire ways of dealing with these problems, but there are ways of getting a purchase on them. The term 'generalisation' is perhaps a misleading one, because a well-phrased generalisation always includes its opposite: a specification. A generalisation in the field of cause and effect, says: 'This happened here under these specific circumstances and it will likely happen generally where something like these specific circumstances obtain.' The key to producing generalisable knowledge thus lies in identifying the specifications. This is something which is unlikely to be possible within the context of a single research study of whatever kind it is. Rather it requires a large number of pieces of research conducted in varying circumstances to discover how 'the same thing' has the same or different effects in different circumstances. This is true whether we are dealing with the development of a theoretical science or of applied research. But it is particularly important for applied research since, without the specifications, practitioners will not know whether some intervention will work in *their* circumstances. It is the specifications which turn research knowledge into recipes for action.

The natural sciences have been characterised by very successful research programmes identifying the specific circumstances under which something will lead to something else, and the circumstances under which it will lead to something different. Thus it is known, for example, what the circumstances are under which water will freeze at 0 degrees Celsius, and what the circumstances are under which it will become 'super-cooled water'. Success in these regards probably owes much to the inherent robustness of the kinds of phenomena dealt with by natural scientists. The social sciences have been much less successful in this regard.

Since there is much less sound information in the social sciences as to the specific circumstances under which something will or will not happen, generalisation has to rely, for the time being at least, on *informed speculation*. This is especially true for applied social research where practitioners simply cannot wait for the outcomes of long-term research programmes in order to decide what to do for the best in the here and now.

Some purchase on the problem of transferring research into practice can be gained by cross-mapping the circumstances of the research against the circumstances of the locale in which someone might attempt to put the research findings into practice. Table 3.5 illustrates the kinds of dimensions such a cross-mapping might have. Here the example is for the property-marking of domestic goods: either by etching or by the use of ultra-violet-sensitive markers. This is an area in which there has been considerable research, sometimes showing that this is an effective way of reducing burglaries, sometimes showing it to be ineffectual (Laycock 1985). Table 3.5 shows the kinds of questions which should be asked by someone considering implementing the same kind of project in another area.

Table 3.5 deals with the problem of generalisation and specification as a practical problem for those who have to make decisions about community crime control. There have been a large number of property-marking projects. None of these has involved controls more powerful than comparing crime rates in a project area with crime rates in adjoining areas or in areas with similar community characteristics elsewhere over the same time period. Nonetheless, by comparing all the projects and looking at the specificities which are associated with success it has been possible to draw some general conclusions as to how property marking might work to reduce crime, and the circumstances under which it is likely to work. As you might have guessed from reading Table 3.5, property marking seems to work to the extent that burglars are locals, disposing of stolen property locally and where they get to know that property has been marked, which in turn depends on how easily information disseminates through a community. Where these crucial conditions cannot be met then property marking is unlikely to be effective. Here are the beginnings of a body of useful theory about criminal behaviour and community structure (Pawson and Tilley 1997).

3.5 Specifying variables

The same kind of approach to that above can be taken in designing research or in assessing research conducted by yourself or someone else. It entails thinking of all the important variables which might have made a difference to the research. You can demonstrate this to yourself by doing the following activity, which builds on your reading of section 3.2 of this chapter. You will see that the grid in the activity specifies the variables in the experiments. Thus the most confident generalisation which could be made about the results of these experiments is that the same would be likely to happen in circumstances with precisely the same constellation of variables. That's not generalising very far! But we can at least speculate in a disciplined way as to the more general circumstances under which something similar would happen. Although I will not deal with this here, an important resource for such generalising is other research about similar topics.

TABLE 3.5	Cross-mapping local circumstances against a research project	
Relevant factors	**In the research area where property marking was associated with a reduction in burglaries**	**Questions for an area considering implementing a similar scheme**
The burglary rate	The rate was high	Do we have a similarly high rate of burglaries?
The burglaries	Mainly opportunistic thefts of high-value domestic goods (the kinds which can be property-marked)	Is our pattern of burglaries similar?
The burglars	Mainly local young people	Are our burglars similar?
The community	A close community, in which potential burglars would know about property marking	Is our target community similar?
Dissemination	Information about property marking was disseminated through the schools, youth clubs, clubs and other places where young people can be contacted	Are there similar opportunities for dissemination?
The victims	Sufficient numbers of local people were persuaded to adopt property marking	Would this be possible in our target area?
The disposal of stolen property	Most stolen property had been disposed of locally to friends, people in pubs and so on, in ways that made it risky to accept stolen property-marked goods.	Is most stolen property fenced locally, or at a distance?
Displacement of criminal activity	There was no increase in burglaries in surrounding areas greater than the county-wide increase	Might our burglars simply shift their attention to houses outside our target area?
Control	Comparison of burglary rate in the target area with that in adjacent areas of similar socio-economic composition over the same time period	Could we set up a similar control in order to monitor the effectiveness of our project?
Resourcing	A high level of funding was put into this demonstration project	Could we/should we invest the same level of funding?
Project personnel	A specially recruited highly enthusiastic team	Could we recruit and enthuse a similar team, or would the project have to be tagged onto someone's existing work?

| Outcome measurement | Results measured via changes in levels of crime reported to the police; there was a high level of house contents insurance and hence a high level of reporting (initially the *reported* level of burglaries increased before declining) | Would people in our area report stolen property in the same way as in the research area? What is the level of house contents insurance in our area? |
| Duration | The demonstration project lasted 18 months and there is data only for this time period. | Would the project have continued to be successful beyond 18 months? Would a project by us be successful in the longer term? |

Source: Based loosely on Laycock (1985).

ACTIVITY 3.1 Specifying the variables which might make a difference to the research

Rosenhan (section 3.2) interpreted the results of his field experiment as showing that even when there were minimal intimations of mental illness this could affect social interaction. I interpreted the results of my field experiment as suggesting that where people *both* gave a minimal indication that they might be mentally ill *and* behaved a little oddly this could affect social interaction. In Table 3.6 I have identified some of the major dimensions in both experiments, so that you can think about how changing a variable on these dimensions might have changed the results. You can add to the list if you like.

For the activity:

1 Identify the variables which differ between the two experiments which might be the most important in producing *different results*.
2 Think more expansively and suggest ways in which variables might have been changed to make either or both experiments more widely generalisable.
3 Design another experiment to investigate whether 'behaving a little oddly' is sufficient of itself to affect social interaction, without the necessity for an intimation of mental illness. For this you might want to depart from the field experiment format, for example, to use video-taped stimulus material. When you have designed your experiment analyse it on the model of Table 3.6 to identity both its weak points and the likely limits to its generalisability.

Table 3.6	Grid for comparing Rosenhan's experiment with Gomm's experiment for the Activity

Kinds of variable	Rosenhan	Gomm	Your notes
Researchers	1 female researcher	18 researchers, 24–32 years old, male and female, various ethnic groups (differences between these variables were not analysed). Alternating as observers and requesters	
Researcher awareness	Presumably the research assistant knew what the research was designed to investigate	The students knew what the research was designed to investigate; some had strong feelings about the unfair treatment of people with mental illness diagnoses	
Locations	University hospital precinct and University campus West Coast America, 1970s	District general hospital (outside and inside in public areas) various locations therein England, 1980s	
Time of day and other temporal variables	Unclear, but presumably daytimes	Weekdays 10 a.m. to 2 p.m. The hospital seemed to be in an ordinary state of busyness	
Targets	People looking like medical staff/people looking like University dons. Chosen as convenient. Exactly who they were is not reported	Anyone wearing a hospital security badge Chosen as convenient but on a strict alternation between request types Exactly who they were was only sometimes recorded.	
Requests	Directions varied according to indication of looking for psychiatrist, or internist, or no such indication. Five other questions	*Excuse me I've got an appointment with a psychiatrist consultant urologist and I don't know where to go.* Other ad hoc questions to clarify directions given.	

Respondent awareness	Respondents were probably not aware that they were subjects of an experiment	Most respondents were probably not aware that they were subjects of an experiment, but we cannot be sure about this
Standardisation	Apart from the above the research assistant was suppose to behave similarly towards all targets	Apart from the above the students were supposed to behave similarly towards all targets, but it seems they did not. There is no guarantee that different students behaved the same as each other except for the standard requests
Recording	By the research assistant herself of targets' behaviour: in terms of eye-contact made, pausing and chatting, stopping and talking and number of questions asked. Pencil and paper record	By observer, in terms of both requester and respondent behaviour: eye contact, register and assertiveness of request,whether and how directions were given. Duration of encounter timed. Pencil and paper record
Number of episodes	Between 10 and 18, 57 in total, see Table 3.1	89 and 91 = 180 in total
Any other important variables		

3.6 Summary

The main theme of this chapter has been about the trade-off between the control over variables which can be achieved with a rigorous control structure and the cost of this in terms of difficulties of generalisation, as against the benefits of more naturalistic investigations at the cost of it becoming difficult to interpret cause and effect. The chapter confined itself to discussing experimental and quasi-experimental designs, but the same issues about relaxed controls apply with even more force to the non-experimental work discussed in later chapters. All the sections looked at the problems which can arise in relaxing control in order to achieve more naturalism, first in relation to field experiments, then in relation to decision-simulation experiments, and third in relation to those experiments which are designed to test the effectiveness of some practical intervention. In connection with effectiveness studies it was noted that there seems to have been a very strong bias in favour of researchers declaring practices to be effective in the fields of medicine, social work, counselling, education or criminal justice, and that this bias shows itself most strongly where controls in the research designs are weakest. This in itself is an important case in favour of more rigour in effectiveness studies, but even outside of applied research, loose control allows for the easy play of bias.

Attention was drawn to the context-dependence of most of the phenomena studied by social researchers, which means that the same event or conditions may have one set of consequences in one context and another set in another. This constitutes a formidable problem when generalising not just from an experiment to 'the real world', but when generalising from naturalistic studies in one place to equally 'natural' circumstances elsewhere. The point was made that to generalise is also to specify and that the development of a body of research knowledge consists in improving our ability to specify the circum stances under which something will generally happen. This was looked at first in relation to practical decision-making among service planners, trying to work out whether some research findings could be applied in their own setting, and then, through the chapter Activity, in relation to how someone designing research or appraising someone else's research might identify the specific factors which produced the results and, from that, make an informed judgement as to how widely the results might apply, or how to construct another piece of research in order to assess its external valid

Further reading

Campbell and Stanley (1996) is a primer on experimental design including the design of quasi-experiments such as those discussed in this chapter and takes into consideration the difficulties of taking experiments 'into the field'. Oakley (1989) is a justification for the greater use of more rigorous experimental research as applied to social work, counselling, education and similar fields and represents experimentalism as a particularly important recent trend in feminist research. Oakley (2000) is a book-length treatment of the same issues containing much interesting information about the history of experimentation in social science. Pawson and Tilley (1997) is an excellent book on evaluation research in general with most of its examples drawn from the field of crime control and the rehabilitation of offenders. Its comments on how to interpret the results of different pieces of research alongside each other are particularly helpful and by not just relevant to applied research. Gomm, Needham and Bullman (2000) is designed to help practitioners appraise published research on practice covering most major research methods.

4 Sample Surveys and Statistical Representativeness

By the end of this chapter, you will:

■ Understand the principle of statistical representativeness, the ways samples can be selected to be representative of populations and how survey non-response can impair representativeness
■ Know the main considerations in determining the appropriate size for a survey sample
■ Know what is meant by confidence intervals, how to calculate these and interpret them in survey research

And know the meaning of the following terms:
Confidence intervals limits ■ cluster sampling ■ design factors ■ non-response ■ probability sampling (random and systematic) ■ quota sampling ■ sampling error ■ sampling frame ■ sensitivity analysis ■ staged sampling ■ stratified probability sampling (proportional and disproportional).

4.1 Introduction

This chapter looks at surveys as attempts to produce accurate estimates of frequency distributions in populations – for example, what proportion of the population suffers from limited and long standing illness, or whether the percentage of poor people who have had their houses burgled is larger than the percentage of rich people who have experienced this. The use of survey data for theoretical purposes is dealt with in Chapters 5 and 6. The key issue for the current chapter is how researchers can select and sustain **statistically representative samples**. For survey research the most usual thing to do with a sample of people is to ask them questions. Asking such questions is dealt with in detail in Chapter 8.

Only insofar as a sample is statistically representative can it be claimed with confidence that what was true for the sample will also be true for the population from which it was drawn. Thus statistical representativeness is the basis for an important form of generalisation – *statistical* or *empirical generalisation*, which is different from the kind of generalisation which can be made on the basis of the results of an experiment (see Chapter 2, section 2.10; Chapter 3, section 3.5).

4.2 **Statistical representativeness**

Imagine that you had to pick a representative bunch of flowers from a garden. There are various ways in which you might interpret 'representative'. The most tempting for gardeners, perhaps, would be to select the best blossoms to represent the best of the garden. There are some researchers who behave rather like this, selecting instances to make a convincing case for some theory they have, or to show the worst of some social evil of which they disapprove (see Chapter 12, section 12.4). Or you could make a selection to show the diversity of flowers in the garden; picking one of each kind. This would be a kind of **purposive sampling**. You would have a scheme of classification in mind – types of flowers – and select one or more to represent each type irrespective of how common or rare they were. Purposive sampling usually appears in social research in the guise of **theoretical sampling** where the scheme of classification is a theoretically interesting one. Sampling in qualitative research often takes the form of theoretical sampling (see Chapter 10, section 10.6) but it is different from the **statistical sampling** which is the main topic of this chapter.

For statistical sampling you would make a selection to represent the **frequency** with which each kind of flower appeared in the garden. If 95 per cent of all blossoms were forget-me-nots, most of the flowers in the bunch would have to be these. Unless the bunch were to be unmanageably large, it might be necessary to ignore some rarer flowers entirely in favour of those most commonly occurring. It is this selection strategy which uses the principle of **statistical representativeness** which is that used in sample surveys. As you will see, there are ways of making sure that the 'rarer flowers' do get included in a statistically representative sample (section 3.8).

Censuses, experiments and sample surveys

The 10-year national censuses in the UK attempt to collect data about everyone. They are enormously costly. Experimental researchers attempt to collect data about all their experimental subjects. This is a feasible aim because, typically, the numbers of subjects in an experiment is rather small – though that may give rise to problems in itself (see Chapter 2, section 2.10). By contrast, sample surveys collect data from just a selection of people to represent their population. Thus statistical representativeness refers to a sample-to-population relationship such that what was true about *frequencies* in the sample will be true also about *frequencies* in the population from which the sample was drawn. For example, a sample which is representative for gender will have a very similar gender ratio to that in the population from which the sample was selected. The art of choosing such samples is to choose those which will accurately reflect their populations in this way. Given the importance of cost, it is part of the art to choose the smallest sample which will do this adequately.

4.3 A population for sampling: young people in Slegborough

For this chapter we will consider the options and the logistics of taking a statistically representative sample from the population shown in Table 4.1. This shows a population of 14–25-year-olds in a town. We'll call it Slegborough. They number 10,796. They divide into two genders, then into three age groups and then into three ethnic groups, though the 'white' category will also include a very small number of people from minority ethnic groups which are neither 'African-Caribbean' nor 'South Asian'. For each category the numbers and the percentage of the *total population* are given, thus white females 14–17 number 1,503, and make up 14 per cent of the population of young people 14–25.

The sampling will be for a survey on drug use by young people. National and local surveys of this kind became particularly common from the end of the 1990s in connection with the government's *Tackling Drugs Together* strategy. Their purpose is to chart the extent and distribution of illicit drug use and, by repeating much the same survey at different points in time, to identify time trends in drug use. Drug use questions are now a standard item in the regular *British Crime Survey* (Ramsay, Barker, Goulden, Sharp and Sondhi 2001) and there is a new series of government surveys on smoking, drinking and drug use among young people (Boreham and Shaw 2001).

To keep things simple there will only be one question on drug use in our survey for the time being. This will be: *During the last 12 months have you used any of the following drugs?* with respondents being shown a list of illicit drugs they might have taken, using a variety of names for each. So the survey will actually have *four* questions: one on gender, one on age, one on ethnicity, and one on drug use. The final column in Table 4.1 shows what the respondents to the survey ought to answer if their answers are accurate and honest. In the survey there would have to be provision for a 'don't know/won't say' response.

The way the population has been divided into categories means that the survey should be able to answer questions about differences in (admitted) illicit drug use as between young people in different age groups, of different genders and different ethnic groups. National surveys on drug use do show that drug use varies with age and gender though there is no clear relationship with ethnicity (Ramsay and Partridge 1999). But age, gender and ethnicity are also, as it were, standard 'currency units' for surveys such that if all surveys on a particular topic collect this information, survey results from one area can be compared with survey results from another, or local survey results can be compared with national survey results. The age, gender and ethnic structure of a population is also something which can usually be estimated independently of the survey and these estimates provide benchmarks against which the representativeness of the survey sample can be judged.

TABLE 4.1	A population for sampling for a survey of illicit drug use by gender, age and ethnicity			
Total	**Gender**	**Age**	**Ethnicity**	**An accurate and honest response to a question**
ALL YOUNG PEOPLE 14–25 10,769 (100%)	FEMALES 14–25 5,341 (49.6%)	Females 14–17 1,656 (15.6%)	White females 14–17 1,503 (14%)	Yes
				No
			African-Caribbean females 14–17 66 (0.6%)	Yes
				No
			South Asian females 14–17 112 (1%)	Yes
				No
		Females 18–21 1,869 (17.4%)	White females 18–21 1,716 (16%)	Yes
				No
			African-Caribbean females 18–21 75 (0.7%)	Yes
				No
			South Asian females 18–21 79 (0.7%)	Yes
				No
		Females 22–25 1,816 (16.9%)	White females 22–25 1,663 (15.4%)	Yes
				No
			African-Caribbean females 22–25 73 (0.6%)	Yes
				No
			South Asian females 22–25 54 (0.5%)	Yes
				No
	MALES 14–25 5,428 (50%)	Males 14–17 1,864 (17.1%)	White males 14–17 1,648 (16.2%)	Yes
				No
			African-Caribbean males 14–17 74 (0.7%)	Yes
				No
			South Asian males 14–17 124 (1.1%)	Yes
				No
		Males 18–21	White males 18–21 1,742 (16.2%)	Yes
				No
			African-Caribbean males 18–21 76 (0.7%)	Yes
				No
			South Asian males 18–21 81 (0.75%)	Yes
				No
		Males 22–25	White males 22–25 1,566 (14.5%)	Yes
				No
			African-Caribbean males 22–25 67 (0.6%)	Yes
				No
			South Asian males 22–25 50 (0.5%)	Yes
				No

As the chapter proceeds we will consider various ways in which a sample might be taken from this population, and the size it would need to be in order accurately to represent the diversity in which a researcher is interested.

Estimating the parameters of the population

How could we know the structure of the population without doing the survey? The figures in Table 4.1 could have been estimated from pre-existing data about Slegborough. Most local authorities and all health authorities maintain a demographic ('population') model of their local populations as a basis for their own planning. Ultimately these are based on the Census returns for the area, so the models will be more accurate in 2003 when the results of the 2001 Census are to be published than in 2002 when the base figures would still be those of the 1991 census. Models are updated by periodic estimates coming from the Office for National Statistics (ONS) (the ex-Office of Population Censuses and Surveys (OPCS)), and by using other data sources such as school rolls, or GP practice lists, or ad hoc local surveys. So the figures in Table 4.1 are estimates and they won't be precisely right. One of the reasons we need to have these figures is in order to check that we have indeed selected something like a representative sample: thus the population estimate is for 32 or 33 per cent of the young people 14–25 being in the 14–17 year category. In checking the representativeness of our sample we will be looking to see that the sample selected shows approximately the same percentage. However, except in the period immediately after a Census , if there are discrepancies we will never be quite sure as to whether they show that the sample deviated from representativeness, or that the population estimates for the area were awry. Even up-to-date Census data may be inaccurate. In England, Wales and Scotland its seems that young adult males were likely to be unrecorded in the 1981 and 1991 Censuses to the extent of 30% in some inner urban areas (OPCS 1994).

4.4 Sampling strategies for statistically representative samples

Box 4.1 gives a synopsis of the methods available for taking a statistically representative sample.

Most social science survey research uses probability sampling so we will restrict our attention for the time being to this, looking later at quota sampling and other kinds of sampling (section 4.13).

The principle of probability sampling is easy to understand. It is that everyone in the population of interest should have an equal chance of being chosen for the sample. It is as if everyone had been given one raffle ticket and it had been arranged to make as many draws in the raffle as needed to make up the sample. In practice, computer generated random numbers are usually used to select a **random sample** of people. For a **systematic sample**

BOX 4.1 Statistically representative samples for surveys

There are two basic ways of selecting statistically representative samples and variations on these: probability sampling and quota sampling

Probability sampling (random and systematic) (see also sections 4.5–4.10)

Each person in the population has as near equal as possible chance of being chosen. This requires some kind of listing (or *sampling frame)* from which people can be chosen, which lists everyone in the population of interest. Complete sampling frames are rare so some kinds of people are likely to get excluded at the outset, reducing the representativeness of the sample, or restricting its representativeness to being representative of just those who are in the frame. Random selection is usually done with a table of random numbers or a computer programme making random selections. Systematic selection is arbitrary selection; for example every 14th name on a list. Fourteen would here be the *sampling interval.* As long as there is nothing special about the way people are ordered on the list, systematic selection works as well as random selection to give everyone in the population an equal chance of being selected.

Not all people selected will be contactable. Some may refuse to co-operate. Thus a sample which starts out as representative may become unrepresentative through non-response (section 4.9).

Very large unmodified (or simple) probability samples are needed to represent diversity within sub-groups or to recruit adequate numbers of people to represent groups which are in a minority in the population. To ensure adequate representation of minority groups stratified probability sampling may be used. Non-proportional stratified sampling might mean, for example, collecting samples of the same size from each ethnic group in the population, even though each makes up different percentages of the population; for example 400 from each ethnic group. Proportional stratified probability sampling means selecting the same sampling percentage from each group, say 10% from each, rather than relying on chance to do this, as in an unmodified probability sample. Either form of stratified sampling

---

where every *n*th person will be chosen from a list. However, it is often difficult to find a list to start with.

4.5 Sampling frames for probability samples

The starting point for a probability sample is called a **sampling frame**. It is often a list of some kind. For the population of young people in Slegborough (Table 4.1) school rolls might constitute a sampling frame for 14–16-year-olds. But that would exclude young people living in the area being schooled out of area, and include young people from other areas being schooled within it, and it would exclude a minority of young people in the area lost to the school system entirely. A question which arises here is whether the kinds of young people likely to be excluded from the sampling

may be used to ensure that the sample adequately represents people across geographical areas, where the *strata* might be wards of a town, or agencies; or cover a diversity of agencies or types of people where the strata might be ethnic groups or age groups, for example; or types of institutions, where the strata might be types of schools or types of hospital.

Two advantages of probability sampling over quota sampling (see below) are that the probability sample is more likely to be representative with regard to previously unknown characteristics (see Chapter 2, section 2.3) and that the results can be subjected to statistical analysis in ways that the results of quota sampling cannot.

Quota sampling (see also section 4.13)

Researchers need to have a good knowledge of the structure of the population in advance of doing research. Quotas are lists specifying the respondents who need to be recruited in order to build a sample which is a small-scale model of the population. Thus if the population has 5 per cent South Asian males between the ages of 14 and 17, then the instruction will be to find as many South Asian males of this age as needed to make up 5% of the sample. Quotas are filled on a first-found first-in basis so there is no non-response (see above) but there are problems of deciding who fits the quotas, and strong dangers of over-representing the easily accessible and co-operative people who meet the quota specifications and under-representing others. The problem of representing minorities adequately can be managed by non proportional quota sampling with the same effect as disproportionate probability sampling.

An advantage of quota sampling over probability sampling is that it requires smaller samples and requires less initial preparation. It is thus cheaper and quicker. Hence it is the method used most often by public opinion polling and market research companies. A major disadvantage is that only a limited amount of statistical analysis is possible with samples which have not been drawn using probability principles.

frame are themselves likely to be *un*representative of the population of young people, in ways relevant to the survey's topic. There is a reasonable expectation that young people of school age, unknown to the authorities, may well have patterns of drug use different from those of their peers. It is also possible that those schooled out of area, or those who come into the area for their schooling, will be distinctive in terms of social class, or in terms or rural or urban residence. Both of these are matters which might be relevant to patterns of illicit drug use.

School rolls are not going to be so much help with those who are 16+. Another, and widely used possibility is GP listings of patients. Roughly 96 per cent of people are registered with GPs: more in some areas and less in others. But people may be registered with GPs in one area and live in another. The use of school rolls and practice lists as sampling frames raises important issues of confidentiality which have to be solved by using an intermediary to select names and send out postal questionnaires for anonymous return, or an intermediary to ask the person's, or the person's parents' permission for the researcher to contact them for face-to-face interviews (Chapter 13). Both these manoeuvres lead to lower rates of response (see section 4.9).

The 'out-of-area' problem is a problem when the population of interest is defined in terms of residence in a particular town or health authority area, or where area of residence is itself an important characteristic relevant to the research. For example, in a national survey of drug use it might be a matter of interest as to whether respondents lived in areas defined as 'deprived' or 'affluent'. For local surveys, out-of-area problems can be solved by looking for the missing subjects in the listings in surrounding areas, and by deleting in-comers from the sampling frame of the area of interest. But this is extremely time-consuming. A much cheaper response is to cite the population of interest in terms of the sampling frame used. Thus instead of claiming that the survey is of the population of young people living in Slegborough, it might be described as a survey of the young people registered with a GP in Slegborough.

A list of residential addresses is another possible sampling frame. The post office maintains a list of all postal addresses – the *postcode address files*, including a 'small-user' sub-set which lists all postal addresses receiving on average less than 10 items of mail per day (Wilson and Elliot 1987). This is almost equivalent to being a list of residential addresses, though it will exclude people living in institutions or who are roofless. Given the problem of finding any other sampling frame for the 16–25-year-olds in the population in Table 4.1, this may be our best option for a sampling frame. Another address-based approach uses a street directory or even just a street map as a sampling frame. Telephone directories are another possibility. But these exclude ex-directory subscribers, people without telephones, and with the many telephone companies today there are many directories. Surveys by e-mail will exclude anyone without access to e-mail.

Starting with a list of addresses gives every residential address an (almost) equal chance of being chosen. But the object was to give every 14–25-year-old an equal chance. There will be a large number of addresses chosen where there are no 14–25-year-olds, so the number of addresses sampled would have to be much bigger than the sample of young people it is intended to recruit. Some households will contain more than one 14–25-year-old. If we were to select all 14–25-year-olds living in any chosen address then those living together would be over-represented. In practice it is likely that a survey researcher will make a random decision as to which of several 14–25-year-olds at a single address should be selected. The standard device for making random decisions about who in a household to interview is the so-called **Kish grid** (Kish 1975), but in principle the operation is similar to drawing lots to select one of several.

In adopting an address-based approach, survey researchers may use a technique called **focused enumeration**, as in the 4th National Survey of Ethnic Minorities conducted by the Policy Studies Institute (Nazroo 1997) for recruiting systematic samples of minority ethnic respondents:

> This involves interviewers visiting every nth (e.g. 6th) address in a defined area and asking about the ethnic origins of those living both at the address and at the n-1 (e.g. 5) addresses on either side of the visited address. Consequently non-visited addresses are asked about at two visited addresses. If positive or uncertain identification [of people being from a minority ethnic group] is made at either of the visited addresses for the non-visited address, the interviewer then goes on to interview them in person.
>
> (Nazroo 1997: 12–13)

This might be a viable option for collecting a sample of young people in Slegborough.

The most important point to take away from this section is that since there are almost never any complete sampling frames for communities, some people are likely to be excluded from the outset, and in this sense the population represented will be a population excluding them, thus creating **sampling bias**. Researchers may devise alternative strategies to contact groups likely to be excluded in this way, creating so-called **booster samples**. In Slegborough we might parallel an address-based survey with a special investigation in hostels for homeless people, and in the areas where roofless people gather. Since the respondents for this will have been selected in a different way, their responses should not be mixed in with the main sample for statistical analysis.

Complete sampling frames are often available for surveys within organisations, or for members of professional associations such as doctors or nurses.

4.8 Multi-stage and cluster sampling

The principle of probability sampling is that everyone in the population of interest should have an equal chance of being chosen – well, as equal as possible anyway. This is less problematic where the population concerned is geographically concentrated, as for our Slegborough population. But following this principle for national surveys means that the people selected will be widely dispersed. There are two problems here. The first is the sampling frame problem already mentioned. It is difficult enough to find an adequate list for a small area. With the exception of the postcode address files or telephone surveys, it is even more difficult to do so for a nation. The second problem is that if people are to be interviewed face-to-face, or if they have to be found by knocking on doors, a widely dispersed sample incurs a high expense. This is not so with postal surveys or telephone surveys, however.

Staging

In order to reduce the expense of travelling widely, survey researchers often **stage** their sampling. First a sample will be taken of *areas*, then probability samples will be taken of *people* within these areas. Thus the interviews will be geographically clustered. The locations might themselves be chosen on probability principles. For example all the wards in England together might be treated as a population of wards and a probability sample of these taken to select wards for the survey. Or the locations might be chosen purposively. For example in the National Survey of Ethnic Minorities referred to earlier, Nazroo and his colleagues (1997) wanted to select a national sample which would be representative of minority ethnic people living in high levels of concentration and in low levels of concentration. They therefore *stratified* their sample of locations into three strata: wards with fewer than 0.5 per cent minority ethnic population, wards with 0.5–10 per cent and wards with 10 per cent +, selecting a sample of wards within each category on probability principles. The data on concentration was taken from the Small Area Census statistics. The next stage was to make a random selection of addresses from the postcode address files for the chosen wards. As you saw earlier, the next stages involved focused enumeration, and the next, where necessary, the random selection of one person within a chosen household to be the respondent. Thus process of sample selection here was like a series of lotteries, with the 'winners' of one being entered as competitors into the next. The sampling was also adjusted – stratified – in order to ensure adequate numbers of respondents from each minority ethnic group. You can read more about this in section 4.8.

Clustering

Sometimes the most convenient way of making contact with respondents is through naturally occurring clusters of them: as pupils in schools, as patients of a GP practice and so on. **Cluster sampling** is common practice. Sometimes it is adopted to avoid the expense of interviewing people in widely dispersed locations. It may achieve economies of scale because making arrangements to interview one person via a school or a clinic costs almost as much as making arrangements to do so for 20. In terms of our Slegborough population most of the 14–17-year-olds would be pupils of say, eight schools. It would be very tempting for a researcher to decide to contact this age group via their schools, and instead of selecting, say, 900 from eight schools to select the same number from just four schools.

The problem here is that no school is a representative sample of all schools. Starting with a selection of four schools is almost certainly starting with a population which is unrepresentative of all the young people of that age in the town. Remember that in this context a 'representative sample' is a sample which shows the *same frequencies as does the population as a whole*, as relevant to the topic of interest: in this case relevant to percentages of young people admitting to using illicit drugs. If, as seems likely, schools have their own distinctive patterns of drug use, selecting pupils from only some schools is likely to produce results which are seriously unrepresentative for the area: another form of sampling bias.

It is very difficult to draw a sharp distinction between multi-stage sampling and cluster sampling. It is better to think of both as 'clustering' the sample. In so doing researchers will inevitably reduce the extent to which the final sample represents diversity within the population. This is because people who live in the same area, or go to the same school, or are registered with the same doctor are more like each other than they are like people elsewhere. Practical considerations of time and money often decide whether researchers use such strategies; and the cheaper the sampling strategy the bigger the sample can be. They may find themselves faced with the choice of taking a larger clustered and possibly less representative sample because of clustering, but more representative because of larger size, as against taking a smaller more dispersed sample, possibly more representative because of its dispersal through the population, but possibly less representative because of its smaller size.

Design factors

Because staging and clustering reduce the statistical representativeness of a sample, survey researchers sometimes provide an estimate of the effect of this called a 'design factor'. For example, in between censuses the quarterly *Labour Force Survey* is the main regular source of information on the number and characteristics of minority ethnic populations. Its results are regularly published in the magazines *Population Trends* and *Employment Gazette*. For this survey the sampling unit is the household and unlike the National Survey of Ethnic Minorities above all people in the households selected feature in the survey. Some minority ethnic groups typically have larger households than others. If each survey 'hit' is a household this will mean that the same number of hits for different ethnic groups would recruit different numbers of subjects. Hence simply grossing up the results of the survey to provide estimates for the population as a whole is likely to over-estimate the total numbers in the population of people from those minority groups with large households. For the *Labour Force Survey* estimates of numbers of people in different ethnic groups are adjusted for with a design factor calculated on the basis of average household size for different ethnic groups (Schuman 1999; Korovessis 2001).

4.7 Unmodified (simple) probability sampling

The minority ethnic groups in the population in Table 4.1 make up only a small percentage of all 14–25-year-olds, though at 8 per cent this is more than the 6 per cent constituted by minority ethnic people in the population of Great Britain (Haskey 1996) and it is four times the percentage found in 80 per cent of local authority areas (Teague 1993). As with other numerically small groups, minority ethnic groups tend to get short shrift in national surveys which use an unmodified or simple probability principle to select a sample (see Box 4.1). For example, the large-scale OPCS, National Psychiatric Morbidity Survey had a sample size in excess of 10,000 (Meltzer *et al.* 1995). It recruited only 460 people from minority ethnic groups of colour. But at 4.6 per cent of the sample this is precisely representative of the frequency of such groups in the adult population of Great Britain. Once 460 people are divided into different minority ethnic groups, into genders, age groups, groups of socio-economic status and groups of differing mental health, very little can be said with confidence as to how far the patterns shown in the sample reflect patterns of mental health for minority ethnic groups in the population.

In a simple probability sample everyone in the population is given an equal chance to be selected. But for the population in Table 4.1 whereas African-Caribbeans as a group only have four chances in 100 of being chosen for the survey, white young people have 82 chances in 100. We don't know how many of these young people have used drugs in the last 12 months: that's what the survey is supposed to find out. But suppose that 50 per cent of African-Caribbean males aged 14–17 should say 'yes', and the same was true for white males aged 14–17. Then yes-saying, African-Caribbean males aged 14–17 would have only 3–4 chances in 1,000 of being selected for the sample, while yes-saying whites of the same age group would have 80 chances in 1,000.

A sample size of 1,000 might sound rather large for the population in Table 4.1 (p. 74). But if it is a sample selected on unmodified probability principles it isn't large enough to produce accurate estimates of drug use within the smaller sub-groups of the sample. If the hypothetical 37 yes-saying African-Caribbean males aged 14–17 had only 3–4 chances to be selected between them, then none of them might come up at all. With an unmodified probability sample we would not be able to draw any conclusions at this level of detail. We could attempt to solve this problem by simply increasing the sample size overall. But in order to get large enough samples for the smaller sub-groups we would then be forced to over-recruit numbers from the white majority groups. What we need is a **stratified probability sample**.

4.8 Stratified probability samples

Table 4.2 shows you what a stratified probability sample would look like for the youth population of Slegborough. Section 4.10 will explain how the sample sizes for each sub-group were decided upon. The strata are gender by age by ethnic group, and the simplest way of thinking about stratified sampling is to think of it as doing several surveys at the same time, one for each stratum: in this case 18 surveys alongside each other. Table 4.2 shows a *disproportional* stratified probability sample, since the sample size for each group is not proportional to the percentage it makes up of the

TABLE 4.2	Disproportional stratified probability sample for the population of young people in Slegborough as shown in Table 4.1: gender, ethnic and age strata						
Age	Females White	African-Caribbean	S. Asian	Males White	African-Caribbean	S. Asian	Totals
14–17	306	56	87	312	64	94	919
18–21	314	63	66	315	64	67	889
22–25	312	62	47	309	57	44	831
Totals (%)	932 (19)	181 (85)	200 (82)	936 (19)	185 (85)	205 (80)	2,639

How to read the table
Each cell in the table represents a stratum defined by age, gender and ethnicity. The figure in each cell gives the sample size needed for this sub-group which would allow estimates to be made with a margin of error plus or minus (±) 5%, which would be accurate 95 times out of 100. Comparing this with Table 4.1, 306 white females aged 14–17, are to be selected on probability principles from a population of 1,503; 56 African-Caribbean females of this age group to be selected from a population of 66 and so on. Notice that the smaller the sub-group the bigger the sample has to be as a percentage. Thus only about 1 in 5 white females or white males are to be selected (19%) but over 80% of members of minority ethnic groups within genders are to be selected. The total sample size needed for this is 2,639 or thereabouts.

The sample sizes here are set to give accurate estimates ±5%. If you were satisfied with a wider margin of error – say ±10%, then the sample sizes could be smaller.

See also section 4.10.

population. For example, there is a 20 per cent sample of white females and an 85 per cent sample of African-Caribbean females. The only point in taking a *proportional* stratified sample, with the same percentage from each sub-group, is that this ensures that indeed there is the same percentage of each sub-group, rather than leaving it to chance. Since the percentage for each sub-group for a proportional stratified sample has to be that required for the smallest group, and in our case that would mean sampling 85 per cent of 'whites', this is not a serious option for us.

The OPCS National Psychiatric Morbidity Survey referred to above used a simple probability sample and recruited only 460 ethnic minority respondents, but the 4th National Survey of Ethnic Minorities (cited earlier) covered much the same ground as the OPCS survey using a stratified sample consisting of 1,205 Caribbeans, 1,273 Indians, 728 Africans, 1,185 Pakistanis, 591 Bangladeshis and 214 Chinese, with a white sample for comparison. The figures for each minority group are proportional to their size within the minority ethnic population, but all together the ethnic minority sample was disproportionately large compared to the white sample selected for comparison. Although those are much larger samples than in the OPCS Survey, they were still too small to investigate differences *within* some groups; for example gender differences within the Chinese group.

4.9 Survey non-response with a probability sample

Survey researchers make great attempts to minimise non-response. This includes making it easy and pleasant for people to participate. Devices include offering incentives for participation, as with many market research surveys conducted by post which use 'prize draws' as an incentive. But, as with paying experimental subjects, this may lead to the over-representation of those who are motivated by gain (Rosenthal and Rosnow 1969; 61–120; Tzamourani 2000; Tzamourani and Lynn 2000). To avoid excluding those whose first language is not English, it may mean producing versions of the survey in several languages and using bi-lingual interviewers (Meadows and Wischer 2000). Once someone has been chosen as a survey respondent, several attempts will usually be made to contact them, if the first approach does not succeed.

An incomplete sampling frame may already have skewed a sample away from statistical representativeness if the people excluded from the frame are unlike those included in ways relevant to the survey. There may be further movement away from representativeness though staged sampling or cluster sampling (see section 4.6). Then some people who are chosen for the sample will not be contactable, and some may refuse to co-operate. With postal questionnaires some may not return the questionnaires. At a finer level of detail some people may answer some but not all questions on a questionnaire, or some may terminate an interview before it is completed (de Leeuw 1999). Hence the representativeness of the sample may vary from question to question. Although they occur at different stages, all of these have the same effect of jeopardising the representativeness of a sample: they are all forms of *sampling bias*. The extent to which this is a problem depends on two factors:

- The absolute numbers of those excluded
- The extent to which those excluded are unlike those included in ways relevant to the survey topic.

The size of the non-response

The first of these relates to the need for statistical purposes to recruit a sample of adequate size. To accommodate for the effect of the absolute size of the non-response, survey researchers often take larger samples than would be necessary with 100 per cent response: for example, larger than those suggested in Table 4.2. You will sometimes read that a 'non-response rate of

20 per cent is acceptable'. But this is extremely misleading. It is not only the size but the shape of the non-response which is important.

The shape of the non-response

The second of the factors above has to do with the shape, or structure, of the group who are initially excluded, or who once selected do not respond. Looking again at Table 4.2 you will realise that 20 non-respondents among white females aged 14–17 will not be such a serious problem as 20 non-respondents among African-Caribbean females aged 14–17. Or if 100 non-respondents were drawn more or less randomly from Table 4.2, this wouldn't matter so much as if all of them were drawn from among South Asians.

For Slegborough we have some estimates of the population parameters for age, gender and ethnicity which are independent of the survey. Apart from the inherent interest of these characteristics in relation to drug use, this gives us an opportunity to compare the sample as it was at the end of the survey with these known characteristics. It is a reasonable assumption that if the sample shows the same age, gender and ethnic distribution as the population, then it will also give an accurate picture of the unknown datum, which in this case is the distribution of illicit drug use in the previous 12 months, subject to the willingness of young people to disclose this information. Equally, to the extent that the sample shows deviations from what is known about the population it is a reasonable assumption that it will also deviate with regard to the unknown pattern. This depends, of course, on making some assumptions about the accuracy of the population data.

Sensitivity analysis of non-response

Non-response can make a survey difficult to interpret. Table 4.3 shows what might have been the result of the survey. It shows that females were less likely to report drug use than males, but there were 15 per cent of females and 20 per cent of males who were non-respondents. The non-respondents have a pattern of drug use or non-use. We don't know what it

TABLE 4.3	Survey results			
	Females (%)		Males (%)	
'Users' – answered 'yes'	223	(17)	229	(23)
Non-users – answered 'no'	893	(68)	740	(57)
Non-respondents – uncontactable or refused to answer	197	(15)	260	(20)
Totals	1,313	(100)	1,299	(100)

TABLE 4.4	Sensitivity analysis of survey results shown in Table 4.3: sensitivity of results to three different assumptions about behaviour of survey non-respondents					
	Assumption 1: No non-respondent males used drugs		**Assumption 2:** Half of all non-respondent males used drugs		**Assumption 3:** All non-respondent males used drugs	
	Females (%)	Males (%)	Females (%)	Males (%)	Females (%)	Males (%)
Assumption A No non-respondent females used drugs	17	23	17	33	17	43
Assumption B Half of all non-respondent females used drugs	28	23	28	33	28	43
Assumption C All non-respondent females used drugs	33	23	33	33	33	43

How to read this table
The survey showed that 17% of females and 23% of males admitted to having used an illicit drug (Table 4.3). But to accept this as an accurate population estimate we have to assume that *none* of the non-respondent females and *none* of the non-respondent males used drugs (as in the first pair of cells in this table). Table 4.4 provides a set of 6 alternative assumptions about the behaviour of the non-respondents, generating 9 combinations. Five of these still leave more males being users than females, but two reverse the picture and one puts males and females as equal.

is, but are there enough non-respondents to suggest that the survey results could be different if we did know their answers to the question.

Table 4.4 shows what is sometimes called a **sensitivity analysis**. It is called this because it investigates how sensitive the results were to something or other. In this case the question is how sensitive were the results to the survey non-response. How different might the results have been had the non-response been different?

This kind of analysis will not provide definitive answers but by disciplined speculation of this kind it is possible to define how big the problem is and how far it should undermine our confidence in the face-value results of a survey. Speculation here can also be linked with other information. For example if you knew that male non-respondents included a large number of school excludees, whereas female non-respondents did not, then you might have reasonable grounds for suggesting that the non-response actually *under*-estimated the differences in drug use between males and females. In our survey we would know whether the non-respondents were drawn disproportionately from particular age or ethnic groups, and that might offer some hints on how to interpret the results.

Imputation

In survey research the term 'imputation' refers to making estimates of the responses which would have been made by the non-respondents, had they in fact responded: imputing answers to them, even though they didn't give any (Martin 1999). If, for example young men of a particular ethnic group and social class are under-represented among respondents, then the simplest imputation might be that those who did not respond would have responded in a similar way to those of the same category who did. Imputation is obviously a rather risky enterprise, but often it can be done with more confidence if there is additional research into the characteristics of the non-respondents. The Census, for example, is followed by a series of follow-up sample surveys designed to estimate both the extent of non-response and the particular characteristics of the non-respondents, in order to form the basis for filling the gaps left by non-respondents.

This section shows how important it is that survey researchers report on non-response in as much detail as possible. If you are writing up the results of a survey you should always cite details of the non-response, and you shouldn't believe the results of any survey which omits to do so.

4.10 Sample size for a probability sample

Representativeness is not an all or nothing matter. A sample which is large enough to produce an accurate estimate of the ratio of males to females in a population may be too small to provide an accurate estimate of the gender ratios *within* age groups in the population. And a sample big enough for that may be too small to give accurate estimates of gender ratios *within* age groups *within* ethnic or social class groups in the population. The smaller the units or the finer the detail you are interested in, the bigger the sample has to be.

Setting the sample sizes

Table 4.5 is useful for judging the adequacy of a sample size.

I used the same calculations as created Table 4.5 to set the size of strata in Table 4.2. Thus there are 1,503 white females aged 14–17 in the population. Table 4.2 tells me that if I was going to do a survey with just this group asking them to answer a yes/no question, then I would need a sample of 306.

TABLE 4.5	Size of a sample required for various population sizes in order to produce an estimate of a dichotomous variable in a population, accurate to ± 5% or better, with 95% confidence about being right		
Population size	**Required sample size**	**Population size**	**Required sample size**
10	10	800	260
50	44	1,000	278
100	80	1,500	306
150	108	2,000	322
200	132	3,000	341
250	152	4,000	351
300	169	5,000	357
400	196	10,000	370
500	217	50,000	381
700	248	1,000,000 or more	384

How to use this table
You can use this table if you want to check whether a sample size in a piece of survey research is adequate for the frequencies being estimated. The heading refers to a 'dichotomous variable' meaning first and foremost, variables with two modalities such as 'yes' or 'no' or 'male' or 'female'. But remember that any set of results can be reduced to dichotomous variables: for example yes/no/don't know can be reduced to yes and no + don't know. White, African-Caribbean, South Asian can be reduced to 'white' and 'all other ethnicities'. In terms of the population in Table 4.1, if we wanted an accurate estimate of the population's sex ratio, we would need a sample of between 370 and 381, since the population is 10,769 in total. If we wanted an accurate estimate of the number of males in the population who should say 'yes' or 'no' to the drug question and the number of females who should say 'yes' or 'no', then we would need a sample of about 720. This is because we need an adequate sample of males to estimate their yes/no distribution, say 360, and an adequate sample of females similarly: 360 + 360 = 720. All this is to produce estimates accurate to ± 5%. If you are willing to tolerate a larger margin of error then smaller sample sizes can be used. You might be willing to tolerate a larger margin of error if you were mainly interested in big differences and were prepared to regard figures showing small differences as equivalent to each other.

Source: After Krejcie and Morgan (1970:608).

So that's the sample size for them. On the same principle, African-Caribbean females aged 14–17 have a population of 66, and the Table 4.2 tells me that I need a sample size of somewhere between 44 and 80. I did a calculation and came up with 56. So that's the sample size for them. I continued doing this for each sub-group, added the results together and ended up with the total sample size of 2,639.

Increasing the response options and increasing the sample size

All this is on the basis that the survey is going to ask just one 'drug question' with yes/no/don't know response options. But that would be a rather odd kind of survey. Let's consider the effects of asking more. Now instead of recording the results yes/no/don't know, we are going to record them in terms of which drugs the young people admitted to taking. This takes us to another level of detail and may require an increase in sample size. Or, at least, it may require an increase in sample size if we want results by gender, by age, by ethnicity and by drug of use. The first three categorisations here have divided the population into 18 groups. Dividing it into users and non-users divides it into 36 as in Table 4.1. Allowing for there being 12 illicit drugs of use would divide it again to create 216 groups, without taking account of the fact that some people might have admitted to using more than one drug. Let's be cautious and just decide to record results in terms of 'cannabis only' and 'all other illicit drugs including or not including cannabis'. Ignoring the don't knows/won't says gives us a survey with 54 unique response possibilities. If there are 54 unique response options then each of these has less of a chance of appearing in the survey than do the representatives of the earlier 36 unique response options. If we go on adding questions or increase the number of response options available for a particular question, sooner or later we will need to increase the sample size, for exactly the same reason as we would need a larger sample size if we divided the population into four age groups rather than three, or cross-classified the three ethnic groups by three social classes.

Ignoring some diversity to accommodate to a smaller sample size

But when faced with this problem, what survey researchers usually do instead of increasing sample sizes will be to ignore out some of the sub-divisions in the analysis. Thus the sample may not be big enough to get accurate estimates of the frequencies with which particular drugs were used by people by gender by age group by ethnic group (216 categories). But it might be big enough to give accurate estimates of use and non-use by gender by age by ethnicity *irrespective of drug of use* (36 categories) and also to give accurate estimates of main drug of use by ethnicity and gender *irrespective of age* (again 36 categories). It is likely that a survey researcher will present cruder analyses like this rather than increase the sample size.

You will often see surveys which include large numbers of questions but have a rather small sample, with the response to each question being analysed separately without any attempt to relate the answers given on one question to the answers given by the same respondents to another. This is for exactly the same reasons as above. In our case, our sample is large enough to add some more questions without deleting any sub-divisions.

This arises from it being a local survey where some of the samples are of a very large percentage size. If you ask questions of 85 per cent of all people in a population, then you can be pretty certain that the pattern of their response will come close to mirroring that for the same category in the population as a whole.

4.11 Statistical testing of survey results and confidence intervals

Statistical significance

Chapter 2, section 2.9 gave a brief explanation of the principles underlying the statistical testing of the results of experiments. In testing survey results for their significance the principle is essentially the same. It aids understanding to think in terms of someone taking the same-sized probability samples again and again and again from the same population. For chance reasons the sample will be different every time; there will be a random **sampling error**. Don't confuse this with sampling bias which is something different (see above). Statistically testing the results of surveys, asks the question

> are the differences between groups in the survey of such a size that they might be attributed to the chancy business of selecting samples (to sampling error), rather than reflecting real differences between groups in the population?

Statistical tests of survey results are presented in the same way as those for experiments, with p or probability values, as shown in Chapter 2, section 2.9. Again statisticians rule that only results less likely to have occurred by chance 5 times out of 100 should be regarded as significant: $p = 0.05$ or less (see pp. 41–2).

There is a close relationship between sample size and statistical testing, since the smaller the sample the more it is the prey of chance factors. Statistical tests take sample size into consideration.

Confidence intervals

Confidence intervals (CIs) give a much more meaningful way of appraising results than figures for p. References in Table 4.5 to margins of error of $\pm$ 5 per cent were actually references to confidence intervals. You are probably familiar with these from television pathologists who say 'time of death 12 midnight give or take two hours'. The formula for calculating confidence intervals is a useful one and it is not very difficult to use as long as you have a calculator with a square root function. Box 4.2 shows how to do it.

Confidence intervals really come into their own in providing a graphic display of differences between groups, as shown in Figure 4.1. As you can see there is no overlap in the confidence limits between males and females in

---

BOX 4.2 Calculating confidence intervals

The survey found that of females 17% answered 'yes', 68% answered 'no' and 15% were non-respondents
The formula is:

$$1.96 \sqrt{\frac{P \times Q}{N}}$$

Where P = percentage you are interested in – here 'yes' sayers = 17%
Q = the percentage the you are not interested in – here 'no' sayers plus non-respondents = 68 + 15 = 83%
N = the size of the sample = 1,313
    1.96 is a 'magic number' adjusting the calculation to provide 95% confidence that the estimates are right. The formula here is for the *95% confidence interval.*
The calculation goes like this

$$1.96 \sqrt{\frac{17 \times 68}{1,313}}$$

$$1.96 \sqrt{\frac{1156}{1,313}}$$

$$1.96 \sqrt{0.88}$$

The square root of 0.88 is 0.94

$$1.96 \times 0.94 = 1.839 = 1.84$$

The confidence interval is 1.84 %
    This means that 17% yeses can be regarded as an estimate running from 17% − 1.84 = 15.16% to 17% + 1.84=18.84%. Thus 15.16% and 18.84% are the *confidence limits.*
    The formula here is for the 95% confidence intervals, giving you odds of being right about these limits of 95 in a 100. To raise the odds to 99 in a 100 substitute 2.56 for 1.96 in the formula. That will increase the size of the confidence interval. The bigger the margin of error you allow yourself – the less precise your estimate, the less wrong you can be !

---

this figure. You can take this as an indication that the sampling reflects a *real difference* between males and females in the population. You have already seen that some of that difference may be due to a larger percentage of males than females not responding to the survey, and some due to males and females having different patterns of use and non-use. In addition, some of the difference may be due to differential honesty between male and female respondents. The warning here is that differences in results may have a number of causes. Neither statistical testing for significance nor calculating confidence limits will tell you the size of the contributions made by different factors.

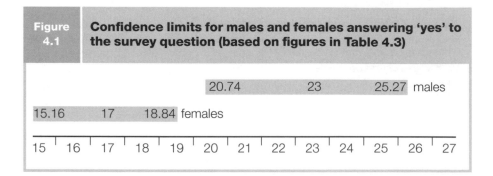

| Figure 4.1 | Confidence limits for males and females answering 'yes' to the survey question (based on figures in Table 4.3) |

You might like to try using the formula in Box 4.2 to calculate confidence intervals for the sensitivity analysis in Table 4.5. That would tell you just how sensitive the results were to survey non-response.

4.12 Selecting interviewees to 'represent' survey respondents

One of the iron laws of research is that for the same quantum of resources you can find out a little each about a lot of people or a lot each about a few people, but not both. Often researchers try to square the circle by doing a sample survey using a questionnaire collecting numerical data from a large sample and then, from the sample, select some few people to interview in depth. This would be very tempting with our survey of drug use among young people in Slegborough. After all, the survey may tell us about the prevalence and the social distribution of drug use but it won't give us much information about practices, experiences and meanings of drug use to the young people surveyed. We could ask a lot more survey questions but we would still probably be dissatisfied with survey results as a way of getting to know the about the realities of drug use for young people. Having the survey data does provide a kind of sampling frame for selecting a handful of respondents for more intensive interviews.

No doubt the interviews would be interesting. But this practice does raise an important issue about the representativeness of those interviewed in this way: 20 interviews is likely to be the maximum; that means either that 20 people have to represent all the 2,639 people in the sample, who in turn represent 10,796 in the population – more credibly, that the 20 people have to represent some sub-group in the sample and population, for example 100 or so young people in the population who actually used heroin in the last 12 months. As you have seen in this chapter the greater the level of detail a sample is required to represent, the *bigger* the sample has to be. But this interview study is going in the opposite direction. First, this is rather like saying that instead of selecting an adequate sample of 200 South Asian young women, I will select just one or two to interview in depth. Second, in the interview, the interviewer will ask a large number of questions to which the interviewees will give answers. For each answer they give, other uninterviewed people might have given different answers. Hence the deeper the interviews go, the more diversity between people they are likely to uncover and the more unrepresentative a group of 20 interviewees will be.

This is not a case against combining survey work with interviewing in greater depth, but it is warning against regarding the interviewees as being statistically representative of the population for the kinds of questions they are asked in the interviews. It would be difficult to say that the data from the interviews *explained* the patterns shown in the survey results.

4.13 Quota sampling and other sampling techniques

The interviewer in the street who approaches you to ask you questions is probably conducting a quota survey. Quota sampling has to start from a sound knowledge of the population to be sampled, much as shown in Table 4.1. Then quotas are defined, much like the strata in a stratified probability sample. Quotas are 'shopping lists' which in effect say things like: 'collect responses from 25 African-Caribbean females aged 14 to 17.' The quotas might be proportional, collecting the same percentage of each population sub-category, or disproportional, collecting larger percentages from some sub-categories than others – again as with probability sampling, and for the same reasons (see section 4.8).

At first sight quota sampling is intuitively appealing. If selecting a sample is building a small-scale model of the population, then quota sampling is building the model respondent by respondent. But there are two problems with quota sampling. First, selection is not blind as it is with probability sampling. Quota sampling relies on the judgement of the interviewer as to who to approach and who to include. It is all too easy to avoid recruiting people who are difficult to get at, or who look hostile. Thus quotas tend to get filled with the getatable rather than with the representative. This is a tendency in probability sampling, too, where there are incomplete sampling frames and/or a high survey non-response (section 4.9). There is no non-response in quota sampling, since the researcher goes on looking for people until the quotas are filled. This may look like an advantage. But survey non-response leaves a record of gaps, so it can be estimated how it distorted the sample from representativeness. Something at least is likely to be known about the non-participants. Because there is no non-response in a quota sample, the extent to which the sample is unrepresentative is unknown if the researcher is successful in filling all the quotas. You should see the parallels here between sampling for surveys and composing comparison groups for experiments (see Chapter 2, section 2.3). The second problem is that because quota sampling is not based on probability principles there is little guidance available as to how large samples ought to be and no way of estimating confidence intervals for them.

All this said, however, surveys using quota sampling by the top opinion poll companies have been as accurate at predicting election results as surveys based on probability samples. Contrary to popular belief, such surveys do give pretty good predictions of electoral out-turns given the small margin there usually is between the two leading parties. The level of success achieved with quota sampling by reputable companies such as Gallop or MORI is due to the way such agencies have built up over time a fund of practical knowledge as to which towns and parts of towns and times of day are particularly suitable for filling quotas to get accurate predictions, or due to maintaining carefully selected , semi-permanent panels of people to interview. Agencies like this do essentially similar surveys week in week out. Quota sampling is cheaper because it uses smaller samples, which makes it attractive to commercial polling and market research companies. It is also speedy, which is important if a survey has to be completed and published within a few days, as with public opinion polls. These never claim to be accurate for more than a short time period. They are often designed to measure the impact of a particular event such as a party political conference, or a budget speech.

BOX 4.3 Samples other than probability or quota samples

Apart from probability sampling, quota sampling and sampling which approaches 100% of the population of interest, no other methods of sampling can claim to be statistically representative in the sense that frequencies shown in the sample can be safely generalised to the population from which the sample was drawn.

Snowball sampling. Most usually used in circumstances where nothing like a sampling frame exists and respondents are a group who are difficult to find. In his study of drug users Gerry Stimson (1972) asked each drug user he met to put him in touch with others, so that he rolled up a 'snowball' sample of drug users in Cheltenham and the surrounding areas. He stopped sampling when contacts were unable, or unwilling, to put him in touch with anyone he didn't know already.

Convenience or 'grab' samples. These are just the people who happened to be around when a sample was needed. Rosenhan's field experiment and my emulation of it (Chapter 3, section 3.2) used convenience sampling. Who gets into the sample depends very much on the processes which brought people to a place at a time when they were available for being recruited. Being there, then, may, or may not, make them unrepresentative of the population they are supposed to represent. Most experimental work uses convenience samples, which are made more convenient by excluding people who are out of the ordinary – or, in medical research, excluding people who have multiple pathologies, or are very sick. All this adds to the problem of generalising from experimental results (see Chapter 2, section 2.10; Chapter 3, section 3.5).

Self-recruited samples. Newspapers, magazines, radio and TV channels often conduct reader/audience surveys. Some of these are done by reputable survey agencies using probability or quota samples. But some rely on people writing or phoning in. The TV and radio versions often offer respondents the option of ringing

Box 4.3 gives a synopsis of other kinds of sampling, none of which can claim to produce statistically representative samples. Hence for none of these could it ever be claimed that what was true about frequencies in the sample would also be true about frequencies in the population from which the sample was drawn; hence they cannot provide a sound basis for empirical or statistical generalisation (section 4.2).

4.14 Generalising and extrapolating from surveys

Imagine we have conducted our survey of the young people of Slegborough and have a set of results which are frequency estimates within margins of error (confidence intervals). If we selected our sample well, if it was of an adequate size, and if the non-response was not too damaging, then we should be able confidently to generalise the frequencies found in the sample to the frequencies for the population. How long such generalisations would remain true depends on the kinds of phenomena being studied. Public opinion

---

one of two telephone numbers thereby automatically recording an opinion. The populations polled are the readerships or the audience – unrepresentative of the population at large, and an unrepresentative selection of these. No conclusions at all about frequencies in the readership/audience can be drawn from such samples, still less about frequencies in the wider population. The kinds of self-completed evaluation forms which are now common in hospital waiting rooms are similar. Nearly all sampling has some element of self-recruitment insofar as people can refuse, but the kinds of people eager to engage in long interviews or focus groups are likely to be unrepresentative in the extent of their co-operativeness. They may be unrepresentative in other ways, too.

Petitions masquerading as surveys. Pressure groups often use what looks like a survey technique to mobilise support for policies they favour or against those they do not. Response will almost certainly be dominated by those who support the aim of the pressure group. It does mean something if 10,000 people register their objection to a by-pass. But this doesn't rule out the possibility that 10,001 others would register their support if given the opportunity.

Theoretical sampling. For representative sampling the object is to produce a sample which represents the frequencies in the population. Theoretical sampling is used to investigate what is theoretically interesting, irrespective of how frequent it is. For example a theoretical sample of schools might include large schools, middle-sized schools and small schools, cross-classified by the social class composition of their pupil intake, if the research was about the influence of either or both of school size or social class composition on educational achievement. Frequency of occurrence of each type would not be an issue (see also Chapters 5, section 5.3; Chapter 10, section 10.6).

changes quickly and erratically, the age structure of a population more slowly and more predictably.

But often people want to generalise further than this, in order to apply the results of a survey in one locality to the situation in another, or to apply the results of a national survey to a local population. This is obviously a more hazardous kind of statistical generalisation.

The two important questions here are:

- Whether the area to which the survey results are to be extrapolated is similar or different from that in which the survey was conducted, and
- Whether the phenomena of interest are of the kind which are likely to show similar patterns in different areas.

Epidemiology is the study of the geographical and social distribution of illnesses and social problems. Medical epidemiology has demonstrated that a very large number of illnesses have a distribution which is very closely determined by the age and/or gender and/or social class structure of a population. For example if you know the percentage of a population aged 65+, and it is an English population, you can produce very accurate estimates for the prevalence of dementia there (Meltzer 1985), or if you know the age structure of an area and how deprived or affluent it is then you can make a good guess as to its rate of mental illness, or angina, or the number of low-birth-weight babies (Benzeval, Judge and Whitehead 1997). Something similar is true of crime rates within Britain which are predictable from the number of 14–18-year-olds in a population, who commit most of the crimes, and the area's deprivation or affluence. Thus the high crime rate areas have youthful populations and high rates of deprivation. With phenomena like this it is possible to take the findings of a national survey, make some adjustments for local differences in age and affluence/ deprivation and apply the national survey results to produce reasonable local estimates; and similarly with applying the results of a survey in one area to the situation in another.

However, it is only sensible to do this when there is a large body of research demonstrating the age-, gender- or socio-economic-relatedness of a phenomenon. For many phenomena we do not have this knowledge, and for some we have knowledge that local factors other than age or gender or socio-economic factors determine the pattern, though we might not know what these are. It is not quite clear at the moment whether drug use by young people is the kind of phenomenon which shows a consistent pattern nationally (Ramsay and Partridge 1999). If it varies systematically according to the age structure populations of young people and according to area affluence or deprivation, then our survey results might been extrapolated to another area after making suitable adjustments for differences in age and deprivation. But it is also possible that drug use by young people has an epidemic pattern, flaring up here, dying down there, for a large number of different reasons. If that is the case our survey results from Slegborough are unlikely to travel.

ACTIVITY 4.1 Guarding against unrepresentativeness

Figure 4.2 shows that the outcome from a sample survey will be a set of frequency statements. These might provide accurate estimates for the frequencies in the population from which the sample was drawn. But it also shows that the results might be shaped by other factors as well. Think of a topic which might be researched using a sample survey and define the population of interest carefully – for example, 'people aged 65 years plus, living in residential care in England and Wales', or 'female medical doctors under the age of 35 whether practising or not, and living in Scotland'.

With your chosen population in mind, for each of the numbered boxes in Figure 4.2, jot down what might be done to prevent the sample deviating from statistical representativeness, or to prevent the drawing of misleading conclusions about population frequencies from an unavoidable deviation. (Ignore Box 6 for now, it refers to a topic which will be dealt with in Chapter 8.)

4.15 Summary

This chapter has been about drawing statistically representative samples from populations for surveys designed to produce estimates of population frequencies. The survey which is successful in this regard will support a valid statistical or empirical generalisation. This would take the form that what was true in terms of frequencies in the sample would be true of frequencies in the population from which the sample was drawn. Since most social science surveys use samples drawn on probability principles most of the chapter was about those. It dealt with the various ways in which probability samples can be selected, with stratified samples, with the problems of survey non-response and with the issue of sample size and confidence intervals. Less attention was given to quota sampling since this is more often adopted by commercial research companies than by academic social researchers. Some other kinds of samples were mentioned as examples of sampling which *cannot* be statistically representative and cannot support statistical generalisations. Theoretical sampling is an important one of these and will be discussed in more detail in Chapters 5 and 9. Finally the chapter looked briefly at the possibilities for generalising from the results of a survey conducted in one area to the situation existing in another. It was suggested that only under some circumstances would such generalisations be sound ones.

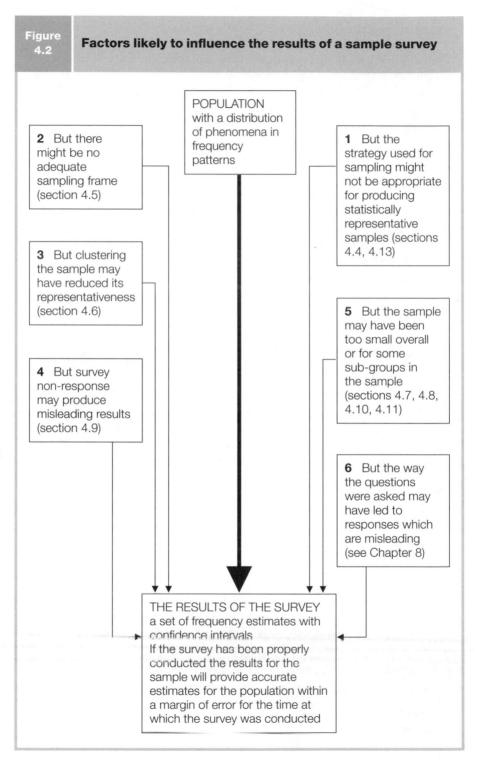

Figure 4.2 **Factors likely to influence the results of a sample survey**

POPULATION with a distribution of phenomena in frequency patterns

2 But there might be no adequate sampling frame (section 4.5)

3 But clustering the sample may have reduced its representativeness (section 4.6)

4 But survey non-response may produce misleading results (section 4.9)

1 But the strategy used for sampling might not be appropriate for producing statistically representative samples (sections 4.4, 4.13)

5 But the sample may have been too small overall or for some sub-groups in the sample (sections 4.7, 4.8, 4.10, 4.11)

6 But the way the questions were asked may have led to responses which are misleading (see Chapter 8)

THE RESULTS OF THE SURVEY a set of frequency estimates with confidence intervals If the survey has been properly conducted the results for the sample will provide accurate estimates for the population within a margin of error for the time at which the survey was conducted

Further reading

Survey sampling is a topic which is well dealt with in many text books; for example Sapsford (1999) gives an overview of both the theory and practice of survey work. Fink (1998) and Thomas (1999) are step-by-step guides to conducting surveys. Fowler (1993), de Vaus (1995) and Alrek and Settle (1995) are survey research handbooks. The design and analysis of surveys is now supported by software packages, such as *Sphinx Survey*, (www.scholari.co.uk). For the analysis of survey data see Marsh (1988). Fink (1998) is particularly helpful in explaining how to interpret computer print-outs from the statistical analysis of surveys, while Babbie and Halley (1994) is a disk and book kit allowing you to practise the statistical analysis of survey data using the main software in this field, SPSS. Quota sampling is usually dealt with best in market research handbooks, for example, Chisnall (1986). Examples of quota surveys, their sample size and the questions asked can be found on the MORI web site, http://www.mori.com.

For the possibilities of generalising from the results of surveys in one area to the circumstances in another, or of applying national surveys to local areas, see Gomm (2000e).

For community surveys, census-based data is often the starting point for designing the samples, and provides some benchmarks against which the representativeness of a sample can be judged. A convenient source for these data and commentaries on the methodology of the census is the ONS Neighbourhood Statistics Service, http://www. Statistics.Gov.uk/nsbase/nss/.

5 Natural Experiments

By the end of this chapter, you will:

- Understand the idea of a 'natural experiment'
- Know what is meant by statistical control
- Understand the use of prediction as a form of explanation
- Know the difference between surveys, case control and population comparison studies
- Be able to state the advantages and disadvantages of a natural experimental approach as compared with controlled experiments.

And know the meaning of the following terms:
ad hocing ■ ascertainment bias ■ case control studies ■ interaction effects ■ internal versus external controls ■ population control studies ■ random error ■ statistical control.

5.1 Introduction

An experimental design is the most adequate for investigating cause and effect but the results of controlled experiments are always vulnerable to the critique that while the experiment might give valid results for the experimental conditions, things would be different in 'real life' (Chapter 2, section 2.10 and Chapter 3). Sometimes a distinction is made between 'experiments' ('true' and 'quasi'), meaning controlled experiments as described in Chapters 2 and 3 and **observational studies,** meaning studies such as surveys asking people questions (Chapters 4 and 7) as well as studies done by observing people going about their everyday affairs (Chapter 10). But when astronomers write about 'experiments' what they usually mean is making some strategic observations of events and entities which would exist whether astronomers existed or not. Of all the sciences astronomy is the one which has most successfully made such **natural experiments** its stock in trade. It is natural experiments of this kind which are the topic of this chapter and of the next. Chapter 6 deals with the control of *time* in natural experiments through taking a *prospective* or *longitudinal* approach.

Natural experiments

The term 'natural experiment' is used to refer to the investigation of configurations of factors of the kind which experimenters would create, if they could, where they can't, but which crop up naturally. The interest is in finding out what causes what. Taking this approach is sometimes called 'the comparative method'. Astronomers can't shove stars and galaxies about so if they want to know what happens when two stellar bodies of particular magnitudes are close together, then they have to look for naturally occurring examples for an answer. Similarly there are often practical, and in addition, ethical, reasons why social and behavioural scientists cannot, or should not, conduct controlled experiments (on research ethics, see Chapter 13). For example they probably could not, and certainly should not, do a controlled experiment subjecting a group of children to extreme social and emotional deprivation to see what effects this has on their social and emotional development, compared with a control group of children raised under more benign conditions. But the collapse of the communist regimes in Eastern European countries has made large numbers of orphans available as a natural experiment of this kind (Rutter 1999). Again we could not divide people among a set of experimental groups and subject some of them to the catholic religion, some to protestant religions, and so on, throughout their lives in order to investigate the effect of religion on suicide rates. But we can analyse the data on suicide to see whether people of one religion rather than another did actually commit suicide more frequently. Durkheim's famous study of suicide at the end of the nineteenth century was an example of a natural experiment of this kind (Durkheim 1952, and see Taylor 1982). In anthropology the migration of people from the same cultural stock across the different ecological circumstances of the Pacific Islands produces something like an experiment for studying the historical development of the same culture in different environments (Thompson 1961).

Again in their well-known *Affluent Worker* studies, Goldthorpe et al. (1968a, 1968b, 1969) chose workers in Luton as their subjects for a natural experiment since they wanted to investigate the notion that manual workers were becoming increasingly middle class, and Luton at the time was a town with cutting-edge industries with manual workers earning wages equivalent to many white-collar workers elsewhere. They reasoned that if manual workers were becoming more middle class, Luton was the kind of place where this trend would be most advanced.

The data for natural experimental research may come from sample surveys, or from routinely collected bureaucratic data such as the registrations of deaths, or the recording of crime (Chapter 7). The practice of 'constant comparison' in qualitative research can also be regarded as conducting natural experiments (Chapter 10, section 10.6).

Table 5.1 gives a synopsis of the difficulties of studying causality using natural experiments, recapping on what was said about controlled experiments in Chapter 2. The table presumes a similar subjects–different treatments design (Chapter 2, section 2.2), but the principles are the same for a different subjects–similar treatments design as illustrated in Chapter 3, section 3.3. As you can see there is a trade-off between, on the one hand, being able confidently to say what causes what, but being unsure as to whether anything similar would happen under non-controlled experimental conditions, and on the other, being sure that what was studied was something that happened under real-life conditions, but being rather uncertain as to what made it happen.

Table 5.1 shows that in controlled experiments, control over variables – experimental control – is exerted by organising people and the environment directly, and that in natural experiments this is replaced with *statistical control*, which involves organising data from naturally occurring situations into categories and analysing them. The topic raised in the first row of Table 5.1 – prospectivity – is dealt with in Chapter 6.

5.2 The idea of statistical control

For social and behavioural scientists the constellation of variables needed for a natural experiment may occur only rarely and, in addition, may be difficult to find. This can be illustrated by the studies of twins conducted from the 1930s to the 1960s. These are important because they were used as the main prop in an argument that intelligence and some aspects of personality are largely inherited, and that therefore there is a biological basis for social inequality and perhaps for criminality (Kamin 1974, 1981; Taylor 1980). Because identical twins have identical genetic endowments the natural experiments constituted by identical twins *reared apart* have been used to study the relative importance of heredity and environment in influencing intelligence and personality.

Table 5.2 shows what 'statistical control' means here. It just means sorting subjects into groups of similarity and difference as relevant to the research topic.

Reading from left to right in Table 5.2 there are three categories of decreasing genetic similarity. This could be continued with first cousins, second cousins and so on. Reading vertically there are two states of 'environmental' conditions: 'reared apart' and 'reared together'. You can think of the table as equivalent to three controlled experiments of the similar subjects – different treatments kind conducted side by side (Figure 2.1). Taken all together similarities and differences *along the rows* should show the influence of heredity, and similarities and differences *down the columns* should show the influence of environment. And, in principle, at least, if there was more similarity in intelligence between identical twins reared apart, than between non-identical twins reared together, that would be presumptive evidence that heredity was more important than environment in determining measured intelligence. By combining and analysing all the data in all the cells it is possible to come up with an estimate of the relative importance of

TABLE 5.1	Controlled experiments and natural experiments compared as ways of studying causality		
Requirement for study of causality	**Approach adopted in controlled experiments**	**Difficulties in natural experiments**	
1 Accurate characterisation of the state of affairs before the causal factors of interest have any impact and after they have had an impact (*prospectivity*) (see Chapter 6)	Controlled experiments are usually *prospective* in that data are recorded prior to the start of the experiment to set a 'base-line' and at the end to measure 'outcomes' Where this is not done the results are less convincing	Researchers often find the right conditions for a natural experiment only *after* the causal factors have had their impact Then they have to collect data about earlier events *retrospectively* It may be difficult to recover accurate data about earlier events Longitudinal designs are sometimes used to avoid this problem; without a longitudinal design it may be difficult to determine direction of effect (see Chapter 6)	
2 Existence of two or more comparison groups of subjects (people, situations, events and so on) similar in all respects which might be relevant to the experiment (*Controlling for differences at the subject level*)	Creation of comparison groups by the experimenter which can be subjected to different experiences, creating the groups using one of the means available for creating comparison groups similar in all respects relevant to the experiment (Chapter 2, section 2.3)	Comparison groups have to be created by the statistical manipulation of data: by *statistical control* It is often difficult to control out important differences between subjects to create groups similar in ways they should be similar and different in ways they should be different as relevant to the research topic The success of statistical control depends on the quality of the data available	
3 All the subjects are the same in ways relevant to the research topic, except with regard to the impact of the causal factor(s) of interest (*Controlling for differences at the 'treatment' level*)	As above, and insofar as the experimenter can control what happens to the subjects it can be arranged that subjects are treated the same where they should be treated the same, and differently where they should be treated differently	What happens to the subjects in a 'natural experiment' happens 'naturally' and is beyond the researcher's control Thus the researcher has to use *statistical control* to separate those to which something happened from those to which it did not happen The success of statistical control depends on the quality of the data available	
4 Other factors which might influence what happens are either excluded, or impact equally on all comparison	As above, and insofar as experimenters can control what happens to subjects, other factors can be excluded	Since natural experiments study what happens naturally, all kinds of other things will have happened to the subjects in	

groups *(controlling out other extraneous variables which might confound the experiment)*	This is where more naturalistic experiments such as field experiments often become most problematic (see Chapter 3, section 3.2)	addition to what is of interest These other factors cannot be excluded from what happens, and it may be very difficult to identify them and to discount their influence in analysing the data
5 Observations, measurements and so on are made of each subject in the same way *(controlling for unreliability in data collection)*	This is usually easy to arrange Where it fails it will be difficult to have confidence in the results of the experiment *(see* Chapter 3, section 3.4, for example)	Often natural experiments utilise data from surveys or from bureaucratic sources (for example from death certification, or crime statistics) Any shortcomings in a survey (for example, non-response, Chapter 4, section 4.9) may undermine the natural experiment The shortcomings of bureaucratic data are dealt with in Chapter 7.
	High degree of control Low degree of naturalism	Low degree of control High degree of naturalism

heredity on the one hand and environment on the other in determining IQ *for the people actually studied*. The classic studies always came up with results which showed that heredity was the more important influence.

Representativeness

There are two kinds of problems here, however. One is a problem of statistical representativeness (see Chapter 4). How representative of all twins are the twins in the sample, and how representative are the twins reared

TABLE 5.2	**A statistical control structure for studying the relative influence of heredity and environment on characteristics such as intelligence or personality traits**			
	Identical twins	**Non-identical twins (same gender only)**	**Non-twin siblings (same gender only)**	
Reared apart	Measure of difference in IQ for subjects in this category	Measure of difference in IQ for subjects in this category	Measure of difference in IQ for subjects in this category	Different environment
Reared together	Measure of difference in IQ for subjects in this category	Measure of difference in IQ for subjects in this category	Measure of difference in IQ for subjects in this category	Same environment

Decreasing genetic similarity ⟹

apart of all twins reared apart, and so on? Since the twins which appeared in the studies were found mainly by advertising in the mass media and offering a financial reward for participation, it seems unlikely that those found are a representative sample, and identical twins reared apart who did not know they had a twin sibling are excluded. Only if they are representative in the statistical sense (Chapter 4, section 4.1) can the results be generalised to the population from which the subjects were drawn: all twins. For a researcher to say that intelligence is 75 per cent heredity and 25 per cent environmentally determined is trivial if this applies only to the small number of people studied and these are not a representative sample of any wider population. It is important only if such an estimate can be generalised to a larger population.

However, even in a small sample there would be something compelling about the demonstration that similarity in IQ always decreased as hereditary difference increased: from identical twins to non-identical twins, to non-twin siblings, to first cousins, to second cousins and so on. But the problem of representativeness has another twist. Because identical twins reared apart are rare, the sample on which such calculations have been based was drawn from several countries at several different points in time. Think of athletics as a parallel example. Sprinters in 2000AD were running much faster than sprinters in 1900. There is no reason to believe that the genetic endowments of people have changed much in the 100 years, so this must be due to environmental factors, including, in this case, the social processes through which people get to be athletic competitors. Thus the contribution of environmental factors to running speeds as recorded in competitive athletics cannot be of a fixed magnitude and must vary from time to time and place to place; so also must the contribution of genetic factors. Hence any calculation of the relative importance of heredity and environment can refer only to a specified population in its social context at a specified point in time. So it is with IQ. But with twin studies it is far from clear as to just what population the people studied represented in place and time.

Statistical control

For statistical control the more important issue is that of getting the right people into the right cells of a control structure such as Table 5.2. There are two axes of difficulty here. First, there used to be a problem of distinguishing identical from non-identical twins. These days this can be done infallibly with DNA testing. But in the classic twin studies it was done by eye. From DNA tests we now know that some identical twins are far from identical in appearance, and that some same-gender non-identical twins look very much alike. Second, there is an even worse problem of drawing a line between 'reared together' and 'reared apart'. These are proxies for the idea of 'similar environment/different environment'. But there are many ways in which similar environments can be different for different people, and different environments similar for different people. There is also a question of time; 'how long should twins be reared separately in order to count as having been reared apart?' or 'how short should a period of separation be, not to count as an apartness?' And there is a problem of *timing*: 'Is being separated from the age of 15 years the same as being separated at the age of 15 months?' Re-analyses of the twin studies (Taylor 1980; Kamin 1981) suggest that relatively brief periods of separation were sometimes regarded as instances of being reared apart. Sometimes living in different households next door to each other were counted as being reared apart. A photo of identical twins reared apart and allegedly having just been re-united by the researcher, shows two boys in identical suits with identical haircuts, which rather beggars belief. It is not clear whether the 'together/apart' distinctions were made even-handedly with regard to identical and non-identical twins. The data were collected retrospectively by the original researchers, either from bureaucratic records or from interviewing subjects or their parents and guardians, so it is very difficult to say much with any confidence as to the appropriateness of the 'reared together/reared apart' distinctions actually made. There is more on the problems of retrospectivity in Chapter 6.

Thus in terms of Table 5.1 (row 2) the classic twin studies seem to fail in creating comparison groups which are similar in ways they should be similar and different in ways they should be different – on the genetic axis. And on the environmental axis, they fail adequately to divide the subjects into groups of pairs who have had similar experiences and to separate these from groups of pairs who have had different experiences from each other (Table 5.1, row 3). It is also unlikely that these studies adequately controlled for the host of other things which might have happened to the subjects which were neither associated with their genetics, nor with their living together or living apart: for example illnesses and accidents. These would probably control themselves out in a large sample by *random error*, since by chance such matters might distribute themselves evenly across all the groups. But here we are talking about a small sample, where a few accidental happenings might have a considerable effect on the overall picture.

Ad hocing and expectancy effects

Not all of these shortcomings would favour the production of results suggesting a hereditarian interpretation. But, in fact, for a long time twin studies were regarded as the definitive proof of the overwhelming importance of heredity in determining intelligence. Wherever data are ambiguous they offer researchers the opportunity to make ad hoc decisions as to where, for example, to locate a case within a statistical control structure, or which data to include or exclude entirely. These are the ideal conditions for expectancy effects (Chapter 2, section 2.6 and see Chapter 3, Table 3.4). Re-analysis of the classic studies (Kamin 1974; Taylor 1980) suggests that the researchers concerned engaged in *unilateral ad hocing*. That means always tending to give the benefit of the doubt to decisions which would favour one interpretation rather than another: in this case, a hereditarian interpretation. For example, Shields (1965) seems to have excluded from his studies identical twins with dissimilar IQs on the grounds that one of them must have misunderstood the test instructions, nor did he note that when he conducted tests himself the IQs of identical twins were more similar than when a research assistant administered tests (Kamin 1981).

Worse than this, the majority of the identical twins reared apart came from the studies of Cyril Burt. It now seems that he invented all or at least some of them (Kamin 1974, 1981; Shipman 1988:119–21). Despite this fraud being uncovered in the early 1970s, many textbooks published up to 12 years later still cited findings based on Burt's data as the truth, some even despite mentioning the fraud elsewhere in the book or article (Gould 1992). More recent twin studies suggest a much lower degree of heritability for personality and intelligence than was suggested in the past (McGuffin 1999).

5.3 Measuring the school effect as a natural experiment

Here I want to illustrate a natural experiment approach with the investigation of 'the school effect' by Jesson, Gray and Tranmer (1992). Do not confuse the school effect with the effect of going to school or not. That would be something different. The school effect is the size of the difference that *attending one school, rather than another*, can make to the educational achievement of otherwise similar children.

This formulation suggests the outline of a controlled experiment: two or more comparison groups of children selected to be as similar to each other as possible in ways relevant to educational achievement, but treated differently by being sent to different schools (Figure 2.1). Because the groups were similar at the outset any differences between the average achievement scores of the groups at the end should then be due to differences made by attending different schools: the school effect. It would be impossible to perform this controlled experiment, but thinking about it makes it obvious why it is difficult to measure the school effect under naturally occurring circumstances. It is because naturally occurring circumstances are unlike those we would create if we were able to do a controlled experiment. The most important difference here is that whereas in the experiment we would arrange for the children in each comparison group to be similar to each other, in reality different schools are attended by different groups of children with different combinations of characteristics known to be associated with differences in educational achievement: characteristics such as ability, social class, gender, ethnicity, ambition and so on. In the vocabulary of controlled experiments there is an acute problem here of controlling prior differences at the subject level (Table 5.1, row 2). In a controlled experiment this would be done by creating comparison groups and organising what was to happen to them. In a natural experiment it has to be done by statistical control (see section 5.2)

The technique used by Jesson and his colleagues is a version of multiple regression analysis called **multi-level modelling**. Many people find the statistics difficult to follow (Goldstein 1987; Schagen 1993). But even if they do, they can still gain from reading this kind of research so long as they understand its underlying logic, which I will explain.

The term 'multi-level' denotes that influences – here on educational achievement – are conceived of as operating at a number of levels. As Table 5.3 shows, at a minimum in school studies there are the *pupil-level variables* (equivalent to the subject level of Table 5.1, row 2) and *school- level variables* (equivalent to the treatment level variables of Table 5.1, row 3). Sometimes school-level variables are divided into Local Educational Authority variables and school-level variables. Sometimes school-level variables are divided into department-level variables and school-level variables, where the latter are those things which are constant for a school, and the former differ from department to department within a school.

At the school level there are all the differences between schools *except* for differences in the characteristics of their pupils. At the pupil level are all the differences between all the pupils in all the schools with regard to the kinds of factors which they 'bring to school with them' which might influence their educational achievement apart from the differences between the schools they attend. I will use the 16+ GCSE examination results as the outcome measure. Statistically speaking, the variation in the results achieved by all the pupils is called the **variance**, and the approach taken is called the **analysis of variance**. Some of this variance will be explained by factors at the pupil level – how schools differ in their intakes – and some will be accounted for at the school level – how schools differ in other respects.

Prediction and explanation

I am going to use the idea of predicting below, so it is important to understand what this means. In research, *prediction* might or might not mean

TABLE 5.3	**Examples of pupil-level and school-level variables**
Examples of pupil-level variables	**Examples of school-level variables**
Gender	Size
Social class	Rural/Urban
Ethnicity	Co oducational/ Single sex
Poverty/affluence	Single sex – boys
Ability	Single sex – girls
Ambition	Selective/ non-selective
Parental interest	Budget per head
Health	Quality of management
	Quality of staff

forecasting the future. What it will nearly always mean is seeing how accurately you can guess one thing from knowing another. If I know someone's gender then I can make a pretty accurate prediction as to which door they will go through in entering public toilets in the UK, or indeed as to which doors they went through over the previous 12 months. Prediction is often phrased as explanation. Statisticians in particular tend to use the two terms as synonyms. So I might say that in using public loos, gender *explains* why someone goes through one door rather than another. My evidence for this would be that knowing their gender allows me to make accurate *predictions*. Making predictions is at the heart of exerting statistical control.

Imagine that the pupils in a sample of different schools have taken their 16+ examinations and we know the results for each. If we wanted to predict the educational achievement of any pupil, not knowing anything else about him or her, then the best bet would be to predict that he or she had achieved the same as the average for all children. Now imagine predicting the result of each child in turn. The most sensible bet is still that each one will obtain the average result. So our best prediction is that all children will all score the same, spot on average. Our basis for prediction here is knowing that they all belong to a data set which has an average score. But that isn't a very good basis for a prediction, since looking at the actual results we see that there is a large spread from worst to best and most pupils didn't get the average result. To the extent that this is a poor prediction a statistician says that it leaves a great deal of unexplained variance.

We can improve our prediction if we take a factor from the pupil-level variables – gender for example – and calculate the average score for girls, and the average score for boys. Then knowing that a pupil is male, and nothing else, our best prediction is that he will score the average for boys; similarly with girls. If we do this for all boys and for all girls then we will still be wrong for most pupils. But are we less wrong in our predictions than when we made predictions on the basis of the ungendered average for all pupils?

If we make fewer errors by gendering the data and improve our predictions in this way, then we can say that the extent of our improvement is the extent to which gender explains the differences in results between pupils. If that were so then the statistician would say that there is less unexplained variance when the data is gendered than when it was not. In fact, for most educational authorities we would indeed improve our power to predict by knowing the gender of pupils.

The next kind of step is fairly obvious. For example, we could now divide the boys into social class groups and calculate the average scores for boys with fathers with manual jobs, those with routine white-collar jobs and those with professional and managerial jobs, and calculate the average score for each of these sub-groups. We could then use knowledge of boys' membership of such sub-groups to predict that they would gain the average for their group, doing the same for girls. The extent to which this reduced our prediction errors and increased the accuracy of our prediction, over using gender groups alone would be the extent to which the variance was explained by social class, net of gender. And there are other sub-groupings which we could use as well. The logic is shown in Figure 5.1. Sooner or later we will run out of pupil-level variables. When we can't find any more pupil-level variables to improve our predictions we will still be left with some unexplained variance. Inside that there will be the school effect.

The school effect in Nottinghamshire

In studying the school effect in Nottinghamshire schools in 1991 Jesson, Gray and Tranmer (1992) went through a process analogous to that in Figure 5.1 but they started with social class. Social class might be defined by parental occupation, or by the educational level achieved by parents. There is a number of different ways of categorising by social class (Reid 1977; Marshall *et al.* 1988 Chapter 1). Jesson and his colleagues used father's current or last occupation – or, in the absence of a father, mother's occupation – divided into three categories: manual, intermediate and professional/managerial.

Table 5.4 was created by classifying the 74 Nottinghamshire schools according to the social class compositions of their pupils at age 16. There are nine logical types but for two types there are no examples in Nottinghamshire. Then for each cell, the average school GCSE score is calculated for the schools in the cell. Thus, for the 13 largely middle-class schools in the first cell of the table, the overall average for all 13 schools was 34 points.

This controls only for the social class differences between schools, and there are other pupil-level variables which are known to affect educational achievement. Jesson and his colleagues followed essentially the same procedures to control for gender differences between schools, for 'poverty' as indicated by the percentage of pupils receiving free school meals, and for the ethnic mix of schools. This allowed them to draw up the ready-reckoner given as Table 5.5. The figures in Table 5.5 are derived from prediction errors as suggested in Figure 5.1. Thus if we predicted all pupils to have achieved the average achieved by working class *girls* not receiving school meals, then we would find that we were wrong about the average for professional managerial *boys* not receiving school meals, by 21.8 – 2.4 examination points. Ethnicity is not shown since differences in achievement by different ethnic groups were very small once social class had been controlled for.

With this additional information we could improve on Table 5.4 as a predictor by calculating average scores for schools according to their social class and gender composition and the percentages of children receiving free school meals. Table 5.5 was only given as an illustration here because in practice all this goes on inside the statistical calculations of a multi-level model.

But that's still only some of the pupil-level variables. Why not go on ? The reason for not going any further is that diminishing returns from doing so set in quite soon. Note that in the ready-reckoner (Table 5.5) knowing

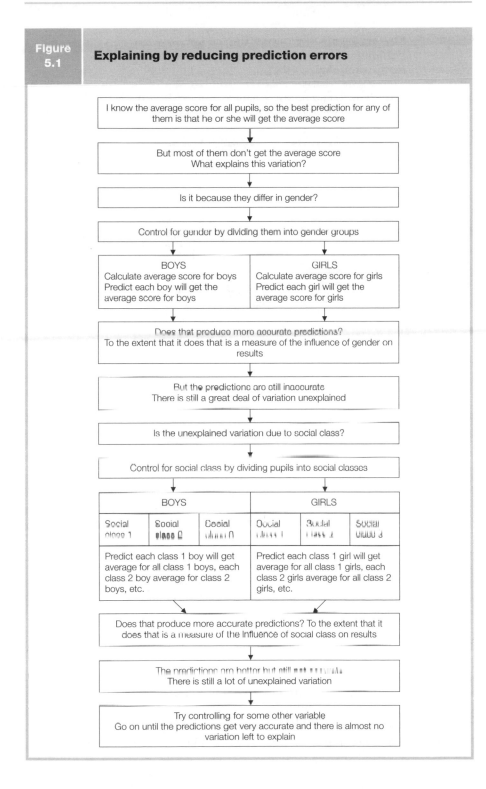

Figure 5.1

Explaining by reducing prediction errors

I know the average score for all pupils, so the best prediction for any of them is that he or she will get the average score

But most of them don't get the average score
What explains this variation?

Is it because they differ in gender?

Control for gender by dividing them into gender groups

BOYS	GIRLS
Calculate average score for boys Predict each boy will get the average score for boys	Calculate average score for girls Predict each girl will get the average score for girls

Does that produce more accurate predictions?
To the extent that it does that is a measure of the influence of gender on results

But the predictions are still inaccurate
There is still a great deal of variation unexplained

Is the unexplained variation due to social class?

Control for social class by dividing pupils into social classes

BOYS			GIRLS		
Social class 1	Social class 2	Social class 3	Social class 1	Social class 2	Social class 3
Predict each class 1 boy will get average for all class 1 boys, each class 2 boy average for class 2 boys, etc.			Predict each class 1 girl will get average for all class 1 girls, each class 2 girls average for all class 2 girls, etc.		

Does that produce more accurate predictions? To the extent that it does that is a measure of the influence of social class on results

The predictions are better but still not accurate
There is still a lot of unexplained variation

Try controlling for some other variable
Go on until the predictions get very accurate and there is almost no variation left to explain

TABLE 5.4	The social class composition of schools and their average achievements in 16+ examinations (GCSEs): Nottinghamshire 1991			
Percentages of pupils with professional managerial background	Percentage of pupils with a manual social class background			Average exam scores
	Low (under 28%)	Median (28-60%)	High (above 60%)	
High (above 28%)	13 schools: average score 34	6 schools: average score 28	No examples	33
Median (8–28%)	5 schools: average score 28	26 schools: average score 26	6 schools: average score 25	26
Low (under 8%)	No examples	5 schools: average score 22	13 schools average score 20	20
Average exam.score	33	26	22	26

How to read this table

Each cell in the table represents a different possible social class composition for a school's pupil body at age 16. The table divides pupils into three social classes, not two. Thus the first cell of the table represents schools where 28% or more of the pupils come from professional/managerial homes, less than 28% come from manual backgrounds and whatever is the remainder in each school come from 'intermediate' backgrounds where a parent is a routine white-collar worker. The first cell in the table then represents the schools with the greatest percentage of middle-class pupils. There were 13 of these in Nottinghamshire in 1991, and the pupil average of all of them together was 34 GCSE points. GCSE scores are calculated on the basis of 7 for an A, 6 for a B and so on, added together for each pupil and divided by the number of pupils in the examination year including those who took no examinations, or gained no passes. The diagonal from the top-left hand cell to the bottom right hand one runs from maximum middle-classness, to maximum working-classness: from schools averaging 34 points to schools averaging 20 points. The average for all schools together was 26.

Source: Based on Jesson, Gray and Tranmer (1992:28).

whether a child has free school meals or not doesn't add a great deal to the ability to predict GCSE results. Since the percentage of children having free school meals in each school is rather few, it adds very little to making accurate predictions for the average score of a school. This doesn't mean that poverty is not an important influence on educational achievement. But the procedures adopted, and the order in which they were adopted, have already controlled for social class. This has already mopped up most of the influence that poverty (measured by free school meals) will have. The effect of poverty on lower-class pupils has already been registered and the negative score of 4.4 points in Table 5.5 is created largely by the lower achievements of *higher*-class pupils in poor circumstances. Again ethnicity would not add much to the ability to predict, since children from ethnic minority

TABLE 5.5	Ready-reckoner for calculating the predicted GCSE scores of pupils from a knowledge of various pupil characteristics
Base score (the pupil is female, from a manual background and does not receive free school meals)	20.5
If the pupil comes from an 'intermediate' background	+10.1
If the pupil comes from a professional/ managerial background	+21.8
If the pupil is male	–2.4
If the pupil receives free school meals	–4.4

Source: Jesson *et al.* (1992: 27).

groups tend to achieve similar scores on average as white children from the same social class. Nationally, Indian and Chinese children tend to achieve more than white children of the same social class and African-Caribbean and Pakistani and Bangladeshi children a little less, though the pattern varies from areas to area (Demack, Drew and Grimsley 2000).

Ability in terms of either an IQ test or some measure of prior achievement is the very best predictor for future educational achievement. Jesson and his colleagues did not use an ability measure, largely because no convenient measure was available. These pupils had not been tested using national standardised achievement tests (SATS). Future cohorts of pupils will have been, so a convenient measure of ability at an earlier age will be available. When a researcher wants to study the school effect with regard to 18+ examinations, the results of the same students at 16+ can be used as the prior ability measure (for example O'Donaghue *et al.* 1997). There is also a conceptual problem here. Should the ability of pupils be regarded as a pupil-level variable, independent of school influence, or as a school-level variable, as something fostered, or inhibited, by attending a particular school? This can be resolved only by chop-logic. If we are interested only in school effects in the GCSE year, then ability shown in previous years belongs to the pupil level. But if we were interested in the school effect for five secondary school years measured in the fifth year, then the problem remains, unless there is a measure of ability for age 11.

In 2003 the Department for Education and Skills began to publish the GCSE results for schools in a way that showed the relationship between pupils' SATs scores in earlier years and their 16+ examination results (DfES 2003). This 'value-added' approach made it possible to see whether schools with intakes of a similar ability, measured by SATs, achieved better or worse 16+ examination results than each other. You can consider this further if you do the activity at the end of Chapter 12.

Social class and ability measures for the same pupils usually correlate quite closely, though not exactly. Thus, following the logic of Figure 5.1 if social class is tackled first, followed by ability, then knowledge of pupils' ability does not greatly increase the accuracy of prediction/reduce the remaining unexplained variance. Knowing the pupils' social class will already put them into groups of predicted achievement fairly similar to the groups of pre-dicted achievement they would be put in on the basis of knowledge of their prior ability. And the same is true if ability is taken first and social class second. Using both social class and ability in such an analysis is interesting because it shows the effect of social class net of ability, and of ability net of social class (see, for example, Smith and Tomlinson 1989). Using both measures takes account of higher-achieving pupils of lower social class, and lower-achieving pupils from higher social classes, who are invisible in an analysis based on only social class, or only ability measures.

Figure 5.2 shows what schools in Nottinghamshire actually achieved in 1991 against predictions for their achievement calculated as described above.

There are two ways of looking at these results. One is to concentrate on the inaccuracies of prediction, the other is to focus on how accurately the predictions were met.

Failure to predict

Failure to predict accurately on the basis of knowledge about one set of factors is taken as evidence about the effects of another set of factors. This is precisely how astronomers identified the presence of planets they could not see, by showing that the orbits of planets they could see could not be accurately predicted from knowledge of the orbits and magnitudes of other known planets. This prediction failure meant there must be some as yet undiscovered body or bodies influencing planetary orbits. Astronomers knew Pluto was there before it was discovered. Predicting from a knowledge of the characteristics of the pupils in different schools did not result in perfect predictions. Somewhere in this prediction error is the school effect.

We would expect chance factors to prevent the estimates from being per-fectly accurate. Jesson et al. (1992) have allowed for this on the scattergram (Figure 5.2), by marking a zone on either side of the prediction (or regres-sion) line. These are actually the 95 per cent confidence limits (see Chapter 4, section 4.11). Within that zone, differences between the results predicted and the results achieved may well be due just to chance. Outside the zone there are 15 schools who show much bigger differences between their predicted and their actual results. Seven of these achieved much more than predicted. It is tempting to suggest that they are particularly *effective* schools. In more everyday terms, these may be the schools which 'do more for their pupils' than others would do for the same pupils. Jesson et al. (1992) suggest that on average these schools boosted GCSE scores by the equivalent of around 4 points per pupil (equivalent to 1 extra D grade each) with the most effective school among them boosting achievement by a maximum of just over 7 points each: the equivalent of one grade B pass extra for each pupil. This most effective school is one which has a middling GCSE score itself, showing that the most effective schools are not necessarily those which achieve the highest results. Eight of the schools achieved appreciably less than was predicted. It is tempting to regard these as

| Figure 5.2 | Actual school average examination scores plotted against scores predicted from knowledge of school's social class and gender composition and percentages of pupils receiving free school meals; 74 schools in the state sector, Nottinghamshire, 1991 |

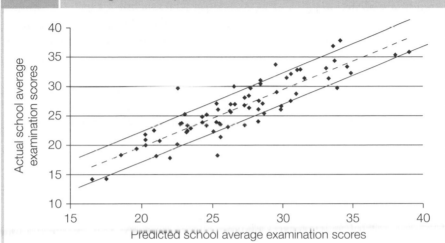

Predicted school average examination scores

How to read this figure

The blocks on the scatter diagram show the average pupil examination score achieved by each of the schools in Nottinghamshire in 1991. They are plotted in terms of achieving higher or lower scores than each other against the vertical axis. The most highly achieving schools are towards the top of the figure. Against the horizontal axis they are plotted in relation to the scores predicted for them. The schools for which high scores were predicted are towards the right of the figure. The dashed diagonal line shows where schools would lie if their results were precisely as predicted: the regression line. If the plots were all on the line, each would have scored exactly as predicted from knowledge about their pupils and there would be no school effect. Thus schools which appear above the line have achieved more than predicted for them, and schools which appear below the line have achieved less than predicted for them. The two other diagonal lines mark the boundaries of a zone in which predictions would be expected to be inaccurate just by chance . For 7 schools which appear above the top line and 8 which appear below the bottom line it seems unlikely that the differences between the prediction and outcome are just a matter of chance: these are statistically significant differences (see Chapter 2, section 2.9). Since the predictions took account of each school's social class and gender composition and the percentage of pupils receiving free school meals, the mismatches between the predictions and the out-turns seem most likely to be due to:

- A failure to control *adequately* for differences between schools for social class, gender and poverty differences
- Some other *uncontrolled factors* at the pupil level: differences in ability not correlated with class, gender and poverty would be the most likely
- Differences between schools (other than differences between their pupils) – the *school effect*.

Source: Jesson *et al.* (1992:29).

particularly *ineffective* schools. Had their pupils gone to a school outside this group they would probably have done better. Jesson *et al.* (1992) suggest that the disadvantage of attending these schools was equivalent to pupils each gaining on average 4 points (one grade D pass) less.

However, we cannot regard these as precise estimates of the school effect. What has been defined by a process of elimination (Figure 5.1) is an amount of variance where the differences cannot be explained by chance, by gender, by social class (as defined in the study) and by poverty (defined by free school meals): the left-overs when these factors have been controlled for. There are three reasons why this unexplained variance will be bigger than the size of the school effect. First, it is likely that the calculations have not *fully* controlled for social class. Pupils were divided into only three social class groups, and each of these will be heterogeneous with regard to parental income, occupation and parental education. Using a six-point social class scale and a more elaborate version of Table 5.3 would have improved the accuracy of the estimates. There are also some problems associated with classing pupils according to the information they themselves provided about parental occupation. Since there are only two genders we can probably be certain that the calculations have controlled for gender adequately. We will look a little more at 'controlling for social class' later in this section and at the end of Chapter 6.

Second, some of the gap between prediction and out-turns is also likely to include the effects of some other *uncontrolled factors* at the pupil level. Remarks were made earlier about this study's failure to control for ability except insofar as ability is controlled via controlling for social class. We know that ethnicity has a small effect after social class and free school meals have been accounted for, and so does coming from a one- or a two-parent family. And no doubt there are some other pupil-level factors remaining uncontrolled and influencing the prediction gap. You can consider this possibility in the Activity at the end of the chapter. Controlling also for these factors would alter the relative position of schools right and left of each other in Figure 5.2, since some schools would be affected more than others according to the make-up of their student body.

Third, there are *interaction effects*. The analysis described so far assumes that each of the factors relates to each other in the same way in all circumstances. But in reality this is unlikely to be so. Being female is different in some South Asian communities by comparison with being female in a white community. Being working class in a largely working-class school is different from being working class in a middle-class school. Matters such as the latter have been investigated in other studies, usually under the heading of 'compositional effects' (Gray, Jesson and Sime 1993). For example, do working-class pupils do worse in predominantly working-class schools: is the effect of social class on achievement multiplied according to the percentage of same-class pupils in a school ? There is some evidence for a compositional effect with regard to social class. With regard to gender, girls in single sex schools do seem to achieve more.

Thus the figures cited in the Jesson *et al.* (1992) study must be regarded as over-estimates of the differences that school factors make, because some of the unexplained variance will be due to uncontrolled variables at the pupil level.

The implications of accurate predictions

In Figure 5.2 note how accurately the GCSE scores of schools were predicted from a knowledge of the school's social class and gender composition and the percentage of pupils receiving school meals. In fact simply knowing the social class composition gives pretty accurate predictions alone. You can see this by looking at the ready-reckoner. The really big figures are those for social class. Compare this with what must be an over-estimate of the school effect. The gap between the most effective and the least effective school was around 12 GCSE points: but the most and the least are only 2 schools out of 74. The overwhelming majority of pupils go to schools which seem more or less equivalent to each other in fostering achievement: the differences between their results might just be a matter of chance. By contrast, the gap between the average for pupils from manual backgrounds and for those from professional and managerial backgrounds is nearly 22 points. Thus social class differences are much more important in explaining educational achievements than are the kinds of factors which are under the control of schools or Local Education Authorities (LEAs) In terms of the logic of this approach the fact that we can better predict a child's educational achievement from knowing his or her social class than from knowing which school they attended is presumptive evidence that social class is more important in determining educational achievement than the influence of the school.

Jesson *et al.* (1992) do demonstrate that there is a school effect: that it does make a difference to children's achievements what school a child attends. And they give an estimate of its size, which turns out to be rather small in comparison with other influences. They identify more and less effective schools. But they do not explain why some schools are more effective than others. To do this they would have to continue the analysis controlling for different school level variables such as those in Table 5.3. For work of this kind see Reynolds *et al.* (1994).

Measuring relativities

Jesson *et al.* give an estimate of the size of the school effect. As they themselves point out, that should be taken as an estimate of the size of the school effect *in terms of the way they measured it*. Controlling variables in different ways would have produced different estimates, but probably not very different. But also this study was only for Nottinghamshire in 1991. In fact their estimates are broadly in line with other local and national studies (Gray, Jesson and Sime 1993; Gray, Goldstein and Jesson 1996). But we would not expect the school effect to be the same size everywhere. There will be some areas where more schools 'do more for' their pupils than in other areas and in other areas there will be more 'failing schools'. In either case there will be a greater school effect, because at base the school effect is a measurement of the distribution of schools above and below an average for all schools in the data set. Changing the schools in the data set will change the average and change the distances by which schools will be below or above average. Changing the boundary of Nottinghamshire LEA in a way that excluded a number of less effective schools would magically reduce the effectiveness of the remaining schools, because some 'weak' competitors would no longer enter into the comparison. But, just as magically, this might increase the effectiveness of all Nottinghamshire schools combined, as against schools in another area.

This is the same kind of problem as arises in making general statements about the relative importance of heredity and environment in determining IQ (section 5.2). It is necessary to keep your wits about you when dealing in relativities. The key question is always: 'what exactly is being compared with what, according to what criteria ?' or 'who's in the data set to be compared with whom, and who's not counted?'

But what are we controlling for in controlling for social class?

Social class is one of the most widely used concepts in social science, but it is rarely clear exactly what it means (Marshall *et al.* 1988 Chapter 1). In the study discussed above, the working or *operational* definition was achieved by asking pupils about parental occupation and then, on that basis, dividing them into three groups: professional, intermediate and manual. The job one's dad does might have some influence on one's educational achievement in itself, but when sociologists think about the 'influence' of 'social class' they are usually also thinking about the influence of family incomes on the one hand and, on the other, the influence of having parents who have had a particular educational experience themselves. So social class is a hybrid concept: part economic, part cultural. If putting families into 'classes' on the basis of occupation or income or parental education always resulted in the same families being in the same groups there would be no problem. But this isn't so. Thus classing pupils by a parent's occupation will fail to control entirely for 'class-as-income' and will fail to control entirely for 'class-as-educational background', as shown in Figure 5.3.

As you might guess, classing people instead by income, or instead by educational level, would again leave bits of 'social class' hanging out.

In addition pupils usually have two parents, often two parents contribute to family income, and mothers and fathers may themselves have different educational backgrounds. There are schemes for classifying pupils by 'social class' using both mother's and father's occupations, or both mother's and father's educational level. But in practice these are rather difficult to use. The reason is that even if we only defined three classes (however defined) we would need 16 categories to accommodate all the possible combinations of mother's and father's 'class' in two-parent families (allowing for either or

Figure 5.3	Uncontrolled aspects of 'social class' when social class is defined by occupation

PARENTAL EDUCATION

(1) Extent to which parental education predicts neither income nor occupation

(4) Extent to which parental education predicts income and vice versa

FAMILY INCOME

(2) Extent to which income predicts neither parental education nor occupation

(5) Extent to which occupation predicts parental education and vice versa but not income

(7) Extent to which occupation predicts income and parental education

(6) Extent to which occupation predicts income and vice versa but not parental education

(3) Extent to which occupation predicts neither income nor parental education

PARENTAL OCCUPATION

How to read this figure

The zone of maximum overlap (7) shows that classing people according to occupation captures something about the relationship between occupation, income and education but not for everyone. Thus if we class people by occupation there will be people with low-status jobs and low incomes but high educational levels and people with high incomes and high-status jobs and low levels of education in sector (6), and people with high educational achievements, high-status jobs with low pay in sector (5) and so on. Whether we class people according to occupation, income or education some aspect of social class will be left hanging out, and hence uncontrolled (sectors (1), (2) and (3)).

both parents to be non-employed), and a further 8 to accommodate pupils from single-parent households. We would have converted social class from being a 3-value variable (as in the Nottinghamshire study), into being a variable with 24 values. To make use of this we would need a very large sample (Chapter 4, section 4.10). Douglas (1964: 69-80) used such a classification but despite having a sample of 5,362 children, he still had to collapse a potential 24-category system into just 4 classes based on combinations of mothers' and fathers' characteristics. However, if we were interested in distinguishing between the effect of mother's social class, and the effect of father's social class, we could follow the logic of Figure 5.1 and see which of the two best predicted a child's educational achievement. Earlier studies suggested that mother's educational achievements were the better predictor.

The general points here are that however social class is operationally defined, it never quite seems to capture everything we mean by 'social class', and that attempts to define it to do so tend to generate more classes that the usual sample size can handle. A more specific point in relation to the school effect study is that, insofar as it failed to control for aspects of social class as shown in Figure 5.4, and for those arising from taking mother's social class into consideration, it will have left some unexplained variance which ought to have been attributed to the pupil level – to diversity between pupils, and will have been wrongly included in the school effect. This a further case for regarding these estimates of the school effect as over-estimates (see also the Activity at the end of Chapter 6).

5.4 Case control and population comparison studies

Case control studies

The examples in this chapter so far have used *internal* controls. That means that statistical control groups are created by dividing the subjects in the research into categories and comparing them. But there are also natural experiment approaches which use *external* controls. **Case control** studies are common in medicine and in criminology. Here a researcher usually allows natural processes to assemble a group of subjects with something in common: all suffering from the same disease, all on the doctor's case load, all in prison, put there by the criminal justice process. These are the *cases*. Then the researcher finds a group of people who are in many respects like the cases, but they don't have that disease, or they are not in prison. The cases are compared with the controls and any other differences between them are candidates for being the cause of the difference of interest. There are two main problems with this. The first is **ascertainment bias**. This is mistaking the characteristics which make people into 'known cases' for the causes of their being in the condition in question. With a criminological study there would be a danger of mistaking the factors which increase the chances of being reported, prosecuted, found guilty and being imprisoned, for the factors which made someone likely to commit a crime. This violates the requirement in Table 5.1, row 2.

Second, there are serious risks of inadequately controlling variables in this way. For example, the study of sudden infant deaths is largely through case control studies (Blair *et al.* 1996). These suggested that parents who smoked were more likely to suffer the sudden death of an infant because there were more smokers among the 'case families' than among the control families recruited to compare them with. But there were also more working-class families among the cases, and working-class people are more likely to smoke. Therefore it is possible that under-recruiting working class families among the controls created the spurious impression that parental smoking is a cause of sudden infant death (Dwyer and Ponsonby 1996). This is the kind of problem which in a controlled experiment is usually avoided by creating comparison groups at random, though it will occur from time to time (Table 5.1, row 2). The same risks occur when using internal controls from survey data, but they are particularly high with the external controls of case control studies.

Case control studies are usually conducted where the condition of interest is rare. It would take a massive survey sample to collect even a few cases of sudden infant deaths, thereby collecting 'cases' and 'controls' in the same operation. With rare conditions and unusual circumstances the only feasible option is to collect cases and then recruit external controls.

Population comparison studies

An even weaker external control device is **population comparison.** For example, a researcher might have access to a number of young delinquents aged 12–16 and want to investigate what characteristics they have which explain their delinquency. To do this the researcher might compare the delinquent group with what is known about the population of 12–16-year-olds in general. This age group in the population in general becomes the control group. The researcher might be tempted to regard any way in which the delinquent group were uncharacteristic of the population at large as 'causes' of their delinquency. There are many studies like this. Durkheim's suicide study (1952) frequently uses this approach. This usually produces lists of 'risk factors' along the lines, for example, that delinquents are more likely to come from poor homes, more likely to come from single-parent families, more likely to have a parent who has experienced imprisonment and so on. But these studies rarely produce any convincing account of what actually causes what to happen. The major problems here arise from inadequacy of information about the distribution of the characteristics of interest in the population at large which is being used as the control (Table 5.1, rows 2, 3, 4, and 5). For the example above, unless we know accurately how many 12–16 year olds there are who come from 'poor homes' according to some precise definition, then we cannot know *how much more likely* are the delinquents to come from 'poor homes'. There is also the problem of ascertainment bias again. The control population is likely to contain an unknown number of unknown 'cases' (Table 5.1, row 2). A third problem is that there are rarely any adequate data either for the group being studied or for the control population as to what they were like before they became delinquent, got the disease, got divorced, or whatever is of interest. If they are contemporaneous studies there will be the problems suggested in Table 5.1, row 1, and discussed in more detail in Chapter 6.

Controlling one study against others

Although the term 'control' might not be used, it is in effect what is being done when one researcher compares his or her findings with what has been found in other studies. Thus in the *Affluent Worker* studies referred to earlier, Goldthorpe and his colleagues had internal comparison groups in the form of both affluent manual workers and white-collar workers from the same industries in the same town at the same time, but no comparison group within the study to represent traditional manual workers. This is important since the heart of the study was about how the well-paid manual workers in the then hi-tech industries in Luton differed from the more traditional, worse-paid manual workers in other industries. For this comparison they had to rely on other published studies, conducted at other times in other places, using other methods of study. If you look back to Table 5.1, you will see that this introduces the kinds of problems identified in rows 2, 3, 4 and 5, with regard to investigating the causal influence of 'affluence' on workers' life-styles, attitudes and beliefs. These remarks are not so much a criticism of these studies as a recognition, first, that the confidence we can have in the conclusions of a natural experimental study relates closely to how successfully researchers have statistically controlled the important variables; and second, that the naturally occurring circumstances with which the researcher works limit what it is possible to achieve.

Figure 5.4	Social class, gender, parental interest and reading scores

Source: Wadsworth (1996a:30).

ACTIVITY 5.1 Activity Controlling variables in explaining reading scores

The data for Figure 5.4 came from Douglas' (1964) studies of educational achievement in the primary school.

1 Just check you understand what Figure 5.4 shows by completing the following:
This display shows the relationship between scores on a reading test and:
Social class after controlling for gender and parental interest
.... , after controlling for .... , and ....
.... , after controlling for .... , and ....

2 The caption given to Figure 5.4 in its original form was:
'The power of encouragement: the level of interest shown by parents in their children's progress at school was more important than their gender and social background'.

  (a) Parental interest is another 'pupil-level' variable in terms of the study described in section 5.4.
  What effect do you think controlling for parental interest, in addition to the other pupil-level variables, would have on the size of the 'school effect'?

  (b) In the original study, level of parental interest was:

  [P]artly based on comments made by the class teachers at the end of the first and at the end of the fourth primary school year, and partly on the records of the number of times each parent visited the school to discuss their child's progress with the Head or class teacher. Parents are said to show a 'high level of interest' if the teachers regarded them throughout the primary school as very interested in their children's work and if they had also taken the opportunity to visit the primary schools at least once a year to discuss their children's progress. (Douglas 1964: 83)

  I Do you think that the procedure described above would give an accurate measure of differences in parental interest?

  II How far do you think differences in parental interest cause differences in children's educational achievement, and how far do you think that differences in children's educational achievement cause parents to be more or less interested in their children's education?

  III How warranted do you think is the original caption for what is shown in Figure 5.4?

If you care to look back to Table 3.5 (p. 65) you will see that the approach of controlling different studies against each other, or indeed of using a series of case studies in the same research programme was what was implied with regard to property-marking projects. The Activity for Chapter 3 took you through the motions of looking for variables which might be the same in different studies or might vary between studies, hence identifying which variables to look for in controlling one study against another.

5.5 Summary

This chapter has been the first of two about natural experiments: the study of naturally occurring constellations of variables in an experimentalist fashion in order to determine what causes what to happen. Social scientists often have to resort to natural experiments since there are practical and ethical reasons why they cannot re-organise the world to create the conditions of a controlled experiment. Apart from necessity, the advantages of adopting a natural experimental approach are that this evades the criticism levelled at controlled experiments that they produce artificial results which cannot be generalised to real life.

As with all experiments, the key issue is that of controlling variables. In a controlled experiment this is done hands-on in a pre-planned way. In natural experiments it has to be done through statistical control, by manipulating the data into comparison groups. Doing this successfully means accurately classifying people (or events, or situations, or organisations) so as to put in the same category those that are similar and to put into different categories those that are different, in ways relevant to the study (Table 5.1). But this is often not an easy task. By necessity much natural experimental work has to be done with incomplete and 'dirty' data. This means that sorting the data into the categories of a control structure may leave the variables identified inadequately controlled and may allow other unidentified variables to confound the interpretation. The particular problems of using data from bureaucratic sources are discussed further in Chapter 7.

The chapter also explained what is usually meant by 'prediction' in social science, which is the extent to which one thing can be guessed from knowing another, and how 'guessability' is taken as explanation. Chapter 6 will introduce some difficulties about doing this which have to do with establishing *time sequences*. This is essential in investigating causation, as you saw in the chapter Activity (2b).

Further reading

It is difficult to recommend reading on the design of natural experiments. Each tends to be determined by what is possible under the circumstances, so the best approach is to read the methodological chapters of particular pieces of research. Gerry Rose's *Deciphering Sociological Research* (1982) is a particularly well-written text helping readers to unpick the methods used in a number of studies summarised in his book. Although written for health researchers Mant and Jenkinson (1997) is a lucid introduction to case control and cohort studies (the latter are dealt with in Chapter 6). Much of natural experimenting depends on the analysis of data to accomplish statistical control. As easy introductions to this try Fielding (1993) and Proctor (1993a); both are articles in Gilbert (1993). For a basic introduction to data analysis, try Marsh (1988). SPSS is the standard software for statistical analysis in social science. Foster (2000) is a good text introduction to the use of SPSS. Both Babbie and Halley (1994) and Field (2000) are book and disk kits which allow you to practise analysing data using SPSS.

6 Controlling for Time in Natural Experiments

By the end of this chapter, you will:

- Understand the importance of establishing time sequences for causal analysis
- Know the difficulties of relying on informant memories for reconstructing the past
- Understand longitudinal surveys and cohort studies as ways of doing naturalistic experiments prospectively.

And know the meaning of the following terms:
cohort ■ contemporaneous or snapshot surveys ■ correlation ■ longitudinal/ prospective/cohort/panel or follow-up surveys ■ pre- and post-data ■ prospective ■ record-linkage ■ repeat surveys ■ retrospective ■ retrospective or recall bias.

6.1 Introduction

Controlled experiments are *prospective* (Table 5.1, row 1). That means that they involve the collection of data *before* the events of interest happen (**pre-data**), then data are collected *after* the event (**post-data***) and the two sets of data are compared to see what effects, if any, the events or conditions of interest had. This enables researchers to establish time sequences of events: to *control for time*. Causality is often difficult to pin down, but one sure rule is that what happened later cannot have caused something which happened earlier. The obverse is not necessarily true. What came earlier will not necessarily be the cause of what came later.

Where there are no trustworthy data on the state of affairs at an earlier point in time it is often difficult to decide what came before what. For example, from studying people at the time of their death we would find that unemployed people tend to die at an earlier age than people in employment (Harding 1995). This is a **correlation**: a statement of what is associated with what. The most common cliché in research literature is that 'correlation is not causation'. Cliché this may be, but it is an extremely important principle. Having data only from the time of death we would have no means of knowing whether being unemployed was in some way a cause of early death, or whether being sick was a cause of both unemployment and of early death. It will be difficult to determine **direction of effect**. We encountered this direction of effect problem in relation to parental interest in the Chapter 5 Activity.

There are often difficulties in making natural experiments prospective. One source of difficulty arises from not knowing where and to whom the naturally occurring events are going to happen, until they have. Then it is too late to collect the data about the situation before the events happened. In the classic twin studies (Chapter 5, section 5.2) what had happened to twins prior to their being discovered by researchers had to be reconstructed by the researchers. Often this was inadequately done with regard to age at separation and length of separation and similarity and difference in environment. Surveys are a common source of data for natural experiments in social research. But most surveys are *contemporaneous*. They are a snapshot about the state of affairs at a particular point in time. They will yield plenty of correlations. But whether the correlations indicate causes and effects and what is the direction of effect, may be difficult to decide.

The Chapter 5 Activity also illustrated another difficulty with studying cause and effect in natural experiments. In controlled experiments the 'causes' in the form of treatments, or sets of experimental conditions can, as it were, be switched on at the beginning and off at the end, so that at the end of the experiment all that are left are the 'effects'. But under real-life conditions there are feedbacks between causes and effects. Thus it is extremely difficult to see whether parents being interested in their children's education is a cause of children doing better at school, or whether children doing well at school is what causes or maintains parents' interest in their child's education (Hage and Meeker 1988).

6.2 Reconstructing the past relying on informant memory

Many surveys actually collect data about circumstances and events which happened before the date of the survey, by asking people questions about the past. But these *retrospective* data may be misleading, partly because people's memories are far from accurate. Box 6.1 outlines the difficulties of relying on memories in order to reconstruct the past.

Box 6.1 relates mainly to the memories of informants. But researchers may misremember the past as part of an expectancy effect (Chapter 2, section 2.6; see also Table 3.4, p. 61). This is the reason for the principle of protecting data collected at one point in time from being altered later.

6.3 Repeat surveys and longitudinal surveys

One advantage surveys have over controlled experiments in studying causality is that they can utilise large statistically representative samples (Chapter 4) while this is difficult in controlled experiments. This means that survey

---

BOX 6.1 The difficulties of relying on memories to reconstruct the past

---

The psychology of memory suggests that it is unwise for researchers to rely on the accuracy of what people tell them about experiences and events in the past (Potter and Wetherell 1987). Here are some of the findings:

- People forget a great deal about what happens to them – nearly everything in fact – but when asked about the past are quite likely to give an answer as if they remembered. This is an aspect of so-called *co-operation bias*. Most respondents try to be helpful to researchers.

- Memory is *re-constructive*. People constantly bring what they remember into line with what has happened to them since. For example, the mothers of children who become delinquent are likely to remember and tell their children's earlier years in ways which are different from the mothers of children who have not become delinquent (West and Farrington 1973). They tell the past in such a way as to provide an explanation for the present. The same seems to be true of parents who have given birth to a child with a disability (Swan, Shaw and Schulman, 1992).

- Memory is *conservative*: people tend to remember in a way that confirms continuities between past and present. This is especially true with memories which bear on what kind of person the rememberer thinks they are. The term *self-serving bias* is used for memories which conserve a self-image.

- Memory is *collective*. What people remember and what they believe about the past depends on who they have discussed it with, and memories tends to be shaped by well-established frameworks for telling stories and giving people characters (Douglas 1987; Wertsch 1987; Middleton and Edwards 1990; and see Chapter 11, sections 11.4, 11.5).

- The telling of memories is shaped by the *immediate circumstances of telling*: for example, by what impression the teller wants to give at the time, what the teller thinks the listener wants to hear, what mood the teller is in and so on (Radley 1990; Shotter 1990; and see Chapter 9, section 9.4).

- What people remember and how they remember often depends on the *cues given by the person asking them about the past*. Cueing and prompting does not necessarily result in accurate recall and can serve to re-shape what people remember, or at least to shape what they tell (Silverman 1989; Davies 1997b; and see Chapter 8).

All the biases above are sometimes collectively called *retrospective* or *recall bias* .

---

findings can be generalised empirically (Chapter 1, section 1.8; Chapter 4, section 4.14) to wider populations with much more confidence than can the results of controlled experiments. With contemporaneous surveys this advantage is usually offset by difficulties in determining direction of effect. By adopting a longitudinal approach, survey researchers can combine the advantages of prospectivity with the advantages of representativeness.

Repeat surveys

The weakest way of adopting a longitudinal or prospective approach with surveys is through conducting **repeat surveys**. This means drawing representative samples from a population in the same way at different points in time. This is quite adequate if the objective is simply to chart time trends, without being particularly interested in what causes them. The large-scale repeat government surveys such as the *General Household Survey* (Bridgewood *et al.* 2000) are primarily designed as time-trend trackers and state of the nation snapshots. But if the interest is causal, then repeat surveys suffer from the problem that what is recorded among one group of people at one point in time has to stand as a base-line for changes which occurred among another group of people studied at a later point in time. Nonetheless, where causal matters are of interest, repeat surveys are usually superior to contemporaneous ones.

Longitudinal surveys

The stronger longitudinal design is one which selects a sample of people at one point in time, and then follows these *same people* through time with repeated surveys, or *sweeps*. It is to these that the terms **longitudinal** or **cohort surveys** or **prospective surveys** are applied. 'Cohort' just means a group of people followed through time. In much American literature **panel surveys** is the term used, and **follow-up surveys** is yet another term for the same. The best known of these are the national birth cohort studies, which are an important source in the fields of developmental psychology, health, delinquency and educational achievement (Davie 1993; Wadsworth 1996b). These are studies through life of all or a large sample of children born in a particular week in 1946 (5,362 children), 1958 (17,000 children), or 1970 (16,000 children). The 1946 cohort was fixed, but for the other two immigrant children with the same birth date have been identified and added in. The 1946 and the 1958 studies have been extended to study the children of the original children. It was from the 1946 cohort that the data for the Chapter 5 Activity were drawn.

The sampling strategy of these studies might be regarded as a kind of systematic sampling with a single sampling interval (see Chapter 4, Box 4.1), or as a form of cluster sample, clustering by time rather than by place (Chapter 4, section 4.6). Systematic samples are as good as random samples so long as there is an arbitrary relationship between the sampling interval and the data collected. However, there are important differences between children with summer birthdays and children with birthdays elsewhere in the year (Sharp *et al.* 1994), hence no single week of birth will produce a sample of children representative of all children born that year. Equally you can see this as a problem of clustering. This is a limitation on the generalisability of these studies, particularly with regard to educational achievement.

These studies together have produced a rich treasure-house of data, but they also illustrate some of the difficulties of adopting a longititudinal approach. A synopsis of these is given in Table 6.1.

TABLE 6.1	Some of the problems of longitudinal survey designs
Sample size	Sample size usually has to be larger for longitudinal surveys since each category in the analysis based on data at one point in time will need to be sub-divided according to differences between members of that category at an earlier or a later point in time – this follows the rule that sample size depends on the degree of diversity in which the researcher is interested (Chapter 4, section 4.9). This is not so much a problem of longitudinal surveys *per se* as of studying causality in detail, where researchers are interested in a wide range of cause and effect relationships. For rare conditions, such as sudden infant death, or Creutzfeldt-Jakob disease (CJD), or the background of serial murderers a longitudinal survey would never have a large enough sample for studying causes: a case control study would be the more feasible option for these topics (Chapter 5, section 5.4).
Time cluster effect	Choosing a cohort with birth dates in a restricted period of the year means that the cohort will not be representative of children born in other periods of the year, and the cohort may not represent children born in other years. This is avoided in the OPCS Longitudinal Study (section 6.5) by selecting four birth dates throughout the year and adding in new births and immigrants for each succeeding year.
Sample attrition	The extent of non-response is magnified as more and more subjects become untraceable through time, though actually sample attrition has not been an enormous problem in the birth cohort studies (Shepherd 1985). In another respect non-response via attrition is less of a problem in longitudinal surveys than in contemporaneous surveys since the characteristics of those lost will be clearly known from previous data collection (Chapter 4, section 4.9).
Subject reactive or Hawthorne effect	There is a possibility that those involved in a longitudinal study behave differently from the ways they would have behaved if not involved. Some of the birth cohort subjects have themselves become interviewers in similar surveys when grown up (Wadsworth 1996a). But in big samples this is unlikely to have large effects.
Irretrievable errors	Bad decisions made at the beginning of longitudinal research may affect the research for a very long time (see Chapter 5 Activity).
Unpredicted relevances	As longitudinal surveys unfold, so questions get posed which suggest that other kinds of data should have been collected at an earlier time. But this simply puts the researcher in the position of one conducting contemporaneous research, and forces the use of the same retrospective strategies as a remedy.
Ageing of relevance	The findings of the 1946 birth cohort may tell us how the circumstances of childhood in the 1940s led to what happened to people in their 50s at the turn of the twentieth century. But the circumstances of childhood in 2000 are very different. So the 1946

Table 6.1 (*Continued*)	
	cohort study might not tell us much about people who will be 50 in 2050. This problem varies according to the length and topic of the study. Longitudinal studies such as the OPCS *Longitudinal Study* (See section 6.5) deal with this by recruiting an additional younger cohort for each year of the study.
Expense	Long-term longitudinal surveys are enormously expensive. Those who conduct them often have constantly to raise funds to keep them going.

Some of the problems of the birth cohort studies arise from the fact that they were open-ended in that they were interested in virtually any differences which might emerge between the children in the sample. At the outset it was not clear what might cause what interesting differences later in life. Thus it was difficult to decide what data to collect at each stage, though each successive birth cohort study learned from the mistakes of the earlier ones. For designing long-term longitudinal studies it would be nice to have the wisdom of hindsight right at the beginning.

But longitudinal studies can be designed to answer sharply focused questions. Then far less information needs to be collected. Because analysis will entail dividing the sample into only a few sub-groups, smaller samples can be used while retaining statistical representativeness (Chapter 4, section 4.2). And the duration of a longitudinal survey does not have to be life-long. The standing panels of respondents maintained by many market research and opinion poll firms serve as the subjects of short-term longitudinal surveys (Hakim 1987: 91-2). They might be surveyed, for example, before the Chancellor's budget statement and then afterwards to judge the effect of the budget statement on public opinion; using internal control to investigate differences between different kinds of people (Chapter 5, section 5.2).

Recapping on Table 5.1, to be adequate as a basis for a natural experimental approach the researcher needs to collect data of the kinds shown in Table 6.2. For examples of studies something like this see Douglas (1964) or Mortimore *et al.* (1988) though the latter is a cohort *study* rather than a cohort *survey* (see section 6.4)

6.4 Cohort studies

The study of the school effect in Chapter 5, section 5.3, was contemporaneous. But Smith and Tomlinson's (1989) study of the same topic was longitudinal, collecting data about the same cohort of 3000 pupils in 20 multi-ethnic inner urban comprehensive schools from entry to secondary school to their 16+ examinations. The schools were not selected by prob-

TABLE 6.2	The kinds of data needed for a longitudinal survey to be adequate as the basis for a prospective natural experiment:
Kinds of data	**For example, in a study of educational achievement 5–11**
To control for prior differences at subject level Base-line data (Table 5.1, row 1) to divide subjects into comparison groups relevant to what is being investigated (Table 5.1, rows 2 and 4)	Measure of ability at 5 years, parental social class, parental education, parental aspirations, gender and ethnicity, season of birth
To control for differences at the treatment level Data on what happened to the subjects as relevant to the investigation within duration of study – dividing the comparison groups above yet again (Table 5.1, row 3)	Characteristics of schools attended, streaming/setting/mixed-ability teaching, parental attitudes to education, measures of reading and maths ability at 8 years, health record 5–11, family crises
Outcome data Data on subjects at end of the study period (or at any interim point) (Table 5.1, row 1)	Measures of, say, reading and maths ability at 11years, child's attitudes to school at 11years
Data of the same kind to be collected from all subjects in the same way (Table 5.1, row 5, and see Chapter 8, section 8.4)	

ability. They were chosen purposively (Chapter 4, Box 4.1) because they had significant numbers of pupils from minority ethnic groups, and ethnicity and education was a major interest of the researchers. In each school the whole year group was studied. Thus this is better called a cohort *study* rather than a cohort or longitudinal *survey*, though often such studies are called surveys (Wall and Williams 1970: 32–7). By contrast with the study by Jesson, Gray and Tranmer (1992) described in Chapter 5, this study allows for children of the same ability at 11, but of different social classes, genders, ethnic groups and schools to be tracked up to their 16+ examinations. And equally it allows children of the same ethnicity but of different ability, social class, genders and schools to be tracked over the same period and so on, with all possible permutations. And hence it allows us to see the school effect over five years in terms of which kinds of pupils, in which schools, made most progress.

However, just as the study of Nottinghamshire schools cannot be generalised to other LEAs, so the results from the schools in the Smith and Tomlinson (1989) study cannot be generalised directly to the secondary education system as a whole. Their study does not represent minority ethnic pupils in schools where they are very much in the minority, or any pupils in schools in more affluent and or in more rural areas (but see Chapter 3, section 3.5). The study which does give a representative picture for the

English educational system as a whole is the *Youth Cohort Survey*, which is a longitudinal *survey* with national samples drawn on probability principles of successive cohorts of students. This provides information on class, gender and ethnic differences in educational achievement nationally (for example, Demack, Drew and Gray 1990, Demack, Drew and Grimsley 2000). But this cannot investigate the school effect, because a nationally representative sample of school students rarely includes more than one student from any one school.

One of the most famous of all cohort studies is that by Doll and Hill (1964), which established the link between smoking, heart disease and lung cancer. This is illustrated in Table 6.3. The study started with a census of doctors rather than a sample, and an incomplete census at that. Doctors cannot be regarded as a representative sample of the wider population, hence the results could not be generalised numerically to a wider population. Thus this study demonstrates a mechanism, smoking–causing–illness, rather than providing an estimate of the size of the effect of this mechanism in the general population. While the initial data were collected by questionnaire, the follow-up data were collected by **record-linkage** (see section 6.5). Deaths of doctors in the study were traced through death certificates (see Chapter 7).

Another large-scale longitudinal cohort study is the so-called *Whitehall study*, which is a study of the occupational mobility, health and other characteristics of 17,000 male government employees from 1967 onwards continuing into retirement and to death (Marmot 1995). It shows, for example, that there is a close relationship between occupational status, stress, illness and premature death, with the government manual employees having much higher rates of all three. These correlations show in contemporaneous studies (Drever, Whitehead and Roden 1996). But as a longitudinal study this one is able to show that differences in health between civil service grades become greater over time, which is presumptive evidence that occupation has an effect in determining health, rather than health determining occupation. This direction of effect is something which cannot be demonstrated so convincingly in a contemporaneous study.

In the Whitehall study, the choice to study civil servants was mainly of convenience and cost. It is easier to conduct such a study where all the subjects have the same employer. For all survey researchers there are costs involved in finding people and travelling to see them. As noted in Chapter 4 these are sometimes reduced by multi-staged sampling and by clustering. In longitudinal surveys these costs are increased by the fact that people have to be surveyed several times. Hence in longitudinal work it is tempting to use convenience samples: doctors, or civil servants rather than the general population. If you like to think of it this way, a cohort *study* is often a longitudinal 'survey' with a convenience sample. The civil service does constitute ideal conditions for a natural experiment insofar as it is a microcosm of the occupational structure. It has workers ranging from low-paid manual workers to highly paid mandarins. But because the civil service

TABLE 6.3	An example of a medical cohort study: Doctors, smoking and death

Cause of death	Deaths per 1000 persons (doctors) per year			
	Doctors smoking more than 25 cigarettes a day	All cigarette smoking doctors	Non-smoking doctors	All doctors in study
All causes	19.7	16.3	12.1	14.1
Lung Cancer	2.2	1.2	0.1	0.7
Coronary Heart Disease	5.0	4.8	3.3	4.0

How to read the table

In 1951 Doll and Hill (1964) sent a questionnaire to all 59,600 doctors on the UK medical register asking about their smoking habits; 68 per cent returned questionnaires. Thereafter the deaths of doctors and the causes of their deaths were monitored, mainly through the death registration process (see Chapter 7). By 1961 there had been 4,963 deaths. These are recorded in the table as rates per 1000. Thus if there were 40,637 doctors in the study and 14.1/1,000 died per year, that is about 500 deaths per year. The table represents a control structure, dividing doctors into smokers and non-smokers and distinguishes heavy smokers from among all smokers. The table shows clearly that the risk of death in all three cause categories increases with smoking. The figures show the pattern predicted if smoking is among the causes of death: a so-called *dose relationship* – more smoking, more death. Most deaths were from causes other than lung cancer or CHD, so that in terms of actual numbers the differences for deaths from lung cancer and CHD between smokers and non-smokers are quite small too. They are statistically significant differences (see Chapter 2, section 2.11), but that has to be read in relation to the 32% non-response rate (see Chapter 4, section 4.9). The pattern of deaths shown by doctors dying after 1961, added to those in the table above, provided more convincing evidence (Doll *et al.,* 1994).

Source: Doll and Hill (1964)

excludes the very poor, the very sick, those working in very hazardous conditions and the unemployed on the one hand, and excludes the very rich on the other, it under-estimates the extent of class-related inequality in health. There are obviously problems of representativeness here, and hence problems of generalising from this study to the wider population. As with the Doll and Hill (1964) study, what is demonstrated is the existence of causal mechanisms and their direction of effect, but not the magnitude of these effects in the wider population. Convenience is traded off against representativeness and generalisability. But something is known about how doctors differ from the population at large, and of how the occupational structure of the civil service differs from the wider labour market. Hence any empirical generalisations can be finessed accordingly, and the theoretical generalisations about what kinds of mechanisms cause what kinds of effects seem credible (see Chapter 1, section 1.5).

6.5 Record-linkage studies

Findings similar to those of the Whitehall study with regard to social class and early death are shown by another longitudinal study: the *Office of Population Censuses and Surveys Longitudinal Study* (Goldblatt 1990; Dale 1992; Harding 1995) This is based on a large representative sample of people, now about 1 per cent of the total population of Great Britain. The study began by selecting from the 1971 Census all those born on one of four birth dates spread throughout the year. It continues by adding in all new births and all immigrants with the same day and month of birth at each new Census. The study is entirely done by *record-linkage*. Data are retrieved about these people from bureaucratic data sets, such as Census returns, birth and infant death registrations (for their children), death certification (for themselves), records of long-stay psychiatric episodes, cancers from the Cancer Registry and so on. Thus the people entered into the survey at the outset can be identified from Census to Census from 1971 to 2001 and onwards, so long as they survived that long, and through various other bureaucratic systems to their death.

Record-linkage is cheaper than interviewing the same number of people. Records will often contain information which subjects themselves could not provide or might forget. And records of these kinds are taken at the time when events happened and then 'frozen' so that they cannot be altered. In these respects bureaucratic records can be very useful in assigning a sequence to events as is necessary for determining direction of effect. But record-linkage studies depend first, on there being records to link with, and for many topics this is not so. Second, access to records about individuals is often difficult to obtain for reasons of confidentiality and because, unlike most industrial nations, individuals in the UK have no single identity number for bureaucratic purposes. Third, such studies rely on the records being accurate and reliable, which is not always the case. The difficulties of using bureaucratic data are discussed in Chapter 7.

ACTIVITY 6.4 Social class as a variable fixed in time or varying through time

Much social science research treats social class as if it were a variable fixed through time. Thus in the study of the school effect in Chapter 5, Jesson *et al.* (1992) divide pupils into three social classes. Yet within each of these

ACTIVITY 6.1 (*Continued*)

social classes there will be pupils who have been in the same social class since birth, and pupils who started life in one social class and were in another at the time they were asked for the information. Presumably educational achievement is influenced by social class experience *throughout life* and not just at the time when 16+ examinations were taken. Similarly the picture given by figures on social class and university entry is of university entrants coming overwhelmingly from middle-class backgrounds. But this is based on parental occupation at time of University entry. My own autobiography shows that at birth my father was a manual worker, at the time I entered primary school he was a routine white-collar worker. He was in junior management at the time I entered grammar school, and by the time I entered University a managing director of a medium-sized company. By the time I graduated he was a managing director of a multinational company. By the time I gained my PhD he was unemployed. Social mobility on this scale is not the norm, but it is not unusual (Heath 1981). The question is not so much what 'social class' influenced my own educational achievements, but when. You will see that this adds yet another set of problems to add to the discussion of controlling for social class in Chapter 5, section 5.3.

The first part of the Activity assumes that you are a University student, but if you are not you can just imagine doing it and then do the second part of the activity:

1 Conduct a survey among undergraduates as to:
   (a) Their social class at birth
   (b) Their social class at entry to University

   In both cases use father's occupation, or in the absence of a father, mother's occupation. Assign occupations to 'Upper Middle' 'Middle' and 'Working Class'. So long as you are consistent in the way you assign occupations to social classes, and these are broadly in line with conventions as to what are higher and what are lower classes, it doesn't matter too much how you do this. But because you will be using your own classification your results will not be directly comparable with anyone else's.

   Use a convenience sample for this (Chapter 4, section 4.13), unless you are willing to invest the time in taking a probability sample (Chapter 4, sections 4.4–4.10) and in chasing up the people chosen in order to minimise the non-response (Chapter 4, section 4.9).

   When you have gathered your data, analyse them to discover what percentage of students from upwardly mobile families there are in the higher class categories at time of university entry.

ACTIVITY 6.1 (*Continued*)

2   If you have conducted the survey consider the results in the ways below. If not, use your imagination to answer the questions:

(a)   What are the implications for sample size of studying social class and University entry using measures of social class at two different times rather than one?

(b)   What would be the difficulties of generalising from the results of the survey above to all undergraduates in British Universities?

(c)   What problems are there of relying on subjects for information on parental occupation?

(d)   What kinds of problems are introduced by their being 'mature students' in the sample?

(e)   What problems did you have/would there be in coding occupations to social classes?

(f)   Despite all these problems, what are the merits of taking this more longitudinal approach to investigating the relationship between social class and University entry?

3   Sketch out a feasible design for research which would avoid the problems identified in (2a)–(2d) above.

Note that it would not be feasible to use a classification of social class combining mother's and father's social class. Following the logic of the discussion in Chapter 5, section 5.3 that would turn the social class of students into a variable with 24×24 values = 576 (or more if you treated mature students differently). But it might be interesting to see which of mother's or father's social class best predicted University entry (see Figure 5.1, p. 111).

6.6 Summary

This has been the second of two chapters on natural experiments. It focused on the problems of controlling for time sequence when studying naturally occurring constellations of factors with a view to establishing causality. This is necessary to make confident statements about the direction of effect and for distinguishing relations of causality among the many relations of correlation to be found among variables. It noted the difficulties of doing this where circumstances in the past have to be reconstructed from memories. Prospective approaches in the form of longitudinal surveys and cohort studies were discussed. These have the advantage of collecting before and after (pre-and-post) data within the framework of the research. But for causes which operate over a long time, they involve a very long-term research investment. The chapter activity drew attention to the way in which much research treats variables such as 'social class' as fixed throughout time, whereas in reality they are not. The British class structure shows a considerable degree of social mobility so that where social class is cited as a cause there is always a question about when in someone's life-time they are classified as belonging to a particular social class.

Further reading

Hage and Meeker (1988) is a thorough discussion of the concept of causality in social research and the strategies of studying it, largely through natural experiments. Taris (2000) is a comprehensive guide to longitudinal research. The methodological sections of particular longitudinal studies are also worth looking at: for example Goldblatt (1990) or Butler *et al.* (1982).

7 Using Bureaucratic Data in Research

By the end of this chapter, you will:

- Understand why social researchers often have to use data collected by bureaucratic organisations as part of their routine operations
- Understand why such data may not be an adequate basis for drawing conclusions
- Have considered the possibilities of cross-checking such data against alternative sources
- Have modelled the production of data by a bureaucratic system.

And know the meaning of the following terms:
ascertainment bias ■ construct validity ■ reliability ■ secondary analysis ■ standardised mortality ratios ■ triangulation ■ validation.

7.1 Introduction

By necessity, social researchers often have to utilise information which has been collected by the bureaucracies of the state. This may be the only existing record of the past, or the only data available at a cost the research budget can afford. Sometimes the use of bureaucratic data in social research is called 'secondary analysis' since the researcher gets the data second hand, though that term applies to the analysis of any second hand data, whatever its source. Bureaucratic data has rarely been collected for research purposes. Before using them, social researchers need to have a good idea as to how bureaucracies work as data producing machines. Studies of the way bureaucracies produce data are useful in remedying the deficiencies of bureaucratic data, but they are also interesting in their own right as studies of the way in which facts about people are socially produced.

7.2 Problems of using bureaucratic data in research

The collection of some data by the state does involve rigorous social science methods. For example, the decenniel censuses and various large-scale repeat government social surveys such as the *General Household Survey* (Chapter 6, section 6.3) or the *British Crime Survey* (Chapter 4, section 4.2) employ the methods described in Chapters 4 and 8. These give rise to relatively few problems when used in secondary analysis. But many such data are collected as a routine part of the way in which state agencies operate in, for example, diagnosing disease and allocating treatments to patients, establishing eligibility for welfare benefits, for deciding what kind of offence has been committed and whether someone is guilty of it, or deciding on the cause of death for legal purposes. Such data are primarily used for internal agency purposes and for the external monitoring of their performance. They are a product of the way such services are organised. They reflect, for example, the way in which clients, conditions, treatments, offences and so on are classified and documented: the decisions made by people to use, or not to use services and decisions which construct this person as a case of this, that person as a case of that, and this potential client as not a client at all. And they reflect the ways in which people become 'clients', 'patients', 'students', 'offenders', 'claimants', 'unnatural deaths' and so on and flow into, through and out of bureaucratic systems according to complex decision-making processes typically involving quite large numbers of people, often making decisions in rather idiosyncratic ways. In assessing the quality of findings from social science we have to ask 'by what methods were the findings produced?'. In assessing the adequacy and the meaning of bureaucratic data we have to ask a similar question.

Flows, filters and data machine

Figure 7.1 is based on Goldberg and Huxley's (1992) 'filter model' of community mental health. It represents mental health services as machines for generating data which sift and sort clients into different types, send them down different routes, collect some information about them on the way and count which of them end up where. Looking at mental health services in this way it is difficult to believe that, for example, a count of psychiatric in-patients over a period of a year is a straightforward measurement of the number of people in an area suffering from 'severe mental illness'. Chapter 5, section 5.4, referred to **ascertainment bias**, which is the bias arising from treating known cases as statistically representative of all cases. Figure 7.1 gives a picture of the way cases become known, and hence how the conditions for ascertainment bias are created.

Thus data routinely generated from bureaucracies may tell us more about the way the bureaucracies operate than about whatever it is that the data are supposed to stand for: levels of crime, number of children at risk, numbers of homeless people or episodes of domestic violence.

7.3 Basing research on bureaucratic data

Sometimes researchers have little choice but to utilise data which are generated by the routine operation of bureaucratic agencies. For example, much of the corpus of epidemiological knowledge is based on data generated by the certification of deaths. Figure 7.2 gives an example of this.

Figure 7.1

Goldberg and Huxley's filter model of mental illness

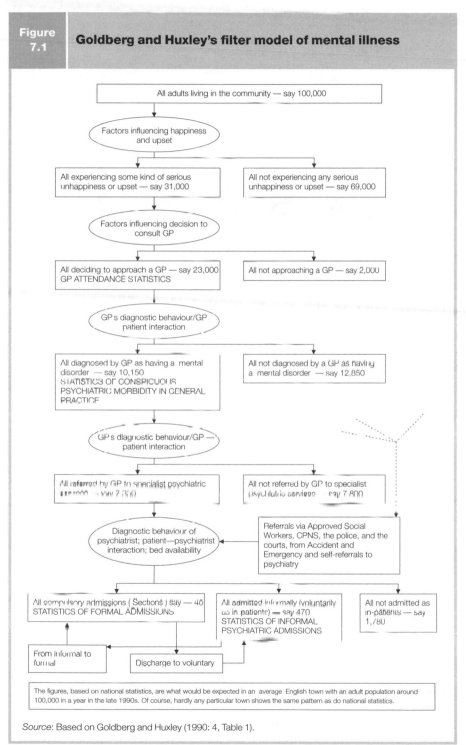

All adults living in the community — say 100,000

Factors influencing happiness and upset

All experiencing some kind of serious unhappiness or upset — say 31,000

All not experiencing any serious unhappiness or upset — say 69,000

Factors influencing decision to consult GP

All deciding to approach a GP — say 23,000 GP ATTENDANCE STATISTICS

All not approaching a GP — say 2,000

GP's diagnostic behaviour/GP patient interaction

All diagnosed by GP as having a mental disorder — say 10,150 STATISTICS OF CONSPICUOUS PSYCHIATRIC MORBIDITY IN GENERAL PRACTICE

All not diagnosed by a GP as having a mental disorder — say 12,850

GP's diagnostic behaviour/GP — patient interaction

All referred by GP to specialist psychiatric services — say 2,350

All not referred by GP to specialist psychiatric services — say 7,800

Diagnostic behaviour of psychiatrist; patient—psychiatrist interaction; bed availability

Referrals via Approved Social Workers, CPNS, the police, and the courts, from Accident and Emergency and self-referrals to psychiatry

All compulsory admissions (Sections) say — 40 STATISTICS OF FORMAL ADMISSIONS

All admitted informally (voluntarily as in-patients) — say 470 STATISTICS OF INFORMAL PSYCHIATRIC ADMISSIONS

All not admitted as in-patients — say 1,780

From informal to formal

Discharge to voluntary

The figures, based on national statistics, are what would be expected in an average English town with an adult population around 100,000 in a year in the late 1990s. Of course, hardly any particular town shows the same pattern as do national statistics.

Source: Based on Goldberg and Huxley (1990: 4, Table 1).

Figure 7.2	Standardised Mortality Ratios (SMRs) for selected causes of death, by social class (based on occupation) men aged 20–64, England and Wales, 1991–3

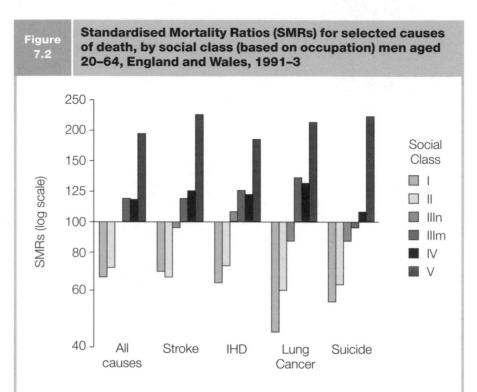

Source: Drever, Whitehead and Roden (1996:16, Figure 1).

How to read this figure

Standardised mortality ratios are calculated to make comparisons in death rates between different sections of the population: in this case between males in different social classes aged 20–64. The line across the figure set at 100 is the death rate for all males in this age group. Thus bars above this line show a higher-than average death rate, and bars below a lower-than-average death rate. An SMR of 50 would be half the rate for all men, and 200 twice the death rate for all men. Deaths are expressed as a proportion (a rate) of all males in a particular social class in this age group: this figure is derived from up-dated Census data. For the method of calculation see Gomm 2000e:181. The causes of death derive from death certification. The social classes are those of the Registrar General's scheme: I – Professional/Managerial, II – Intermediate (e.g. Teachers), IIIn – Routine white-collar workers, IIIm – Skilled manual workers, IV – Semi-skilled manual workers, V – Unskilled manual workers. The figure does not show deaths for a further 'Unoccupied/Other' category.

One of the most telling demonstrations of class inequality in Britain and in other societies is that people of different social classes have different life-expectancies and that poorer people suffer more illness and disability than richer people do. For example in 1996 men in the higher social classes had an average life expectancy of 77.7 years and those in the lowest social classes only 68.2 years. The equivalent figures for women were 83.4 and 77.0, respectively (Goldblatt and Whitehead 2000). A major data source for such findings is the routine certification of deaths by cause (Drever, Whitehead and Roden 1996). Figure 7.2 cross-classifies cause of death for males between the age of 20 and 64 with social class. The data for these two addresses come from different procedures. That for cause of death comes from judgements made by a certifying doctor making entries on a death certificate assigning a cause of death. This is then converted into the codes of the International Classification of Diseases (of the World Health Organisation (WHO)) by an official in the death registry. In Figure 7.2 these codes have then been translated back into verbal labels such as 'Stroke'.

Michael Bloor realised that only a small number of doctors account for a large percentage of all certificates completed in any health authority area. Idiosyncrasies among this small group would be likely to have large effects on the local data about the cause of death, and that in turn on national patterns. His study of death certification in Scotland (Bloor 1991, 1994) was conducted using a simulation experiment on similar principles to that conducted by Atkinson and his colleagues with English and Danish coroners (Chapter 3, section 3.3). He found that, confronted with the same evidence, on paper, doctors often reached very different conclusions about the cause of death. Bloor also notes, from interviews with the doctors, that they regard death certification as a routine chore, and not something to be done very assiduously. They are much more interested in treating live people than in completing paperwork on dead ones. He also points out that there are only weak mechanisms to hold doctors to account for the accuracy of their assignation of the cause of death. As a GP, Howard Shipman murdered a large number of his elderly patients over a long period of time. His death certificates were accepted without question until an inquiry into one such death was forced by pressure from the deceased's relatives.

There is an important general methodological point to be made here. When researchers involve practitioners in controlled experiments (Chapter 2), as often happens in medical social work or educational research, they do all they can to make sure that all the practitioners involved make the same judgements in the same way as each other and that each makes judgements in a consistent way each time. That is, they attempt to make practitioners into *reliable* decision-makers, where 'reliable' means 'consistent' (see Chapter 2, section 2.7). But all research studies of practitioners in normal circumstances show that they are most unreliable judges, different doctors confronted with the same evidence often reaching different diagnoses (Bloor, Venters and Samphire 1978; McPhearson, Strong and Epstein 1981; Dingwall and Murray 1983; Jenkins *et al.* 1985; Sackett *et al.* 1991). Studies of judgements in social work (Dingwall *et al.*1983; Campbell 1991), coroners (Atkinson 1978, Taylor 1982, and see Chapter 3, section 3.3) and in the criminal justice system (Maynard 1989) give the same impression.

The unreliability of judgements in practice is not only a matter of differences between practitioners, but relates also to the general messiness of real-life practice, unlike the more simplified environment of a controlled experiment. Practitioners in practice would usually fail an inter-rater reliability test (Chapter 2, section 2.9).

The other references in Figure 7.2 are to the personal characteristics of the deceased. Gender will rarely be wrongly recorded. Age at death can usually be cross-checked against birth certification for people born in Britain or in another country in which births are certificated and copied forward onto passports or visas. There is some room for error here. A few years either way for occasional cases will not make much difference to the interpretation of the general relationship between social class and early death, though in a study of death rates and ethnicity it might be more important, where many of an ethnic group were born outside the UK. The data from assigning social class are much more problematic.

In the UK this is usually based on information provided to the Registrar of Births Marriages and Deaths by whoever registers the death (Prior 1989). This is usually a kinsperson who is asked to give the current or last occupation of the deceased. Sometimes those who register a death only have a hazy idea as to the occupation of the deceased, when what is needed is some information which can be accurately coded in the registry into the six categories of the Registrar General's Social Classes (see Figure 7.2). 'He worked for the Council' is not adequate for this purpose. Thus there is bound to be some inaccuracy here, and many people are allocated to a seventh, 'Not occupied/Other' code. Classing women is particularly problematic since there is an option to class them according to their own or their husband's – or, in the case of young women, their father's – occupation. Research on how deaths are classed through these procedures suggest a general tendency to report occupations higher rather than lower in the social class scale. One aspect of this relates to early retirement. Thus miners, police officers, fisherfolk and people in the military tend to take on less-demanding occupations before their final retirement, but at death are frequently reported according to their earlier more 'notable' occupation. This means, for example, that the records show deaths among miners or police officers disproportionate to number of miners and police officers there are in this age group and thus gives such occupations spuriously high premature death rates (Bloor, Samphire and Prior 1987).

This in turn raises an issue as to what data about death and social class are supposed to show. Recording attempts to tie death and social class to the final pre-retirement occupation of the deceased but it is social class position throughout working life which provides the substrate for the class-related causes of death, not just the final occupation. Most men change their social class by at least one step in the Registrar General's scheme during their lives from birth to death (Heath 1981; Goldthorpe and Payne 1986). Social class assignation, based on current or last occupation recorded at the time of death, doesn't seem a very adequate way of controlling for the effect of 'social class' on life-expectancy if 'social class' is thought of as a life-time of experience (recall the Activity for Chapter 6).

A further problem with regard to social class and early death raised by Figure 7.2 is that the number of deaths is expressed as a proportion of all people in that social class in that age group at that point in time; the so-called **population at risk**. This means that the statistics in Figure 7.2 include data from yet another source: from the questions about occupation in the Census. As soon as the Census is conducted, reality begins to depart from what the Census shows, since the occupational and social class structure are constantly in a state of flux. This is the same problem as noted with population comparison studies in Chapter 5, section 5.4.

The relationship between social class and premature death is such an important topic, and the system of death certification is such a convenient source of data on this, that there has been much research investigating how far the certification data can be trusted. This research has taken the form of studying how certification data are produced, as with Prior's (1989) study of death certification in the Northern Ireland Registry, Atkinson's (1978) or Taylor's (1982) studies of coroners' investigations and decisions, simulation experiments as with Bloor's research reported here or M.W. Atkinson's simulation experiment (Chapter 3, section 3.3), and by cross-checking samples of certification data against different sources, such as more detailed interviews about the occupation of the deceased with samples of kin who register deaths, or checking cause of death on death certificates against independent post-mortem examinations.

With regard to the relationship between social class and early death, the overall conclusions are, first, that many of the errors are random and simply cancel each other out, which has the paradoxical effect that data which might be inaccurate at the level of individuals, are nonetheless accurate in aggregate. And, second, that the main direction of systematic error in the certification data tends to *under*-report the extent to which lower social class membership is associated with earlier death. This is partly because of the tendency to elevate the occupation of the deceased on registration, and partly because the 'Not occupied/Other' category is dominated by people from lower social classes, who ought really to be added in as deaths among those of social classes IV and V (Bloor, Samphire and Prior 1987). And it is partly because much of the impact of social class on life-expectancy occurs in childhood and is not captured in the registration procedure for the deaths of adults many years later. most social mobility is upwards. The same picture of social class conditions causing illness and premature death is given by studies such as the OPCS *Longitudinal Study* referred to in Chapter 6, section 6.5 (Harding 1995). But this study in turn relies on linkage to death certification to attribute cause of death.

Note the relationship between the precision with which a claim is made and the confidence we can have in it. We can be fairly confident that, for adult males at least, the death certification data give a fairly accurate picture of the relationship between the fact of death between 20 and 64 and having had a manual or a non-manual occupation. It becomes less accurate the more we elaborate these two addresses. Thus on the one hand the more causes of death we allow for, the more disagreements there will be between doctors about the cause of death. And on the other hand the more finely we divide people into socio-economic categories – 'classes' – the more errors can be made about these.

7.4 Checking bureaucratic data against alternative sources

The discussion above illustrates something general about what is needed in order to use bureaucratic data for research purposes. Unlike data produced by quantitative social science research, these data do not have a clearly articulated audit trail showing how they were produced. In this regard they are more like the data produced by some forms of qualitative research (see Chapter 8, section 8.5 and Chapter 10). Thus using bureaucratic data requires this deficit to be remedied by studying the process of data production to see what the data actually mean and by checking the data produced against alternative sources.

A very common kind of research project involves comparing bureaucratic data with data produced through some alternative means, called either *triangulating between sources* or *validating*. For example Payne and Saul (1997) used a questionnaire sample survey to estimate the frequency of angina in Sheffield (see Chapter 8, section 8.4). This showed that angina was more common among people living in the poorer wards of the city. By contrast, health service records showed that it was the people living in the more affluent wards who were more likely to be receiving treatment for heart disease. Again, information on the incidence of crime, collected independently of the criminal justice system is what is needed to check whether some group in society is disproportionately likely to be arrested and charged in relation to their actual level of offending. The only way in which such data can be produced is through self-reporting. The regular *British Crime Survey* is a sample survey which collects information both about whether people have been the victims of crime and whether they have committed crimes themselves. The victimisation data show that the majority of crimes go unreported and unrecorded (Mayhew, Elliot and Dowds 1989; Mirrlees-Black *et al.* 1998).They also suggest that a major consideration in reporting crime is whether insurance is involved, since insurance companies often require police authentication for a settlement. That in turn suggests that poorer people, who are less likely to have insurance, are also less likely to report crimes where they are the victims. Again, the fact that the majority of crimes go unreported creates a kind of permanent reservoir from which spurious crime waves can be created with crime remaining stable but people becoming more likely to report it. Large increases in the recorded incidence of sexual assault (Harris and Grace 1999), domestic violence (Mirrlees-Black 1999) and racially motivated crime (FitzGerald and Hale 1996) in the 1990s may have been due more to increases in reporting than to increases in commission.

The *British Crime Survey* also asks people to admit to committing crimes. It seems reasonable to assume that these data are less accurate than those on crime victimisation, but they are the only data source which allows rates of commission of crime for particular groups as recorded via the police and the courts to be compared with an independent source of information (Bucke 1997). One of the problems with self-report data of this kind is that it assumes that different levels of reporting reflect different levels of offending rather than different degrees of self-disclosure in various social groups.

Both the angina survey used by Payne and Saul, and the *British Crime Survey* have a further problem. This is that respondents are not 'expert' in classifying their illness, in the one case, or their offences, in the other. In practice what 'heart disease' is, what kind it is and what its severity is, is something which will be decided by doctors. The way the WHO *Angina Questionnaire* was designed seems to make it a fairly reliable indicator of the amount of heart disease which would be diagnosed by competent doctors if they examined the people concerned, though with a consistent over-estimate (see Chapter 8, section 8.4). But it is much more difficult to achieve a similar kind of matching in the *British Crime Survey*. This is because the police, the Crown Prosecution Service, or, in Scotland, the Pro-curator Fiscal, and the courts have so much discretion in how to categorise crime into particular types and particular levels of severity, and the dis-cretion seems to be exercised differently in different areas of the country and at different points in time. Asking people what crimes they have com-mitted for which they have not been prosecuted is asking them a question they cannot answer, since the answer could be determined only by their being caught and prosecuted. Nonetheless, the exercise does produce a useful point of reference on the extent of crime which is independent of the activities of criminal justice agencies.

These remarks raise important issues about *construct validity*: a question about what a datum is supposed to measure. Suicide statistics, for example, measure the number of suicide verdicts reached by coroners, not the number of people who intentionally kill themselves. Reports of crime statistics measure reports of crime recorded by the police, arrests measure the number of arrests, and so on. Only with difficulty can data measuring one kind of phenomenon – say verdicts, be used as a measure of another kind of phenomenon – say self-homicides.

ACTIVITY 7.1 Modelling the production of official statistics on crime

1 Select any kind of crime.

2 Look again at the filter-diagram of Figure 7.1 and draw up something similar to show how the official statistics for this particular crime might be produced. Include at least three levels: 'reported to the police', 'charged with the offence', 'found guilty of the offence'.

ACTIVITY 7.1 (*Continued*)

3   Look at the diagram you have produced:

(i)   For this crime two police divisions show radically different levels of reports to the police (after taking into account differences in the size of the population). What alternative kinds of explanation might be given for this?

(ii)   For this crime there is a very large rise in guilty verdicts from one year to the next. What alternative kinds of explanation might be given for this?

(iii) For this crime the statistics from a particular police division show that some sub-group of the population (for example, African-Caribbean males, aged 17–25) are much more likely to be charged with the offence, than other people. What alternative kinds of explanation might be given for this?

4   Look up the meaning of ascertainment bias in Chapter 5, section 5.4. Use your diagram to explain what it means, and note down the problems this kind of bias might cause in studying crime.

7.5 Summary

Data deriving from the routine activities of bureaucratic agencies are often used in social science research: because they are cheap or because they may be the only data available, particularly about past events. But these data are not usually produced for research purposes. They are often produced in a haphazard way, with contributions by many different functionaries in different agencies classifying events and people differently, and rarely in ways that are consistent through time. Unlike well-conducted research there are rarely any clear protocols for recording, rarely any checks on the reliability of recording and little to control the effects of bias on the recording process. There may also be problems associated with the political aspirations of governments, who require that data is collected to produce positive pictures of the success of government policies, and with the desire of agencies to make sure that the data they collect and report on reflects well on their activities (see Chapter 12, Chapter Activity). The latter is becoming an increasingly important issue with the spread of 'performance management', where agencies are 'named and shamed' in terms of the data they themselves produce. Thus there have been examples of schools cheating on SATs tests, or under-recording truancies, hospitals lying about their waiting lists, and police forces maximising the number of crimes they charge each offender with in order to boost arrest rates (Davie 1999).

The problems of using bureaucratic data for research purposes can be ameliorated, first by studying the way in which the bureaucracies in question produce data, and second by checking bureaucratic data against alternative sources. It is rare that either method can provide a precise numerical correction of bureaucratic data, but either can be very suggestive as to the directions in which bureaucratic data may be misleading: more likely to over-record this, or to under-record that.

Further reading

Dale, Arber and Proctor, *Doing Secondary Analysis* (1988) is a good introduction to secondary analysis as a whole, although mainly about the re-analysis of survey data. *Demystifying Social Statistics* (Irvine, Miles and Evans 1979) is now very out of date in the examples it uses, but nonetheless does identify a wide range of ways in which bureaucratic data may be misleading. Various studies of how data are collected in bureaucratic contexts are noted in the text in this chapter. On crime statistics see Muncie and McLaughlin (2001: Chapter 1) and Bottomley and Pease (1986), which remains a model for how to understand crime statistics: worth looking at after you have completed the Chapter Activity. The substantive data in their book are out of date, but crime statistics are always 'out of date' because the law, policing and criminal justice procedures change rapidly. What were 'robberies' in 1980 were what were constituted as robberies by the criminal justice system of the 1980s. They cannot be directly equated with 'robberies' of the 2000s, which would have been constituted as such though the criminal justice system of the time. See also Muncie and McLaughlin (2001: Chapter 1).

8 Questions and Answers

By the end of this chapter, you will:

- Have a good understanding of the considerations which shape the questioning strategies of researchers conducting social survey research and be able to contrast these with …
- … the considerations which shape the questioning strategies of those who conduct the more discursive interviews of qualitative research
- Know the main factors which might give misleading results from questioning respondents and the measures researchers may take to manage such problems.

And know the meaning of the following terms:
acquiescence bias ■ construct validity ■ co-operation bias ■ Delphi group ■ demand characteristics of an interview ■ focus group ■ forced choice (or closed) questions ■ incorrigibles ■ interviewer effects ■ leading questions ■ open-ended questions ■ pre-structured data ■ random error ■ scaling ■ self-serving bias ■ social desirability bias ■ systematic error.

At the end of the chapter there is an Activity which asks you to practise framing the kinds of questions which appear in social survey questionnaires. In Chapter 9 you will look at the kinds of responses which arise from the questions asked in qualitative interviews and the activity at the end of Chapter 9 features a transcript from a focus group.

8.1 Introduction

Many data come from asking people questions and recording their responses. Whether this is experimental research, social survey research or through the longer more discursive interviews of qualitative research (see Chapter 9), in each case the data collected are shaped by the way the questions are posed, and the manner and the context in which they were asked. Much bureaucratic data arises from asking people questions too (Chapter 7). This chapter examines the implications of data being responses to questions in the circumstances under which the questions were asked.

8.2 Validity and reliability in questioning

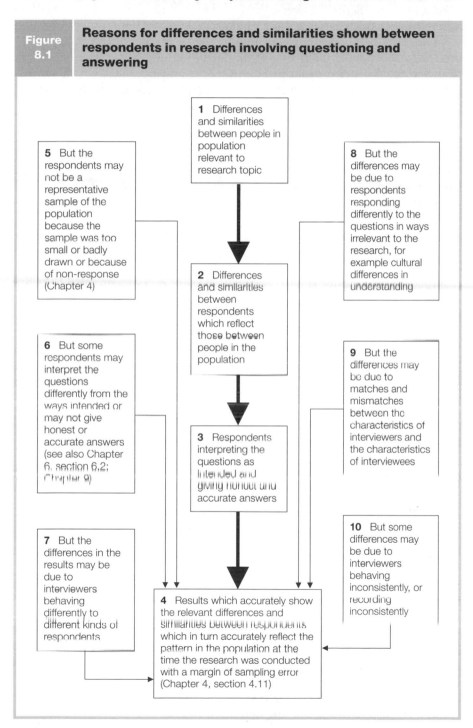

| Figure 8.1 | **Reasons for differences and similarities shown between respondents in research involving questioning and answering** |

1 Differences and similarities between people in population relevant to research topic

5 But the respondents may not be a representative sample of the population because the sample was too small or badly drawn or because of non-response (Chapter 4)

8 But the differences may be due to respondents responding differently to the questions in ways irrelevant to the research, for example cultural differences in understanding

2 Differences and similarities between respondents which reflect those between people in the population

6 But some respondents may interpret the questions differently from the ways intended or may not give honest or accurate answers (see also Chapter 6, section 6.2; Chapter 9)

9 But the differences may be due to matches and mismatches between the characteristics of interviewers and the characteristics of interviewees

3 Respondents interpreting the questions as intended and giving honest and accurate answers

7 But the differences in the results may be due to interviewers behaving differently to different kinds of respondents

4 Results which accurately show the relevant differences and similarities between respondents which in turn accurately reflect the pattern in the population at the time the research was conducted with a margin of sampling error (Chapter 4, section 4.11)

10 But some differences may be due to interviewers behaving inconsistently, or recording inconsistently

Figure 8.1 shows that, at the end of research involving researchers' questions and respondents' answers, there will be a data set for which it will be possible to say that there are these similarities and these differences between respondents. If the research was a controlled experiment (see Chapter 2) then the important differences and similarities would be between members of different comparison groups composed in advance. If it was a sample survey then the interesting differences and similarities are likely to be between categories already provided for in the survey design: between genders, age groups or ethnicities, perhaps (see Chapter 4). And in some more open-ended research there may have been no prior assumptions as to what groups would emerge as interesting and what would be the differences between them, and the researcher will be looking to discover this in the data (see Chapters 9 and 10). This chapter will concentrate on the differences and similarities in the data *put there through the processes of questioning and answering*.

What the researcher hopes for is that any differences and similarities in the data will accurately reflect something real: that they won't simply be *artefacts* of the way the data were collected: that the research will go straight down the middle of Figure 8.1: Box 1, 2, 3, 4. Suppose that the research is on alcohol consumption and one of the questions is 'how many pints of beer do you drink a week?' The hope might be that the responses obtained could be added up and divided to provide an estimate of average beer consumption for all respondents, and separately for different types of respondents: for example, young men, young women, Muslims, Hindus and so on. Further, the researcher might hope that these estimates accurately captured how much the respondents really did drink and that if the respondents constituted a representative sample (Figure 8.1, Box 5), that their drinking habits could stand for the drinking habits of similar groups they were taken to represent in a much larger population (Chapter 4).

Validity and reliability

Apart from the issues of representativeness which were discussed in Chapter 4, there are two main kinds of ways through which all this might go wrong. The first is an issue of **validity**. The term 'validity' has many meanings but for this example it would refer to a relationship of accuracy between the *responses* and the *reality the responses were intended to capture*: **construct validity**. There is a difference between the act of downing pints and the act of answering a researcher's question about this. The latter has to stand for the former but there are many ways in which it might not: they include that the respondent:

- Doesn't know the right answer, but gives an answer nonetheless –
  co-operation bias.
- Gives an inaccurate answer which he or she thinks is accurate. There is a tendency for people to believe that which supports some preferred beliefs about themselves – **self-serving bias**.

- Knowingly gives an inaccurate answer in order to present a favourable impression – **social desirability bias.**
- Is unwilling to give (what he or she thinks) is the right answer, but gives another, perhaps one which the respondent thinks the interviewer wants – **acquiescence bias.**
- Refuses to give any answer at all.
- Doesn't interpret the question as it was intended and gives an answer based on a different interpretation, unbeknown to the researcher.

Validity is always relative to the intentions and assumptions of the researcher. Thus it would be invalid for the researcher to assume that an inaccurate response by the respondent was an accurate indication of their drinking habits. But knowing that it was an inaccurate response, and some other things as well, the researcher might rightly assume that this was valid evidence of, say, the way people very often do not know how much they actually drink, or, say, of the way in which people are often inhibited about disclosing the amount of their alcohol consumption.

Reliability refers to consistency of approach. Suppose that for some respondents the question was asked privately and for others it was asked in the hearing of their friends or relatives. That is likely to inject a considerable amount of unreliability into the research. Then it might not be clear as to whether differences in numbers of pints, recorded between respondents, derived from differences in how many pints they actually drink, or whether, alternatively, it derived from differences in response to a confidential situation, as opposed to a situation in which there were reasons to understate or overstate their level of consumption. In circumstances like this it would be an invalid assumption on behalf of the researcher to assume that the data obtained gave an accurate picture of the pattern of differences in beer consumption between different respondents.

As the last sentence suggests, it is actually extremely difficult to distinguish unreliability from invalidity. Treating these as different issues gets really difficult when a researcher does all that can be done to treat each respondent exactly the same – behaves reliably – but where the same situation is experienced as importantly different by different kinds of respondents. For example, however successful a white interviewer is in behaving similarly towards black and white respondents, there will still be important ways in which the combination white and white is different from the combination white and black, and this might create differences in response.

Now here comes a problem which is more fundamental than deciding on the meaning of the terms validity and reliability. Suppose a researcher recognised that the ethnicity of the interviewer was likely to be an important factor in influencing responses, and for this reason used black interviewers with black respondents and white interviewers with white respondents. Would this solve the problem? The answer is that it would swap one problem for another. With only white interviewers we might speculate that differences in responses between black and white respondents have something to do with black respondents being confronted with white interviewers. But in using interviewers matched to the ethnicity of the respondent, we might also speculate that, of any differences, some were owing to black respondents being interviewed by black interviewers and white respondents being interviewed by white interviewers. The best way of deciding matters here would be through setting up a control structure (Chapter 2). This would involve four situations: white interviewer: white respondent, white interviewer: black respondent, black interviewer: white respondent; black interviewer: black respondent; and analysing the data from each to see whether ethnic matches and mismatches were important.

Unfortunately there are practical limits on how far this kind of strategy can be built into research programmes. Ethnicity is not the only kind of factor which might influence responses. Gender, age, social class and other 'interviewer' characteristics might also be important. Again there are bound to be differences among people as to the way they respond to self-completed questionnaires as against face-to-face interviews, or to one-on-one interviews as opposed to the group interview situation in a focus group. And what about responses varying with time of day and day of week and venue of interview, or differences relating to language use or ways of interpreting questions? A control structure to manage all this diversity would be impossible to create for most kinds of research. There is, however, piecemeal evidence from research done to specially to investigate such matters. For example, there is research on the influence on response of ethnic matches and mismatches between interviewer and interviewee (Finkel, Guerbock and Borg 1991) or gender matches and mismatches (Padfield and Proctor 1996). This can be drawn on by other researchers, somewhat speculatively, to interpret their own results.

Validity and right or wrong answers

The researcher would have been unwise to ask: *How many pints of beer do you drink per week?* because it is unlikely respondents would be able to answer this accurately, short of the respondent having an extremely accurate memory and taking pencil and paper and adding up all the pints consumed over a long time period and dividing by the number of weeks (see also Chapter 6, Box 6.1). But the researcher could have asked a question for which a correct (or incorrect) answer could be given: *How many pints of beer have you drunk in the past seven days including yesterday, but not today?* Then, in principle, there would be no doubt as to what a valid set of results would be. They would be results mirroring some very tangible activity, describable in a widely understood vocabulary.

Researchers often do investigate matters where it is reasonable for them to behave as if there were some 'right answers'. Much of the basic data collected about respondents and used to put them into categories for analysis are of this kind. This includes those data used to divide people into age, gender, ethnic, or occupational categories. And in policy-oriented research, researchers often collect the kind of information which grants, or should grant, someone eligibility for some kind of service – for example, degree of disability, housing condition, length of period of unemployment. While various decisions might be made about definitions here, once a decision had been made about this, it would be possible to say that the researcher had made an accurate or an inaccurate count.

However, there is much of interest in social research where it would be impossible, *in principle*, to find any means of independently verifying what respondents say. These include matters of 'self-knowledge', or **incorrigibles** ('uncorrectables') such as opinions, attitudes, experiences, intentions, feelings, beliefs, values, ideas and ways of understanding. These are the opposite of **corrigibles**: matters about which there can be wrong, and hence correctable, answers. The problem of *incorrigibles* is discussed further in Chapter 9. But here it is worth noting that distinguishing between the kinds of bias listed earlier requires evidence of beliefs and motives which is not usually available.

8.3 Two different approaches to eliciting information from respondents

Social research includes three different approaches to the problem posed above. I shall deal with two of these here. The third is that taken by ethnomethodological researchers and is discussed in Chapter 9.

The first approach is of a piece with experimental research, and is followed by most researchers doing research using questionnaires with forced-choice questions, which is most survey researchers. For convenience I will call this a *social survey approach* to questioning, though it is usual for collecting data in controlled experiments too. Here a premium is placed on standardisation and reliability: on doing as much as possible to make sure that every respondent is asked the same questions in the same way, departing sometimes from this where it seems necessary to cater for major differences between respondents; for example, where it is necessary to translate questions into different languages.

Since they recognise that different respondents will experience the research situation differently, and that differences between interviewers might create misleading effects, researchers may make provision to collect information to judge whether this is happening. For example, they might analyse the results from different interviewers separately and compare them, in the same way as national examination boards analyse results to see if any marker is marking more or less leniently than others. Well-conducted research in this genre, then, involves exerting some statistical control over the research process in order to detect matters such as different responses to the same situation by different kinds of respondents, or differences in performance between different interviewers. In these ways this approach employs something like the same safeguards against error as were described for experiments in Chapter 2.

The second approach is to regard standardisation of the kind above as itself being a process of distortion. The argument goes that approaching respondents like this creates a thoroughly unnatural situation, so whatever the results, they won't have much bearing on what respondents usually think, generally feel, normally experience, or really believe. The criticism here is similar to that sometimes made of experiments (Chapter 2, section 2.10 and Chapter 3). It is important to note that this criticism is applied particularly in the context of research on matters of 'self-knowledge' (see above). The approach suggested instead is to develop close, friendly, trusting, relationships with respondents, and to vary interviews from respondent to respondent in order that they will make authentic disclosures about their thoughts and feelings. The logical conclusion of this policy is not to conduct interviews with respondents at all, but to share their lives via some kind of participant observation research (Chapter 10) or though some kind of collaborative research activity (Chapter 12). But many people who hold this view do conduct interviews, though interviews which look much more like ordinary conversations. For want of a better term I will call this **qualitative interviewing**, since the users generally identify themselves as qualitative researchers, and the results are usually expressed in non-numerical terms.

The two approaches can be regarded as representing different ideas about the efficiency of different methods for eliciting information from respondents. But, in addition, the positions also entail different ethical ideas about the way researchers ought to treat the subjects of their research. This is discussed further in Chapter 13. For the time being it is worth keeping issues of expediency separate from ethical issues. Below I will take each of the two approaches in turn.

8.4 Standardisation and control in eliciting information in survey or experimental research

Social survey research has a long history. Part of that history is a body of research on research identifying what can go wrong in a social survey, and suggesting improvements to technique (de Heer, de Leeuw and van der Zouwen, 1999; Kalton 2000). In addition, experimentation, in psychology in particular, has generated a literature explaining why it sometimes happens that when experimenters ask subjects questions, the results prove difficult to interpret. The lessons taken from both sources are that when it comes to asking people questions what is needed is more rigour, more standardisation and more control over confounding variables. Note here the similarities between this approach to collecting information and a 'similar treatments/different subjects' experimental design (see Chapter 3, section 3.3). In both cases the aim is to treat the subjects similarly so that any differences in results are attributable to relevant differences between the subjects, and to nothing else.

The problems addressed in this genre of research are of a number of kinds. The first of these concerns failures of representativeness, including the problem of non-response (Figure 8.1, Box 5). These were discussed in Chapter 4 and will not be discussed further here. But remember that usually people who are asked questions are being taken to stand for larger groups of people and only if they are representative can what was discovered about them be generalised more widely. Other kinds of problems are those associated with:

- Effects deriving from the way questions are framed and posed and the way they are administered
- Uncontrolled differences in the circumstances in which different respondents provide information; for example, with a postal questionnaire some may complete it alone, and some together with others
- Uncontrolled interviewer variables – characteristics of interviewers and their behaviour which should be irrelevant but actually influence the results (Figure 8.1, boxes 7 and 9)
- Uncontrolled subject variables – characteristics of respondents which cause differences in response but are not the differences the researcher is interested in – for example, differences in proficiency in the language used for the research, or differences in responses to being a research subject (Figure 8.1, Boxes 6 and 8).

Designing the questions and administering them in survey or experimental research

Much has been written about the relative merits of using postal questionnaires as opposed to face-to-face interviewing and of the latter as against telephone interviewing. The different methods have different implications for survey non-response as noted in Chapter 4, but in terms of eliciting accurate information there seems to be little difference between well-designed versions of each, except a hint that the more distance that can be placed between the respondent and the questioner, the more likely respondents are to disclose information embarrassing to them. Table 8.1, for example, compares the results of three methods of eliciting information about their smoking habits from pregnant women. As you will see, the greater the distance between the questioner and the respondent, the higher the level of smoking admitted. It seems reasonable in this case to assume that the higher levels are the more accurate ones.

Anonymous postal questionnaires seem to win out on this criterion. But this can be established only where researchers have some independent means of verifying what respondents told them, which is rarely.

Each mode of delivery gives different opportunities for researchers to control the research situation. With a postal questionnaire, the characteristics of an interviewer cannot influence the response except through what appears on paper. But nor can the researcher control the circumstances under which a questionnaire is completed, or even who actually completes it. Moreover, the only guidance the researcher can give to the respondents has to be written in advance on the questionnaire. Telephone interviewers cannot influence responses by their appearance or gestures, and can offer

TABLE 8.1	**Intimacy and anonymity in disclosure: reports of numbers of cigarettes smoked daily at the beginning of pregnancy as reported in hospital records, by mothers interviewed at home and in postal questionnaires**		
Number of cigarettes smoked daily	**Hospital records (%)**	**Home interviews (%)**	**Postal questionnaires (%)**
1–9	23	21	11
10–19	57	57	42
20 +	20	22	47
Total:	100	100	100
Average	11.7 cigarettes	13 cigarettes	16.6 cigarettes

How to read this table

Information about smoking at the beginning of pregnancy was sought from the same group of 75 women in three different ways. Very similar results were obtained through the two face-to-face methods, but the anonymous postal questionnaire suggested much higher rates of smoking. Since it is difficult to imagine these women exaggerating their smoking under circumstances of anonymity it seems reasonable to assume that the postal questionnaire gives the more accurate figures. There is evidence to suggest, in addition, that many smokers do not know accurately how many cigarettes they smoke, and that they consistently underestimate this.

Source: After Oakley, Rajan and Roberson (1990): 483.

supplementary guidance as to the meaning of questions – for good or ill. Face-to-face interviews may offer considerable opportunities for the interviewer to control the circumstances of the interview, especially if interviews are conducted at a venue chosen by the researcher, though less so if conducted in the respondents' home or work place, and even less so on a busy street. Face-to-face interviews also offer greater risks that what should be irrelevant characteristics about interviewers will influence responses.

Question formats in survey or experimental research

Closed or **forced choice** questions are usually preferred by survey researchers (see Box 8.1). This is because the object of most survey work is to make point-by-point comparisons between different kinds of people, or between the same kinds of people at different times. This can be done precisely only if the same questions are asked of everyone, and if respondents are restricted to a limited number of responses. The responses from forced choice questions are easily coded into numerical forms. Sometimes researchers begin by designing the tables in which the results are to be expressed, and then devise questions to generate the numbers to fill into the tables. How the

BOX 8.1 Question formats

Closed, or forced choice questions – all permissible options are provided for

Dichotomous
Are you male or female ?   Male ☐   Female ☐

Multiple Choice
How many cigarettes did you smoke yesterday?

None	1–5	6–10	11–20	21–30	30+	Don't know
☐	☐	☐	☐	☐	☐	☐

Likert Scale
How strongly do you agree or disagree with this statement?
   Young people these days have no respect for older people

Strongly disagree	Disagree	Don't know	Agree	Strongly agree
☐	☐	☐	☐	☐

Semantic Differential
Tick the box which is closest to your feelings
        Doctors are...

Warm [ ] [ ] [ ] [ ] [ ] [ ] [ ] [ ] [ ] [ ] [ ] *Cold*
Wise [ ] [ ] [ ] [ ] [ ] [ ] [ ] [ ] [ ] [ ] [ ] *Foolish*

Rating Scale
Please rate the quality of the accommodation as:
Excellent 1 [ ]   Good 2 [ ]   Fair 3 [ ]   Poor 4 [ ]   Very Poor 5 [ ]

Open-ended Questions

Unstructured (or better, 'loosely structured')
What does it mean to you to be a woman in a profession dominated by males?

Sentence Completion
To me a good day at work means.....................

Repertory Grid Technique
Can you tell me in what way these two [people] are alike, and unlike this other [person]
Kelly (1955).

In addition, responses can be elicited by asking respondents to complete half-finished stories, or to describe what is shown in a picture. Instead of answering questions respondents may be asked to put cards in rank order or, in experiments, to press buttons.

researcher intends to analyse the results statistically will also influence the way the questions are framed.

In a survey, **open-ended questions** may sometimes be asked. But if respondents are allowed to use their own words, what these words mean may not be clear to the researchers. And when they analyse the results they will have anyway to reduce the diverse responses to a much smaller number of categories. There is a strong possibility that a large percentage of the responses will end up in the 'miscellaneous' category and not really con-tribute to the results at all. Probably some respondents will provide more than one answer to a question. If all the answers are counted this will over-represent the responses of the loquacious as against those of the more reticent, thus undermining the representativeness of the sample for this question. Or, if only one of several answers from some respondents is to enter the analysis, then it is difficult to find principles for choosing and excluding responses.

The use of closed questions often gives rise to the criticism that these force respondents to express ideas they may not have, in words they would not normally use and that they are thereby misrepresented. Whether this is an apposite criticism depends on the purpose of the research. Consider, for example, research designed to establish the extent of 'homelessness' and the risk of being 'homeless' among different categories of people, and con-ducted to influence policy in this field. Here it would produce meaningless results to allow each respondent to define 'homelessness' differently, because the purpose of the research implies that the results should be meaningful in policy terms and meaningful to policy-makers. The most appropriate approach here might be to elicit from respondents the kind of information which a housing officer would ask for in order to determine someone's eligibility for housing: either under a current policy, or according to one the researcher thought should be adopted. Here it would be appropriate to force respondents to use response categories provided for them.

However, in a piece of research designed to capture something of what it was like to experience homelessness it would prejudge what this experience was to ask respondents closed questions. The results from closed questions might then be meaningless in the sense of not capturing the meaning of 'homelessness' to those experiencing it. It would be better to get them to use their own words, even if it might sometimes turn out to be uncertain as to what they meant. Many surveys include both closed and open questions according to the use to which the resulting information will be put. Research using open questions is often a preliminary for the design of a closed-question questionnaire.

Different questions, different answers

The use of closed as opposed to open questions can certainly give rise to different answers about the same matters. For example in a Finnish study of the menopause Hemminki and colleagues (Hemminki, Topo and Kangas 1995) found that when given a list of symptoms to tick, 45 per cent ticked tiredness, 41 per cent hot flushes and 35 per cent headaches as symptoms they had experienced in the previous two weeks which they associated with the menopause. But when asked an open-ended question only 9 per cent mentioned tiredness and only 4 per cent headaches, though about 40 per cent mentioned hot flushes.

The use of closed questions is also a response to the problem of collecting data from large numbers of people with a limited amount of time for each. In addition, closed questions can be constructed to force respondents to make themselves comparable with others by expressing an opinion or belief on a scale from very strong to very weak: so-called **Likert scales** and similar scaling devices (Box 8.1). Without this it would be very difficult to distinguish between those who forcefully express an opinion not very important to them and those who reticently express an opinion dearly held.

Table 8.2 illustrates the different kinds of results which might come from asking yes/know/don't know questions, as opposed to asking a scaled question. With the unscaled questions there seems to be little difference in 'satisfaction' between males and females, but with a scaled question large differences show themselves. However, to use scaled questions it is necessary to use larger samples, for reasons explained in Chapter 4, section 4.10. The strength with which an opinion or feeling is held is virtually impossible to determine with open questions, where the different ways respondents use for expressing themselves add a complicating factor. Of course, scaling does not entirely solve this problem.

Researchers have to frame questions in terms which are likely to be understood by respondents. That includes avoiding ambiguity, except in those kinds of research where the object is to see how different kinds of people resolve an ambiguous stimulus differently, as in some psychological research. Sometimes it is necessary to produce questionnaires or interview schedules in various language versions. This can introduce confounding factors into the research. Differences between languages are not just differences between words, but also differences between ideas. A directly translated question may not be the same question as the original (Meadows and Wisher 2000). Differences in the results may reflect this, rather than whatever it was that they were supposed to reflect. For example, in the national survey of minority ethnic mental health Nazroo (1997) found that those respondents who were asked questions in South Asian languages appeared to be more mentally healthy than were either other minority groups interviewed in English, or the 'white' respondents. These South Asians were the more recent arrivals so this might be taken as evidence that the longer you live in Britain the more mentally unhealthy you become. But, equally the finding might be an artefact of the way the ideas in the interview were conveyed differently in different languages.

Producing 'user-friendly' questions by phrasing them in colloquial terms also has problems. Several questionnaires still used commonly in health services research use 'feeling blue' instead of sad or depressed, and are very out of date in this respect (for example Jenkinson 1994: 69). Yet using

TABLE 8.2	A comparison between results which might be obtained from yes/no/don't know questions as opposed to scaled questions: invented data				

QUESTIONNAIRE 1 – UNSCALED			QUESTIONNAIRE 2 – SCALED		
	Males	Females		Males	Females
Satisfied (S) (%)	32	31	Very Satisfied (%)	4	4
			Moderately satisfied (%)	14	9
			Neutral (%)	59	20
Not satisfied (NS) (%)	63	65	Moderately dissatisfied (%)	14	24
			Very dissatisfied (%)	4	39
Don't know/won't say (DK) (%)	5	4	Don't know/ won't say (%)	5	4

How to read this table

Questionnaire 1 offered three response options: S/NS/DK. The results suggest no significant difference between males and females. Questionnaire 2 offered 6 response options. Now it appears that females are much more dissatisfied than males. So long as the sample sizes were adequate an analysis of the first set of results would show no statistically significant differences between males and females, but an analysis of the second would show a statistically significant difference (see Chapter 2, section 2.9).

the term 'sad' for its more usual meaning might cause confusion for those young people for whom it meant 'pathetic' or 'despicable' in the year 2002. Generally 'user-friendly' language is more exclusionary than standard English. The same is true with regard to colloquial Hindi as compared with educated Hindi which is much more widely understood.

Leading respondents to appropriate answers

Similar problems may arise with expert terms. For example, it would be no good asking people if they had angina because there will be people who have been diagnosed with angina, but who don't know this, people who have been diagnosed and do know it and, of these, some will have been correctly and some incorrectly diagnosed. And there will be people who have not been diagnosed with angina who actually have it, some saying 'yes' and some saying 'no', and some people who haven't been diagnosed, haven't got angina but say they have. To make matters worse, as with most illnesses, people don't just have it or not. They have heart conditions ranging from very mild to very severe. Somewhere on this continuum a line is drawn between 'angina' and 'not-angina'. Different doctors are likely to make such 'casing' decisions differently (see Chapter 7, section 7.3).

Payne and Saul (1997) were particularly interested in whether, in Sheffield, the people most in need of coronary care services were those who received them most frequently. To find this out they had to know who suffered from angina. It was impossible to use medical records, since part of the problem was that doctors were not picking up all the cases. It would have been much too expensive to send teams of doctors out into the community to examine people. Instead they sought information directly from people in the community, using a sample survey technique (see Chapter 4). It would have been silly just to ask: 'Do you have angina?', but people do know sufficient about their own bodily experiences to be able to provide the kind of information which an expert can use to judge whether they have angina or not. Payne and Saul used the WHO Angina Questionnaire (Rose, McCartney and Reid 1977) for this purpose. This asks people questions about their experience of what doctors usually take to be the symptoms of angina. What Payne and Saul actually found was that poorer people were much more likely to report the symptoms of angina than richer people, and much less likely than richer people to have been diagnosed by local doctors or, even if they had been diagnosed with a heart condition by local doctors, to be less likely to be receiving coronary care.

The Angina Questionnaire also illustrates the use of standard data collection instruments by different researchers. The WHO Angina Questionnaire had been developed for international use by trialling various draft versions, comparing each with the results of medical examinations of the respondents. The final version was one where there was a good match between diagnosis via medical examination, and diagnosis via questionnaire response. This process is called **validation**. In other fields the development of questionnaires often begins with a survey using open-ended questions, or several versions of the same question, in order to see what kinds of phrasings are understandable by respondents, before producing a forced choice questionnaire. Using unstructured interviews or focus groups is not an uncommon first stage the development of such instruments – asking people what they think the questions mean, or what difference it would make if a question was phrased in a different way. Instruments produced in this way are never perfect, but at least researchers know something about their imperfections. For example, the Angina Questionnaire usually produces an over estimate of the number of cases of angina in the community by comparison with doctors' diagnoses.

Using standard instruments also allows direct comparisons to be made between the results of two different pieces of research using the same data collection instrument. Experimental researchers, in particular, tend to use standard questionnaires for this reason. But the same principle is applied in various repeated 'state-of-the-nation' surveys such as the *General House-*

hold Survey, the *Labour Force Survey* or the *British Crime Survey*. These have some new questions on each occasion but there are also standard questions. A major objective is to measure trends over time. With differently worded questions it would be difficult to say whether any differences from time to time were real or merely due to asking different questions.

There are two reasons, then, for using standard questions in survey and experimental research:

- To ensure *comparability* between different pieces of research
- To *share 'tried and tested' questions* among researchers.

To these ends, those who design British government surveys draw on and contribute to a central question bank (http://www.statistics.gov.uk/harmony/harmonfp.asp). The CASS question bank (http://qb.soc.surrey.ac.uk/) provides a wide selection of previously used survey questions together with commentaries on what happened when they were used, their strengths and shortcomings.

The term **leading question** is usually used pejoratively to refer to questions which lead the respondent towards giving a misleading response. This is usually if the phrasing of the question implies that the questioner will think better of the respondent for answering one way rather than another, provoking an acquiescence or a social desirability bias (see above). For example, 'Do you ever get drunk?' is probably a leading question in this sense, and 'Do you ever get rat arsed?', is certainly one. But these questions wouldn't necessarily 'lead' everyone in the same direction. Some people would be ashamed of getting drunk, others proud. So the idea of a leading question is a problematic one. The Angina Questionnaire example shows how researchers have to lead respondents towards giving the information required. So all questions lead: they lead to an answer. The important issue is whether they lead to the truth.

The lead of a question may not be immediately obvious. For example, it makes a difference whether questions are framed positively or negatively. Figure 8.2 shows the difference in administration and wording of two Scottish NHS consumer satisfaction questionnaires.

The Lothian Survey showed much higher rates of dissatisfaction with the NHS than the all-Scotland Scottish Users' Survey. But Cohen and his colleagues (Cohen, Forbes and Garraway 1996) found that people from Lothian who were polled in the all-Scotland survey were no more dissatisfied than people in Scotland as a whole. They concluded that the differences had to do either with one survey being conducted face-to-face, and the other as a self-completed, self-return, anonymous questionnaire, or it had to do with the different ways the questions were posed. There were important differences in responses to only some questions, which suggested that it wasn't the mode of administration making a difference to the results. The main differences were associated with questions which were framed positively in one survey but negatively in the other, as in the examples in Figure 8.2. Cohen *et al.* conclude:

| Figure 8.2 | **Differences in questioning strategy and wording between an NHS consumer satisfaction survey in Lothian and one covering the whole of Scotland (NHS Users' Survey)** |

The Lothian Survey: a self-completed postal questionnaire survey

The *questionnaire* asked:

'Thinking generally about your experience in hospital last year, please tell us if you agree or disagree with the statements below'
One of the statements was:
You were encouraged to ask questions about your treatment.

And the questionnaire asked:

'The National Health Service in Scotland published a booklet called 'Framework for Action'. They listed some of the things which upset patients. In your experience of hospitals in Lothian are any of these a cause for concern ?'

One statement was:

Doctors have no time to listen

The NHS Users' Survey: a survey in which a questionnaire was filled in by an interviewer face-to-face with the interviewee

The *interviewer* asked:

'Thinking about the information you were given at the hospital, did any of these things happen at your visit?'

The interviewer then showed interviewees a card with a number of negative statements including:

I was not given enough information

I was not encouraged to ask questions

I was not encouraged to get involved in decisions about my treatment

There was not enough time for me to be involved

Source: Based on Cohen, Forbes and Garraway (1996: 843).

Whereas only 5.6% of respondents in the Scottish Users' Survey agreed with the statement: 'I was not encouraged to ask questions', 23.9% of the Lothian respondents disagreed with the statement 'You were encouraged to ask questions about your treatment'. Thus substantially different conclusions can be obtained if patients are presented with a negative statement about care and asked to agree that something 'bad' happened, as opposed to presenting them with a positive statement and asking them to disagree that something good happened.

(Cohen, Forbes and Garraway 1996: 843)

Here a fourfold difference in dissatisfaction is attributable to a difference in the way questions were asked about similar issues. However, this is a problem only when comparing the results of the two different surveys. Results from the same survey questions administered in the same way at different points in time would be adequate for showing time trends in consumer satisfaction.

Interviewer effects and respondent reactions

Interviewer effects include some which are directly equivalent to the **expect-ancy effects** referred to in the context of experiments in Chapter 2 (Box 8.2). In survey interviews, too, what interviewers expect and how they would prefer the results to come out may influence the results. A classic example here is Kinsey's huge research programme on human sexuality. Kinsey believed that child sex abuse was extraordinarily rare but that sex with animals was common. Although there was a standard schedule of questions, Kinsey frequently departed from these, apparently asking many supplementary questions about bestiality and cutting short respondents who claimed to have been sexually abused as children, who he regarded as deluded. Not surprisingly, the *Kinsey Reports* give a picture of Americans who rarely engaged in child sexual abuse and often had sex with animals (O'Connell-Davidson and Layder 1994: 83–113).

Interviewer effects also include the effects created inadvertently by the interviewer's gender, ethnicity, social class, age, accent, demeanour and so on. We could force the comparison with experiments further and say that respondents may also show *Hawthorne effects*, answering questions in a way most unlike they would do otherwise, because they know they are being researched. But since the context of questioning and answering is a *social relationship* between questioner and respondent it is better to think in terms of interviewer effects and respondent reactions together.

Whatever a respondent does, he or she will set themselves up as being a particular kind of person. It is an issue for a respondent, then, as to what kind of person they are going to represent themselves as being at the time of the research. Everyone is quite capable of representing themselves in differ-ent ways in different situations, so this doesn't necessarily suggest attempts to mislead, though some people may use the opportunity to tell outrageous untruths, or to fantasy role-play being the kind of person they usually aren't. There are at least two audiences for these performances. One is the inter-viewer, or in the case of a postal questionnaire, the person the respondent

---

BOX 8.2 Some circumstances leading to large interviewer effects: that is when there are large differences between the responses elicited from the same kinds of people by different interviewers, using the same questions

Interviewer effects are greatest when:

- Sensitive or emotional topics are investigated
- Open, rather than closed questions are used
- Questions are ambiguous or difficult to understand
- Interviewers have received little or no training
- Interviewers adjust their performance to the demeanour of the interviewee.

Source: After Groves (1989).

imagines will read it when completed. The other is the respondent himself or herself. The answers tell the respondent what kind of person they are. When I fill in market research questionnaires I am inclined to lie when I wouldn't like the look of myself given by answering correctly. Sometimes there are additional members of the audience. A one-on-one interview overheard by others adds another audience to posture to. A focus group provides a very complex audience to perform in front of (Green and Hart 1999).

Researchers speak of the **demand characteristics** of an interview situation. This is what it is that the respondent thinks the situation demands – or, rather, what it is that the respondent thinks the situation demands if he or she is going to come across as sensible, competent, moral, and otherwise OK, or as put-upon, neglected and abused, or as strong and resilient, or whatever impression he or she would prefer to make. Part of the demand structure will have been put in place intentionally by the researcher explaining what is necessary, and indeed in the phrasing of each question. But part will consist of all the *cues* which the respondent will pick up as to what would be appropriate and inappropriate behaviour and what answers will lead the respondent to be viewed as he or she would prefer. The usual bias here is towards *social desirability*, but some respondents will want to shock and scandalise their interviewer.

The sources of such cues include the characteristics of the interviewer. Research suggests that white respondents are less likely to express racist views in the hearing of a black interviewer (Finkel, Guerbock and Borg 1991), and that males are more likely to express weaknesses to female interviewers (Nathanson 1978). Again, drug users seem more likely to describe themselves as having a problem they can't handle and as being in need of treatment when interviewed by social worker interviewers than when interviewed by someone representing themselves as an 'ex-user' (Davies 1997b). Other cues will come from the behaviour of the interviewer, and yet others from the venue of the interview. Interviews in pubs seem to produce higher estimates of alcohol consumption than interviews at home (Crawford 1987). Respondents are always likely to be looking for 'a lead' from the interviewer or from the questions (see also Chapter 6, Box 6.1).

Controlling the interview situation

The way in which survey researchers try to manage such problems is through controlling the circumstances of the research directly by standardisation – by the equivalent of experimental control (see Chapter 2), and by monitoring closely what happens, to see if control has been effective – by statistical control (see Chapter 5, section 5.2). Controlling the circumstances mainly means training interviewers to give a standard, courteous, non-judgemental performance. This may mean getting them to learn a script to recite, though they usually find they have to depart from the script from time to time (see below). Attention may be given to the clothing, cleanliness, hairstyle and so on and to the furnishings and layout of any venue. Standardisation doesn't rule out using interviewers who are ethnically or gender matched to respondents, but researchers recognise that this may introduce a confounding factor. In surveys with several interviewers, monitoring is likely to include separate analysis of the results for each interviewer to see if there are any consistent differences between them. Even with one interviewer it is not uncommon to analyse separately the results of interviews conducted early in the programme compared with those conducted later, since interviewers may significantly change their style as time goes on. If there are worries about particular categories of respondents responding to the research situation in a way that might produce misleading results, then again the results for them can be compared with those for others: recall the example of those who were interviewed in South Asian languages in the National Survey of Minority Ethnic Mental Health (Nazroo 1997). All this is the exercise of statistical control over the results in order to detect any *distorting factors* at play.

Increasingly, however, those who conduct large-scale surveys are regarding this as inadequate, since it can only be inferred from the results as to what might have happened in the interview. Thus it is becoming common practice to tape or video-record at least a sample of interviews for each interviewer and subject these to detailed analysis. With telephone interviewing this can be done unobtrusively.

The research interview as fact-producing interaction

Transcript 8.1 is an example of an interview involving the use of a questionnaire. The questionnaire here is from the large-scale *American National Health Interview Survey*. The actual interview was not part of the survey as such but conducted in order to investigate the interview process.

Transcript 8.1 The research interview

1 **Interviewer**: During those two weeks did she [daughter] miss any time from a job because of illness or injury?
2 **Mrs. E** [pause, looking to Mr E]: I don't know. I don't know if she did have one day when she didn't go to work, when she didn't feel too well. I think one day, she didn't.
3 **Interviewer**: one day?
4 **Mrs E**: Mm hm
[portion omitted, during which it appears that the daughter may have missed two weeks' work]
5 **Interviewer**: what condition caused her to miss work, and stay in bed during those two weeks?
6 **Mrs E**: [smiles, looks to Mr E]
7 **Mr E**: I think she had ... : She had a sore throat
8 **Interviewer**: Sore ...
9 **Mr E**: Sore throat or cold, yes.
[portion omitted]

10 **Interviewer:** when did [your daughter] last see or talk to a doctor or assistant about her sore throat?

11 **Mrs E:** Well, she didn't talk to one, to a doctor about the sore throat at this time, but in the fall, I believe it was in October [looks to Mr E] she had flu. She was run down. And she was. I believe she was ill for about a week. She had flu, and she had a fever. And she went to Dr C. Twice she went to Dr C.

12 **Interviewer:** this was, uh, you stated in the fall …

13 **Mrs E:** in the fall of the year

14 **Interviewer:** Has she seen the doctor about uh her sore throat?

15 **Mrs E:** no, not this week, no. Not this last time

16 **Interviewer:** What was the cause of her sore throat?

17 **Mrs E** [shrugs] She had a cold. I don't know

18 **Interviewer:** Did the sore throat result from an accident or an injury?

20 **Mrs E:** No

Source: Suchman and Jordan (1990: 236, numbering added).

This transcript illustrates how a carefully constructed set of questions proves awkward to use in actual interviews, and how the interviewer has to depart from the script and use ad hoc methods in an attempt to find answers. One question sounds quite daft (18): How could a sore throat be caused by an accident or injury? But the question the interviewer is trying to find an answer for is something like *'whatever the condition which caused the person to see the doctor*, was it caused by an accident or injury?' In many circumstances it wouldn't have been a daft question. Even though it is a silly question in this context, the interviewer has been instructed to ask all the questions of all the respondents.

A more important point is that the transcript shows how 'an interview' isn't just one person asking questions, and another answering them, but a *co operative activity* in which interviewer and interviewee work together to establish the truth of the matter of interest. The interviewer here is just as important as the interviewees in providing the answers. Indeed it is the interviewer who makes a fact of the daughter's sore throat, while the interviewees leave it as ambiguous as to whether she had a sore throat or the flu or both. The interviewer needed something to be established as a matter of fact by point 10 in the transcript in order to pose the questions she poses at points 14, 16 and 18, all of which require her to ask a question about an illness or injury which has already been established as real and relevant to the survey. The daughter seems to have had three, perhaps four, episodes of illness, one involving time off work and perhaps a different episode associated with seeing the doctor. But in the survey results she will appear as having had just one episode of illness, necessitating two weeks' absence from work and causing her to consult a doctor.

A further feature illustrated by the transcript is of the *co-operative bias* shown by many respondents. Mr and Mrs E don't seem at all sure about the facts of the matter, but since the interviewer wants some facts they willingly serve some up. The interviewers for the *American National Health Interview Survey* are experienced and highly trained. Even with well-designed questionnaires and experienced interviewers what are supposed to be highly structured interviews, in a series attempting to engage each respondent in the same way as each other, often show messy sequences like this when transcribed.

So from this example we can see how the performance of the interviewer and the interaction between interviewer and interviewees can influence survey results in a way not intended by the survey designers. We can only see this, of course, because the interview was recorded and transcribed. Usually such effects disappear. They may leave their traces on the results but it may be difficult to see them for what they are.

Random and systematic errors in survey research

However, for the *American National Health Interview Survey* things are not as bad as might first appear. This is a large-scale survey which attempts to build up a picture of how things are in aggregate. For this it is not essential to produce entirely accurate data from each individual respondent. A large percentage of the errors in such surveys will be 'one-offs' and each affect so few people that they won't affect the overall results much at all, and a large percentage will be **random errors** where what is recorded wrongly for one respondent will be compensated for by an error in the opposite direction for another. Much more worrying to survey researchers than random error is undetected **systematic error** where some feature of the research creates a bias always in one direction (see the example from Cohen, Forbes and Garraway above). However, if systematic errors are detected the results can be adjusted accordingly. For example, once it is known that the *WHO Angina Questionnaire* over-estimates the prevalence of angina, as it does, and by how much it usually does so, this is no more of a problem than having a watch which is consistently ten minutes fast.

Focus groups

Some of the issues discussed above can be revisited by considering situations where interviews are conducted not with individuals or couples, but with larger groups of people.

Focus groups have a long history in market research and have recently become popular in mainstream social research (Kruger 1994; Barbour and Kitzinger 1999; Bloor *et al.* 2000), and in testing political public opinion in Britain (Jenkins 1997). They consist of a group discussion focused on topics provided by the researcher and sometimes involve the use of stimulus material, such as problem scenarios for participants to discuss, or videos for them to comment on. The group discussion will probably be audio or video recorded and the write up is most likely to be qualitative rather than quantitative, although there are exceptions. Typically group size is between 8 and 12. Focus group method raises three important methodological issues.

First, there is an issue of the representativeness of the group and generalisability of the findings (see Chapter 4, section 4.1). Are the people who are recruited to be focus group members representative of anyone but themselves? Would the information derived from the focus group apply to anyone but them? In Chapter 4 this was discussed in relation to selecting samples for surveys of individuals, but the same principles apply. For *statistical representativeness* and *empirical generalisation*, large samples are needed. Ideally these are selected on *probability principles*. But in market research and political opinion polling it is typical that participants are selected on *quota sampling* principles (Chapter 4, section 4.13) to create a representative mix, either within groups or of groups within a research programme. Large numbers of focus groups tend to be run for the same research programme by market research and opinion-polling companies. With regard to sampling it is important to note that, while a focus group might involve 10 participants, it is still only one interview for the kind of statistical analysis used by survey researchers. If statistical representativeness and empirical generalisation are the aim, there are no merits in the claim that conducting 20 focus groups of 10 people each is a cheap way of recruiting a sample equivalent to 200 individuals.

With *theoretical sampling* and *theoretical generalisation* (Chapter 4, Box 4.3; Chapter 10, section 10.6) the researcher has reason to believe that the people of interest fall into a number of different types in ways that are relevant to the research, and decides to investigate each type. For example, in her study of the response of medical students to a new problem-based learning curriculum Lloyd-Jones (2002) suspected that this would differ according to various differences among students influencing their peer-group membership and their study habits. Therefore she arranged different group interviews with, for example, overseas students and UK students, students living at home and students living on campus, and so on. It might have been better for her to have conducted individual interviews, but as a single-handed researcher with limited time available, group interviews increased the range of types of people she could interview and allowed her to cover the dimensions of diversity which seemed most relevant to her research topic.

Second, these are *group* interviews. A number of people are involved and encouraged to vocalise, so there are plenty of opportunities for all of them to influence each other as to what is said. This is like the problem of the 'interviewer effect' but on a larger scale. From the viewpoint of the orthodox survey researcher, the focus group looks like a hopelessly uncontrolled environment in the sense that it will be difficult to work out what in the results reflects whatever was the research topic, and which derive from the 'chemistry' of the group. Mortimore and Atkinson (2000) of MORI Polls report: 'not all groups work as they should. On one occasion, two strangers seduced each other as the group was going on. Everyone pretended not to notice.' The activity at the end of Chapter 9 offers you an opportunity to look at interaction within a focus group.

The influence of the participants on each other is a problem if the object of the research is to discover what each one thinks or believes individually and independently of the others. In groups there are often very strong pressures towards conformity, even if this means conformity to one or other of two opposing views taken by members. Lloyd-Jones (2002) also collected some information from individually completed questionnaires. This allowed her to judge how far the group situation had influenced what people said. Thus she controlled responses elicited in a group situation against individually elicited responses. Mutual influence also raises issues of *reliability*. In one-to-one interviews it is always an issue as to whether the same interviewee would have given the same response on a second occasion. Group discussions twist and turn and group dynamics ebb and flow, so it must be the case that what anyone says is closely determined by the state of the group at the moment when they say it. In a different group, or in the same group run on a second occasion, they might have said something very different.

Sometimes however, the researcher's interest will be precisely in how people express themselves in group situations. David Morgan (1988: 12, original emphases) says: 'The hallmark of focus groups is *the explicit use of group interaction to produce data and insights that would be less accessible without the interaction found in a group.*' For example, focus group members might be recruited from within an existing organisation – a school perhaps, or a firm. Then the way they discuss issues in the focus group is likely to provide some insight into how these same issues are discussed in the everyday circumstances of the organisation. In the group they may 'talk the talk' of the organisation, in ways that would not happen in one-to-one interviews. If a researcher cannot directly observe what happens under naturally occurring circumstances (Chapter 10) a focus group may be the next best approach. But, of course, in these circumstances there are likely to be important topics which are unmentionable in the group, but which might be disclosed one-to-one.

In more general terms it can be argued that what people do is nearly always influenced by the social setting in which they find themselves. Thus what people say in a focus group may be more like what they would say in real-life settings than what they would say to a researcher in a private one-to-one interview, and a better guide to their actions. On this consideration it is the private one-to-one interview that looks problematic rather than the group interview. This point is sometimes made by describing one-to-one interviews as 'decontextualised', meaning that they are off-stage, artificial situations removed from the normal contexts in which people interact with each other. This argument usually continues by describing focus groups as a 'contextualised' method for research (Wilkinson 1999). This argument stretches the meaning of words to breaking point, since there is nothing which has no context. But if the claim is that the focus group situation is more like the everyday lives of the participants, then this will vary from focus group to focus group, and the more 'everyday' the focus group is, the more it will reproduce any of the inhibitions which prevent these particular people from being open and honest with each other. Such matters might be the topic for research, but this argument is usually made in favour of focus groups facilitating open and honest communication.

Focus groups, and other group interviews, raise issues of confidentiality and participant welfare which are not raised to the same extent by individual interviews. In one-to-one situations interviewers are able to promise confidentiality and are in a position to keep the promise. Where information is shared with other participants there is no guarantee that they will respect each other's confidentiality later. Again, in a one-to-one interview it is easier to minimise the chances of any distress being caused to the interviewee – only two people are involved. Ensuring this in a group situation means controlling the behaviour of a number of people towards one another. This may call for very skilful group facilitation. It is sometimes argued that in group situations participants find it easier to articulate their views because they feel supported by the group. This has been claimed with regard to research with minority ethnic groups (Chiu and Knight 1999) and children (Kitzinger and Farquhar 1999) and similarly where sensitive issues are the topic (Farquar and Das 1999). But at the same time participants take risks in disclosing themselves in a group situation which are not present in a private one-to-one interview. This is particularly so if groups are composed of people who will be in contact with each other later. Issues of confidentiality and participant welfare are discussed further in Chapter 13.

Action research is discussed in more detail in Chapter 12 (Section 12.5). The main purpose of action research is to effect some worthwhile change while studying how this does (or does not) come about. Here focus groups may be used as part of the change process, for example as ways of getting groups of people to define what they want to happen, commit themselves to action or to sort out misunderstandings between them. When focus groups are used in health promotion research, part of the aim is often that the members will learn more about healthy behaviour and will become more committed to healthy lifestyles.

Third, unlike most other kinds of group interviews, in a focus group the facilitator *focuses* group discussion on a set of issues for discussion, rather than just asking questions. There is an expectation that what participants know and believe will be transformed by hearing what other people say and by their own responses. This is probably not very different from most one-to-one interviews. These often ask people questions they have not thought of before, and thinking up an answer on the spot may change and add to what they originally thought. However, in the focus group research, this becomes explicit and the data will show how people stake out and argue positions, how they are convinced by others, negotiate compromises, and so on. In this regard focus groups are not very different from some of the group interviews and task groups used in psychology to study group decision-making, group problem-solving, or group dynamics in general. However, in these examples it is likely that the researcher will use a structured observation technique (Chapter 10, Box 10.1) and produce quantitative data rather than, or in addition to, qualitative data, and most such psychological research on groups involves some of the usual control devices of experimentation (see Chapter 2).

A 'Delphi' group looks and is operated very much like a focus group. The participants will be experts in their field and the object will be for them to reach a consensus about the issues discussed. The participants might, for example, be a group of doctors developing some guidelines for the treatment of a medical condition, or a group of economic forecasters producing a report for a government department or a merchant bank. 'Nominal groups' involve participants coming to some agreement about the ranking of options or preferences. This might involve voting for different versions of the same package design in market research, or ranking the importance of various options for service development in consumer research in public services. Whether Delphi groups and nominal groups are regarded as 'focus groups' varies from author to author. But in both cases the interest is in the results of the group discussion rather than the process of the discussion. The same is true of focus groups used to trial different versions of a questionnaire for later use in a survey. But in much focus group research it is the group process which is of greater interest to the researcher.

   While much group interviewing in psychology and some in market research and opinion polling generates quantitative data, as does nominal group technique, focus groups usually produce qualitative data and are best regarded as within the genre of qualitative interviewing discussed below.

8.5 Making close relationships with respondents: qualitative interviewing

So one approach to the possibility that the research situation may be distorting of the truth is to try to exert more control: either directly or by collecting information about it, as described earlier. The other approach goes entirely in the opposite direction. If the research situation is artificial and distorting then it should be made less 'researchy' and more like 'real life'. People who hold this view prescribe that interviews should be more like ordinary conversations, with no pre-set questions, and respondents allowed to decide topics and ask questions themselves. **Loosely structured interviews** is probably a better term for this than '*in-depth*'. First, because psychoanalysts and police investigators also conduct in-depth interviews, but certainly not on the same egalitarian terms as being suggested here; second, because what is deep and what is shallow depends on the analogy in use: a brain-scan might be regarded as in-depth in some ways and superficial in others. For a loosely structured interview there will usually be a list of topics the researcher hopes to cover, though in no particular order, and with no particular wording. Since each interviewee is regarded as being different it makes sense to treat each one of them differently.

Margaret Andersen describes the way she, as a white and middle-class researcher interviewed poor African-American women:

> it is impossible even to count the exact number of interviews in my project and to report the amount of time they took. Many of the women included in this research refused to be interviewed formally, but were willing to talk with me for hours. One woman asked that the tape recorder be turned off at various places in our conversation. With the tape recorder turned off, she spoke freely about information she thought should remain confidential, although it revealed important yet sensitive information about race and gender relationships in the community. Another woman told me her long and intriguing life history and talked openly about class and race relations in the community, but refused to be taped. We sat in my car for most of the afternoon, in subfreezing winter temperatures. Other important information and ideas in this project came from many days and hours of informal discussion with these women at the local senior centre ...
>
> Several talked at length about how my 'personality' made them more trusting, open and willing to speak with me. These comments made me think about what I was doing – consciously and unconsciously – to elicit their reported trust ... In sum, what seems to have made these interviews possible was my direct violation of the usual admonitions to social science researchers. During the interviews I answered questions about myself, my background, my family, and my ideas. In the interviews and during the field research, the women and I exchanged our feelings and ideas about many of the ideas we were discussing. At times, I showed the emotion I felt during very moving moments in their accounts of their experiences.
>
> (Andersen 1993: 47–50)

For the orthodox social survey researcher, interviewers getting over-involved with respondents looks like a problem. There are two reasons for this. First, there is the worry that if respondents get to know too much about inter- viewers they will begin to care too much what they think about them, and answer questions accordingly. In focus group research the equivalent worry is that respondents will care too much about the opinions others in the group form of them. Second, there is the concern that interviewers will make better relationships with some respondents than others, and hence introduce a confounding differentiating factor into the research (Figure 8.1, Box 9). However, for those who believe that the problem lies in the artificiality of the research situation the policy is again entirely opposite. The argument is that only by developing intimate, trusting and empathetic relationships will respondents feel able to disclose the truth. This is some- times applied to encounters between researchers and interviewees which last for only an hour or so, but the preference is for longer and more intense encounters. For the orthodox survey researcher the personal characteristics of the interviewer are regarded as something to be controlled out of the way by standardising their performance. But here the personal characteristics of the interviewer may be regarded as either an asset or an outright disqualification. Thus it is may be argued that only women can successfully interview women, and only black people can successfully interview black people, and that the more the interviewer and interviewee share in the way of characteristics and previous experience the more successful the interview is likely to be (Oakley 1981). Similarly in favour of focus groups it may be claimed that people will be more comfortable in sharing their thoughts if supported by a group.

Interviewing for understanding

One-to-one qualitative interviews are usually conducted with the aim of producing a picture of the interviewee as a person with their own way of understanding the world, although usually as having a way of understanding which can be taken as characteristic of people of the same category or in the same social circumstances: the kind of mind-reading research referred to in Chapter 1, section 1.4. And the main interest is in incorrigible matters. The relationship which the interviewer wants to make is a befriending one, on the assumption that people are more likely to disclose themselves 'authentically' to friends, as in the quotation from Andersen (1993) above. It is worth thinking here how we get to know our friends and what we get to know about them. The psychology of person perception and of the development of inter-personal relationships tells us that how others are to us is very much a product of how we behave to them (Blumstein 1991). Thus it is possible for someone to appear differently in the context of different intimate relationships. Making a befriending relationship with a respondent may then elicit data as to what they say in the context of a relationship with one friend (the interviewer), but not what they are like in relation to another friend (someone other than the interviewer). Again, being 'friendly' over any period of time is a learning process for both parties. Thus the respondent will learn what to say and do which seems to please the interviewer, and hence consolidate the relationship. Moreover as Madeline Grumet (1991: 69) says: 'telling a story to a friend is a risky business; the better the friend, the riskier the business.' So 'friends' may be the last people someone will disclose intimacies to. It is a common experience that people will disclose some things to a stranger which they will not disclose to a friend, and vice versa, and probably people differ in this regard. Thus all in all, although the befriending interview will produce more and richer data than the social survey interview, it will remain a question as to how much of the extra data are an artefact of the relationship made between interviewer and interviewee.

What kind of problem this is depends on whether a researcher subscribes to the view that inside every person there is a real person hidden beneath a misleading exterior, which has to be penetrated by making an empathetic relationship with them. On that assumption the considerations above are really fundamental, since there will never be any way of knowing whether the researcher has been successful. Alternatively we might assume that people are always who they are in the context of relationships they make, whatever these may be. On that assumption the more impersonal relationship of the social survey interview tells us how people behave in that context, and the more personalised relationship of the qualitative interview tells us how people behave in that kind of relationship: they are no less 'themselves' in the former than in the latter; they simply show different aspects of themselves. Rather than assume that adopting a befriending relationship will elicit truthful accounts it can equally be argued that for some respondents a befriending relationship is precisely the kind where they feel more comfortable about telling lies and, if they value the 'friendship', may be most motivated to lie in order to elicit the good opinion of the interviewer (Sikes 2000).

Some researchers seem to evade this problem by conducting research not as a way of getting to understand people as they are, but as a way of changing people (Lather 1986 – see also Chapters 12 and 13). This doesn't evade the problem, however, since the success criterion is whether the person really changed or not. To judge that it is necessary to know how they really were at the beginning, and how they really were at the end, and that takes us straight back into the problems discussed in the previous paragraphs.

8.6 The accountability of interview research

Table 8.3 gives a synoptic contrast between survey interviewing and qualitative interviewing. Many of the points have already been dealt with and the important points for this section concern differences in the way in which the research is made accountable.

To be able to judge the credibility of research, readers need to be given information as to how it was conducted. It is relatively easy for survey researchers to show readers what was done to produce the results. Social survey interviews are protocol-driven – there are rules to follow, often written down, and the questions are printed out. These can simply be shown to readers. Although limits of publication space often mean readers have to apply for copies of the questionnaire, those for most recent large-scale surveys are available via the World Wide Web. Sometimes the raw data can be made available too, after anonymisation. Survey researchers orient to confounding variables as a set of problems to be solved and are therefore able to tell readers how they addressed such problems and with what results. The interview transcript presented earlier showed that not everything that might have influenced the results will be made available to readers, but there is usually enough for readers to make a considered judgement as to whether the differences and similarities shown between respondents in the results were due to the reasons attributed by the researchers, or due to other reasons.

TABLE 8.3	A comparison between interviewing for social surveys and qualitative interviewing	
	Interviewing for a social survey	**Qualitative interviewing**
The sample (see also Chapter 4)	Typically a large representative sample of people	Rarely a large and rarely a representative sample (Figure 8.1, Box 5)
The interviews	Organised to be as similar for each respondent as possible with the same instructions, the same questions and the same sequence	Different for each respondent although probably involving the same set of key topics for discussion Respondents will be allowed to raise their own issues (Figure 8.1, Boxes 6 7 8 and 9)
The interviewer	Will attempt to behave in a standardised way, disclosing as little as possible about his or her personal characteristics: an impersonal relationship	Will adjust his or her performance to each interviewee. Will use his or her own characteristics as a resource for making a relationship with respondents: a more personal relationship (Figure 8.1, Boxes 6 7 8 and 9)
The data collection instrument	Typically a questionnaire dominated by forced choice questions asking for brief responses from each respondent. Sometimes a questionnaire which has been tested and validated in other studies	Typically just a list of discussion topics, probably a tape recorder
Comparability	The interviews will have been designed to ensure that point-by-point comparisons can be made between all respondents in terms of a standard vocabulary.	Point-by-point comparisons may not be possible if each interview is different, with different topics being discussed at different levels of detail and not using a standard vocabulary
The data and analysis	Most of the analytic decisions will be made before the interviews are conducted and the questions designed on that basis, thus the data will be 'prestructured' before it is collected The data will be framed in the categories and expressed in the language decided by the researcher	There will be many on-the spot intuitive analytic decisions made during the interviews but the data from the interviews will be loosely structured, and most of the explicit analytic decisions will be made after the interviews have been conducted

Table 8.3 *(Continued)*

		The data will quite likely be framed in categories and expressed in the language of the respondents (see Chapter 9)
Control measures	Care is likely to be taken to control confounding variables such as interviewer effects and erratic or idiosyncratic behaviour by the interviewer Data will be analysed to detect any such distorting effects –as described in the main text	Little in the way of control measures
Accountability	*Readers*: are usually able to access the questionnaire used, and any details about its validation They are usually given details of the analyses undertaken to scrutinise for confounding variables *Subjects* of the research: will be given a standardised explanation, and may or may not be sent a copy of the completed research	*Readers*: are often asked to take it on trust that the researcher did not do anything untoward in conducting the research Readers may not know what questions were asked, and often have to be satisfied with selected quotations from the interviews *Subjects* of the research: some qualitative researchers believe that their prime accountability should be to the subjects; thus subjects may be treated as co-researchers, may be allowed to vet the material before publication and may be allowed to be the final arbiters as to what is published (see Chapter 13)

By contrast, it is much more difficult for those who do qualitative interviews to make themselves accountable to readers. Margaret Anderson (1993), quoted earlier, says she did not know how many interviews she conducted, and for the many which were unrecorded she would be unable to provide an accurate account of what she and the respondent said, or in detail how her own behaviour produced particular responses. Since each interview will be different there is no interview protocol or list of questions which will serve as a summary of all of them. Some agencies which fund research do make it a condition than transcripts of qualitative interviews are archived so that other researchers can consult them (Hammersley 1997). But 20, 1-hour-long, qualitative interviews can convert into 1,000 pages of transcript. The central issue running through this chapter is the question of what in the results is an artefact of the research and what reflects the reality of whatever it was that the researcher set out to capture. All the matters which survey interviewers take pains to control are allowed free play in the qualitative interview or focus group. Without analysing transcripts in detail, it is extremely difficult to see how the researcher's behaviour shaped the data and whether this was in a misleading way. You will be able to examine this in more detail in Chapter 9, section 9.4. It is perhaps worth drawing a parallel here between the reader confronted with some statistics of medical diagnoses or statistics of crime on the one hand (Chapter 7), and the reader confronted with some claims about the findings from a study based on qualitative interviews with only minimal indications of what happened in the interviews. In both cases the reader's problem is not knowing how the data were produced, and hence not knowing how much credence to give the results.

This is not a case against qualitative interviewing. Sometimes, as Andersen implies, this is the only kind of interviewing which respondents will agree to. Such interviews produce interesting results and give us access into the lives of other people, in ways that other approaches do not. But it is a case for saying that the results of well-conducted research using qualitative interviews should be regarded with less confidence than those from well-conducted survey research. Probably the appropriate analogy to draw here is between qualitative interviewing in social research and the kind of interviewing a biographer does with the subject of the biography, associates and confidants. Many famous people are the subjects of several biographies, which give rather different pictures of the person concerned (Plummer 1983). In the same way it is to be expected that qualitative interviews conducted by one person would give a picture different from those conducted with the same people by another researcher: and it would be very difficult to say which one was more accurate.

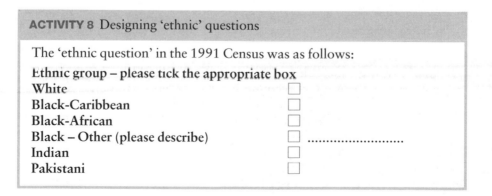

ACTIVITY 8 Designing 'ethnic' questions

The 'ethnic question' in the 1991 Census was as follows:

Ethnic group – please tick the appropriate box
White ☐
Black-Caribbean ☐
Black-African ☐
Black – Other (please describe) ☐ ....
Indian ☐
Pakistani ☐

ACTIVITY 8 (*Continued*)

Bangladeshi ☐
Chinese ☐
Any other ethnic group (please describe) ☐ ....

'If the person is descended from more than one ethnic or racial group, please tick the group to which the person considers he/she belongs, or tick "Any other ethnic group" and describe the person's ancestry in the space provided.'

This 1991 question proved controversial. Simply asking an 'ethnic question' led to some Census enumerators being physically attacked. But the classification is probably that most widely used in survey research conducted in the 1990s. The 2001 Census, in addition, provided boxes to allow for people in England and Wales to identify themselves as Irish – the largest single ethnic minority in England, Wales and Scotland, 'mixed race' and as 'Black British' or 'Asian British'.

1 Comment on the usefulness of this question for producing data to classify respondents:
  (a) For an investigation into ethnic differences in levels of educational achievement
  (b) For an investigation into racial harassment
  (c) For an investigation into how people experience their own ethnicity.

2 Try designing a different approach for the purpose of:
  (a) Collecting information about the 'race'/ethnicity' of the perpetrator of a 'racial attack'
  (b) Collecting information as to how people experience their ethnicity – remember that from this point of view ethnicity is relational and people may regard their ethnicity differently according to whom they are comparing themselves with.

You may use as many questions as you like and forced choice or open questions, but remember that if you use open questions, you will have to close them down again by classifying the respondents' replies into a single framework.

On the classification of ethnicity in surveys and government statistics see Smaje (1995 Chapter 1); Kertzer and Arel (2002).

8.7 Summary

This chapter has been about two different approaches to asking people questions. On the one hand there is the approach adopted for questioning in social surveys, or often for collecting information from the subjects of experiments. This approach is shaped to avoid or minimise problems which might derive from poorly designed questions, differences between interviewers, or from different kinds of respondents reacting to the research situation in different ways. The main devices for managing such problems are to standardise the research situation for all respondents and to collect data about the research process and analyse it to detect any factors likely to confound the results. This approach is also shaped by the need to generate numerical data which allows for point-by-point comparisons to be made between different respondents or between the same kinds of respondents at different points in time.

The other approach is that of the qualitative researcher conducting longer, more discursive interviews, usually directed at discovering how respondents understand their lives. For this purpose interviewers usually consider that a personal engagement with the respondent is necessary to develop a relationship of trust, and that it is necessary to allow each interview to vary according to the particularities of each interviewee. Thus, while for survey researchers interviewer effects are a problem, for qualitative researchers, 'interviewer effects' are what deliver the truth.

With social survey interviews it is usually possible for readers to reach a judgement as to how the methods used generated the results, and whether they will bear the researcher's interpretations. By contrast it is often very difficult for readers to do this with qualitative interviews, unless readers have access to transcripts of the interviews. Qualitative interviewers can claim that their methods are more naturalistic and therefore more likely to produce research which captures the realities of people's lives as they experience them. This is probably so, but it is very difficult to verify this claim with regard to any particular piece of research. The claims made by survey researchers are usually more modest. They are quite willing to admit that the data they produce are superficial. But providing an insight into the meaning life has for people is rarely an objective of survey research and, if it was, this would be a poor vehicle for investigating it. Thus, as at other points in this book we meet the trade-off between rigour, standardisation and control, to produce results which can be regarded with considerable confidence, but which don't seem to get close to the fundamentals of the human condition, and on the other hand, naturalism, empathy and intuition which seem to produce results which are rich in meaning, but in which we can have only limited confidence.

In questioning for social surveys most of the important analytic decisions are made *before* the interviews begin; the data are pre-structured. But in qualitative interviewing most such decisions are made during the interview as the interviewer decides what to say next, and afterwards as the researcher analyses the data. Chapter 9 looks at ways in which the data from a loosely structured interview might be analysed. It should also give you a better insight into what loosely structured interviews sound like.

Further reading

There is no shortage of books on designing questionnaires; Alreck and Settle (1995: Chapter 6); de Vaus (1995: Chapters 7, 8); Newell (1993) provide excellent advice. Arksey and Knight (1999) is a guide to conducting interviews of all kinds. Fielding (2003) offers four volumes of papers on interview research. Bulmer (2002) consists of four volumes of key articles on questionnaire research. Berg (1995: Chapter 3); Flick (1998: Chapter 8) or Mason (1996: Chapter 3) give treatments of qualitative interviews in particular. Kruger (1994) and Bloor *et al.* (2000) are comprehensive manuals on focus groups and Barbon and Kitzinger (1999) provides a selection of papers featuring focus groups used in a wide diversity of research.

The Centre for Applied Social Surveys (CASS) question bank (http://qb.soc.surrey.ac.uk/) contains a large battery of previously used survey questions together with commentary on their effectiveness. The following web sites provide access both to the questionnaires used in many large-scale social surveys and the data produced by using them:

http://www.data-archive.ac.uk – University of Essex Data Archive
http://www.mimas.ac.uk/ – Manchester Information and Associated Services
http://www.statistics.gov.uk/ – Office for National Statistics (for UK Government social surveys)

These three sites and others can be accessed from the CASS home page http://www.natcen.ac.uk/cass/.

9 Analysing the Results of Qualitative Interviews

By the end of this chapter, you will:

- Understand the implications for conducting interviews of coding in advance or coding in arrears, and hence more about why survey questions are different from the questions in qualitative interviews
- Know what is meant by thematic analysis
- Know what is meant by, and have practised, linguistic analysis of, the Conversation Analytic (CA) kind
- Be able to make a point-by-point comparison between thematic and linguistic analysis in terms of their underlying assumptions, procedures, strengths and limitations.

And know the meaning of the following terms:
account ■ adjacency pairs ■ characterisation ■ coding ■ corrigibles and incorrigibles ■ discourse analysis ■ grounding ■ intuitive data processing ■ locution and illocution (or speech act, or performative) ■ preference order ■ recipient design ■ respondent validation/member-checking/fallibility testing ■ sequential analysis ■ speech exchange ■ theme ■ triangulation of sources.

9.1 Introduction

Chapter 8 looked at asking people questions. This chapter is about analysing the responses. Where researchers use forced choice questionnaires, the way the questions are posed *follows* from decisions about how the responses will be analysed. The data are *pre-structured* by the way the questions are designed and most of the important analytical decisions have already been made before any questions are asked. By contrast, where researchers use open-ended questions on a questionnaire, many of the important analytic decisions are made *after* the data have been gathered (Chapter 8, section 8.6). Where researchers engage in semi-structured or qualitative interviews, most of the important analytic decisions are made *while* the data are being collected, and *after* the data have been collected. The kinds of analytic decisions made while the data are being collected are those which lead to the interviewer deciding what question to ask next, when to speak, when to remain silent and so on. Respondents to an interview will be making the same kinds of decision. As you saw in the transcript in Chapter 8, section 8.4, even in highly structured interviews with forced choice questions, interviewers and interviewees will be engaged in this kind of *intuitive data processing*. In the highly structured interview this is not supposed to happen very much. But in the qualitative interview it is regarded as an important facility for making relationships between interviewer and interviewee and for allowing the interviewee's ideas and understandings to be articulated without being distorted by a more structured framework. This chapter will throw more light on this intuitive data processing (section 9.4, and see Chapter 10) but its main topic is the more explicit process of analysing the results of qualitative interviews after the data have been collected.

We will look at three main ways of analysing such data;

- As a set of *reports* about states of affairs and matters of facts – section 9.2
- *Thematic analysis* as a way of describing what things mean to people – section 9.3
- *Linguistic analysis* which treats the interview as a display of the use of language in context – section 9.4.

9.2 Analysing interviews as reports on states of affairs

Corrigibles and incorrigibles

There are many things which researchers cannot investigate at first hand, and can find out about only by asking people questions. These include some which, in principle, could be verified as matters of fact – **corrigibles**, and some which in principle are unverifiable because they are matters of self-knowledge – **incorrigibles** (Ayer 1956). The former include matters such as how many cigarettes someone smoked in a week. The latter include opinions, attitudes, beliefs, understandings and so on. The incorrigibles are incorrigible because it is built in to the definition of, say, an 'opinion', that it is something which is first and foremost known by the person who holds it, and known by others only insofar as that person discloses it. We could not logically say 'I know what your opinion really is, even though you don't know yourself'. Between the corrigible and the incorrigible is an area of disagreement as to those matters about which an individual must be regarded as the authoritative source of information, as against those intimate details of their own lives about which they can be regarded as mistaken. For example, someone who adopts a psychodynamic point of view can logically say: 'You are out of touch with your true feelings' and imply that he or she is a better judge of those 'true feelings' than the person who allegedly has them. For a researcher who assumed that feelings were the kinds of stuff about which feelers themselves could not be mistaken, this would be an illogical claim. The border is not something which doing research can decide. Rather it is something which is decided by an *a priori* decision – that is, independently of doing the research. For this section we will concentrate on what are conventionally regarded as verifiable facts and corrigible. Section 9.3 strays into the field of incorrigibles.

Some possible facts about George

I interviewed George as part of a local census of roofless people, people crashing out with friends and relatives and people living in hostels and night shelters. This used a questionnaire with forced choice questions. But a few people were selected for longer loosely structured interviewing, largely to collect some 'quotable quotes' for the research report. George was one of these people.

In an early draft of the final report George appeared as follows:

It is notable how often homelessness is preceded by one or more traumatic events. For example:

> ... then my wife died, unexpectedly and that threw me. It was stomach cancer, which was common in her family but I didn't see it coming [so] it was a great shock, and I reacted badly. I began hitting the drinking very hard, but not for the same reasons as earlier ... and then when I was just getting over that I got made redundant, which knocked the stuffing out of me. And what with the drink and the [lack of] money I just ended up here in [hostel] which is just one better than being on the street, but only just.

(George: male, aged 69: resident in hostel for single homeless men)

George is made to stand here as an example of how predisposing events of particular kinds may lead to homelessness. But is it true that these events actually happened to George, and in the order described ? Asking this is prior to asking whether this is a sequence of events which *caused* George's homelessness.

Some things George reports could in principle be checked for their veracity. These are matters for which there are socially organised processes for producing authoritative versions of the truth. For deaths, the identity of the deceased, the date of death and the cause of death are all produced as factual matters by a process of death certification. Illness leading up to death and family histories of conditions may be inscribed in medical records. Redundancies are recorded in personnel files, and often in social security records. Place of residence may be given a factual status by tenancy agreements, rent-books and, in the case of hostels, hostel records. As discussed in Chapter 7, there are problems with these kinds of data.

For reasons most unusual in research of this kind, I actually knew about the timing of some events in George's life. For others I checked his story out. In fact George's wife died several years after separating from George, and moving 150 miles away. He became aware of her death several years after it happened and long after he became homeless. George was not made redundant but dismissed for persistently failing to turn up for work, and before he learned of his wife's death.

Factual facts and interesting stories

My reconstruction of George's CV suggests that we cannot take his story of the events leading up to his homelessness as a straightforward factual account of what happened. This illustrates something referred to earlier (Chapter 6, Box 6.1) which is the way people take 'facts' and turn them into meaningful stories and invent facts to plug the gaps in stories which would otherwise be less credible. This does not necessarily involve them in lying. It may do (Sikes 2000), but we could rarely know whether someone had the intention to deceive us, or genuinely believed the untruth he or she was telling (Miller and Stiff 1993). The more important point is that 'facts' are told in some context and the context is likely to shape what is told as 'the facts' (Peneff 1990). As you saw in the transcript in Chapter 8, section 8.4, the facts about the daughter's illness were shaped first by the structure of the questionnaire, and then by the efforts of the interviewer to find some facts in answer to the pre-set questions. In loosely structured interviews, interviewees and interviewers have even more latitude to turn facts into what seem to be interesting and relevant stories, and hence further to depart from what might be inscribed as the facts in an independent record.

But what kind of problem is this? It is a really serious problem if the purpose of the interview is to draw information from informants to build up a picture of some factual state of affairs. As noted in Chapter 6, survey researchers often try to elicit accurate information about antecedent events in order to identify causal factors, by asking respondents to draw on their memories. I was doing much the same in the quotation from the draft report earlier. In these circumstances the data are likely to suffer from **retrospective or recall bias** (Chapter 6, Box 6.1) and from other biases determined by the **demand characteristics** of the interview – that is, from the way in which people will modulate and finesse what they say in order to shape it to what they understand to be the context of the interview (Chapter 8, section 8.4, and section 9.4 below). One way of evading some of the problem is to collect data *prospectively*, both before and after something has happened (Chapter 6). But that resolves only problems of accuracy in timing and sequence, and only some of them, because people may give factually misleading accounts before and after. And remember that if bureaucratic data are used for establishing time sequences, much of this too is interview data or data from self-completed questionnaires, though the interviews may be medical consultations, or the questionnaire may be an application for housing benefit (see also Chapter 7).

Triangulating between sources and judging credibility

I was able to correct the historical sequence of events in George's life by finding independent sources of information, much of which happened to be in my filing cabinet since I had represented George in his claim against 'unfair dismissal'. But, of course, the usual reason for relying on informant accounts is that there are no easily available independent sources. However, sometimes survey researchers will adopt the strategy of collecting most of their information from informants via a questionnaire, and checking a random sample of responses against some independent source. This is often done in health services research where levels of illness in a community are estimated from questionnaire responses, but a level of confidence is assigned to the responses by medically examining a sub-sample. As noted in Chapter 8, section 8.4, many standard data collection instruments have been produced though a process of *validation* like this, but only for instruments producing quantitative data.

Validation is a matter of **triangulating** evidence from different sources about the same events. Historians often do this, cross-checking news reports against official records against contemporary diaries and memoirs (see Chapter 11, section 11.7). American news media (but not usually British ones) employ researchers whose entire job is doing something like this. Triangulation raises the problem of what to do when sources disagree. In their study of dual-career families, Rona and Robert Rapoport (1971, 1976) carried out something which is variably called **respondent validation, member-checking,** or **fallibility testing,** which is allowing respondents to comment on the results prior to publication. They found that couples often disagreed with each other as to what was 'the truth' about events which had happened in their relationship. Where accounts are discrepant, *and as long as we assume that there is only one correct account of the truth*, then some decision has to be made as to which account to believe. Then in analysing the accounts and trying to reconcile them, the analyst has to have some *theory of witnesses* as a guide to deciding which account is the more credible. Researchers rarely make their theory of witnesses explicit. It is usually a fairly commonsensical and ad hoc set of assumptions about which people were in the best position to know the truth, which are the kinds most likely to tell the truth, what are the likely reasons why someone may have a distorted view of the truth and so on (see also Chapter 10, section 10.5, Chapter 11, section 11.7). Researcher bias in favour or against particular kinds of people may play a part in the decision as to which person to believe (Chapter 12, section 12.4).

The above is problematic only if researchers are trying to use informant accounts as evidence about some factual matter. That is what I was doing in the way I used the quotation from George: using George's words to imply a cause–effect relationship between antecedent and consequent events. Worse, I was offering George's words as a generalisation about cause and effect to apply to other homeless people too. This was entirely unjustifiable, and would have been so even if George had himself provided an accurate CV (see Chapter 4 on representativeness).

However, I might instead have said something like this:

It is notable how often homelessness people *attribute* their homelessness to sequences of traumatic events.

... then my wife died, unexpectedly and ...

(George: male, aged 69: resident in hostel for single homeless men)

Here the interest is not in what caused what, for which it is necessary to pin down the facts of what happened and when. Rather, the interest is in how someone understands – or at least, describes – what happened. Here it doesn't matter whether what George says is true in an historical sense. Not only does its factual accuracy not matter, but it is actually very interesting if what he says departs from what might be taken as a factual account. But now we face another problem. Is what George said in the interview to be taken as evidence of what he usually, ordinarily, generally, believes: of how he understands his situation in some general sense? Or is what George said in an interview to be taken as evidence just of what was going on in the interview, without begging questions as to what he might think, feel or say in other situations? These two different orientations lead to two different ways of analysing data. The first usually leads to a **thematic** analysis or something similar, the second to a **linguistic** analysis. These will be demonstrated in the next two sections.

9.3 Thematic analysis of qualitative interviews

What I shall call 'thematic analysis' is a version of **content analysis**, though that term is more usually used for the analysis of written and broadcast materials, but content analysis doesn't have to be quantitative (Chapter 11, section 11.2). Thematic analysis will be familiar to anyone who has studied literature as a subject: the theme of 'betrayal' in Shakespeare's plays; the theme of 'renewal' in the poetry of T.S.Eliot, and so on. The analyst looks for themes which are present in the whole set of interviews and creates a framework of these for making comparisons and contrasts between the different respondents.

Sometimes themes are inspired by a set of theoretical ideas already espoused by an analyst. For example, someone may already be suspicious that teachers have stereotyped views about girls and boys, may look for evidence of this, and label different utterances by teachers as examples of different kinds of themes such as 'Proactive boys' 'Passive girls' 'Girls as non-mathematical' and so on. Sometimes themes just seem to float up from the data. But, wherever themes come from the mechanics of thematic analysis are similar:

- Deciding what themes will be
- Deciding what will count as evidence of a theme
- Coding a transcript to indicate that this passage is an example of this

theme, and that passage is an example of another theme; sometimes this just means writing a code word for the theme in the margin of a hardcopy transcript (see below), but nowadays it often means assigning a database fieldcode to a passage so that the analysis can be automated (Fielding 1993)

- From then on the analysis is in terms of which kinds of people said what, which relates to a particular theme, and how saying something with regard to one theme relates to saying something with regard to another theme.

Some writers use the term code – in the sense of something to be cracked – rather than theme, but this tends to confuse something which is allegedly in the data with the technical process of indexing the data: coding it to show what is where. One of the many uses of the term 'discourse' is an alternative to 'theme' (Chapter 11, section 11.1).

Coding a transcript thematically (Transcript 9.1)

Transcript 9.1 Transcript coded for themes in a thematic analysis

Speaker and utterance number	Speech	THEME
RG1	So, hmm, you were aware that you had a drinking problem. That was the wor-d you used wasn't it ?	ADDICTION
G1	Yea [2 seconds]	
G2	I mean it took me a long time to accept it, to really accept it that is as, hmmmm a problem to be solved sort of problem. An derrr then I said, well [Georgie] boy you gotter do somethink about this. Sssss so I spose I got myself dry for about en year	CHARACTER TRAIT: PERSONAL DETERMINATION
RG2	Uhhm	
G3	Well occasional lapses, but nearleee dry. It was o.k.	
RG3	Yeahh	
G4	Hmmm, then my uh, wife died [3 seconds]	VICTIM OF CIRCUMSTANCES:

Transcript 9.1 (*continued*)

Speaker and utterance number	Speech	THEME
G5	Unexpectedly and derr that threw me. It was stomach cancer which was common in her family, but which I didn't see it coming [untranscribable] it was a great shock, and I yh reacted badly. I began to hit the drinking very hard, but not for the same reasons as ear[lier]	LOSS OF RELATIONSHIP
RG4	[ear]lier. Hhh, earlier you said drinking was about stress. Stress at work.	
G6	Yea. I told you. But I got to handle that see. That was behind me. Then this thing with [wife's name]. And then when I was just getting over that, I got made redundant, which knocked the stuffing out of me.	VICTIM OF CIRCUMSTANCES: LOSS OF RELATIONSHIP/ LOSS OF JOB
G7	[Omitted passage on redundancy and how badly it affected many people. How it was caused by bad management and greedy unions, ending on 10 second silence]	VICTIM OF CIRCUMSTANCES: LOSS OF JOB/ACTS OF OTHERS
G8	And what with the drink and the [lack of] money I end up here [in the hostel] which is just one better than being on the street but only just.	VICTIM OF CIRCUMSTANCES: FINANCIAL CRISIS
	(5 minutes' more interview talk. RG5–RG9 G9–G14)	
RG10	So in more general terms, what do you think makes people homeless ?	
G15	Oh, oh, mmmm, there's lots. Everyone's got their own. Hmmmm hhhhhher. I mean some it's really a lack of character. I mean little things which anyone else could	FLAWED CHARACTER (attributed to other people)

hmm, anyone with a bit of
character could cope with. But me
hhhhm, all though my life my
luck's been against me. It's almost
as if I was heading for the bottom
all the time and now I've pretty
well reached it. At least there's
nothing to be afraid of any more
[2 seconds]

GOOD CHARACTER
(attributed to self) ???

G16   That's what I tell myself
[3 seconds]

G17   I mean, everything I've tried to do,
just when I was succeeding has
been snatched away from me. It's
been me getting it together, and
then the slap in the gob. The
mistake was trying to get it
together. Ider bin much happier if
I'd just accepted I was a loser from
the start
[2 seconds]

VICTIM OF
CIRCUMSTANCES:
GENERAL AND
FATE/LUCK

G18   Hmm ?
[3 seconds]

G19   Someone up there's laughing at me

RG – Roger Gomm, G – George, [2 Seconds] – 2 seconds' silence;
[ ] encloses overlapping speech.

The transcript gives an example of a segment of interview coded thematically. The inspiration for the themes is attribution theory (Kelly and Michella
1980). This is the idea that people have many options available to them as
to what to attribute as the cause of their misfortunes or advantages, including their own character and actions, the actions of others, luck, the will of
God and so on. Particular people tend to use only some of these options, or
some in some situations and others in others. Some tend to attribute all the
good that happens to them to their own actions, and all the bad that
happens to them to the actions of others, or to discorporate entities such as
'fate' or 'society'. Some people show the opposite tendency, rarely crediting
themselves as the cause of good happenings, and usually blaming themselves for bad occurrences. The extreme version of this is symptomatic
of clinical depression (Beck 1970). In the literature of addictions it is a
common idea both that addicted people tend to think of themselves as *non-
agentive* (as the victims of forces they cannot control), and that people who
think of themselves in this way are rather unlikely to be able to throw off
their addiction (Davies 1997a, 1997b).

TABLE 9.1	Agentive and non-agentive attributions: coding frame for a thematic analysis

Causes of misfortune	
Non-agentive attributions: victim of circumstances	**Agentive attributions: victim of own behaviour**

■ Loss of relationship
■ Loss of job or other valued activity
■ Disability/limiting illness
■ Addiction
■ Financial crisis
■ Discrimination on basis of: Age
                Gender
                Race
                Other
■ Bad luck, fate or supernatural agency
■ Other eventuality (specify)
	■ Loss of relationship
	■ Loss of job or other valued activity
	■ Disability/limiting illness
	■ Addiction
	■ Financial crisis
	■ Criminal offence
	■ Supernatural punishment
	■ Flawed character
	■ Other eventuality (specify)

Causes of advantage	
Non-agentive attributions: beneficiary of circumstances	**Agentive attributions: self-made good fortune**
■ Good will/philanthropy of others ■ Good luck: being in the right place at the right time ■ Good luck – treated as an agency, e.g. 'Lady Luck' ■ Supernatural intervention	■ Good character accounting for good fortune (specify character traits)

The coding in the transcript derives from a model like that shown in Table 9.1. The codings are at the bullet points. If you are puzzled as to whether the codes equate with themes, or whether the themes are 'victim of circumstances', 'victim of own behaviour' and so on, don't worry. There can be themes within themes within themes.

To show how this coding scheme might generate similarities and contrasts between different respondents, consider how this passage from an interview with Lara might be coded and compare Lara with George:

> It's because I'm a shit. I was a shit to my ol' man and a shit to my kids. I've let down every employer whose been good enough to employ me even if I haven't ripped him off as well. Which is probably that I was born that way.

(Lara: female aged 35, living rough)

These procedures may look radically different from asking people questions using forced choice questionnaires. They are different but not radically so.

The thematic framework in Table 9.1 constitutes a kind of questionnaire, answered by the analyst while reading transcripts of interviews. The 'questionnaire' asks the analyst: 'Is this an example of this theme, this theme, this theme or this theme?' The major difference is that with forced choice questionnaires all the *permissible* responses from interviewees are decided in advance, whereas with thematic analysis the range of *interesting* responses is decided after the interview data are available. Insofar as themes suggest themselves to the researcher as a result of reading the data, this is sometimes described as **grounding** theory/concepts/categories, and so on **in data**, meaning the opposite of imposing theory/concepts/categories on the data (see also Chapter 10, section 10.6). However, the contrast is not so sharp as the words imply. The difference is really one of timing. Even with thematic analysis there comes a point at which the analyst imposes a structure on the data. It will only be one of many structures he or she might have imposed.

Forced choice questions aim to provide *measurements of variables*. There is also something rather 'variable-like' about a theme. It is fairly easy to imagine converting the themes in Table 9.1 into forced choice questions, using them and counting the responses. Indeed there are many 'attribution questionnaires' generating numerical data used in psychology, psychiatry and in the study and treatment of addictions.

A disadvantage of delaying the making of analytic decisions until after interviews have been conducted is that it may mean that different interviews take different paths, so that it may be impossible to find examples of variants on the same theme in all the interviews. This leads to puzzles as to whether what was missing from an interview was unimportant to the interviewee, or important but just didn't come up in the interview. For example, if an interviewee doesn't attribute blame for the breakdown of his marriage to himself, his wife, social circumstances or to other people, does this mean he doesn't usually attribute any particular cause, or that the interview didn't make it appropriate for him to do so? This is the obverse problem of that arising from asking a forced choice question along the lines of : 'To what do you attribute the breakdown of your marriage: to your own character or actions/ to those of your wife/.../don't know? The forced choice question may lead a respondent to give an answer to a question he doesn't usually pose to himself; an answer made up on the spot to satisfy a researcher's question, but that may happen in a qualitative interview too (see section 9.4).

It wasn't particularly difficult to use the coding framework in Table 9.1 with the interview with George. But sometimes it is quite difficult to know which codes, if any, to attach to a particular passage of speech. Since nothing is going to be counted this isn't so much of a problem as it would be in research generating numerical data. Nonetheless, there are still opportunities for coding to be slipshod, or for analysts to code in such a way as to massage the data so that it shows what they want it to show. Because of the sheer bulk of the data from qualitative interviews, readers are sometimes not shown the coding at all – or, more often, have to be satisfied with some examples of speech which exemplify the coding. Only rarely do thematic analysts subject their coding to blind independent scrutiny and conduct inter-rater reliability tests to measure the degree of agreement between different people doing the same coding (see Chapter 2, section 2.9). Armstrong *et al.* (1997) have suggested that this should be standard practice in this kind of research.

The coding demonstrated above is only the beginnings of a thematic analysis. It is quite common to subject the same data to analysis using several different coding frames. The analyst is likely to go on to ask questions such as: 'what themes tend to cohere with what other themes; which never occur together; what kinds of people provide the examples of these themes and not those?' and other questions. Eventually the analysis will be written up; qualitatively rather than quantitatively. For example, the paragraphs below might have resulted from continuing the thematic analysis begun above, applying it to the transcripts of other interviews as well:

> In summary then, in the study two distinctively different groups of homeless people can be identified. First there were a group who might be called 'self-blamers' who mainly attributed their misfortunes to personal failings. They had very low self-esteem, and seemed to be inhibited from trying to improve their situation, partly because they had no confidence that they could do so, and partly because they did not seem to believe that they deserved anything better:
>
> > It's because I'm a shit. I was a shit to my ol' man and a shit to my kids. I've let down every employer whose been good enough to employ me even if I haven't ripped him off as well. Which is probably that I was born that way.
> >
> > (Lara: female aged 35, living rough)
>
> These were in the minority, however and were more likely to be women than men. Much more usual was the person who attributed homelessness and other misfortunes to bad luck, and to the machinations of other people. In one sense they had a high opinion of themselves, since they often explained how they had made determined efforts to deal with problems, and it was despite this that adversity had nonetheless beset them: they were 'persons of character but victims of circumstances'. In representing the forces acting against them as extremely powerful they also represented themselves as having shown admirable character traits such as perseverance, determination and so on. However, in this sense they 'lived in the past'. They faced the present and the future having learned lessons from the past to the effect that the forces acting against them were just too great for them to prevail. As one of them said:
>
> > I mean, everything I've tried to do, just when I was succeeding has been snatched away from me. It's been me getting it together, and

then the slap in the gob. The mistake was trying to get it together. I would have been much happier if I'd just accepted I was a loser from the start.

(George: male aged 69: resident in hostel for single homeless men)

What do themes stand for?

The paragraph above describes types of people: people with particular ways of thinking, understanding the world, acting and so on. The data source would have been an hour-long interview with each person, and only some of what they said would have entered the final analysis. Yet the implication is that by looking through that 1-hour window, the analyst was able to discover what each person was like, 24 hours a day, 7 days a week and over some period of their life-span. The credibility of this rests on a number of assumptions:

- That people think, feel and act much the same in most or all of the situations in which they find themselves, such that studying them in one situation will tell us about them in other situations.
- Or, failing this, that the qualitative interview is an especially effective way of finding out about how people are in general, underneath some misleading appearances, or despite their acting in ways uncharacteristic for them in some situations. (Note the remarks about the importance, and the problematic, of making close relationships with interviewees in Chapter 8, section 8.5)
- That the themes in a thematic analysis are not merely convenient headings for use in writing up the results of an interview study, but actually stand for something about the way the minds of interviewees are organised. I have used the term 'theme' where others might have used terms more strongly implying that what was being discovered was the structure of people's minds: terms such as 'world-views', 'perspectives', 'typification schemes', 'actor social theories', 'interpretive frameworks', 'schemes of relevance', 'cognitive frameworks' or 'representational structures' or 'discourses'.

Whichever term were used the implication would be that George would have a mind organised such that being 'a person of character but a victim of circumstances' is a persistent characteristic of the way he thinks about himself and understands his experience.

These assumptions cannot be tested while all we have from each interviewee is a small sample of their speech, elicited in what may be a highly unrepresentative situation when judged against the spectrum of situations in which they usually find themselves. Commonsense suggests, anyway, that had a different person done the interview, then the interview talk might have been different (see Chapter 8, sections 8.4 and 8.5). And had a different thematic framework been used, then the themes claimed to be persistent features of the respondents' consciousness would have been different themes. Whether a different interviewer, asking different questions, analysing the results in terms of different themes, would nonetheless produce similar findings must be an open question. But this seems rather unlikely.

This kind of mind-reading approach has been the traditional approach in qualitative sociological research. While it was being abandoned by many 'mainstream' qualitative researchers in the 1980s (Hammersley 1992) the tradition was renewed by feminist researchers thereafter (Oakley 1981). But the idea that underneath appearances there is a 'real person' is also held by attitude researchers and personality researchers in psychology who believe that they have the psychometric tests to delve beneath appearances to find out what people are really like underneath (Procter 1993b). There is widespread belief in there being 'real people beneath misleading appearances' but less consensus as to what they are like and what are the best methods for finding out about them.

The next section turns to a different kind of analysis which doesn't require such assumptions. It is far less interested in people and much more interested in situations. It is sceptical about the underlying and interested in the superficial on the grounds that all there is which can be researched is on the surface, to be observed. This orientation runs from the dramaturgical approach adopted by Goffman (Burns 1992: 106–40), to ethnomethodological approaches. For this chapter it will be represented by Conversation Analysis (CA).

9.4 A linguistic, or sequential analysis of a qualitative interview

Ethnomethodology and Conversation Analysis (CA)

The term '**ethnomethodology**' was coined by Howard Garfinkel (1967) to designate the study of the methods (the methodology) that people (ethnos) use to make their lives sensible. An ethnomethodologist would not be interested in what life meant to George in particular, or even in what life meant to George as an exemplar of homeless people, or people with 'drink problems'. Rather an ethnomethodologist would be interested in a transcript of an interview with George for what it might tell us about how people in general go about making sense – or, what is the same thing, how people make what they do sensible to other people. One of the tenets of ethnomethodology is that action is always **occasioned** and **situated**. It is what it is, when it is, where it is. Thus ethnomethodologists would say that an interview with George is an interview with George. It cannot tell us much about what happened to George previously, or what George would be like in another situation. What such a transcript does best is to stand as evidence of what happens when a researcher interviews a respondent (Cicourel 1982).

Conversation Analysis (CA) is a development of ethnomethodology to deal with spoken language data. The 'conversation' does not mean that attention is restricted to what we call 'conversations'. Rather it deals with all kinds of **speech events** or **speech exchange systems**, including interviews.

From pragmatic linguistics (Levinson 1983) comes the idea that speech should be analysed for what people are doing with speech, rather than what they mean by what they say, as explained below.

Locutions and illocutions

In everyday life, and in psychological and sociological research, there are at least three ways of reading or hearing words. One is in mind-reading mode as evidence of the thoughts, mind, mental state, mood, personality, ways of understanding and such like mentalistic characteristics of the speaker. People who engage in this kind of analysis are wont to say that what they are studying is what things 'mean' to people, or how they 'experience' their lives. They pursue the topic of meaning by asking a question something like:

> What must have been in that person's mind in order that they said this or did that?

Thus the topic of meaning is approached by building *models of the minds* which are supposed to lie behind and give rise to what was said, as in the thematic analysis above.

Another approach to language is in *locutionary*, or referential fashion. This is hearing words as intended to refer to something. So a locutionary reading of:

> G2   I mean it took me a long time to accept it, to really accept it that is as, hmmmm a problem to be solved sort of problem. An derrr then I said, well [Georgie] boy you gotter do somethink about this. Sssss so I spose I got myself dry for about err year

is as a report by George which refers to something which happened to him earlier in his life. This was the approach adopted in section 9.2 of this chapter. For this reading we dis-attend to when George said this in the sequence of the interview, and hear it instead in terms of a different sequence of events: the sequence of George's life. Treating language in a locutionary way usually directs our attention to the question of whether the speech is an *accurate* report about whatever it is that it refers to (see section 9.2).

The third way of hearing words is as **illocutions**, or 'speech acts', or 'performatives'. What is important is not what someone means by the words, but what is accomplished by saying them. The classic source for speech act theory is J. L. Austin's *How to do Things with Words* (1962). What Austin says people do with words is to issue commands, give compliments, ask questions, make promises, provide excuses and such like. For example, as a locution, *I'm very busy* is a report on the state of one's commitments. *We're going to lunch*, as a locution, reports on an intended action. But put the two phrases together one after the other:

> We're going to lunch
> I'm very busy

Now the two are hearable in an illocutionary way: the first as an invitation; the second as a refusal to accept the invitation with a reason for the refusal: a so-called 'reasoned refusal'.

Turn-taking

An illocutionary reading of the utterances in the transcript would pay attention to what George and the interviewer are doing with words in the context and sequence of the interview. For this reason the term **sequential analysis** is often used. One thing they are doing is to create and sustain the kind of social situation we recognise as 'a research interview', with people playing the social roles of interviewer and interviewee. Part of this is done by taking turns in the interview, which is structured in a turn-by-turn fashion. This may seem obvious, but it is actually very important. The principle of turn-taking is one of the most fundamental principles for understanding how people organise their interaction one with another:

> Turn-taking is used for the ordering of moves in games, for allocating political office, for regulating traffic at intersections, for serving customers at business establishments, and for talking in interviews, meetings, debates, ceremonies, conversations etc. – these last being members of a set which we will refer to as 'speech exchange systems'. It is obviously a prominent type of social organisation, one whose instances are implicated in a wide range of ... activities.
> (Sacks, Schegloff and Jefferson 1974: 710)

As you will see, taking note of turn-taking in the transcript of the interview with George gives an interpretation of what is going on, which is different from that derived from the thematic analysis.

Adjacency pairs

In a speech exchange whatever is said by the first party is likely to shape what is said by others. This is often referred to in terms of **adjacency pairs** (Schegloff and Sacks 1973). Everyday speech consists of a large number of paired utterances where the second may be predictable from the first, or at least where a later utterance may be predictable from an earlier one.

Even if a 'second' cannot be predicted it is usually unsurprising. Thus:

- A first which is a greeting will most likely be followed by a second which is a greeting
- A question will most likely be followed by an answer (or an apology for not being able to give an answer, or a reason for not giving an answer, or a joke about questions and answers, and so on)
- A complaint will most likely be followed by a denial, a justification, an excuse or an apology
- A compliment will most likely be followed by a combination of a thanking and a diminisher such as 'thank you, no, no but you are too kind', or a return such as 'you're looking very pretty yourself'.

What is predictable is not the locutionary meaning of an utterance, but its illocutionary meaning (sometimes called its illocutionary 'force' or 'intention'). Thus we can predict with a fair degree of accuracy that a question will be followed by an answer, or by one of the other illocutions which often follow questions. But we are much less able to predict what the answer will be.

Of course, the second party's utterance cannot always be predicted from the first party's utterance. Sometimes verbal interchanges do take surprising directions. Sometimes people make sure that what they say is unpredictable when making jokes, catching others out and so on. Nonetheless, illocution-wise everyday language is probably more predictable than most other things studied by social scientists. That this is so relates to the fact that people have to be able to predict responses in order to have coherent conversations with each other. If I could not, to some degree, predict that what I intend as a question will elicit an answer, then I could not engage in questioning. Indeed almost by definition what a question is is that kind of utterance which elicits an answer. And what an answer is is that kind of response which is elicited by a question.

Not only is speech fairly predictable in illocutionary terms, but people do predict in order to determine the sense of another's responses. Thus if I ask a question, *however the other person responds* I am most likely to regard the response as being one of the kind which usually follows questions – or, in the last resort, to regard the response (or no response at all) as evidence of a mishearing or a misunderstanding, a rudeness or an evasion on behalf of the other person. Thus by the act of asking a question I severely limit the number of categories for classifying the response of the other. Whatever they say after my question it is an utterance following a question. In the interchange below, for example, what the second speaker says does not at first seem to be a response to a request for information:

> Speaker 1 What's the time?
> Speaker 2 About 180 degrees

But since the provision of information is what is most to be expected following a request for information, we can probably work out that what Speaker 2 means is 'turn around there's a clock behind you'.

Accounts and self-presentation

Whatever we say, even if we stay silent, we nonetheless give off evidence which other people will take as evidence of our character. This is no mystery to ordinary folk, who always engage in some degree of **impression management**. Goffman's book *The Presentation of Self in Everyday Life* (1959) suggests that people know they are likely to be judged by others and respond to this by putting on a show. Many of the examples which Goffman gives might suggest that people are poseurs and seek either to mislead others about what they are really like, or that they fool themselves. These assumptions, however, do not necessarily follow from the idea of self-presentation. It requires just as much of a performance to show to others what one believes to be the truth about oneself as it would to mislead other people.

By a strange coincidence George used to be an accountant, but in sociology and psychology the terms **account** and **accounting** mean that people monitor the impressions they make on others, and adjust their behaviour in order to *give an account* of themselves as being the kind of person they would prefer others to think they are; those particular people in that particular situation:

I'm sorry it's such a mess, but we've got the builders in

We're not usually so behind but it's this latest 'flu thing

These are accounts (Buttney 1993). They are instructions to another not to judge by appearances, which give an adverse impression, but to take some additional information into consideration in order to reach a different judgement. As these examples suggest, accounting often has to be done under difficult circumstances where all else which is assumable or observable looks discrediting. Indeed the more discrediting the circumstances seem to be, the more an account seems to be called for. People who don't give accounts when all the evidence seems against them are likely to be regarded as 'brazen', 'uncouth' 'not respectable', 'unrepentant', 'insensitive' and so on. George, as a person with a known drink problem, living in a hostel for homeless single men, is the kind of person who has to work harder than others to give an account of himself as being other than a worthless derelict.

Accounts in word form may take any of the forms below:

Self-commendations: attribute meritorious characteristics to oneself, or describe the results of one's own actions as benign.
Denials: refuse to accept that anything is wrong or refuse to accept that anything which is wrong is any fault of one's own.
Disclaimations: a particularly common kind of denial, they take forms such as:

'I know it might sound racist to say this but ...', followed by something which might be interpreted as racist.

Blames: attribute moral fault to others, or attribute blame to circumstances such as 'the recession', 'capitalism', or 'modern society'. Blames are common adjuncts to excuses, justifications and denials.
Justifications: may accept that something unfortunate has happened, but refuse to accept any moral fault by providing good moral reasons for one's own actions.
Excuses: accept moral faults, but offer mitigations for them: 'I was feeling under the weather when I was rude to you.'
Apologies: accept blame for what is wrong, perhaps completely, but perhaps for only part of it.

Self-blames: accept one's own culpability and are often associated with apologies, self-blames without excuses are particularly self-blaming. *Promises of remedial or reformatory action:* often associated with self-blames, apologies and *expressions of remorse.*

There is no precise way of dividing these up, or of allocating particular utterances precisely as being one kind of account or another. They are better thought of as lying on a dimension running from self-commendation through denial ('nothing to blame me for') down to self-blame ('it's all my fault, I can't excuse myself').

A linguist would say that the list is a **preference order** (Levinson 1983: 332–45). People would prefer to give an account of themselves which attracts commendation, failing that they would prefer to give an account which denies any moral fault, but failing that a justification, and so on down the list. Giving an account which is not acceptable to others may be worse than not giving an account at all. Thus, where an excuse would not be believable it is preferable to own up and promise to make amends. One's past moral faults may then be balanced out by one's present and future moral actions and there are brownie points to be had for 'coming clean' (Snyder and Higgins 1990).

We can now apply some of these ideas to the transcript.

Producing characters through interviews

I want to focus on the beginning of the transcript: **G1–G5** (pp. 190–1). From now on ignore the 'thematic' codes. The general question I am going to ask about this sequence is:

> What does this sequence tell us about a social situation in which a researcher interviews another person who lives in a hostel for homeless men and has a known and self-confessed drink problem?

To say that a speech exchange is an 'interview' is to say that it is a form of social organisation in which one person plays the role of the interviewer, who asks questions and determines the topics to be discussed, and the other person plays the role of the interviewee, who is to answer questions and otherwise provide information on the understanding that the information given will be 'on the record'. It is not too difficult to see this social structure in the transcript. Even if the speakers were not identified in the transcript you would have no difficulty in deciding who was playing which role. Moreover, once we know what this social structure is, we have little difficulty in allocating most of the silences as between the speakers. If it is the prerogative of the interviewer to ask (most of) the questions then (most of) the silences will be attributable to the turn of the interviewee and interpretable as failures to answer questions adequately.

To be interviewed is to be required to give some kind of account of oneself. To be interviewed as a homeless person and a person with a drink problem is to be required to give an account of oneself in stigmatising circumstances. None of this requires any particular account to be given, but it does seem likely that in such an interview such stigmatising circumstances will frequently be oriented to and this will be seen in transcripts in the form of excuses, justifications, self-blames, apologies and promises of reform. There is little difficulty in seeing the transcript in terms of George accounting for his discrediting situation, sometimes by giving answers to questions which haven't actually been asked. Thus **G4** seems to be a response to the accusatory question: 'Why didn't you *stay* dry?'

At **G3**, George says:

well, occasional lapses, but nearlee dry. It was o.k.

Why does George say this at precisely this point in the interchange? We must look for the answer in what came before. What came before was:

G2   I mean it took me a long time to accept it, to really accept it that is as, hmmmm a problem to be solved sort of problem. An derrr then I said, well [Georgie] boy you gotter do somethink about this. Sssss so I spose I got myself dry for about err year

Here George is telling a story about how he did what 'everybody knows' is difficult for an alcoholic: staying dry. And the story he tells is one of some success. It is a self-commendation. The most predictable responses to stories like this are either congratulations, or they are commiserations that the effort was not more successful than it was. Or it might be some combination of the two; for example, perhaps: 'Well done, that must have been difficult, but it shows you can do it.'

But what George actually gets as a response to his story of determined effort is a non-judgemental, non-committal:

RG2   (0.5) Uhhm

Let's use a course-grain size of analysis and say that, following a self-commendation, the most predictable response is a positive evaluation.

Positive and negative evaluations are important forms of illocution. They may be explicit ('Thanks: jolly good') or executed in the form of other kinds of utterances, for example by matching one story with another; for example: 'Yes I felt exactly the same when ...' The possibility for a negative evaluation may be evaded by a rapid change of topic, or a negative evaluation may be executed by saying nothing at all; for example:

The teacher asks the pupil a question. The pupil gives an answer. The teacher says nothing. What is the most usual interpretation of this nothing-saying by the teacher?

Marion tells William some good news. William does not indicate that he has heard it, but launches into a story of his own. What is Marion likely to feel about this ?

Claudette tells a joke. No one laughs. Unbeknown to Claudette everyone has agreed not to laugh when she tells a joke. The joke's on her. What principle is being exploited by Claudette's friends?

George tells a story of his determined effort to overcome a problem. RG says 'uhhm'

A rule for covering all these situations is that where an evaluation is expected, the absence of a positive evaluation is usually taken as a negative evaluation. Thus a highly typical classroom sequences runs:

1 Teacher question

2 Pupil answer/failure to answer

3 Teacher evaluation of pupil's answer or failure to answer.

This is so common that virtually anything a teacher says or does in the third slot is heard as an evaluation of the pupil's answer, even if – perhaps especially if – what the teacher says is nothing at all. Teacher silence at this point is usually to be heard as an indication that the pupil's answer was wrong or incomplete. The silence offers the pupil an opportunity to extend or amend the answer (Coultard and Mongomery 1981). Similarly whether people find jokes funny or not, common politeness requires people to laugh on the punch line. No laugh – no positive evaluation – is hearable as a negative evaluation of the joke and/or of the joker – it wasn't funny. Perhaps it wasn't taken as a joke, but as an insult.

In **G2** George tells a story for which it is reasonable to predict that the other party to the interchange will give a positive evaluation. Nothing recognisable as a positive evaluation is forthcoming. The minimal utterance by RG and RG's status as interviewer, leaves the turn with George and the topic still the same: George's drink problem. What does George do ? He does one of the things we might expect. He amends his story as if its first version had been regarded as an exaggeration or an untruth. He diminishes his claims of success a little (**G3**):

Well occasional lapses, but nearleee dry. It was o.k.

Something you might realise from the example of teachers' questions and pupils' responses is that positive evaluations often also serve as *topic change markers*: as in 'yea, thanks that's great. Now another thing'. Silence or minimal responses, whether taken as negative evaluations or not, usually indicate that the topic has not been exhausted. In the case of teacher questions and pupil answers, the teacher silence is likely to imply that the pupil's answer was wrong and the pupil should correct it, or that it was incomplete and the pupil should complete it. Either way the turn stays with, or returns to the pupil for him or her to offer a completion or a correction. Something like this seems to be happening in the transcript. RG's minimal and non-responses are responded to by George as if they meant: 'what you have said so far is incomplete, insufficient, incredible or otherwise inadequate: redeem yourself.'

As the interview unfolds George's responses slide down the preference scale of accounts, from a self-commendation at **G2**, which is then amended to become less self-congratulatory at **G3**, is replaced by an excuse at **G4**, with excuse piled on top of excuse from **G5** to **G8**. At **G15** George is back to self-commendations, characterising himself as someone 'fighting against the odds' – the 'person of character, but victim of circumstances' theme of the thematic analysis (see Transcript 9.2).

Transcript 9.2 Transcript coded for illocutions: sequential analysis

Speaker and utterance number	Speech	ILLOCUTION
RG1	So, hmm, you were aware that you had a drinking problem. That was the wor-d you used wasn't it ?	Question
G1	Yea	Response
	[2 seconds]	No positive evaluation/no topic change signal from RG leaves the silence with George, and implies that his response was inadequate or incomplete
G2	I mean it took me a long time to accept it, to really accept it that is as, hmmmm a problem to be solved sort of problem. An derrr then I said, well [George] boy you gotter do somethink about this. Sssss so I spose I got myself dry for about err year	Self-commendation
RG2	Uhhm	No positive evaluation of the self-commendation

Transcript 9.2 (*continued*)

Speaker and utterance number	Speech	ILLOCUTION
G3	Well occasional lapses, but nearleee dry. It was o.k.	Amendment of self-commendation to be less self-congratulatory
RG3	Yeahh	No positive evaluation of **G3**
G4	Hmmm, then my uh, wife died [3 seconds]	Excuse No positive evaluation of excuse
G5	Unexpectedly and derr that threw me. It was stomach cancer which was common in her family, but which I didn't see it coming [untranscribable] it was a great shock, and I yh reacted badly. I began to hit the drinking very hard, but not for the same reasons as ear[lier]	Elaboration of excuse
RG4	[ear]lier. Hhh, earlier you said drinking was about stress. Stress at work.	Topic change, which might be heard as rejection of the **G5** excuse on the grounds that a different excuse had been made earlier
G6	Yea. I told you. But I got to handle that see. That was behind me. Then this thing with [wife's name]. And then when I was just getting over that, I got made redundant, which knocked the stuffing out of me.	Excuse
G7	(omitted passage on redundancy and how badly it affected many people. How it was caused by bad management and greedy unions, ending on 10 second silence)	(Several more excuses)
G8	And what with the drink and the [lack of] money I end up here [in the hostel] which is just one better than being on the street but only just.	Rounding up of narrative – implies this topic is exhausted

[5 minutes' more interview talk. RG5–9 G9–14]		[new topic introduced by new question from RG]
RG10	So in more general terms, what do you think makes people homeless ?	Question
G15	Oh, oh, mmmm, there's lots. Everyone's got their own. Hmmmm hhhhhher. I mean some it's really a lack of character. I mean little things which anyone else could hmm, anyone with a bit of character could cope with. But me hhhhm, all through my life my luck's been against me. It's almost as if I was heading for the bottom all the time and now I've pretty well reached it. At least there's nothing to be afraid of any more	Self-commendation in terms of response to the challenges life has thrown at him/self-characterisation as victim fighting against the odds

RG – Roger Gomm, G – George, [2 Seconds] = 2 seconds' silence [ ] encloses overlapping speech.

But by **G17** George is characterising himself as a pathetic victim, someone foolish even to consider he could beat the odds against him.

> I mean, everything I've tried to do, just when I was succeeding has been snatched away from me. It's been me getting it together, and then the slap in the gob. The mistake was trying to get it together. Ider bin much happier if I'd just accepted I was a loser from the start

Then, towards the end of the interview, and beyond our transcript, George is at the bottom of the preference scale with a self-blaming account:

> G32: Yah, well you know Roger this old guff that people like me give you, its all about refusing to confront, what's in the personality, of hhh, y'h average alcoholic. I mean you talk to an alco, and what you probably get is a lot of excuses and justifications and when it's really down to a failure of will power, which is hhhhh, which is something we don't want to confront. I mean that's my story
> (5 seconds)

> G33: In a nutshell.

Aha, at last, George is revealing his true authentic self which he has been dissimulating previously. But why should we assume this ? It would perhaps be better to think of George trying out various ways of presenting himself, none of which seem to elicit any validation from RG and at **G32** trying yet another tack. It is worth noting here perhaps, that what George says in **G32** is cast in the genre of Alcoholics Anonymous meetings of which George attended from time to time. Other research has suggested that something which people with drug and alcohol problems learn from their contacts with members of the helping agencies is that they get a better deal from them by describing themselves in this way. In professional circles it is described as 'showing insight' (Davies 1997b). Thus there is a case for regarding **G32** as 'off-the-peg' drink-problem talk appropriate for an alcoholic to use in talking to members of the helping professions and not as George finally disclosing his 'true self'.

Rather than puzzling about which is the 'real George' it might be better to consider instead how it is that characters are *realised* or *produced* in an interview, or in any other kind of speech exchange. The term 'produced' is used here in the same sense as in dramatics where it refers to a producer enabling an actor to realise a character in a play. In the same way, in an interview, an interviewer and an interviewee enable or disable the realisation of characters. For example, if you are part of the audience for a lecture, this offers only limited opportunities for producing yourself as a character, except by breaking all the conventions of playing the rather passive role of audience member. As you have seen, how George comes across depends on what the interviewer does and how George responds to this. How his interviewer – that's me – behaves depends on how he thinks such interviews should be conducted. As far as I can remember, I thought it was important to say as little as possible, but to make encouraging and non-judgmental noises in order to 'draw interviewees out' on interesting topics. That was the basis of my on-the-spot intuitive data analysis which determined what I said next. You might say that it all went horribly wrong. I would agree. And it may be that my performance was influenced by a scepticism about the truth of what George was saying, developed over several years of inter-action with him. But, whatever I might have said differently, I would still have been involved in the production of George as a character. Note also that George is also partly responsible for how I come across as an inter-viewer.

9.5 Thematic and linguistic analysis compared

One of the main devices George uses to give himself character is that of telling stories in which he is the leading character. So far as the transcript is concerned, a reasonable synopsis of the overall plot would be that this is a story of someone beset with such a sequence of misfortunes that 'anyone' under the same circumstances might turn to drink and become homeless. As you saw from section 9.2 of this chapter, this sequence of events is not an accurate one in historical terms. Having looked at the transcript in terms of the interaction between interviewer and interviewee, you may now be suspicious that the 'one thing on top of another' impression is created by

George piling excuse on excuse in response to what seems to be a rather unsympathetic interviewer. With a more sympathetic response, George might not have depicted himself as beset with so many adversities. Nor perhaps, would he have finally ended up with a self-blame.

This story line is picked up by the thematic analysis in section 9.3. It is the grand theme of 'persons of character as victims of circumstances'. But the assumptions underlying the thematic analysis force us to accept that the stories people tell about themselves have their foundation in some general ways in which the tellers understand themselves and their lives. The linguistic analysis, however, suggests that such stories are devices adopted in particular circumstances as seem appropriate to perform immediate tasks, such as to entertain, to commiserate, to show solidarity, to persuade, to show good character traits; or, in George's case, to find some kind of personality to occupy which would provoke a positive evaluation from his interviewer. Another way of saying this is that what George says is **audience directed** or **recipient designed** in terms of what George understands to be the **demand characteristics** of the interview.

In addition, from the linguistic point of view, what we hear when we hear people telling stories is that they know how to tell stories: that is how to use *narrative conventions* to tell plots and depict characters; to know what is a credible out-turn from an antecedent state of affairs, and to know what motivations people usually assume to lie behind what actions. For example, George does not have to spell out in **G8** that being made redundant and being short of money are conventionally regarded as stressful and among the candidate causes for homelessness. Nor does he have to say, in so many words, that staying dry is difficult for an alcoholic, and that succeeding to some degree is a matter for commendation.

The result of a thematic analysis is usually the delineation of a *type of person* or of a range of types of persons. These are usually the types of person who are assumed to be as they are because of their social location or biographical experience – because, for example, they have been socialised as doctors they think the way they do; because they were abused as children they are anorexic adults, or because their teachers have a poor opinion of them they have gained a view of themselves as stupid and this explains why they engage in disruptive behaviour. The typification is likely to be in terms of mentalistic characteristics, such as personality traits or ways of understanding, together with a causal theory as to how they got that way. In an analysis like this the generalisations run from someone who is interviewed to a much larger number of people, allegedly of the same sort, who have not been studied. Thus the generalisation would be from the 13 homeless people I interviewed to other homeless people. The generalising claim would be that some of them would be of the 'self-blaming type', and some of the type who are 'persons of character but victims of circumstances' and that for both types, homelessness (or some other set of adversities) gave them these characteristics (or that these characteristics explain the state they are in).

The linguistic analysis, however, is framed around the idea of a *type of situation.* In this case, the situation is the type of speech exchange system called 'a qualitative interview'. Thus what has been found more generally about linguistic behaviour in such situations might be applied to, or tested against, the interview with George. What is discovered about the interview with George might be claimed to be true also of other, as yet unstudied qualitative interviews. But there are also likely to be some things which are true of qualitative interviews which are also true of other speech exchange systems: perhaps of job interviews, academic tutorials, radio interviews and so on. Here the generalising movement is from one kind of speech exchange system to another. Just as I used teacher–pupil exchanges in classrooms to inform my analysis of the transcript of a qualitative interview, so ideas arising from the analysis of a qualitative interview might be used to inform the analysis of say, classroom interaction, counselling sessions, or medical consultations. Carrying this sequence on, we reach the most general level which is about the general properties of spoken communication, and includes such general ideas as turn-taking, adjacency pairs, preference orders, accounts and accounting, narrative conventions and many others not dealt with here, which seem utilisable for explaining speech interaction in a wide range of circumstances.

A final difference relates to the researcher's **accountability**. Those who do thematic analysis typically work on a large data set, even if it is drawn from only a few tens of interviews. Considerations of space usually prevent them sharing much of their analysis with their readers. Hence readers have to take much of it on trust. The linguistic analysis has demonstrated the crucial importance both of what is said by the interviewer and what was said previously by the interviewee for understanding any particular utterance by the interviewee. Whereas those who conduct surveys with forced choice questionnaires usually tell readers what the questions were, thematic analysts rarely show what it was that the interviewer said which shaped the interviewee's response.

By contrast, conversation analysts, and others of similar ilk, typically work intensively on small segments of data and provide their readers with all the data which they have analysed. I have followed this practice here. You may not agree with my analysis, but since I have provided you with all the data you are in a position to analyse it yourself and come to your own conclusions. My analysis may not be valid, but at least it is objective.

Chapter 9 Activity Analysing data from a focus group (Transcript 9.3)

This Activity shows some of the differences between the two party-speech exchange system of the one-on-one qualitative interview and the orchestrated, multi-party speech exchange system of the focus group: 'orchestrated' because there is a facilitator to allocate turns when this is necessary, to designate topics and so on . The activity asks you to try analysing a short extract from a focus group. This was actually run as a telephone conference. Participants were not in face-to-face contact with each other. This doesn't seem to show itself in the extract here, though elsewhere in the transcript it does. The speakers are older, housebound women and the general topic is their experience of hospitalisation.

For the George transcript, we got some mileage out of imagining George having a problem of giving an account of himself while occupying a stigmatising status. For this transcript I suggest you think of these women as having the general problem associated with complaining. If one makes a complaint which others find unjustified, one produces oneself as having the character of an ingrate or whinger, or as a busybody if the complaint is on behalf of someone else. And if one reports not making a complaint when others think one should, then one characterises oneself as a sucker, a coward or someone of unreasonable fortitude, or as uncaring or irresponsible if the complaint would have been on behalf of someone else. Thus either reporting oneself complaining, or reporting states of affairs which might be complained about, but were not, is hazardous for the character until one knows what other people think. Bear this in mind while you analyse the transcript.

I suggest you analyse it by coding utterances as 'speech acts'. Use your own vocabulary, but always to indicate what was *done* with the words: that is, what was accomplished by saying them, rather than trying to reconstruct what was in the minds of the women. Thus **3.10** is a self-characterisation – a self-commendation, perhaps.

Transcript 9.3   Extract from focus group for analysis in Chapter 9 Activity

Turn number and speaker	Utterances	Your notes
3.10 Mrs Bloor	When things are not right I'm afraid I'm not one to stand by. I'm a right busybody when I like ? .hhh	
3.11 Mrs Roberts	You have to be	
3.12 Mrs Bloor	So when the poor old thing couldn't feed herself I called the nurse over and told her straight [0.5]	
3.13 Mrs Farmer	You could starve to death [in that place]	
3.14 Mrs Roberts	[no one gives you] hhh any help if you can't get your food down [you]	

Transcript 9.2 (*continued*)

Turn number and speaker	Utterances	Your notes
3.15 Mrs Farmer	[I] didn't get a proper feed 'til the Chaplin came and helped me mm?	
3.16–3.18	[talk establishing Chaplin's name and character]	
3.19 Mrs Bloor	So I told her straight =	
3.20 Mrs Farmer	= Quite right too Minnie	
3.21 Mrs Bloor	I don't think that was out of turn [do you?]	
3.22 Mrs Roberts	[They] need telling a thing or two. Like dead man's meals, like the way you have to eat what someone before you ordered, in your bed before you. I told them off about [that]	
3.23 Mrs Bloor	[That's] right Mavis [but]	
3.24 Mrs Roberts	[My] husband used to say. 'you're a terror when your dander's up =	
3.25 Mrs Bloor	= But it's all right for us because we can stand up for ourselves. But there are some of the old dears that get in there, well they really don't know what time of day it is, really, so they really get put upon (0.5) hhh.	
3.26 Mrs Farmer	Like the one I was telling you about when the nurse gave her her pills and she dropped them and she said 'O well I don't suppose it matters' and walks AWAY =.	
3.27 Facilitator	= Did you do anything about that ?	
3.28 Mrs Bloor	If the doctor gives you the pills, you're SUPPO :::: SED to have them. Isn't that RIGHT ? [2.0]	

3.29 Mrs Farmer	Well, you don't like to interfere too: much do you I mean .hhhh [0.5]
3.30 Mrs Bloor	No you don't want to be too:: interfering
3.31 Mrs Roberts	Not if it isn't any of your business [you don't]
3.32 Mrs Bloor	[no you]don't. That's VERY true.
3.33 Someone	.hhhhhhhh [5.0]
3.34 Mrs Bloor	And some of them in there, that has sort of [0.2] lost their marbles, they complain about every little thing [0.2]
3.35 Mrs Roberts	Every lit::tle thing.

[ ] means overlapping speech; [0.5] means 0.5 of a second silence; (5.0) means 5 seconds silence; = means that there was no gap between one utterance and another . Upper case as in SUPPO:::SED indicates words spoken more loudly than the surrounding speech . Colons as in SUPPO:::SED indicates that the preceding sound was prolonged; .hhhh is a sounded in-breath; hhhhh., is a sounded out-breath ; ? indicates an interrogative tone. For other transcribing symbols not used here see Sacks, Schegloff and Jefferson (1974), or Heritage (1984).

9.6 Summary

This chapter looked at three different ways of analysing the results of qualitative interviews, while making some comparisons with the analysis of data generated from forced choice questionnaires. One mode of analysis was to treat the interviews as evidence of matters of fact. Some such matters might be verified by reference to other sources. But where sources conflict this leaves analysts with a problem of deciding which source to believe. Matters of 'self-knowledge' such as opinions, or feelings, might be regarded as unverifiable or incorrigible in principle, though some traditions in psychology and sociology credit researchers with insights into the inner lives of subjects, superior to those of the subjects themselves.

Instead of regarding what people say in interviews as reports on matters of fact, analysts may analyse interviews as evidence of how people understand their experiences or of what things 'mean to them'. Thematic analysis makes the assumption that a well-conducted qualitative interview opens a window on what interviewees usually and generally think, such that themes identified in interview talk can be regarded as standing for the way thoughts are organised in people's minds, or for the sense-making procedures they use in their everyday lives. Linguistic analyses, particularly those inspired by ethnomethodology, do not make this assumption. Analysts of this kind start from the assumption that an interview is an interview, and that studying interview talk tells us first about how people 'talk-up' an interview, and how they realise themselves as personalities or characters within its confines, and second tells us how, more generally, people use language to create forms of social organisation. The difference between these two approaches is also an important theme in Chapters 10 and 11.

Further reading

I used the term 'thematic analysis' to cover analyses with the objective of finding out what was and generally is in the minds of interviewees. It is not necessarily the term you will find in other books, where instead of themes researchers write about the interviewees' perspectives, social theories, typification schemes, world views, schemes of relevance, interpretive frameworks or use other words implying that people's minds have structures and that these are knowable from analysing what they say in an interview. What I have called 'thematic analysis' is not restricted to the analysis of interviews, but is also applied to talk in non-interview situations and in the analysis of texts (see Chapter 11). Strauss (1990) and Miles and Huberman (1994) demonstrate a much wider range of approaches than was possible in this chapter.

Most modern texts on the analysis of qualitative interviews are strongly influenced by the ideas of linguistic analysis. Silverman (1993) is a very accessible text, linguistically sensitive without having a through-going commitment to Conversation Analysis. Silverman (1997) is a companion volume of papers demonstrating different kinds of qualitative data analysis.

Conversation Analysis now has a huge literature. Hutchby and Wooffitt (1998) is a comprehensive introduction. Membership categorisation analysis (MCA) is a common adjunct of CA. It is dealt with in Chapter 11. The term discourse analysis is sometimes used for something very similar to Conversation Analysis, though with roots more firmly grounded in linguistics; for this see Brown and Yule (1983) or Stubbs (1983). Levinson (1983) is again similar though called *Pragmatics*. Sometimes, however, the term 'discourse' is used as a modern synonym for what would previously have been called 'ideology'. Discourse analysis in this sense uses procedures and makes assumptions much more like those I have called 'thematic analysis', particularly where the enterprise is called 'critical discourse analysis' – for example, van Dijk (1993). Similar remarks can be made about narrative analysis. In CA narrative analysis is an interest in the linguistic devices people use for telling stories and depicting characters, and for the uses people make of storytelling to accomplish interactional effects, such as entertaining people or making complaints. But the term may also refer to the idea that the way people tell stories in one context is evidence about how they think in general: for example Holloway and Jefferson (2000); or that the stories they tell are elements of an ideology which oppresses them (Mumby 1993). See also Chapter 11, section 11.1.

There are several computer software packages for analysing qualitative data, including *Ethnograph 5.0, QSR NVivo 1.2,* and *QSR N5* which used to be NUD*IST). All can be viewed at <www.scholari.co.uk>.Bazeley and Richards (2000) is a handbook for using QSR NVivo.

10 Observing Naturally Occurring Events

By the end of this chapter, you will:

- Understand the idea of ecological or naturalistic validity and how studying naturally occurring events are an attempt to achieve this...
- ... but recognise that researchers will vary in their assumptions of what is there to be naturalistically observed
- Understand that a picture of things as they 'naturally' are, is produced by a large number of selection decisions and interpretations on behalf of the researcher
- Know the problems qualitative researchers have in making any empirical generalisations
- Know how the ideas of theoretical sampling and theoretical generalisation feature in some qualitative research
- Have practised observation of naturally occurring events.

And know the meaning of the following terms:
breaching (or disruption) experiment ■ constant comparison ■ ecological (or naturalistic) validity ■ ethnography/ethnographic research ■ generalising within the case ■ grounding theory in data/grounded theory ■ multiple realities ■ observer expectancy effects ■ participant and non-participant observation research ■ reflexivity ■ Rashomon effect ■ sympathetic bias (or over-rapport)

10.1 Introduction

Experiments, surveys and interviews are all events set up by researchers to generate research data. They attract the criticism that they give only a distorted picture of what usually goes on – for example, that:

- Experimental situations are so unlike 'real life' that their results cannot easily be generalised beyond the experiment (Chapter 2, section 2.10), and that this problem persists even when attempts are made to make experiments more naturalistic (Chapter 3, sections 3.2, 3.3). Experimentalists have their own response to this charge (Chapter 3, section 3.5).

- The opinions, attitudes and so on 'discovered' in surveys using forced choice questionnaires are actually conjured up and brought into being by the questions the researchers ask and the way they ask them (Chapter 8, section 8.4).
- The data generated by an interview are just a record of the interaction between interviewer and interviewee, with only a doubtful relationship to whatever it was the interview was supposed to be about (Chapter 9, section 9.4).

An antidote prescribed for these problems is for researchers to study 'naturally occurring' situations which would have happened whether researchers had been around or not, and which are as influenced as little as possible by research activity. The case in favour of naturalistic observation is often expressed using the terms **naturalistic** or **ecological validity**, meaning that a study will be valid insofar as it accurately captures how things would be irrespective of research activity. There is a close analogy here with the critique of studies of animal behaviour under conditions of captivity, coming from researchers who prefer to study animals in their natural habitats.

Research based on naturalistic observation is often called **field research** or **ethnographic research**, though the latter is also used for studies combining observation with qualitative interviews. The term **ethnographic data** is often a general-purpose term for any qualitative data. However, sometimes the term 'ethnographic' is used in contradistinction to 'ethnomethodological', the former attempting to study meaning by getting into the minds of the people observed, the latter looking for what it is that makes actions meaningful. This is the distinction between thematic analysis and conversation analysis in Chapter 9 (see also Chapter 1, section 1.4). In the social sciences what observers most usually 'observe' is speech and other communicative behaviours, so the analysis of data collected from naturally occurring events is often very similar to the analysis of interviews as described in Chapter 9.

Researchers cannot simply go and look at 'naturally occurring' events and write an account of these 'telling it like it's at'. Their report will be a report by them, based on what was observed by them, excluding what they did not observe, informed by the sense they made of their observations. If the results of surveys are shaped by the way the questions are asked, and the results of interviews reflect the performance of the interviewer then, equally, the results of a study involving the observation of naturally occurring events will be determined by the way the researcher did the observing. Various aspects of this are discussed in this chapter.

An observation study is as much a process of *excluding* data as accumulating them and entails selection decisions at many levels (Figure 10.1). This is true of all kinds of research, of course, though the selection decisions may be made in different ways and at different stages. At the end of a study involving observation there will be a research report which is, among other things, a result of making such selection decisions. There is an important general question:

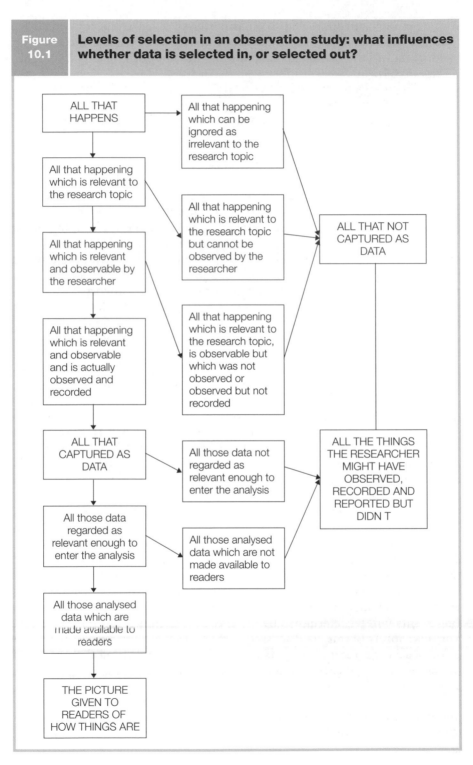

Figure 10.1 Levels of selection in an observation study: what influences whether data is selected in, or selected out?

Are the findings of the study the result of the observer collecting sufficient relevant data, and excluding all irrelevant data, *or* did the study result from the exclusion of relevant data which, had it been included, would have produced a different picture of how things 'naturally are'?

There is something analogous here to the problem of non-response in survey research (Chapter 4, section 4.9), though in a more acute form.

10.2 Outside looking in or inside looking out

All those who favour naturalistic observation would agree, first, that this is sometimes the only way of studying some kinds of people and some kinds of activities, *and* second, that it is a way of doing research where the researcher makes the minimal possible impact on what is being researched, and hence can claim to be giving an account of what ordinarily happens: that is, an account with a high level of ecological validity.

Beyond this, researchers divide. One way of getting at the distinction is to consider whether the appropriate position for the observer is as an insider looking out or an outsider looking in.

Insiders looking out

To claim to study things naturalistically is to make some assumptions about how things 'naturally' are. Chapter 9 dealt with the analysis of qualitative interviews making a distinction between two very different ways of looking at the same interview data which derive from radically different views about the nature of social phenomena. What I called 'thematic analysis' proceeded from the assumption that social events happen as they do because the participants have particular ways of understanding the world. 'Actor theories', 'interpretive frameworks', 'perspectives', 'typification schemes' and many other terms, are used to express this idea of 'ways of understanding'. From this point of view 'how things naturally are' is people interpreting their experiences in terms of their particular ways of understanding and acting on the basis of this. The answer to the question 'Why did s/he do that?' is 'because this is what the situation meant to her/him'. It is a matter of research interest as to how and why people acquired such ways of understanding. These are usually attributed either psychologically – to their upbringing or to the more immediate psycho-dynamic context of a family or an organisation – or sociologically – to their being in a particular location in a social structure which shapes their experience and understandings: for example, being female in a patriarchal world.

But here the first target for research is finding out what these ways of understanding are. For this reason many researchers regard it as sensible to combine naturalistic observation with qualitative interviews. They observe people to see what they *do*. They interview them to discover *why*. This is where the 'why' question is answered in terms of meaning, and 'meaning' means what must have been in the mind of the person in order for them to have done what they did. Some regard the approach to interviews here as 'naturalistic' in the sense that interviews should be more like conversations or chats, and the relationship between interviewer and interviewee modelled on a friendship relationship (Chapter 8, section 8.5).

This is research which seeks explanation through understanding, where 'understanding' means being able to see the world from the point of view of the people being studied. So if what is important is the way some groups of people understand the world, then why not join them, learn their ways of speaking and acting, experience their experiences, learn to understand things as they understand them and then report back as a 'member' of the category of persons being studied? This is what I mean by 'observing as an insider looking out'. It is best exemplified by participant observation research: joining in with the activities being researched (see section 10.4). The justification for this approach may not entirely rest on it producing explanations for what happens in social life. It may be extended with the argument that the purpose of such research is also to foster human under-standing by enabling readers of the research to understand things from the viewpoints of others (see also Chapter 12).

All this assumes that the important topics for research are found in what members know or experience which a researcher can discover by learning to be a member. But there are limits to members' knowledge, as discussed below.

Outsiders looking in

I conducted research on educational assessment in participant observation roles as lecturer, as an examiner and as a chair of an examination board (Gomm 1986). To preserve confidentiality (Chapter 13) I anonymised tran-scripts and field notes of events in which I had participated so that I became 'examiner 3' or 'lecturer 1'. I often found it very difficult to work out who was me in a transcript without looking this up in my secret code book, although there was rarely any difficulty in deciding what roles people were playing. Even if I did know who was me, it was no good relying on my experience of having been there and done that to answer questions such as 'why did you say that, then?' or 'what did that mean to you at the time?' The only way I could find of explaining what was going on was to look at the data from an outside point of view and treat myself as just one among others all equally mysterious. Similarly, I was the interviewer in the transcript with George (Chapter 9). I might have been interviewed after the interview. I could have answered questions as to what I was trying to achieve, how I thought the interview went, what it felt like to do the interview, what kind of person George was and so on. But it would have been pointless to ask me how my performance produced what George said, when he said it and how that produced particular versions of George. For that I would have had to look at the transcript and analyse it as if I had been 'any old interviewer' (Chapter 9, section 9.4). And, of course, had I been interviewed thus, I would have given answers to interviewers' questions, shaped by the way the questions were asked of me.

For many social activities people do not know how they do them, or notice what they have done. This is why it is often held that in participant observation research the early stages of learning to be a member are the important ones (Schutz 1964). What experienced members do without thinking about is strange and difficult for the newcomer. And because it is strange and difficult it is noticeable. For example, as a newly appointed teacher I felt thoroughly inadequate in the face of my more experienced colleagues' ability to give definitive sounding descriptions of pupils. Pupils seemed so diverse and individual to me. But I soon learned the trick. It was to locate any particular pupil in terms of two dimensions, one running from bright to dull, and another running from well-behaved to naughty (Becker 1952). There were some helpful local phrases for doing this, for example 'puddings' were good girls who weren't very bright, 'bitches' were bright but unruly girls. Had I not been a sociologist I would probably not have noticed the mechanics of this. Even though I was a sociologist I soon fell into the same habits of description without thinking much about what I was doing. On these considerations the *last thing* a naturalistic observer should want to do is to become a fully experienced member of the group who are being studied, because fully experienced members are the kinds of people who take for granted the things which researchers ought to regard as puzzling.

Many anthropologists have remarked that it is much more difficult to do anthropology in your own society than in one exotic to you, because doing so requires an effort to unlearn what you have learned to take for granted (Barnard 1994: 154). Garfinkel (1967:9) makes the same point by saying that it is the purpose of ethnomethodology to render the mundane anthropologically strange. Dr Spock in the first series of *Star Trek* is only one of a large number of aliens and androids who serve to make what humans take for granted look anthropologically strange in sci-fi works. As you saw from the exercise in conversation analysis in Chapter 9, section 9.4, ethnomethodologists adopt an outsider's point of view in doing naturalistic observation on the assumption that it wouldn't help the analyst to experience the interview as if they were George or as if they were me. That probably wouldn't have been possible, and anyway, it would be impossible to know whether one person had indeed re-created another person's experience in their own mind.

The outsider-looking-in position is preferred by those who assume *both* that it is important to study naturally occurring events *and that* the people involved would not themselves be able to provide information for a satisfactory explanation, and hence where becoming one of them would not be enlightening. This includes psychologists studying, for example, group dynamics or children's play through one-way mirrors or on video tape.

10.3 Windows of observation, sampling and generalisation in observation research

To avoid a horrible mix of metaphors, put the notion of insiders looking out and outsiders looking in to one side, and try thinking about observation research in terms of there being a 'window' of observation: a set of circumstances making it possible for observers to observe some things but not others. An important issue is how far what is *un*observable can be legitimately inferred from what is observable, sometimes called **generalising within the case** (Gomm, Hammersley and Foster 2000). For example, what does knowing what someone does when we can see them tell us about what they do when we can't see them?

As Figure 10.2 suggests, the duration of a study is important in shaping the window for observation. For example, a large number of ethnographic studies of schools purport to explain why some categories of pupils do better than others in national examinations, attributing this to the way teachers treat different kinds of pupils in different ways: working class as opposed to middle class, girls as opposed to boys, black and Asian pupils as opposed to white. But the groups studied have often been in the lower school years, and the researchers left the scene long before the pupils studied received their results in 16+ examinations. Thus what was observed to happen in earlier school years was used as a basis for explaining what was assumed to be going to happen in the future – what was actually happening to pupils some years older than those studied. This had particularly embarrassing consequences for feminist

Figure 10.2	The window of observation in observation research

| BEFORE All that happened before which is relevant to the topic of the research and is unobservable | What is directly observable | AFTER All that happens afterwards which is relevant to the topic of the research and is unobserved |
| | DURING What is going on at the same time as the research which is unobservable or unobserved | |

researchers who had conducted studies of lower school pupils explaining that the ways that teachers treated girls led to girls achieving less than boys at 16+. By the time the girls they had studied were 17, girls nationally were achieving more than boys (Foster, Gomm and Hammersley 1996).

One way of avoiding this problem entirely is for the researcher to disclaim any interest in what comes before or after the period of study and to claim merely to give an accurate account of happenings during the research period. Ethnomethodologists assume that the past is what is created as the past in the present – for example by people telling stories about the past for some immediate purpose (Chapter 9, section 9.4), while the future is something which people appeal to in the present as a way of justifying their actions as actions which will 'lead to' or 'avoid' some future happening. All the 'past' and all the 'future' *relevant to the study* are observable.

Timing and duration shape the study as a **time sample**. What is an appropriate time sample depends on the topic of the research. If the topic implicates a long-term causal sequence such as the events leading up to differences in educational achievement at 16+ then that suggests the need for a series of time samples, perhaps one each for 11 years for the same cohort of pupils. If the topic were 'pupil–teacher interaction in 1999 in year 9 of an inner urban comprehensive school', and the study was conducted only in the summer term, there might be questions as to how typical the summer term was of other terms in the school for the year 9 pupils.

It is the size and the shape of the window of observation which provides the basis for drawing general conclusions from the study. This idea is elaborated in Table 10.1. This distinguishes between 'time', 'place' and 'people' sampling. But any decision made on one of these dimensions will have implications for the others.

Of all the dimensions in Table 10.1 the one which generates the most discussion is what I have called the 'angle of view' of the researcher. This includes discussion of the relative merits of participant as against non-participant observation.

10.4 Participant observation and non-participant observation research

Covert electronic surveillance apart, there are some areas of social life which can be studied naturalistically only by the researcher becoming a member of an otherwise closed social group; as a participant observer. These include stigmatised and deviant groups and elite groups where the presence of an outsider would be so disruptive that observing things 'as normal' would be impossible.

Many studies of deviant gangs and religious cults have been conducted by researchers who join up as members. Sometimes such participation has been *covert* or known about only by a few insiders and not the rest. Covert participant observation has the difficulty that researchers cannot ask the kinds of questions they might want to ask for fear of 'blowing their cover'

TABLE 10.1	Sampling, representativeness and generalisations from observation research		
What shapes the window of observation?	**Examples (from ethnography in the sociology of education)**	**Limits on confident generalisations from sample observations**	
Time: The historical moment of study Questions: What changes and what stays the same? How and in what ways is what happens at one historical moment representative of what happens at others previously or later?	In what ways do the earlier ethnographies of schools such as Hargreaves (1967) or Lacey (1975) provide insights into the life of schools in the 2000s?	What is observed at one time cannot form the basis for confident generalisations about what has or will happen at another time, unless either the observations constituted a statistically representative sample of some unchanging phenomenon, or the researcher can specify the characteristics of time, place and people which caused the events to happen, and can specify where else in time these same circumstances will occur (Chapter 3, section 3.5).	
Time: The duration of the research study Question: How and in what ways was the time period of the study representative of other time periods relevant to the topic of the study?	How far does a study of one year in the life of a year 9 class represent their 9 years of compulsory education?		
Time: Timing of observations within the study Question: How and in what ways were the episodes observed representative of the episodes not observed?	Several American studies of 'progressive' primary school education in England were conducted by observation Tuesday to Thursday. They gave a very misleading picture of laissez faire practices, because they missed the sessions on Monday when tasks were set for pupils and the sessions on Fridays when the pupils' progress was reviewed (Berlak et al., 1975)	What is observed at one time cannot easily be attributed as caused by something unobserved happening at an earlier time, nor as the cause of something which will happen in the future, without knowledge of causation derived from experimental (Chapters 2 and 3) or natural experimental (Chapter 5) research.	
Place: Social location of the study Question: How and in what ways is this location representative and unrepresentative of other locations?	How far would a study of interaction in a boys' public boarding school throw light on interaction in a custodial institution for young offenders?	What is observed in one location cannot form the basis for confident generalisations about what will happen in other locations, unless either the observations constitute a statistically representative sample of the population of locations to which the generalisation is addressed, or the observer can specify the characteristics of time, place and people which caused the events to happen and can specify	
Place: Settings within the location studied Question: How and in what ways were the settings actually observed representative or unrepresentative of the settings not observed?	Can observations of English lessons and Maths lessons stand as representative of all lessons?		

Place: Angle of view within the settings observed Question: Would an observer differently located physically and/or socially have produced essentially the same description?	Would a researcher playing the role of a teacher observe more or less or differently compared with an observer sitting in the back of the class? Would either provide the same data as a fly-on-the-wall video camera?	that much the same will happen in another location with the same constellation of factors (Chapter 3, section 3.5). What is observed from one location cannot form the basis of a confident generalisation about what would be observable from a different location, without some additional evidence.
People: Social composition of the location studied Question: How in its social composition is the research location representative or unrepresentative of other locations?	Are studies of ethnic differences in pupil–teacher interaction in schools with large percentages of ethnic minority pupils relevant to understanding ethnic differences in pupil–teacher interaction in schools with small percentages of minority ethnic pupils (Gomm and Hammersley 2001)?	What is observed to happen among some people, cannot form the basis for a confident generalisation as to what would happen among some other group of people, *unless* the people are a statistically representative sample of the population to which the generalisation is addressed, *or* unless the researcher can specify the time, place and people characteristics which caused what was observed to happen, and can specify that much the same is likely to happen where this constellation of factors occurs elsewhere (Chapter 3, section 3.5).
People: Characteristics of those observed Question: How representative or unrepresentative of those unobserved are those observed?	How far will what was observed of these 15 teachers in this school also be true of these 35 teachers who were not observed?	
People: Characteristics of those most closely studied within research location Question: How representative or unrepresentative of those who are less frequently or less intensively observed are those who are more frequently or more intensively observed?	How far will what was true for a set of detailed case studies of 25 pupils, stand for what was true of 100 pupils observed but not made the topic of case studies? How far will the comments of a handful of pupils who have a close relationship to the observer throw light on the understandings of the pupils less close to the researcher?	

(Patrick 1973). Rosenhan's pseudo-patient experiment (1973 and see Chapter 3, section 3.2), involved infiltrating 'sane' people as patients into various American mental hospitals to see what would happen to them. This could not have been done overtly. When they asked questions of staff and noted down the responses, this was treated as a symptom of their insanity rather than blowing their cover, but this is a rather odd example. Covert research has the advantage that the researcher can be fairly sure that what he or she observes is not a Hawthorne effect (see Chapter 2, section 2.6) created as a reaction to the subjects' knowledge of being under observation. It raises important ethical issues which will be discussed in Chapter 13.

For anthropologists, becoming a member of a social group exotic to them is both necessary and difficult. The sociologist already has a huge stock of cultural knowledge to draw on in making sense of observations even in rather unusual situations in his or her own society. This can lead the sociologist to take for granted what could be a matter for investigation. By contrast, the anthropologist working in a culture exotic to him or her has to start from scratch. The only way of doing this is by immersion in the life of the people studied. Typically the field-work for an anthropological study is measured in years rather than in months. The trauma of 'culture shock' is not uncommon. My own experiences of this as an anthropologist on the Kenya coast is best described as the experience of being an adult baby; a baby because one simply did not know what was going on, an adult because one knew one was socially incompetent. Coping with this was largely through dreaming up credible stories as to what people were doing and why. I found most of these initial theories to be wrong, but I cannot guarantee that some of the ideas adopted as psychological coping strategies early in the research did not survive to distort the end results (Gomm 1976). Total immersion may be the best way to enter into another social world as a questioning stranger, but it can certainly be distressing.

Researchers may use pre-existing memberships to do participant observation research. Roth's study of a tuberculosis sanatorium (1963, 1974) was done while he was a patient there. There are many studies of schools conducted by teachers and of health care settings by nurses. There are some situations in which some researchers can never participate as members or quasi-members. Males are excluded from all female groups. Lay people cannot take the participant role of a doctor or nurse. Participant observation studies of schools have by necessity been conducted by researchers occupying the role of teacher rather than pupil, even where pupil behaviour is the topic of the research.

Where researchers place a strong emphasis on the need to understand the experiences of those they research, they may argue that only researchers with particular social characteristics and previous experiences are qualified to do the research: for example, that only black women can understand black women (Collins 1990) or only people with disabilities can understand what it is like to be disabled (Beresford and Evans 1999). The end-point of this argument is that the only person who can understand anyone is that person themself and leads to research which consists of the researcher 'ghosting' the autobiographies of those studied, or of the researcher's own autobiography being presented as a research report (Stanley 1992). If you are willing to accept that an autobiography is based on a series of naturally occurring events then autobiographies must count as naturalistic observation research (see also Chapter 11, sections 11.6, 11.7).

Against the assumption of the need for empathetic understanding, it may be argued that the more understandings researchers share with those they research the more likely it is that their research will be restricted to being a re-description of a rather narrow, local and unsociological way of understanding the world and that they will come to share the same biases and prejudices as those they research; what Miller (1953) called **over-rapport** or Becker (1967) called **sympathetic bias** (Lidz 1989).

Participant observation research requires the researcher to find a role to occupy in the setting studied. This is at least so that they can fade into the background and not disrupt 'things as usual' except in the ways that ordinary members influence each other. It may be so that the researcher can experience what it is like to do the kinds of things done by those researched. Some settings naturally include people standing around with clip boards. Hospitals and clinics have an abundance of such roles. There is not much 'participation' to being a participant observer in these circumstances.

Finding a role in other settings can be much more challenging. Laud Humphreys (1975) studying male homosexual liaisons in public toilets took on the role of 'watch queen': the person who keeps look-out in return for satisfying his voyeuristic tendencies. This absolved Humphreys from actually engaging in homosexual acts. Julia O'Connell Davidson (O'Connell Davidson and Layder 1994) in her study of prostitutes and their clients conducted her research from the position of the prostitutes' receptionist (see also Chapter 13). As these examples indicate, there can be dangers in being a participant observer, including those of being drawn into illegal activity. Both Patrick (1973) and Yablonsky (1967) ran close to breaking the law in their research with gangs of young men, and Yablonsky narrowly avoided being seriously injured when gang-members found out about him being a researcher.

The role occupied as a participant shapes what is and what is not available for study. For example, Dingwall's study of health visitor education (1977) was conducted with him playing the role of a health visitor student. This was just after males were permitted to become health visitors. In his student role his experience was close to that of the other students. But because he played the role of a student he was usually excluded from activities privy to staff. Something which Dingwall purports to describe is the way health visitor tutors and other staff *view* the world. His main resource for this was listening to staff talk to students in lectures and tutorials.

My own study of health visitor education (1986, 2000d) was conducted by participant observation as a lecturer, an examiner and a chair of examination board. These were roles I occupied anyway. Whereas the staff world was closed to Dingwall it was open to me, and vice versa. From my participant role I did not feel able to say anything at all about what it was like to be a health visitor student. I found that the worldview of staff *conveyed by staff to students* several years later and in different colleges was remarkably similar to that in Dingwall's account. But I could also say that what staff said when students weren't around was something different again. Thus it could hardly be said that what Dingwall had discovered was the way staff *viewed and understood* the world. Interestingly what health visitor tutors said to me *in interview* was very similar to what they told the students. The difference between this and what they said to me as a colleague and to each other gave me a healthy sense of scepticism with regard to the capacity of interviews to capture what people 'really think' (see Chapter 9, section 9.3). Dingwall's research is a good piece of ethnographic research, but it has to be read as research conducted from a particular observation point, as indeed does my own study.

A common experience for an overt participant observer is that the people researched make efforts to direct the researcher's interpretations, usually with the aim of being helpful. I can almost guarantee that when I visit a school or a clinic or a youth club in a research role, someone will tell me that today is 'not a typical day' with the implication and that I should not rely on what I am seeing, but listen to them instead (see also Chapter 9, section 9.4 on accounts). In addition, participant observation researchers often make closer relationships with some of the people they are studying than with others. There is a danger, then, that the researcher comes to see events through the eyes of only some participants and with their prejudices. Much of William Foot Whyte's classic ethnographic study *Street Corner Society* (1981) is 'through the eyes' of Doc, his key informant and there are some indications that Doc was not entirely truthful (1981, see also *Journal of Contemporary Ethnography* 1992). Labov (1973) warns that the kinds of people who make close relationships with researchers are most unlikely to be typical of the category of people being researched. Similarly, making close relationships with some participants, will often restrict a researcher's relationships with others. In my research on an island off the Kenya coast, before I realised it, I was 'captured' by one of two political factions in the village, who housed me in their part of the village and gave me an honorific kinship title in their clan. This made it extremely difficult to interact with the other faction. Being co-opted to one faction or another is a common problem in evaluation research (see Chapter 12, section 12.3):

> [Tenge] said something to the effect that even if I pulled my weight as a worker I would still as an evaluation researcher have been 'beamed in' by the bosses to check up on them. So that 'this would go against the trust we have to have in each other'. [Tenge] said that they would prefer to select their own evaluation researcher who 'would stand up for the staff against the "suits"' [management].
>
> (Note on negotiations to operate as participant observer evaluation researcher in drugs project: 1989)

Participating can get in the way of observing. It usually rules out using audio or video. If the medium of recording is written notes, it is sometimes difficult both to participate and take adequate notes. Hammersley, for example, found that he had to make frequent trips to the toilet in order to write up his notes of observations of staffrooms, with a cover story about a medical condition (personal communication). Note-making entails on-the-hoof analysis with split-second decisions on what to record and what to ignore. Most of what is preserved as a record of what happened will be that field note. With electronic recording researchers do have to make decisions about where to site the recording apparatus, when to switch it on and when to switch it off, but electronic records can be reviewed at leisure. As against the benefits of the hard data produced through electronic recording, there are the disadvantages that this is likely to be more disruptive of 'things as normal'. In their video-tapes of market traders Pinch and Clark (1986) found examples of traders orienting to the fact of being recorded, with jokes about selling goods 'as advertised on TV'. However, as this example shows, some at least of the disruptive effects of electronic recording produce data themselves, so that the effects of recording can be seen in the data. This is less likely where note-taking is the medium of recording. Electronic recording also limits the angle of view of the observer to that in the view-finder of the camera, or within the range of the microphone.

10.5 Representativeness in qualitative research

Table 10.1 frequently uses the term 'representative'. There are two main kinds of representativeness, statistical or empirical (Chapter 4) and theoretical (Chapter 3, section 3.5).

Statistical representativeness and empirical or statistical generalisation

Chapter 4 dealt in detail with the idea of *statistical* representativeness. What is statistically representative depends on the definition of the 'population' of which a sample is supposed to be representative. Typically those who do naturalistic observation study smallish, naturally occurring groups of people, who for this reason are unlikely to be a statistically representative sample of a wider population. It is doubtful, for example, whether any school class of 15–16-year-olds in the UK is a representative sample of all 15–16 year olds in the population. However, if the 'population' is a population of classes (rather than of pupils) within a particular school then it is conceivable that a researcher might be able to select a statistically representative sample of these. Box 10.1 and Table 10.2 give an example of the systematic sampling of points in *time* to produce a statistically representative sample of teacher behaviour within a lesson.

BOX 10.1 Structured observation to produce numerical data from naturally occurring situations

There is no inherent contradiction between studying naturally occurring events and recording observations in numerical form. An observation schedule is just another kind of questionnaire. The one in Table 10.2 would ask the observer the question: 'At this point in time, was the teacher doing this, or this, or this …?' Using an observation schedule like this requires a great deal of preparation in deciding what will count as being an action of a particular kind. If the observations are made in real time, rather than in viewing a video, then using the schedule requires some split-second decisions to be made. As Scarth and Hammersley (1993) comment, this observation schedule is rather difficult to use, since it is difficult to decide what counts as a *question* and what as a *statement* when spoken questions do not come conveniently marked with a question mark.

Despite the difficulties of this particular example, the use of structured observation illustrates the merits of taking an outsider-looking-in approach. No insider would ever view a situation in this way, and no insider would ever be able to provide the information captured by a structured observation of this kind. From tape-recording lessons Hammersley and Scarth (1986) found that teacher talk made up over 90 per cent of all talk, but the teachers interviewed immediately after their lessons rarely gave estimates greater than 60 per cent. Again it is a common finding that males often believe females spoke more than males in a discussion or a lesson, when a transcript shows the opposite (Spender 1980).

Qualitative researchers are rarely able to study statistically representative samples. Nonetheless, they often write as if they had managed to do something like this, and in two ways. First, even the most qualitative of qualitative researchers still use quantitative terms such as; 'most', 'many', 'few' or 'rarely'. Such usage presupposes some '100 per cent' in terms of which something is 'many' or is 'rarely'. There are many ethnographic studies of classrooms which make claims that teachers *more often* do something with regard to that kind of pupil, or *rarely* do that with regard to this other kind. For example, that they pay less attention to certain types of pupils, or are more likely to criticise some other kinds (see Chapter 12, section 12.4). Most of these claims are made on the basis of *unstructured* observation, usually using written field notes rather than hard records (Foster, Gomm and Hammersley 1996: 107–38). These claims are rarely restricted just to the instances the researcher has observed, but are usually generalised to situations they have not observed. But, for this, it is really necessary both to have an accurate count and to count what is a representative sample of instances. Something we know about human beings is that they are impressively *incompetent* in making accurate judgements about the frequencies and durations of events (Sadler 1981), unless using some kind of aid to structure their observations. One of the routes through which expectancy

TABLE 10.2	Observation schedule for observing teachers' behaviour in the classroom	
Conversation	**Silence**	
QUESTIONS	**SILENT INTERACTION**	
Task Q1 recalling facts Q2 offering ideas, solutions (closed) Q3 offering ideas, solutions (open)	Gesturing Showing Marking	
Task supervision Q4 referring to supervision	Waiting	
Routine Q5 referring to routine matters		
STATEMENTS	STORY READING	
Task S1 of facts S2 of ideas	Not observed Not coded	
Task supervision S3 tolling child what to do S4 praising work or effort S5 feedback on work or effort	Adult interaction Visiting pupil Not interested	
Routine S6 providing information, direction S7 providing feedback S8 of critical control S9 of small talk	Silence	

The observer has a pad of sheets like this with boxes against each category. An observation is made at each 25 second sampling interval, the time being recorded in the appropriate box (Boydell and Jasman 1983: 104)

effects flaw the results of experiments is through biased time measurements *even when experimenters are using some aid to structure observation* (Barber and Silver 1965; Chapter 2, section 2.6). There is no reason to believe that researchers engaged in naturalistic observation are any better at judging frequencies and durations, *without observation aids*, than are experimental researchers when using such aids.

Much of anthropology consists of studies of a few families, perhaps in only one village, yet the write-up may be as if what was discovered would be true of a population numbering tens of thousands. This is a second way in which qualitative researchers behave as if their observations have the quality of statistical representativeness. The claim to generality is often indicated in the title of a book, such as 'The Swazi' or 'The Nuer'. Similarly many ethnographic studies in the sociology of education, while based on observations of a few classes in a particular school, imply general claims that the findings will apply to large categories of pupils in many different schools. Thus Paul Willis' (1977) *Learning to Labour* has the sub-title *How Working Class Kids Get Working Class Jobs* . It is actually a study of 12 pupils who seem to be very untypical of the other working-class pupils even in their own school. Mary Fuller's studies of the education of African-Caribbean girls seems to be based on a sample size of five in a single school (for example, Fuller 1982). Both were widely cited and influential studies and, irrespective of the authors' intentions, were taken as pictures of the general state of affairs in British education at the time they were published, and for some time afterwards.

The first column of Table 10.1 contains a series of questions. The empirical or statistical generalisation from small-scale to large-scale assumes that the researcher knows the answers for all these questions and that the answer to each is that what was observed was indeed representative of a larger population in a statistical sense. But qualitative researchers often do not have answers for these questions.

The Rashomon effect

Margaret Mead's *Coming of Age in Samoa* (1948) is the most famous of all ethnographic studies. Translated into at least 16 languages, it has never been out of print for the 70+ years since its publication in 1928. It gives a picture of adolescent life in Samoa as being without the difficulties associated with adolescence in America or Europe and of a free-and-easy pre-marital sexuality engaged in with the tacit consent of parents. *Coming of Age* was subjected to caustic criticism by Derek Freeman (1983), a researcher who had been conducting research in Samoa on and off since the 1930s. Freeman gives a picture of Samoan society in the 1930s (and earlier and later), as one with a strong puritan morality, severe punishments by parents of their children's pre-marital sexual adventures, chaperonage of young people to prevent sexual liaisons and rape as a common crime.

Putting the two studies side by side creates what Heider (1988) calls the *Rashomon Effect*. This is named after a film by the Japanese director Akria Korosawa, which presents several incompatible versions of the same events, leaving viewers wondering whether they have viewed a murder or a suicide, a seduction or a rape. As Heider says, when we read two accounts of the same society by two different anthropologists we often get incompatible pictures like this.

Looking again at Table 10.1, it shows that incompatible accounts are exactly what is to be expected when two ethnographic researchers look through different 'observation windows' by basing their research on different statistically unrepresentative samples of time, place and people, but both claiming that what they have discovered is true for the same larger aggregate of people, times and places: for example 'Samoa'. Or looking at Figure 10.1 we can see that this is to be expected when researchers or their circumstances, make different selection decisions influencing the inclusion and exclusion of particular kinds of data. Thus although Freeman's research was based on a rather larger population than Mead's, both were geographically restricted: Mead's on an island in Eastern Samoa, Freeman's on islands in Western Samoa, some hundreds of miles distant from each other. Mead's account is almost entirely based on what was told her by the group of 31 adolescent girls she befriended, only 12 of whom admitted to being sexually experienced. Freeman's is based on talking to adults remembering their adolescence. Both project their picture of Samoan society backwards into a past period when they could not have observed what happened, though Freeman draws much more extensively on what historical records were available. The duration of Freeman's research was longer. Freeman is a fluent speaker of Samoan; Mead was only a novice. Mead as a female had access to situations that Freeman could not access: vice versa for Freeman as a male. Neither could directly observe the sexual behaviour of young people. Although there are other reasons why Freeman's account of 'Samoan society' in the 1920s and 1930s seems more believable, some such discrepancies are inevitable if researchers study statistically unrepresentative bits of a society and then gross these up to stand for the society as a whole. The same might be said of school ethnographies where some study, of, say, some of the working-class pupils in a particular school is grossed up so that these pupils stand for most working-class pupils in most schools.

It is important to distinguish the Rashomon effect from the idea of *multiple realities*. The Rashomon effect arises when two different researchers make contradictory claims about what is represented as a single reality. Other researchers avoid the problem by saying that different participants will have different views as to what is going on , and that their account is either only from the viewpoint of one kind of participant, or that it is an attempt to document the contradictory views of many kinds of participants (for an example see Chapter 12, section 12.3). But there is still a potential for something like a Rashomon effect on a smaller scale, for it would be possible for two researchers to make incompatible claims about the viewpoint of the *same* group of people.

Theoretical representativeness, theoretical sampling and theoretical generalisation

Statistical representativeness is not the only kind of representativeness . In qualitative research, as in experimental research, **theoretical representativeness**, and **theoretical sampling** are much more important. Theoretical sampling entails a classification of phenomena into a set of types, such that what is observed can be classified as one type or another. For example Cicourel and Kitsuse (1963) believed that the process of schooling in the USA was becoming more bureaucratised with the careers of pupils being increasingly monitored and directed by specialist staff – counsellors – using tests and performance measures. To study this ethnographically, they did not choose a school of a common type but one of a type which they believed would be more common in the future: a large school with a specialist staff of counsellors doing what in other schools might have been done by classroom teachers. It was also a school taking pupils only from affluent backgrounds: Lakeside High. These characteristics could generate a classification of 8 types of school (Table 10.3)

The ethnographic study of Lakeside is of the processes through which pupils come to be classified into those who are expected to go to elite universities and do well there, and those who are labelled as less clever, and the way in which these definitions determined the educational treatment they received. Thinking of Lakeside as being only one type of school out of 8 possible types addresses some of the problems raised by Table 10.1. If the social composition of the school, if its size and the presence and absence of counsellors makes a difference to the way pupils are processed as successes and failures, then Lakeside cannot represent schools with a non-elite social composition, of a small size or without counsellors. Cicourel and Kitsuse are reticent about generalising their findings to schools of types other than the 'elite-large-with-counsellors' category. Any generalisation based on a study of Lakeside would be a theoretical generalisation. It would entail theorising that different ways of processing pupils were associated with the variables school size, elite or non-elite composition and presence and absence of specialist school counsellors and that, if this were so, the same kind of processing would occur in schools showing the same constellation of variables. As noted in Chapter 3, section 3.5, this is the kind of generalisation which makes an attempt to specify the circumstance under which it is claimed to be true.

Frequencies of occurrence are not important here. Lakeside might be the only school of its type in America, but it would be interesting nonetheless. And there might be no real schools in some of the other categories. That would make it impossible to study examples of the type, but they would still

TABLE 10.3	Theoretical sampling frame implied by Cicourel and Kitsuse's (1963) study of Lakeside High	
	Elite schools	
	Large	**Small**
With specialist counselling staff	Type 1 - Lakeside High studied by Cicourel and Kitsuse	Type 5
Without specialist counselling staff	Type 2	Type 6
	Non-Elite Schools	
With specialist counselling staff	Type 3	Type 7
Without specialist counselling staff	Type 4	Type 8

be theoretically interesting categories. Particle physics, for example, largely proceeds by generating theoretical frameworks which logically predict the existence of particles, and then trying to see whether they actually exist or not.

Sociological researchers often have limited choice over where and when they can do research, or do not develop a theoretical framework until long after the research is underway. In both these circumstances researchers do not so much use a theoretical sampling frame to select an example of a theoretical category to study; instead they decide where it is in such a framework that what they are already studying actually fits. In terms of conducting natural experiments (Chapter 5) researchers often do not start by asking 'where can I find the right naturally occurring constellation of variables for my experiment?' but by asking 'what constellation of variables is there here, and what natural experiment could I do with them?'

10.6 Structuring observation and grounding theory

Figure 10.1 includes the term 'relevant' several times. But qualitative researchers often begin research with the very broad question: 'what of interest is going on here?' As the research proceeds, and as they hit on something interesting, they ask more specific questions. This is somewhat grandly described as **progressive focusing**, though often it is a rather desperate attempt to reduce the complexity of what is observable to something which is manageable. In this process what are regarded as 'relevant data' shift throughout the research study, so that selection decisions made early may turn out to have been the wrong ones with regard to what was relevant at the end. A common response to this problem is to do 'vacuum cleaner' observation at the beginning in the hope of sucking up anything that might turn out to be relevant later. It is an old joke among ethnographers that one thing which is reliable is that 90 per cent of the data collected will turn out to be useless, but that you never know which 90 per cent until the end of the research.

The justification for starting research with a vague question again invokes the idea of ecological validity (see Section 10.1). The notion is that, to achieve ecological validity, it is necessary first to find out what things are like, and then to develop a theoretical framework to explain that – **grounding theory in data** – rather than assuming what things are like in advance and forcing observations to fit these preconceptions. It is, of course, impossible to begin research with no preconceptions, but there is still a persuasive argument that sometimes it is useful to start research with a more rather than a less open mind.

But at some stage in the research, researchers have to structure their observations to focus on what has emerged as relevant to the more specific questions driving their research. There are three closely linked reasons for this.

The first is that observations have to be observations of *something*, and the something they are observations of derives from a framework of ideas developed by the researcher. Thus it is necessary for researchers to develop clear criterial rules for what counts as an observation of this, and what of that. These are the same kind of 'coding' decisions dealt with in Chapter 9. Thus what counts as an instance of a teacher ignoring a pupil, or what counts as an instance of a male behaving in a patriarchal way?

Second, this is a way to control for the effects of the *observer's observation behaviour*. Any text on the psychology of perception details how attention is *selective* – people see only some of what there is to see; how perception is *constructive* – people tend to see what they expect to see; and how memory is *reconstructive* (see Chapter 6, Box 6.1) – people re-organise their memories in the light of subsequent happenings. This is the psychology lying behind the **experimenter expectancy effects**, discussed in Chapter 2. The potential for **observer expectancy effects** in naturalistic observation research is much greater than the equivalent in experimental research (Sadler 1991). Structuring the way observations are made can control for these to some extent. Again the problems are more acute where field notes are the medium of recording and coding decisions have to be made on the spot, rather than on an audio or video record where the same record can be analysed again and again in different ways (see also Box 10.1).

Third, adopting a structure for observation is the only way to test out the *theories* being developed by the researcher in this kind of research.

Theoretical sampling and constant comparison in a hospital study

As an example of observation structured for theory testing purposes, consider Anne Other's ethnographic study of hygiene procedures in a district general hospital (1999). This is an extremely important topic given the prevalence of hospital-acquired infections. Her initial impression was that the lower the status of the staff the more assiduously they followed the laid-down hygiene procedures, such as wearing gloves for patient contact, changing gloves in between patients or, alternatively, scrubbing up in between patients. Conversely, it seemed to her that the higher the status of the staff the less likely they were to do this. This was in contradistinction to the results of a recent test of knowledge administered by the infection control staff of the hospital studied which showed that the higher the status of the staff, the better their understanding of cross-infection. It seemed that those who knew most did least and those who knew least did most in the way of preventing cross-infection.

Initially this was just an impression, and one which was gained from observing situations in which there were many other variables at play, such as the busyness of the ward, the topicality of cross-infection as a problem, the recency of training events, wards running out of gloves (which was common), the composition of bedside congregations of staff, open multiple-bed wards and single-bed side wards and so on.

In these terms any observation of staff hygiene behaviour was a type in a very complex theoretical sampling frame (see section 10.5) , such that, for instance, what was observed with regard to health care assistants on the open wards under the observation of senior nurses might not be true of the behaviour of health care assistants working alone in single-bed side wards. Or what was true of day shift behaviour might not be true of night-shift behaviour. Thinking of the many variables which might influence hygiene behaviour gave Other a structure for her observations. She wanted observations to cover all of the diverse factors which might have been relevant, either to modify her theory, or to 'eliminate them from her enquiries'. The framework also indicated what had to be recorded in addition to the hygiene behaviour: personnel, place, time, audience and so on and whether the member of staff made physical contact with a patient or a patient's belongings. Most of the required observations cropped up without her having to go out of her way to look for them, though for some, such as nightshift observations and those in intensive care she had to make special arrangements. Over a three-month period she accumulated over 5,000 observations representing most of the important constellations of factors. This wasn't a statistically representative sample but the large number of observations made it possible to make frequency statements with some confidence. She wasn't claiming that all senior staff were negligent, merely that they were *more likely* to be negligent than junior staff. But for this kind of statement a large sample size is still necessary.

Only up to a point did her observations substantiate her initial impression. She did not find that senior staff were *less* likely than junior staff to follow hygiene procedures; merely that as a group there were no more likely to do so. This illustrates a tendency for people's impressions to mistake what is interesting for what most often happens:

> had I not attempted to produce quantitative data I might well have allowed my initial impressions to influence my later observations, noticing examples which supported them, and ignoring examples which did not.
>
> (Other 1999:4)

She also found that while some senior and some junior staff were lax, others were punctilious, so that her generalisations would not apply to whole categories of staff. The generalisation would not hold in the intensive care wards where everyone was careful to abide by hygiene protocols. Something which appeared to affect the hygiene behaviour of all staff was having an audience of other staff. All kinds of staff were less likely to follow the rules when no other staff seemed to be around to observe them. For these observations Other had to adopt strategies to avoid being seen to be observing. As she says:

> A reasonable case can be made that I under-recorded such instances, since in order to make observations of behaviour un-observed by staff,

I, as a member of staff, had to be around observing !

(Other 1999: 5)

Again, senior nursing staff sometimes made a great show of following hygiene procedures. This was either where a consultant was present, who nonetheless might not wash his hands between patients, or as part of a dressing-down of a junior member of staff for not following the procedures, or part of inducting new staff or students.

The structuring of observations in this way gave Other's theory abundant opportunities to be falsified. This forced her to move from the claim that senior staff were less likely to follow hygiene procedures to the claim that they were no more likely than junior staff to do so. Had she not structured her observations in that way her findings would have been vulnerable to the suggestions that what she observed could be put down to, say, the over-busy state of the ward at the time of the observation; but given the 'audience effect', staff were actually less likely to follow hygiene procedures when the ward was less busy. Or her findings might have been vulnerable to the suggestion that she observed only particularly punctilious juniors and particularly negligent seniors. But her observations included virtually every member of staff on the shifts she observed. She herself draws attention to the dangers of being biased:

> towards findings which show the great and the good as no better than they should be, and towards those which show inferiors as misunderstood and put-upon (Becker 1967).

(Other 1999: 15)

This is a particularly strong bias within sociology with its tradition of favouring 'underdogs' and drawing attention to social inequities (Hammersley 2000b). Hence Other felt it was particularly necessary to counteract the possibility of a personal bias of this kind.

The theory Other was testing was a low-level one without much explanatory power: a theory about what was actually happening. She found a partial explanation in listening to the senior nurses talk. From this it became evident that they believed that cross-infection was brought into the hospital by outsiders; patients, relatives and agency staff, and spread by the poor hygiene practices of junior staff. In this respect their ideas matched a folk model, common world-wide, attributing pollution, infection and other troubles to 'dirty' 'immoral' low status outsiders such as immigrants, or travelling people (Douglas 1966). On this Other remarks:

> it seemed important to make special efforts to substantiate the claim across a wide range of circumstances in the face of the possibility Mary Douglas' ideas about pollution, which seemed so seductively appropriate, were distorting the way in which I observed what was going on.

(Other 1999: 17)

This example illustrates much of what is referred to as the development of **grounded theory**. The theory, such as it is, is rooted in the data. The observation is structured by a theoretical sampling frame, which allows for a process of **constant comparison**. This involves the comparison of what happens under one set of circumstances with what happens under another set of circumstances different in only one regard: akin to imposing statistical control (Chapter 5, section 5.2). This allows inferences to be drawn as to what are the consequences of the differentiating factor. For example, when everything else is the same what difference does being knowingly observed make as compared with not knowingly being observed?

Other's research does not represent the final stage of a grounded theory approach, which is taking the theory and applying it to what happens in another location, and perhaps in another kind of setting entirely. The study which gave rise to the idea of grounded theory was by Glaser and Strauss (1964) and about how people behaved when they were uncertain as to whether their doctors considered them to be in a terminal state. The same ideas have been transferred fairly successfully to research in other hospitals, and also to other situations such as students in a state of uncertainty as to whether they have passed or failed their examinations, or parents uncertain as to whether their newborn child is handicapped or not. This last stage of 'grounded theory' is precisely the opposite of 'discovering the theory in the data', since it entails taking a theory developed to explain data from one set of circumstances and applying its ideas to another. But that is how theories with a general application are developed.

These remarks indicate that discovering theory in the data is not the only legitimate approach in qualitative research. Good arguments can be made for entering the field with a theory which is already well developed and testing it against the findings. What is important is to adopt a strategy which gives the theory the best possible chances of being disproved. Much social psychological research proceeds in this way.

As Lyn and Tom Richards remark, the term grounded theory is 'widely adopted as an approving bumper sticker in qualitative studies' (1991: 43, cited Bryman and Burgess 1994: 6). There are many studies based on naturalistic observation which include no attempts to test ideas rigorously by looking assiduously for data which would falsify the ideas and consist instead of researchers having ideas and then cherry picking the data to find good examples to illustrate these. Many such studies claim to be exercises in grounded theory, but they aren't (Bryman and Burgess 1994: 4–6).

Accountability and reflexivity

The accountability of research by naturalistic observation can be very high where researchers use electronic records, which can be made available in part or in total to readers and where the claims made are restricted to what the reader can see is in the data. Ethnomethodological studies often achieve this level of accountability. These studies are replicable to the extent that readers can subject the same data to their own analysis. By contrast, the accountability of participant observation research conducted over a long period of time, where the medium of recording is field notes, is very low, because the reader has to rely on the researcher both to describe what was found and to describe everything that was going on from which someone else might have collected different data and might have made a different kind of sense. Such research is, of course, unreplicable. However, researchers can make themselves more accountable by being explicit about their observation strategy and their coding rules, answering readers' questions such as 'where and when was she in order to observe that?' and 'how often?' and 'by what criteria did he recognise this as an instance of that?'.

The term **reflexivity** is used in a wide variety of ways. Its basic meaning in research is that researchers adopt a third-party viewpoint on their own research activities: they treat themselves, as it were, as research subjects in their own research. In that sense my analysis of my own performance as George's interviewer in Chapter 8 (section 8.4) is a reflexive account.

Often, however, reflexivity takes the form of extended philosophical discussions in the field of epistemology – about how anyone can know anything about anything, or ethics – about the moral implications of doing research in general and this research in particular (see Chapter 13). And sometimes reflexivity is interpreted as the need to tell 'the inside story' of the research, its thrills and spills, sometimes extending to telling how the author became a researcher, or what it is like to be a female researcher, how it felt to do the research and so on. These accounts can make interesting reading. But there is an issue here as to whether they put the reader in a better position to evaluate the research. Such accounts are often based on 'field diaries' or other kinds of records made about the process of the research at the time at which it was conducted, but as Bryman and Burgess say:

> It is important to remember that it is *post hoc* reflections which are provided, with the result that projects are tidied up by their authors before being presented to a wider public. (1994: 8) (see also Chapter 11, section 11.6)

Researchers making themselves accountable to readers are also researchers making themselves accountable to themselves. The field research I did in Kenya in the late 1960s was done through unstructured observation research. In the year 2002 I have my yellowing field notes. I have the publications (for example, Gomm 1975) and I have my memories. What I do not have is access to the situation from which I drew the data. For many of the questions posed by Figure 10.1 as to how selections were made I do not have satisfactory answers. Thus I find it difficult to have any great confidence in my account of spirit possession on the South Kenya coast. And if I don't have any great confidence in it, why should anyone else?

ACTIVITY 10.1 Observing and disrupting turn-taking

This is an activity which can be done in an hour or so, or longer if it interests you. It starts from the comments by Sacks, Schegloff and Jefferson (1972) in Chapter 9, that turn-taking is a basic constituent of a wide range of forms of social organisation, from traffic at roundabouts, to lunch queues, to deciding who should go first through a door. There are many situations in life where, momentarily at least, it is an important organisational consideration as to whose turn it is, because someone has to take the turn, or if no one does, something has to be done about this, and where it is an important moral consideration, because people will have ideas as to who has the right or obligation to take the turn. Because turn-taking is a moral matter, whenever turns are being taken people are vulnerable to be evaluated as being particular kinds of personality – 'pushy', 'reticent', 'polite' and so on.

1 Observation
Find a situation in which turn-taking is implicated: for example, turn-taking by precedence order in a queue, goes in a game, sorting out who goes first through a crowded doorway, who gets served first in the restaurant. Observe how people offer each other turns, take turns when offered, how people otherwise know when it is their turn, how long people wait without complaint for another to take a turn, how they grab turns, complain that someone has taken their turn and such like. You will be observing the minutiae of social organisation as social organisation is done. Against this background observe how people come across as being particular kinds of personalities according to expectations about how people should behave in this kind of turn-taking situation. People are realised as the characters they appear to be in terms of how things are being organised.

2 Breaching experiment
For this, you need to be braver. Garfinkel (1967) developed a strategy for studying what usually happens by disrupting it and seeing how people try to put it together again – so called **disruption** or **breaching experiments**. The best-known is the lodger experiment. Students were asked to behave in their own homes as if they were a guest or a lodger, for example asking permission to have a glass of water, or asking questions to which, as a family member, they would be considered to know the answer. In behaving like this they threw into stark relief unstated and unnoticed expectations about how family members should behave. A common way in which families restored the disrupted social order was by invoking the idea of mental illness, such that there was again a 'normal family' but one with a mentally ill member.

ACTIVITY 10.1 (*continued*)

For your breaching experiment try disrupting a turn-taking situation. Don't take a turn when it is obviously your turn. Offer no explanation for this. Record what happens. What does this tell you about the way the local social organisation is put together? How does this cast you as being a particular kind of character? If nothing seems to happen, consider why it does not and the conditions necessary under which not taking a turn would have observable consequences.

Before you do this, consider carefully where you are going to do it. The lodger experiment sometimes provoked violent reactions.

10.7 Summary

This chapter has been about the observation of 'naturally occurring' events in attempts to achieve ecological validity. This is often prescribed as an alternative to other kinds of research critiqued as producing artificial situations and or artefactual data. But while researchers may be able to arrange that their actions have little influence on what happens in the setting they are observing, their accounts of what happens are still written by them and will be the result of their ideas about what the observations mean, and of their selection decisions as to where, when, who and what to observe, which are equally decisions about where not, when not, who not and what not to observe. There is also a potential for the equivalent of a Hawthorne effect (Chapter 2, section 2.6), or an interviewer effect (Chapter 8, section 8.4) arising from the people being studied behaving differently from the way they would if they were not under observation. Covert observation solves this problem of subject reactivity, but there are ethical objections to this (Chapter 13, section 13.5). Participant observation is supposed to reduce subject reactivity as the observer becomes a taken-for-granted member of the setting.

The various of kinds of sampling decisions will make a difference to what is observable and what is observed, and if close relationships are established with the people studied there are possibilities for sympathetic bias. In these regards there is an observer expectancy effect. This is analogous to expectancy effects in experiments (Chapter 2, section 2.6) but the circumstances of much naturalistic observation provide the potential for observer expectancy effects to be much more powerful than these. One main safeguard against observer effects is structured observation designed to avoid observers merely looking for observations to confirm what they believe or would like to be true. This is also the way in which researchers can subject their emerging ideas to a rigorous test, by looking particularly for observations which might falsify their ideas and, if they find them, developing better ideas.

A programme of structured observation also makes observers accountable to readers (and to researchers themselves) as to how they went about their observation activities. By contrast with data in the form of field notes, hard data in the form of transcripts makes the observer much more accountable to readers insofar as less highly processed data can be shared with them. Sometimes naturalistic observers attempt to make themselves accountable via providing a *reflexive account* describing how they went about doing their research. Such 'inside stories' about how the research was done can be interesting and are often useful in conveying the tricks of the research trade and something of the experience of doing the research. But if it is difficult to know whether to believe a researcher's account of some events he or she observed, then it is equally difficult to know whether to believe the story of what it was like doing the observation (see also Chapter 11, section 11.0).

Further reading

On doing ethnographic research in sociology see Hammersley and Atkinson (1995) or Silverman (1997). Burgess (1982) is a collection of papers covering a wide range of practical research issues in ethnographic research, such as those about 'participating' in participant observation research, or making field notes. Hammersley (1998) provides a readers' guide to ethnographic research and Hammersley (1992) a discussion of the problems of the genre. For ethnographic research in anthropology see Barnard (1994). Miles and Huberman (1994) is a handbook containing a wide range of techniques for analysing qualitative data.

A comprehensive guide to doing grounded theory is Strauss and Corbin (1998), though this tends of make it look more special than it is. The literature on observation research of an ethnomethodological kind is often difficult for beginner readers, because of the mind-numbing jargon in which it is expressed, however Heath and Luff (1993) is a fairly pain-free introduction illustrated with the analysis of video-taped material. Many of the data observed under naturally occurring circumstances are speech data, so books on this listed at the end of Chapter 8 are equally good as guides to analysing talk in naturally occurring situations. Ethnographic research is a very literary enterprise; to a great extent its credibility rests on the ability of the researcher to tell a good story. Atkinson (1990) examines the literary devices used by ethnographers to present convincing pictures of real scenes and real people and real research going on. This point is picked up again in Chapter 11.

11 Analysing Written Documents

By the end of this chapter, you will:

- Know more about the differences between data which are produced by speaking and data which are produced by writing
- Know enough to be able to conduct a simple content analysis
- Be able to analyse a text by interrogative insertion
- Be able to conduct a simple version of analysis by membership categorisation
- Be able to conduct the analysis of a problem–solution discourse
- Understand what is meant by rhetorical analysis and be sensitive to the ways in which writing constructs an impression of the author
- Know the difficulties of using written documents as sources of evidence about what is referred to in the writing.

And know the meaning of the following terms:
category bound activity (CBA) ■ content analysis ■ discourse analysis ■ interrogative insertion ■ membership category (MC) and membership categorisation device (MCD) ■ narrative analysis ■ problem–solution discourse ■ rhetoric ■ standardised relational pairs (SRPs) ■ triangulation ■ trope.

11.1 Introduction

Very similar techniques can be used for analysing both speech (Chapter 9) and written materials. But in applying them it is important to bear in mind the way the original data were produced. For example, in his interview (Chapter 9, section 9.4), George told a series of stories or narratives. But these were told through the medium of a two-party, face to face, exchange where the performance of the interviewer was important in shaping what George said. Had George written his life story instead, he would have written it with some kind of audience in mind. But otherwise, the audience would not have had an opportunity to shape the writing.

Again, speech is usually produced with each utterance building on the last, in an open-ended and emergent way. At the beginning, speakers do not know what will be said at the end. But in writing, authors can usually change the beginning to be consistent with the end. And again, speech erodes away as it is spoken. Speakers have to rely on their imperfect memories (Chapter 6, Box 6.1) of what has been said, in order to make what they say next relate to what was said previously. With text, writers can read back, and so can readers.

It is not surprising, then, that sequences of speech are usually marked by inconsistency and incoherence. Most of this is only noticed if the speech is recorded and transcribed, and our impressions of incoherence come mainly from *reading* later what was produced as speech, rather than *hearing* it as it was produced. The sequential analysis of the interview with George showed that whatever he said could be made out as consistent with whatever was going on at the moment immediately before and as he said it (Chapter 9, section 9.4). It would be wrong, therefore, to regard inconsistencies in George's speech as evidence of his inconsistent mind or of the incoherence of his self-image.

By contrast, in writing, authors do have an opportunity to impose a beginning-to-end consistency on the text and to compose the text as an artful display of the kind of person they want readers to think they are, and or as a persuasive version of the truth. Many documents go through several drafts, involving several people, with distinct stages of composition, editing, styling and printing. Some are written into a template or according to a given pattern.

The important distinction, then, is not between speech and writing but between communications produced in different ways for different purposes. Text messages are more like spoken conversation than book writing, and a spoken lecture can be more like a chapter in a text book than a conversation. Broadcast speech is often 'de-ummed' with the hesitancies edited out. It may be re-ordered. Interviewers' questions may be dropped in later, and interviewees' nods and grunts replaced from a series of 'yeses' and 'nos' recorded before or after the interview. The whole interview may be introduced by a 'reverse': an introduction composed after the interview. Thus broadcast speech can be more like written text (Heritage 1985). In transcribing interviews researchers often clean them up, making them read more like text than speech, thereby risking misrepresentation by detaching the data from the context in which they were produced (Chapter 9, section 9.5).

This chapter will centre on written documents which have been produced in a way that allows authors to revise them before releasing them to readers. From time to time I will refer to these as *texts*. I prefer to restrict this term to written materials. But some authors use it to include speech, pictures, films and anything which has been composed to convey a meaning, or even anything which can be interpreted as meaningful, however it was composed. For example, Fiske (1993) refers to, and analyses a holiday beach as a 'text'.

The chapter deals with the use of documents as sources of evidence about events (section 11.7), with content analysis, analysis by interrogative insertion, membership categorisation analysis, problem–solution discourses and rhetorical analysis. But beware: there are no fixed meanings for some of these terms. You will find other authors using the same terms in different ways, and yet others giving different titles to the same kinds of analysis.

The term 'discourse'

The term **discourse analysis** is sometimes used to refer to the analysis of speech or texts or broadcasts. But it is used in so many different ways that it is almost meaningless until you see what the analyst means by it. An important distinction between different kinds of 'discourse analysis' can be made by asking what kind of thing the analyst thinks the discourse is. There are three main possibilities:

- Discourses are assumed to have an existence independent of individuals and of their speech and writing. Thus a piece of writing is treated as a manifestation of a more general way of thinking, understanding or doing things: as an aspect of culture. Here the term 'discourse' has replaced the more traditional term 'ideology'. Today writers tend to write of 'patriarchal discourses', rather than of 'patriarchal ideologies'. Michel Foucault has been a major influence here (see section 11.7) Much of such writing goes under the title of critical discourse analysis (Wodak and Meyer 2001), where the assumption is always that the ideas and practices constituting the discourse favour the powerful and mislead the powerless.
- Discourses are seen as evidence of ways individuals or groups interpret the world. They are manifested, patchily, in particular pieces of speech or writing but have an existence independent of them. Here the term 'discourse' has been added to the already over-loaded set of synonyms, including, 'perspective', 'world-view', 'interpretive scheme' and such like (see Chapter 8, section 8.3). Speech and writing are here studied mainly in an attempt to gain insight into the minds of speakers and writers (for example, Reissman 1993).
- Discourses are the words and the way they are arranged. The interest here is in how particular kinds of communication are put together, how these formats convey the meanings they convey, and the uses to which such communications are put (see sections 11.3, 11.4, 11.5, 11.6).

Similarly, the term **narrative analysis** is used for a wide range of approaches to speech or writing with plots and characters (narratives), but again falling roughly into the three kinds of approach suggested above.

11.2 Content analysis

Indexing a book is a kind of content analysis. Though the name dates back to the 1960s the technique has a long history in biblical scholarship in the Jewish and Christian traditions, cross-referencing various parts of the bible in order to discern its hidden meanings, and especially in the scrutiny of texts with a view to censoring them for heresy (Krippendorf 1980: 13).

Today content analysis refers first and foremost to the quantitative analysis of documents or broadcast media – something gets counted. But much the same approach is adopted by qualitative researchers using what I called 'thematic analysis' in Chapter 9, section 9.3. And most quantitative content analysis begins with a qualitative analysis of the data to discover what they might contain which could be counted.

Representativeness

Usually a content analyst wants to make some claims about the representativeness of the data entered into the analysis (Chapter 4, section 4.1). If the interest is in producers and the products, this is fairly straightforward. For example, in a study of the way newspapers present stories about HIV/AIDS, the analysis might be conducted on all HIV/AIDS stories in a sample of all national newspapers, selected by systematically sampling the dates in January and February in a particular year, with a sampling interval of eight (see Chapter 4, Box 4.1). That would result in seven days' worth of newspapers, each batch on a different day of the week. And it would be a 'blind' sample preventing the analyst from cherry picking newspapers for particularly juicy, but possibly unrepresentative, stories. Such a sample would probably be representative only of the time period from which it was drawn. If the interest was in changes in the newspaper presentation of HIV/AIDS, then it would be necessary to sample from a much longer time period. There are several interesting studies of 'news cycles', charting the rise and fall in topicality of a particular issue (for example Lythgoe 1979; Hall *et al.*1978; Fishman 1981: 71).

But it may be that the analyst is most interested in the influence of these stories on those who read them. In that case, logically, more widely read stories, in more widely read newspapers should feature in the analysis more than little-read stories in minority newspapers. Published readership figures could be used to weight a sample in favour of those papers with the bigger readership, or papers with readerships below a certain level could be excluded. For example, in her study of images of women in women's magazines Majorie Ferguson (1983) restricted her content analysis largely to *Woman, Woman's Own* and *Woman's Weekly*: the three largest-selling women's magazines in the period. Actually, more women read other women's magazines, though each of these had lower sales, and Ferguson's study does include content analysis of less well-read journals. But sales figures are not a particularly good basis for selecting a sample to represent articles and stories proportional to the numbers of people reading them, because they don't tell us who actually read the magazines they purchased, or what they read in them. Most people only read a tiny proportion of their newspapers, but different tiny portions each.

Content frames and coding

Table 11.1 gives an example of a content analysis framework – usually called **content frame** for short. A 'content frame' is essentially a question-

TABLE 11.1	Content analysis frame for preliminary analysis of newspaper stories on HIV/AIDS (code NI (not indicated) where the story features HIV/AIDS but contains no information for any columns)

Story No.	Who get's AIDS/is at risk of getting AIDS	Why/how ?	Who's in the right ?	Who's in the wrong ?	NI
1					
2					
3					
4					

Coded example 1

THE SADDEST little girl in the world sat alone with her Cabbage Patch doll yesterday because her friends won't play with her. Pretty four year old [. . .] is a victim of AIDS. The tragic tot, believed to have caught the disease from her drug-taking mother, is banned from school, shunned by friends and victimised by ignorance.

Who	Gets	At risk	Why/how	Right	Wrong	NI
Child (F)	–	–	Parent child	Innocent child		
Parent (F)	Drug-taker	–	Drug-taking		Drug-taking parent	
Friends, parents of friends, school authorities (?)	–	–	–	–	Ignorant public	

Source: Daily Express (June 1985)

Coded example 2

CHARLES GIVES BLOOD TO STEM AIDS SCARE

PRINCE CHARLES gave a pint of blood yesterday to try to stop a panic over the killer disease AIDS. The number of donors has fallen dramatically as fears of catching the gay plague have spread . . . So the Prince made a surprise visit to a blood donor centre to prove there is no danger . . . Afterwards staff joked about the Royal pint, saying 'Look it's not blue' . . . Prince Charles's blood, which was anonymously bottled, was then added to other pints given by ordinary people.

Who	Gets	At risk	Why/how	Right	Wrong	NI
Homosexuals	Homosexuals		Homosexuality		Homosexuals?	
Prince Charles	–	–		Celebrity		
Health care staff	–	–	–	Health care staff		
Blood donors	–	–	–	–	Ignorant public	

Source: Daily Express (2 March 1985)

naire which is filled in by the analyst. The general question asked by this frame is 'What's in the stories about innocence and guilt?' For each column there is a more specific question to answer. This is only one of many themes which might be examined in analysing the same news stories. The frame is filled in for two examples.

The examples have been coded. If the analysis is done manually, then the next stage would be to draw up an index, so that all the examples, say, featuring children as innocent victims would be listed together, all those featuring celebrities listed together and within that category, all those featuring celebrities as victims would be distinguished from celebrities featured in other ways. Celebrity children would, of course, need their own index label. All this is much easier done electronically where the codes are field codes in a database, and indexing is thereby automated. Then the computer can print out a list of all the examples for any mixture of codes.

Coding is crucial (Fielding 1993) but is usually an awkward and tedious process because when the codes are most useful is while the analysis is in progress, but the analyst is in a good position to decide on an appropriate set of codes only when the analysis is complete. The example here suggests two different sub-themes within the theme, one about who contracts HIV and one about public attitudes to HIV. If the analyst wants to separate these out, maybe a different coding scheme would be more appropriate.

Reliability and validity

Reliability is an important consideration. Would other people concur on the way the analyst used the content frame and coded the examples? For this, inter-rater reliability checks (Chapter 2, section 2.7) should be conducted for at least a sample of the news stories. This might go some way towards showing whether or not the analyst had been consistent herself (**intra-rater reliability**).

In classifying and coding stories there are particular difficulties in knowing how far to go in 'reading between the lines' and coding for what seems to be implied rather than what is explicitly said; a problem of **construct validity** (see Chapter 8, section 8.2). For example, does the Prince Charles story actually blame homosexuals for contracting HIV? This becomes even more difficult where pictures are involved, and even more so with television and film, where camera angles and soundtrack music can contribute to the message.

Moving from the examples to the entries in the content frame loses information or *degrades* or *reduces the data*. Unlike the situation where someone takes notes as an observer, nothing is actually lost (Chapter 10, section 10.1). The news stories are still there and can be looked at again. But much of the detail drops out of the analysis. For example, the way in which an 'innocent child victim' is characterised as 'a tragic tot', 'pretty' and playing with a Cabbage Patch doll, is likely to disappear when this example is combined with other examples of innocent child victims. But some data degradation is necessary if generalisations are to be made about large numbers of news stories. This is particularly so if the data are going to be translated into numbers.

The results of quantitative content analysis

Table 11.2 gives an example of what part of a numerical display of the results of this content analysis would look like.

Quantifying the results of content analysis raises some issues. First there are problems of classification. Is everything which is counted as being the same, really the same ? When a result is quoted as a total of, say, 36 instances, readers may have no way of knowing whether they themselves would count all 36 as being sufficiently similar to be added together. These are issues of *reliability* and *construct validity* again.

Second, there is an issue about units of analysis. In Table 11.2, the basic unit is the news story. But dividing one news story from another is not always easy. Some sections of newspapers consist of a single headline, followed by a number of different, unrelated or only loosely related stories. Here if there are two paragraphs referring to HIV, is this one story or two ? Again, sometimes the same story appears in different forms in the same newspaper. The 12 April 2002 edition of the *Sun,* featuring a foot injury to the footballer David Beckham, might have been counted as having between 10 and 17 'Beckham' stories, or one Beckham story spread over seven pages. Sometimes the unit used is column-centimetres. This does mean that long stories count for more than short ones, and that stories in big type (presumably regarded as more important) count more than stories in small type. But in this analysis of HIV stories, using column-centimetres as a measure would cause some problems, if attempts were made to count the number of centimetres devoted to a 'theme'. In the 'tragic tot' story, is the whole story to be counted as an example of a child being infected by a parent, or only the eleven words explicitly stating this?

Third, there are decisions to be made about how to combine data and compose '100 per cents'. In Table 11.2, stories which feature both children infected with HIV and spouses/partners infected with HIV, will count twice. So longer and more complex stories will contribute more to the overall analysis than shorter and simpler ones, and columns will add up to more than 100 per cent. If newspapers of different kinds are combined in the analysis then, just because they are bigger, the bigger newspapers are likely to contribute more to the results than smaller ones, unless each newspaper is tallied separately. If the interest is in the percentage of all stories of whatever kind constituted by stories about HIV/AIDS there is also some difficulty of deciding what is 100 per cent of all stories, whatever their topic. Often this is done by estimating the number of words/column inches in a typical edition of a newspaper, then counting the number of words/ measuring the column inches in the stories of interest, and expressing the latter as a percentage of the former. But again, combining different news-papers for this purpose could be misleading. The problems here are similar

TABLE 11.2	Table for presenting some results of a quantitative analysis of news stories about HIV/AIDS			
Themes		**No of stories of HIV/AIDS with theme**	**Stories with theme as per centage of all stories featuring HIV/AIDS**	**Stories with theme as percentage of all stories, all topics**
Children infected by parents/carers/older siblings				
(1) Parents'/carers'/older siblings' sexual behaviour implicated				
(2) Parents'/carers'/older siblings' drug-taking behaviour implicated				
(3) Both of parents'/carers'/older siblings' sexual and drug-taking behaviour implicated				
(4) Total				
(5) Children infected as victims of blood transfusion service				
(6) Children infected as victims of rape (not by parents/carers/older siblings)				
(7) Children infected 'innocently' by other means				
(8) Total children infected as 'innocent victims'				
(9) Children infected from own drug-taking behaviour				
(10) Children infected from own sexual behaviour				
(11) Total children as victims by infection				
(12) Children victimised by HIV/AIDS infection of another, for example, orphaned.				
13) Total children in adversity because of HIV/AIDS				
Spouses/partners infected by spouses/partners				
(12) Implicating spouse/partner's sexual activity				
(13) Implicating spouse/partner's drug-taking activity				
(14) Spouse as victim of blood transfusion service				

to those associated with handling the responses of open-ended questions in questionnaires (Chapter 8, section 8.4).

Effects on readers

These considerations, however, become rather trivial if what is of interest is not what is in the newspaper for the analyst to discover, but what is in the newspapers which influences newspaper readers. Newspaper readers do not read by conducting content analyses. There is no basis for assuming *a priori* that what the analyst finds in the stories is what the readers will find there and what will influence their thinking. But a very large number of content analyses of mass media products assume just this.

To study the influence of any kind of media on audiences it is necessary to add to content analysis other kinds of investigations where representatives of the audience are the research subjects. These can include experimental studies, questionnaire research, face-to-face interviews, focus groups, observation studies, or asking people to author news stories themselves and comparing these with those that appear in the papers (Gunter 1999).

This kind of research usually raises an issue about **direction of effect** (see also Chapter 6). For example, do newspaper readers learn to see the world in the way described to them by newspapers, or do journalists describe the world in a way they know their readers will believe, or both – and, if so, which is the stronger influence?

Experimental approaches are usually the best way to settle questions about direction of effect, but only about direction of effect under experimental circumstances (Chapter 2, section 2.10). There is a strong tradition of experimental research on topics such as whether media exposure to violence leads to violent behaviour. But the experimental conditions adopted are so unlike real-life circumstances that the results may not have much bearing on life outside the lab. Natural experiments (Chapter 5) are common in media research, dividing people into comparison groups such that one group has had first-hand, direct experience of the issue of interest plus information provided by the media, while the other gets its knowledge only from media sources (for example, Hartman and Husband 1981; Philo 1990; Philo *et al.* 1994). Comparing the knowledge, attitudes, beliefs and opinions of the two groups gives an estimate of the influence of the media net of direct experience. This approach might explain otherwise curious findings such as that in NHS consumer satisfaction research, that the people who express most dissatisfaction are the people who have had least recent contact with the NHS (Bosanquet and Zarzecka 1995). This might be explained in terms of an unrelentingly negative picture of the NHS given by the mass media, unmodified by direct experience for those who express most dissatisfaction. But there is still a direction of effect problem here. Perhaps the people who express most dissatisfaction are those who, uninfluenced by the media, avoid visiting doctors or who use private health care facilities.

At first sight HIV/AIDS might seem to provide the ideal conditions for a natural experiment on media influence. In the 1980s, from when the examples above were drawn, hardly anyone had any direct experience of HIV/AIDS and the media were the main source of most people's knowledge. Thus it might be argued (as by Vass 1986) that what people thought about HIV/AIDS must have been put in their minds by the mass media. But on closer inspection the way the mass media handled such stories at the time was in terms of very traditional formats used for hundreds of years for telling about epidemic diseases (Herzlich and Pierret 1985) and about crime and other undesirable phenomena (for example, Pearson 1983). These formats divide people into innocent victims and those afflicted because of their own moral shortcomings. They associated disease with immorality, and sourced disease or crime from strangers within the country, or from foreigners outside. There is an argument here in favour of saying that the way the popular media handled the topic of HIV/AIDS was strongly influenced by journalistic need to communicate in ways readers would find meaningful.

By itself, the analysis of the content tells us nothing for sure about what is conveyed to readers by a text or to listeners or viewers by a broadcast. Nor does it necessarily tell us about the thoughts in the author's mind, except something about the author's thinking about how to convey something to an audience. For example, many journalists who write for right-wing newspapers, write under other names in left-wing minority journals. Many people write documents with styles and contents determined by their employers which they themselves would not otherwise choose. Many educators write texts for students which contain what they think students ought to know and what students will understand, which is different again from what they themselves know and believe. And just whose thoughts, ideas and beliefs does a TV programme express when many people have been involved in its production?

But what content analysis can do is to show how communications are put together and what are the communicative conventions which authors use to produce particular effects. The examples in this section give a glimpse of one kind of communicative convention – *news angles* (Galtung and Ruge 1965, 1981; Hall *et al.* 1978: 51–138) or 'news conventions' which journalists use to judge the newsworthiness of events and to write them into what are distinctively newspaper news stories. Thus celebrities – Prince Charles here, are always good copy. People with problems are nearly always divided into innocent victims on the one hand and those who are to blame for their own misfortunes on the other. And there are no better innocent victims than children, unless they are dogs, cats or horses. There are many content analyses of news which use news angles as the categories in the content frame (for example, Best, Dennis and Draper 1977; Hall *et al.* 1978; Hartman and Husband 1981; van Dijk 1991).

The advantage of content analysis, as described above, is that it allows for generalisations to be made about large quantities of data. But to do this it is necessary to extract the data from their immediate context. There is a risk then of losing sight of how the stories are put together to convey meanings.

The approaches described below are all attempts to analyse how meaning is produced through the forms taken by writing. Since the attention is given to the way the texts are *con*structed, the analysis is often called **deconstruction**: taking them apart to see how they work.

11.3 Analysis by interrogative insertion

This kind of analysis shows one of the ways in which a written text hangs together coherently. Most written texts are presented as monologues, but interrogative analysis thinks of the text as a dialogue between the writer – whose words you can see – and an invisible reader, who the writer imagines is asking questions. Few writers actually write this way, except when they write the answers to those FAQs (Frequently Asked Questions) now common on many web sites. But the skilful writer does put questions into the mind of the reader, and then answers the questions the writer wants the reader to ask.

Interrogative insertion goes like this:

1 **Writer**: PRINCE CHARLES gave a pint of blood yesterday.

2 *Reader*: *why did he do that ?*

3 **Writer**: To try to stop a panic over the killer disease AIDS.

4 *Reader*: *How would giving a pint of blood do that ?*

5 **Writer**: The number of donors has fallen dramatically as fears of catching the gay plague have spread. So the Prince made a surprise visit to a blood donor centre to prove there is no danger[. . .].

6 *Reader*: *What was special about it being a member of the royal family giving blood*

7 **Writer**: Afterwards staff joked about the Royal pint, saying 'Look it's not blue' . . .

8 *Reader*: *Would anyone know they were being transfused with Prince Charles' blood?*

9 **Writer**: [No] Prince Charles's blood which was anonymously bottled was then added to other pints given by ordinary people.

This suggests that this is a story written by someone who thinks readers are more interested in Prince Charles, than in HIV. At 7 the writer answers an imagined reader's question (6) about Prince Charles's celebrity status, rather than a further imagined question about HIV and public attitudes to it: such as '*Do you think Prince Charles's action will be successful?* or '*What other measures are being taken to allay fears among blood donors?*'

Interrogative insertion gives an indication of the **recipient design** of a text. That is both how the text was written for a particular readership imagined by the author, and how the text was written to shape the mind of the reader to find each passage in turn appropriate. Recipient design is also a feature of spoken communication. In Chapter 9 (section 9.4) George tried, rather unsuccessfully, to recipiently design his speech for me as the interviewer.

This kind of analysis also shows us why we sometimes find written texts incoherent and disjointed, when we 'can't see what the author is getting at'. This is often when we can't ourselves see what 'reader's question' each passage is answering. Interrogative insertion has a practical as well as a research usage. If your writing is disjointed try inserting 'reader's questions'. You will locate the problem where you can't do this, or where the reader's question the text seems to be answering appears 'out of the blue' and doesn't relate to anything previously.

If writers can lead readers to expect answers to particular questions, then they can also give them expectations that they then thwart in order to make a joke, or say something surprising:

Writer There's a name for people who won't pay standing charges.

Reader: And what is this pejorative name?

Writer: British Gas customers. (British Gas poster, August 2002)

'There's a name for' sets the reader up to expect an insulting name. The joke, such as it is, comes from violating this expectation by giving a name which isn't insulting.

Red-herrings in detective stories are produced by writing in ways that distract the reader from seeing the information given as relevant to answering the overall 'who dun it?' question, or by encouraging readers to see irrelevant information as relevant to this. In many detective stories this is done by putting the 'reader's questions' in the voice of one or many of the characters, which is why so many fictional detectives have rather unintelligent side-kicks

11.4 Membership category analysis

Consider this newspaper headline:

MUM'S WARNING TO BEWARE OF DAUGHTER
(*Stevenage Comet*, 20 June 2002)

This is newsworthy because it violates taken-for-granted expectations about the way mothers behave towards their daughters, which *does not* include warning others to beware of them. By 'taken-for-granted' I mean what we assume unless we are told otherwise: a kind of default understanding. The same default understanding might lead us to read this headline as misleadingly phrased; as referring to one mother warning people about *another* mother's daughter, but it does not.

Membership category analysis (MCA) attends to the way in which authors and readers (and speakers and listeners) draw on common ideas about social organisation: about what kinds of people there are, about how these kinds of people relate to each other and about the kinds of things which different kinds of people do (Lepper 2000). MCA is an important part of Conversation Analysis (CA) discussed in Chapter 8, section 8.4. Table 11.3 provides some of the basic ideas of MCA.

The headline suggests some rather odd behaviour for the mother. But in the story below it is consistent with more usual expectations for the behaviour of mums towards daughters. It is about a mother's resistance to her autistic daughter being removed from a special educational unit and placed in mainstream education. Her 'warning' can be paraphrased as:

> Beware of my daughter if she is placed in mainstream education. She will be violent towards your children and that won't be good for her either.

Hence the story itself fulfils expectations for SRPs and CBAs where 'Mums' and 'daughters' are categories belonging to the MCD 'family', while the headline does not.

You have no difficulty in understanding the Prince Charles story given earlier, because you are a highly competent reader of such stories, but how do you do it? Let's say that the term 'Prince Charles' allocates someone to the membership category 'celebrities'. The opposite MCD is 'ordinaries'. The important thing about celebrities is that they are not ordinary, and when they do ordinary things, they are doing something rather special: the CBAs for celebrities are different from the CBAs for ordinaries. Paradoxically 'an ordinary family Christmas' for the royal family is a most extraordinary ordinary family Christmas. The more like the Christmas of ordinary people it is, the more remarkable it becomes. You know this already and on this basis you know, that when Prince Charles gives a pint of blood, this isn't the same thing as an ordinary person giving a pint of blood. You do not have to be an ardent royalist to do this reading. It doesn't rely on your beliefs and attitudes, but upon public knowledge of categories which are available to those who believe in them and approve of them, and to those who do not.

So the story juxtaposes the social meaning of activities for members of the category 'celebrities' on the one hand and 'ordinaries' on the other. Giving a pint of blood, in order to allay public fears about blood donoring is only a sensible motivation (CBA) for celebrities. To describe this as the motivation of an ordinary would be to describe him as misguided or foolish. Then there are the references to 'blue blood' and the only point of mentioning that Prince Charles's blood was anonymously bottled is that it was celebrity blood.

This may all seem very obvious. But if you were an anthropologist raised in an entirely different culture, you would find the story very difficult to understand until you had cracked the code of MCDs and CBAs. Garfinkel

TABLE 11.3	Some ideas from membership category analysis	
Idea	**Explanation**	**'Mum's warning to beware of daughter'**
Category	Any person can be labelled in many ways, so readers assume that the way they are labelled is important	'Mum' and 'daughter' *
Category modifiers	Finesse the meaning of a category	No examples in this headline, but note '*Saddest little* girl' and '*tragic tot*' in the earlier example
Membership categorisation device (MCD)	Categories are (usually) written and read as grouped together in collections (MCDs)	'Mum' and 'daughter' imply the MCD 'family'
Consistency rule	If one member of a collection is identified then, unless there are indications to the contrary, the next person is likely to be a member of the *same* collection	Although the headline does not explicitly say so, we read the daughter as this mum's daughter. We read them as of the same MCD 'family'
Standardised relational pairs (SRPs)	Pairs of categories are linked together in taken-for-granted ways	Our default expectation is that 'mums' will support and defend their daughters. Warning others against your own daughter violates this expectation. That is why this is newsworthy
Category-bound activity (CBA)	Activities may be read as tied to or 'bound to' certain categories	Warning others against their own daughters is not an activity commonsensically tied to 'mums': not a CBA for mums. This is why this is newsworthy

* Note Note how the category 'Mum' raises our expectations for a loving relationship to a greater extent than would the category 'Mother'. This heightens the contrast between our default expectations for the CBA and SRP and the actual activity described.

(1967: 9) says the task of sociology is to *render the ordinary anthropologically strange*. This means viewing what is familiar from an alien point of view. MCA is one of the ways of making visible the very important taken-for-granted notions on which the communication of meaning relies. MCA is also a way of understanding how authors do *characterisation*. Even when writing purports to be about real people and real life events, in the text the characters have only the existence granted to them by the writer. It is the writer who provides them with personalities, moods and motives. This point will be picked up in the next section.

11.5 Problem–solution discourses

The anthropologist Gregory Bateson (1972) suggested that most statements have two kinds of implications. They have *report* implications about how things are, and *command* implications, about what ought to be done about them. Consider this advertisement:

Sensitive teeth ?
Sensodyne

                (Toothpaste poster advertisement, August 2002)

Here the 'report' is in a conditional form: 'if *you have* sensitive teeth'. And the 'command' is not a command as such but a suggestion: '*why not try* Sensodyne'.

Michael Hoey (1983) elaborates the same basic idea and suggests that a very large variety of texts can be read as what he calls '**problem–solution discourses**' (PSDs). He includes as examples, advertisements, Mr Men books, detective novels, instruction manuals and government reports. For the advertisement above, the first line is the 'problem' and the second the 'solution'. But most PSDs have other components, or if they do not, their absence is noticeable and gives rise to particular effects.

The first column in Table 11.4 gives the major components of a *full* problem–solution discourse (PSD).

The example is taken from a case study by a student health visitor submitted as part of her assessment towards qualification. These case studies are some 2000 words long. Each consists of a large number of PSDs intertwining and threaded through the episodes of visiting the families concerned. They are written in a distinctive health-visitorly way. For example, the *situation* is a health visiting situation – a health visitor visiting a pregnant woman. Elsewhere in the case study, the student will have described a very large number of things which health visitors are supposed to take note of as relevant to the practice of health visiting. The *problem* is the kind of problem that health visitors claim the expertise to deal with: anxious mothers, clingy toddlers. And the *response* is the kind of response which is stock in trade for health visitors.

TABLE: 11.4	Components of a complete problem–solution discourse	
Components	**'Reader's' questions**	**Example: extracts from a student health visitor case study (Gomm 1986)**
SITUATION	*What was the situation?*	'I was visiting a family where the mother was pregnant and had a history of miscarriages' 'There was a two year old child . . .'
PROBLEM	*What was the problem?*	'The toddler reacted by being 'clingy' and unwilling to let her mother out of her sight' 'Mrs Green was herself rather anxious about this pregnancy and I felt she was conveying this anxiety to the child'
RESPONSE	*What was done about the problem?*	'I suggested that Mrs Green should make sure that she put some time aside each day to play with Louise, and that it might be a good idea for the play to be about babies to prepare Louise for the forthcoming event'
RESULT & EVALUATION	*What was the result of the response?* (Result) and *Was the result benign or adverse?* (Evaluation)	[on a later visit] 'I was pleased to see that Mrs Green and Louise were playing at bathing baby, so I knew my advice about involving her in the birth of a sibling had had some effect'

Put another way and recalling section 11.4, the student describes herself engaged in approved-of, category-bound activities for health visitors. What she describes herself as doing is, she hopes, what her examiners will agree a health visitor faced with this problem, in this situation should do. The mother is displayed in terms of an important CBA for pregnant mothers in health visitor lore – being anxious – and a health visiting SRP for mother and child: mothers conveying their anxiety to their children. The child is displayed in terms of another health-visitorly CBA for children – being upset by their prospective displacement by the birth of a sibling. The same situation could have been told very differently by a GP, a double-glazing sales person, a police officer and so on.

As you can see from the second column in Table 11.4, interrogative insertion is part of Hoey's approach (section 11.3). Hoey argues that readers expect these kinds of questions to be answered, and where they are not they feel a sense of incompleteness. The readers for this particular example are health visitor examiners. It is recipiently designed for those. They will certainly read such case studies to see whether the student has indeed answered all these questions in a health-visitorly way.

The example ends with a *positive* evaluation: 'I was pleased to see...' and 'I knew my advice [ ] had had some effect'. Positive evaluations are the usual finishing point of PSDs. For the toothpaste advertisement the *result* and the positive *evaluation* are provided by a picture of a woman happily eating an ice-cream. In writing, writers can supply their own positive evaluations without requiring a confirmation by another at the time. Compare the health visiting example here with its written-in positive evaluation, with George's first story in Chapter 9, section 9.4. There the story fell flat because of the absence of a positive evaluation by the interviewer.

In the student case study, if there had been were no evaluation at all then any reader, let alone examiners, would feel that the discourse was incomplete. Recall the news story of Prince Charles (section 11.3). There was no 'result' or 'evaluation' component to the story and the question of whether his intervention had any effect was left hanging.

Negative evaluations, where they occur in text, are often followed by another PSD which tells of a different response (to the same problem, though perhaps re-conceptualised), the result of the new response and then a positive evaluation. The cause of the negative evaluation is then the 'problem' in the new PSD. For example:

> **Negative evaluation/(new) problem:** There was no evidence that Mrs Green accepted my advice
>
> **Response to new problem:** So I introduced her to another mother who had had similar problems, who I knew would reinforce my suggestions about play to prepare the toddler for the birth of a sibling
>
> **Result/Positive evaluation:** On visiting just before the birth I was pleased to see that Mrs Green and Louise were playing at bathing baby

Positive evaluations are not always possible. If the action which did not lead to a positive result was described as taken by the author, or someone with whom the author feels solidarity, then a negative evaluation is likely to be followed by an *account* mitigating the blame for failure – as described in Chapter 9, section 9.4. In health visitor student case studies, something like the following often appears after a negative evaluation:

> 'There was no evidence that Mrs Green accepted my advice and I realised that I would have to develop my relationship skills further.'

In the language of accounts (Chapter 9, pp. 200–2) this is an *acceptance of blame* mitigated with a promise of reformatory action, and scores some brownie points for honest self-appraisal and willingness to learn, which always goes down well with teachers. In the language of PSD it is, of course, a *response* to an unstated but implied *problem*: the problem of inexperience. In her aural examination, a student who wrote the above would likely be asked 'What did you do to improve your relationship skills?' and 'Was it successful' – completing the written PSD through verbal interaction.

If the action which did not lead to a positive result was taken by someone else, then the negative evaluation, and the whole story, can stand as a complaint that someone has done other than they should have done. For example:

> **Situation/Problem**: THE SADDEST little girl in the world sat alone with her Cabbage Patch doll yesterday. Pretty four year old . . . is a victim of AIDS
>
> **Response/negative evaluation**: The tragic tot, believed to have caught the disease from her drug-taking mother/ . . . her friends won't play with her/ [she] is banned from school, shunned by friends and victimised by ignorance.

Here the response is the response of friends, their parents and the school authorities. As this shows, the components of a PSD do not necessarily appear neatly distinguished from each other, nor necessarily in the order given in Table 11.4.

Many news stories can be regarded as *incomplete* PSDs, mentioning a problem without mentioning a satisfactory solution. There is usually more 'bad news' in newspapers than there is 'good news'. The format of bad news is that of a PSD missing a positive evaluation component.

Now consider the following example:

> [the consultant psychiatrist] considered he had three options. Firstly, he could allow the patient home untreated, putting at risk not only the residents of the [residential] home, but his residential place. Secondly, he could call on several nurses to be on hand while he attempted to inject haloperidol. He had little doubt that [the patient] would have put up a determined resistance, leading to risk of physical injury to [the patient] and the staff, loss of rapport, and an insult to [the patient's] self-respect. Thirdly, he could give him 10mg of liquid haloperidol disguised in a cup of tea.
> (Kellett 1996: 1249)

Figure 11.1 shows how Hoey (1983) might have shown this in PSD terms: You can probably guess which option was taken: the one without the negative evaluation. The whole structure of the passage serves to rule out the other two options as unacceptable. It also follows a common 'rule of three' found in many texts where three things are mentioned in ascending

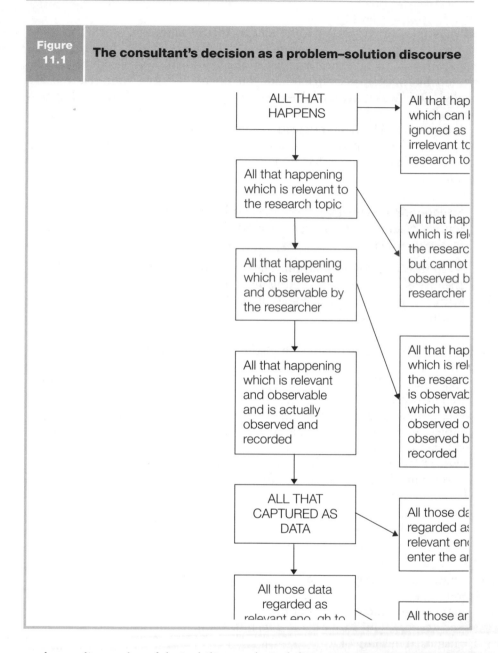

Figure 11.1 The consultant's decision as a problem–solution discourse

or descending order of desirability, undesirability, size, or something – as in *Goldilocks and the Three Bears*. Although Hoey does not himself use MCA (section 11.4) we could say that, to be convincing, the passage relies on its intended audiences' notions about the SRP 'doctor– patient' as the basis for the negative evaluations (Table 11.3). The story appeared in the *British Medical Journal* and the SRP can be regarded as rules for good conduct for doctors which include: not putting patients, or others, at risk, not undermining patients' self-respect, maintaining rapport with patients, and treating their illnesses successfully – later in the story we are told that the option chosen improved the patient's condition. The author of this passage does not explicitly describe the consultant's personality, but does give the consultant a character. First, the consultant is displayed as a judicious man, carefully considering all the options before making a decision. Second, he is shown as motivated by good professional reasons for ruling out some of the possibilities.

But something you may not realise is that it is the third option (*Response 3)* which is ethically most suspect: tricking patients into taking medication they have previously refused. The story goes on to tell how doing this led to disciplinary proceedings against the consultant and against the nurse who it was who administered the medication hidden in a cup of tea. Against the reasonableness of the consultant's reasoning the disciplinary proceedings seem unreasonable. The whole story then can be read as a defence against a complaint of professional misconduct. In the language of accounts (Chapter 9, section 9.4) it is a justification, which might be paraphrased as 'after due consideration of all the options available, the consultant took the one most likely to be the least harmful'. The 'good character' given by the author to the consultant is important therefore in strengthening the defence of the action taken.

This example draws attention to the *pragmatics* of writing. That is to the purpose for which the text is composed and how that purpose is likely to influence the way in which one event is told as leading to another, and what personalities and motives the characters had. A barrister acting for an aggrieved patient might have told the 'same' events very differently, perpetrated by the same consultant but characterised with a different personality and motives.

11.6 Rhetorical analysis

Sometimes people use the term 'rhetoric' as if it were the opposite of 'truth'. But it takes just as much rhetoric to convince people of the truth as it does to convince them of the verity of a lie. When someone draws a distinction between 'the rhetoric and the reality' what they really mean is that they are going to undermine one kind of rhetoric by using another, usually by drawing attention to the tricks and artefacts of the first, but not to those they use themselves. Indeed, contrasting 'rhetoric with reality' is itself a rhetorical device, or **trope**: a way of doing things with words.

Rhetoric lessons, from ancient Greece to the contemporary French school curriculum, are lessons in how to speak and write in a way that gives a preferred impression of the speaker or writer. The impression desired is usually of being the kind of person who can be believed. Public relations firms train industrialists and politicians with the same intention, and some social researchers see their brief as helping oppressed groups to improve their public image, or to make a convincing case for some policy which will benefit them (see Chapter 12).

Rhetorical analysis sometimes refers to a very broad-ranging analysis of speech or writing in terms of the traditional vocabulary for figures of speech, such as metaphor, or irony, metonymy, or synecdoche, or using alternative schemes (Burke 1966). There are some excellent analyses of these kinds in the social sciences (Edmundson 1983; van Maanen 1988; Atkinson 1990), but in this book there is insufficient space to explain the very large vocabulary such analyses use. Instead I will focus on what is at the heart of the idea of rhetoric which is about the way communications convey impressions of their authors. I shall take it for granted that spelling, punctuation, use of vocabulary and sentence construction are important. This is a matter of appropriateness. For example, someone who presents their own diary which is correctly spelt, well-punctuated and full of difficult words correctly used may not be believed if they claim that at the time they wrote it they had received no education.

A key question in rhetorical analysis is 'What makes this document believable, *to some readership?*'. The phrase 'to some readership' is important. What is believable to one audience may undermine the confidence of another. Rhetorical skill inheres partly in recipiently designing a communication for a particular audience. Since research reports are themselves documents I will use them as an example here.

Chapter 12, section 12.4 deals with feminist, anti-racist and other kinds of **partisan research**. A quick scan of this literature shows that it is marked with 'believe me' signals, or **credibility markers** of the kind which imply 'believe me, I'm on the right side', and 'don't believe them, they're on the wrong side'. Table 11.5 gives some examples.

Signals like this are likely to convince some people of the good moral character of these authors and hence of their believability. But for other readerships they smack of over-involvement, bias and hence of unbelievability.

The equivalent 'believe me' signals in more mainstream social science writing are not quite so easy to see (Table 11.6). One reason for this is that such authors often give no explicit characterisations of themselves at all. Or, if they do, these are separated from the main text and put in a foreword, a footnote or a pen-picture at the end, which rarely gives any more information than their institutional position and the other things they have written. But the absence of self-characterisation is itself rhetorical. It goes with the notion that too much personal involvement in research is likely to lead to biased and erroneous results, and with the idea that who the researcher was should be irrelevant with regard to the truthfulness of the account. Thus the absence of self-characterisation excludes from the report what should have been excluded in doing the research – the personal characteristics of the researcher (though these were almost certainly not excluded). The use of the third-party format, as in 'it was found that' (rather than 'I found'), serves to give the impression that the truth is

TABLE 11.5	Credibility markers in feminist, anti-racist and other critical texts
Markers	**Examples**
Markers of correct moral position	*Writing from a commitment to 'women's emancipation'* Or *'work such as mine which is firmly grounded in the anti-racist struggle'*
Markers of alliance with oppressed groups	*Although we take responsibility for the finished product, this research has at every stage been produced through intensive consultation with disabled people*
Markers of privileged understanding of oppression	*Writing as a black woman . . .*
Deconstructions of alternatives as unbelievable	*[Our] experiences have been named for us by men: but men have used what Sheila Rowbotham has called 'the language of theory' and not the 'language of experience' (1973) Our experience . . . is removed from experience altogether by being cast in abstract and theoretical terms. We need a women's language, a language of experience, and this must necessarily come from our exploration of the personal, the everyday, and what we experience – women's lived experience* (Stanley and Wise 1993:146)

speaking for itself, undistorted by human agency. Implicitly rather than explicitly, the research comes across as believable because it is told as the result of a disinterested technician competently following the kinds of methods which that audience will believe usually lead to the truth (Halliday and Martin 1993).

Most researchers deploy another rhetorical strategy, which is to co-opt other writers to agree with them. This can be done as simply as prefacing their own ideas by writing 'As so and so said . . .' thus underpinning their own credibility with that of others. But different readerships will find different co optees more or less acceptable. Each genre of research has its own set of particularly authoritative figures who get enrolled as allies and supporters of the author. Many classic studies get bent into new shapes in this way. Again, a bibliography of a research study is a rhetorical device insofar as it shows how well-read the author is, and whether the author has read the works of which the readers approve.

The research reports of quantitative research usually read as if they were stories of how the research was actually done. But we are almost never told about the aborted questions which didn't get into the questionnaire, or the blind alleys pursued by the researcher, still less about conflicts of person-

TABLE 11.6	Credibility markers in mainstream social science research
Markers	**Examples**
Markers of objectivity	Reports: ■ Rarely include material on the authors' subjective feelings or personal lives ■ Rarely level blame ■ Often include descriptions of measures taken to exclude personal bias
Markers of methodical practice	Reports are usually dominated by descriptions of the methods used
Markers of logicality	Authors show themselves taking pains over ensuring that conclusions follow logically from evidence
Markers of circumspection	Authors limit what they claim, since making grandiose claims throws doubt on the credibility of the report as a whole.

ality, or early analyses of data which didn't make sense. Research always seems a much more trouble-free activity than it really is. These reports are better read as sets of instructions as to how someone else *could* do the research to reach the same conclusions, but told rather misleadingly in story format; what Kaplan (1964) calls the 'reconstructed logic of research'.

Many researchers who do qualitative research, particularly using participant observation, give much richer accounts of themselves doing the research, so that readers can visualise, in realistic detail, the researcher being there, finding things out. It all seems so believable. TV companies sometimes screen programmes to show how another programme was made. And it is easy to be lulled into the belief that these programmes about making programmes get straight to the truth without the intervention of directors directing cameras or editing tapes. But, of course, behind the shots of camera crews taking shots there is another hidden camera crew, and screened discussions of how a programme was edited are themselves edited. And in the same way, the inside story of a piece of ethnographic research is just another story. It probably won't be untrue, but it might have been told in a large number of other ways.

Much writing in ethnographic studies is concerned with establishing that the ethnographer has been to the place and seen what is described. Geertz (1988:4–5) says about anthropological ethnography:

The ability of anthropologists to get us to take what they say seriously has less to do with either a factual look or an air of conceptual elegance than it has with their capacity to convince us that what they say is the result of their having actually penetrated (or, if you prefer been penetrated by) another form of life, of having, one way or another, truly 'been there'. And that, persuading us that this offstage miracle has occurred, is where the writing comes in.

(Cited in Hammersley 1992:52)

Why for example, do Rex and Moore (1967), towards the beginning of their study of ethnic relations in Sparkbrook, tell readers about cats foraging in gardens? This is an inconsequential detail with regard to ethnic relations but consequential in the sense that it gives an impression that they really were there, on location, doing the research (Edmundson 1984:38).

Rhetoric in unavoidable. However authors write, they will convey some impression of themselves to readers, and that in turn will make their accounts more or less believable. But in evaluating research reports, of whatever kind, it is important to see the rhetoric for what it is.

This brief consideration of the rhetoric of research reports should have sensitised you to the rhetorical features of other kinds of documents. For example, how advertisers associate a product with what they imagine an audience will value, how newspapers use quotations (often invented) to suggest that what they report is not made up by journalists, how those who write press releases include material which will serve as quotable quotes, how the consultant in the example earlier was given a good character to strengthen the defence or how political speeches include markers of solidarity with the audience, such as 'speaking as a parent myself'.

Writings as evidence

The sections above treated writing as evidence of itself, of how writing is written. Writings were treated as a *topic*. But social scientists frequently make use of writings as a *resource* of evidence of the events or experiences the writing refers to. Now you have considered writings as a topic, you will see the difficulties associated with using writings as a resource, if the object of doing this is to derive accurate information about something from what has been written about it.

Historians in particular have little choice but to use ready-made written documents as resources of evidence and this is true of other social scientists where they cannot gain direct access to what is being described. But, as you have seen, writings are not necessarily well designed to be sources of evidence in this way:

■ Writers will have their own schemes of relevance. They will tell what they think is important and interesting, and perhaps ignore much of what is of central interest to the researcher. Bureaucratic records (Chapter 7) record what is useful for the workings of the bureaucracy, and sometimes to the political party in power, in categories which may be awkward for social scientists to use. Newspapers are a poor source of direct information about the ordinary and mundane, because what is news is the opposite of this. A naïve historian reading the news media of the years 2000–2 might gain the impression that children being abducted and murdered was common, whereas the number of children murdered by strangers has remained constant at around 8 per year since 1975. Again, many of the things which are of particular interest to social scientists are important because people take them so much for granted, and are the very things which don't get recorded.

- Writers write for particular purposes, which are rarely those of being a resource for social scientists. What they tell as the 'facts' may be presented as part of a text with purposes such as celebrating their own achievements, complaining about the state of the world, to amuse and entertain, or as in the consultant story (section 11.5) as a 'case for the defence' and so on. Sometimes writers write with the deliberate intention to mislead (Platt 1981), but whatever the purpose for which a text was written it will usually influence the way that one thing is said to have led to another, and the way the people described are attributed with motives and personal characteristics.

- Only some people write and publish. Thus what is made available as evidence in this way will be presented from some vantage points and not others.

- Writers write for particular audiences, and rely on what they imagine the audience will understand and find credible. For example, it is now extraordinarily difficult to read the writings of early experimentalists such as Sir Isaac Newton as he intended them to be understood, since we do not share his world view, and often do not recognise the references he makes to other texts and debates of his time. Or again, the minutes of most meetings give only a parsimonious account of what happened, and rely on the memories of the people present to fill in the gaps, including the gaps left by not mentioning matters too contentious to be recorded in the minutes.

Ethnographic studies of how people actually speak and behave can be compared with what is written about this. Linday Prior (1993) gives a qualitative content analysis (section 11.2) of psychiatric, mental health nursing and mental health social work text books. But what they contain bears rather little relationship to what is said and done in mental heath practice as observed in ethnographic studies (Byrd 1981; Barrett 1996; Griffiths 1997). For example, the formal diagnostic categories of psychiatry, such as schizophrenia, or bi-polar affective disorder, seem rarely to be used, except by consultants teaching medical students and junior doctors. Again, what scientists write about doing science bears little similarity to what has been observed in ethnographic studies of natural scientists at work (for example, Woolgar 1982). People's everyday practices, and the way they think and speak while they are carrying them out, can rarely be reconstructed adequately from what they themselves write about them. This is important. For example, the French scholar, Michel Foucault has been immensely influential on sociological thinking about crime and punishment (1977), sexuality (1979), mental illness (1967) and medical practice (1973). But his work is based entirely on the analysis of writings. What he says about what is *in these texts* may well be appropriate, but what these texts say about everyday practices and experiences may be misleading.

Using ready-made writings thus gives rise to questions about the accuracy and completeness of the evidence they provide. The first step in evaluating this must always be to consider the kind of writing it is, the purpose for which it was produced and the audience to which it was directed. For example, once we realise that the story of the consultant's decision was being told as a defence against a charge of professional misconduct, we know that we must treat with some suspicion the description of him judiciously weighing the options *before* making his decision. Perhaps this is what he did. But it is also exactly the kind of post hoc reconstruction of events we would suspect to appear in a justification.

As in Chapter 8, section 8.2, it is worth making a distinction here between, on the one hand, what are conventionally regarded as 'matters of fact' – such as the date, time and sequence of events or who was present – and, on the other hand, incorrigibles such as feelings and beliefs and experiences. With regard to the former, ideas such as 'accuracy' make some sense. If the party really started at 19.05, British summer time on 21 August 2002, then that's when it started. Writing saying that it started at another time is simply wrong.

There are actually rather few phenomena which allow for reports about them to be easily arbitrated as 'accurate' or not. Even for timing 'events', it is necessary to decide what constitutes the event. Until this is done we cannot decide when 'it' started or finished. Historical writings are full of discussions about when the 'Middle Ages' or 'Industrial Revolution' started or finished. Most of what are regarded as 'matters of fact' are amenable to a range of quite reasonable but different interpretations. Nonetheless, this problem can usually be managed by imposing a definition. We could say, for example, 'taking the arrival of the first guest as the starting point, the party started at …', or 'defining the "audience" as all those seated in the auditorium when the curtain went up, the audience numbered 253'.

For matters like this, where it is possible for there to be an accurate datum, it is possible to **triangulate** different sources of evidence to decide on which are accurate. This is also called **validation** (see also Chapter 7, section 7.4, Chapter 8, section 8.4, Chapter 9, section 9.2). For example in their study *Belfast in the '30s: An Oral History,* Munck and Rolston (1987:12) write:

In the first place we carried out … 'investigator triangulation'. That is each transcript was checked by two or three researchers to ensure that what was said was what people had meant to say. In the second place, we systematically did a cross-method triangulation, in that every piece of oral evidence that could be, was checked against a range of written sources: newspapers, parliamentary reports, documents etc. Finally there was a considerable amount of 'data triangulation' possible within the oral sources themselves.

(Cited in Macdonald and Tipton 1993:199)

Here written sources were used as a point of triangulation for judging the accuracy of interviews: their 'cross-method triangulation'. Investigator triangulation would more usually be called 'inter-rater reliability testing' (Chapter 2, section 2.7). These researchers do not say that they conducted 'data triangulation' *among* the written sources, but they probably did pay attention to the points of agreement between them.

The problem with triangulation is always that of deciding which of several discrepant possibilities is the accurate one (Chapter 8, section 8.4). This usually has to be decided in an ad hoc manner as appropriate to the puzzle at hand, speculating about which authors were in the best position to know the truth and which were most likely to tell the truth – much after the manner in which the police and the courts decide between the accounts of different witnesses (Platt 1981; Plummer 1983: 99–109). Nor is it necessarily safe to assume that because several accounts concur that they must be the accurate ones. Several sources might be erroneous in the same way. A large number of news stories can be generated from a single misleading press handout, errors are copied from one text to another or several writers may share the same prejudices. Discrepancies can be an interesting topic of research in their own right. Why do some people say one thing, and others another?

When it comes to using writing as evidence about incorrigibles such as feelings or experiences then there are no conceivable ways of judging the accuracy of written descriptions of these. Feelings are felt, and experiences are experienced, and they are so at the moment when they are felt and experienced. Remembering transforms a feeling or an experience into a memory (see Chapter 6, Box 6.1). Writing down the memory transforms it yet again. When social scientists write that their research 'captures the experience' of some group of people they commit a category error: they mistake one kind of thing for another. What they must mean is that they have collected some *stories* which people tell about their experience. Whether these stories are spoken or written they will be *tellings* of experience, shaped by the linguistic and social conventions available for telling experiences and told in order to have some effect on an audience in terms of presenting the teller as being a particular kind of person. The difference between writing and speaking here is that writers have a longer period of time to compose what they want to convey. As Ann Oakley says of autobiographies:

Stories about people's lives are simply one special kind of story. They are, in principle, no different from any other kind of book. All books

depend for their success on the narrative strength of their story telling
... the standpoint from which the story is told will, of course, always
be partial. Autobiographies are the most partial ways of representing
life, since their writers are usually striving in the very act of writing to
make sense of their own lives in a way which offers them the most
congenial justification for living them as they did.

(Oakley 1993: 414)

And as Ken Plummer writes of letters:

[E]very letter speaks not just of the writer's world, but also of the
writer's perceptions of the recipient. The kind of story told shifts with
the person who will read it – witness the different letters produced by
Robert Burns to his mistress, his friends and his wife on the same day.

(Plummer 1983: 23)

This is not to say that the analysis of writings about feelings and experiences is not worthwhile. First, it tells us the ways people have for telling
such stories. The stories show us a cultural repertoire which people use and
how they use it and for what purposes, which is suitable material for
analysing in the ways suggested in this chapter. For example, rather than
analysing autobiographies for telling us about the lives of the people who
wrote them, we can analyse them for what they tell us about the practice of
autobiography writing, or how, for example, the genre of scientists' autobiographies differs from that of feminist autobiographies.

Second, they provide a glimpse of a process through which people try out
versions of themselves, by characterising themselves in particular ways
and writing themselves into particular story lines. In this sense what people
write about themselves, as in autobiographies, or how they construct themselves as authors in writing about someone or something else, is a stage in a
process of becoming someone. But it is not one which stops when the
writing is done. Another piece of writing, another conversation, allows for
another self-characterisation. In this regard there is something rather dis-
respectful in social scientists claiming that they have pinned down the essence
of someone else on the basis of a small sample of their speech or writing.

ACTIVITY 11.1 Deconstruction through reconstruction

This is an activity based on a research technique pioneered by Richard
Winter and Michael Hoey (Hoey 1983: 3–16).

Find a piece of writing which is more or less self-contained and runs to
about 1000 words. Avoid writings which consist of numbered lists and
ideally choose a piece with largish print and double-spacing. Make two
photocopies. Take one of these and cut it up into sentences. Then trim the

ACTIVITY 11.1 (*continued*)

edges of the cut-up pieces so that they cannot be re-assembled jigsaw style, or paste each sentence on a strip of card for the same purpose.

Give the cut up pieces to someone else and ask them to re-assemble them.

When they have completed the task, check it against the uncut copy and ask them what clues they used to accomplish it, with 'how did you know that went there?' questions.

You will find that people use a large variety of different sorts of clues. They will follow 'way-markers' such as 'There are three main points about . . .' They will know what kinds of sentences are likely to precede a sentence beginning 'However'. They are unlikely to explain to you that they used interrogative insertion (section 11.3) but they might say; 'that went there because it seemed to complete what was said in that earlier sentence'. This is much the same as saying that it answered a question which an earlier sentence provoked the reader to ask. They are even less likely to explain how they used MCA (section 11.4), but in deciding to whom a pronoun referred, they may explain that it had to be that person, because what was described of him was consistent with the personality, situation or role of a person named earlier. They probably won't know about PSDs (section 11.5) but they are quite likely to use their intuitive sense of what makes a complete PSD to recognise a passage as, say, a *response* which they predicted would follow a *problem* described earlier. Or they may grasp the overall purpose of the writing, or recognise the genre and use this as a guide to re-assembly.

That people can re-assemble a cut-up document is witness to the fact that writing has a structure – or rather, many structures – and that people know about these. This is the knowledge which allows them to create texts which others find meaningful and find meanings in texts written by others.

Summary

This chapter picked up themes and issues concerning the analysis of speech data raised in Chapters 9 and 10 . Some of the kinds of analysis described in this chapter could be used with speech data also (content analysis, MCA, rhetorical analysis). But in analysing any kind of communication it is important to consider how it was produced. The structure of conversations with their turn-by-turn characteristics is quite different from the structure of a text which has been written backwards and forwards creating consistencies from beginning to end.

The chapter dealt with content analysis, the most traditional way of analysing writing, but most attention was given to kinds of analysis where the interest is in the way writings are structured so that readers can find meaning in them – though what the author intended by the text may not be what the reader finds in them. As in Chapters 9 and 10, emphasis was placed on recipient design, but here on how writing assumes a readership who will understand it as it was intended to be understood: and on self-presentation in communication – here on the way in which authors writing about themselves write themselves characters, or in writing about other matters convey impressions of themselves as authors. These features of writing, and others discussed in the chapter, often make ready-made documents a difficult resource for social scientists to use as evidence about the events and people referred to in them.

Further reading

As a source for a large number of different ways of analysing writing you might try Titscher et al. (2000). For content analysis, Neuendorf (2002) is a very detailed text, with 'how-to-do-it' advice. Berger (2000) is a thorough introduction to mass media research.

For MCA the classic text is Sacks (1992a, 1992b), but Lepper (2000) gives a very full treatment. Hoey's (1983) On the Surface of Discourse is the best reference for problem–solution discourses. Edmundson (1984), Atkinson (1990) and van Maanen (1988) are all books on the rhetorical analysis of social science texts and Halliday and Martin (1993) on the rhetoric of natural science writing. Wodok and Meyer (2001) explain and illustrate what is meant by critical discourse analysis.

Kenneth Burke's scheme for analysing texts (1966) is quite widely used though not described in this chapter. Also missing from this chapter are semiotics or semiology. For an entertaining introduction to these try Fiske (1989). Nor does the chapter deal with the forms of structural analysis associated with the analysis of myths and folk-tales which are often extended to other kinds of narrative (covered in Titscher et al. 2000). Different ways of analysing pictures and other visual materials are well explained in Rose (2001).

WinMAX and MAXoda (www.scolari.co.uk) are software packages for analysing texts, and the software packages noted at the end of Chapter 10 will also deal with written materials.

On using ready-made documents as a resource of evidence Platt (1981) remains a sensible source of advice on the evaluation of authenticity and accuracy. Plummer (1983) or (2000) are useful sources on use of documents in life-history research.

12 Evaluative and Emancipatory Research

12.1 Introduction

A piece of research can be evaluated for its quality in terms of how well it was conducted or how credible are its results. But the term 'evaluation' is also used in a narrower sense to mean making *moral judgements*. This is the important sense of the term for this chapter which is about the ways in which value judgements are involved in research, apart from those which have to do with the way researchers treat those they research. This latter is usually termed 'research ethics' and is dealt with in Chapter 13.

Value judgements may be explicitly made, where those who make them lay out a moral case for what they are doing. Or they may be made without people recognising that values are influencing their judgements. So far in this book values have usually appeared in relation to the way experimental and survey researchers take such pains to avoid the researcher's hopes and desires, preconceptions and prejudices biasing research findings. But matters of value cannot be entirely excluded from research. For example, to be worried about values of one kind influencing research findings is to be signed up to some other values, such as the value of truth.

Options for managing values

I shall assume that all researchers are committed to the value of finding out the truth, and to some values about not harming the people involved in the research (see Chapter 13). But otherwise researchers might:

- Try to exclude issues of value entirely from decisions about what topics to choose, what methods to use, how the data are interpreted, and how they are made public – **value-free research.**
- Allow issues of value to be involved in selecting topics for research and in deciding how to make the findings public, but exclude values from influencing the way the research is done and the conclusions reached – **value-relevant but value-neutral research.**
- Specifically select topics for research on the basis of their moral or political values, do the research in such a way as to maximise the chances of findings which promote these values and use the findings in ways that will have the moral or political consequences they desire – **value-led,** or sometimes, **partisan research.**

There is one step further down this path. This is where researchers conduct research not so much to produce findings but in an attempt to make the world a better place in the very act of doing the research. Thus the research may be directed towards improving the knowledge of the people who are the subjects of the research, or their self-image, or their public reputations, or of winning some resources for them, or of helping them to win some political conflict. When it is done by feminist, or anti-racist or disability researchers it is often called *emancipatory* research, making the claim that it frees some people from some kind of oppression, or *empowering* research, making the claim that it increases the capacity of those researched to improve their situation.

Without the use of terms such as 'emancipation' or 'empowerment', much the same kind of activities are engaged in by the people employed by political parties whose job it is to find the information which will help their party to win, and which can be 'spin-doctored' and published to improve the party's ratings or to smear the opposition, and by the public relations departments and consultants employed by large corporations to manage the company's public image and to enhance its relationships with governments and international agencies such as the EU or UN. People employed in this capacity are also often called 'researchers' and call what they do 'research'.

12.2 Value-relevant, value-neutral research

The naturalistic fallacy

Philosophers warn against the **naturalistic fallacy**, which is fallaciously arguing from 'is' to 'ought'. It is fallacious to say: 'It is raining and therefore you ought to get the washing in.' A complete and logical formula would be: 'It is raining *and* it is a bad thing for washing to get wet, *and* it is your moral responsibility to prevent this, *therefore* you ought to get the washing in.' The naturalistic fallacy entails the missing out of the moral component of an argument, hiding it away so that it might be accepted as if the argument was entirely factual. A more common form of the naturalistic fallacy in the social sciences is: 'It is a fact that these people are disadvantaged, therefore something should be done about it.' But the fact of disadvantage is not in itself an argument for alleviating it. For that, a moral justification is necessary.

It is probably impossible to do research which is entirely value-free. It might seem that whether the sun goes round the earth or vice versa is an issue which is easily abstracted from moral and political concerns. But that was not what Galileo found. It is particularly difficult at the front end of research where topics for research are chosen, and at the rear end where findings are published. Researchers might wish to pursue knowledge for knowledge's sake, but those who fund research programmes usually want something which will suit their interests. Governments usually want research which will be relevant to whatever they define as the most pressing social and political problems. Companies prefer to fund research which will have some relevance to their profitability. For example, Conversation Analysis (CA), which you encountered in Chapter 9, has been has been very heavily funded by telephone and computer companies in connection with the development of voice recognition and generation by machines; market research is the major application of survey technique and user of focus groups; much psychological research is involved in the design of products and marketing campaigns. Thus the pattern of options available for the researcher is partly determined by the values and interests of the kinds of people and agencies who control research funding. Options may also be limited by the kinds of people who can deny a researcher access to a particular research location. There are very few published sociological studies of corporate boardrooms, for example, and none from within the state security services. (For influences on publication see Chapter 13.)

The Weberian position: value relevance and value neutrality

The mainstream position on values and social science is that based on the thinking of Max Weber (Weber 1949; Bruun 1972). Weber is sometimes represented as being an advocate of 'value-free research'; but that was not his thinking. Weber recognised the difficulty of preventing values from determining the choice of topics for research. And he recognised that if research was to have any benefits, someone would have to make value decisions as to the best ways to put the findings to practical use. Therefore what he prescribed was research which was 'value-relevant but value-neutral'. By 'value-relevant' he meant that researchers might and often should select research topics according to value decisions about the kind of research which would be of social benefit. By 'value-neutral' he was referring to setting up a kind of exclusion zone for values, to insulate the way the research is conducted, and the way the data are interpreted, from being influenced by what the researcher, or the research funders, *desire* the findings to show.

Throughout this book there have been examples of devices used to maintain and police such an exclusion zone: blinding to control experimenter expectancy effects (Chapter 2, section 2.6), blind methods of selecting participants as with randomisation (Chapter 2, section 2.3) or with probability sampling (Chapter 4, section 4.4), standardised performances for survey interviewers, the separate analysis of interviews from different interviewers to check that none of them was conveying their values to respondents and thereby influencing responses (Chapter 8, section 8.4), inter-rater reliability tests to check that coding decisions are not biased in analysing data (Chapter 2, section 2.9) and a falsification programme to avoid researchers simply cherry picking data to produce the results they want to see (Chapter 10, section 10.6); see also Table 3.4. These are all modulations on standard practice within scientific research in general.

Puzzles, problems and the attribution of blame

There are always multiple options for framing a topic of research. Some will frame in more moral assumptions than others. Physicists and engineers sometimes draw the line between themselves by saying that physicists pose and solve physicists' *puzzles* and engineers accept and solve other peoples' *problems*. The point being made is that physicists are usually able to select topics for research less influenced by wider moral, political and commercial considerations. Their puzzles are generated by the theoretical development of the subject. By contrast, the kinds of topics worked on by engineers are framed by the practical interests of other people. Hence doing engineering assumes that some people have a moral and political right to have their problems solved (by engineers), which may sometimes be to the disadvantage of some other people.

In everyday social affairs the idea of causation is nearly always double-barrelled. Whenever it is said that this is the cause of that, the implication can be drawn at the same time that someone is morally responsible for either causing it, or has an obligation for doing something about it (see Chapter 11, section 11.5). Such implications will probably commit the naturalistic fallacy (see above) but that doesn't stop people making them.

At first sight the causes of heart disease in later life might merely appear to be a biological issue. An evolutionary biologist might frame this as a puzzle, abstracting the topic as far as possible from any immediate practical concerns of solving it as a problem. The biologist might argue that evolution proceeds by favouring those characteristics which maximise reproductive success. In the evolutionary past there have been no reproductive advantages in developing mechanisms which keep the heart in good repair beyond the age at which people are most fertile, therefore there has been no mechanism for favouring the transmission of any genes which do this, therefore it is understandable that human hearts wear out. This wearing out is 'heart disease'.

This solves a biological *puzzle* but it hardly addresses the *problem* of heart disease as most people would like it addressed: that is, in terms of finding a solution to something which they find undesirable. As soon as we move from puzzle to problem we make a moral judgement that heart disease is a bad thing, and that reducing its incidence would be a good thing. And we narrow the objectives of research in such a way that successful research is the kind of research which has morally desirable pay-offs. However, all phenomena have multiple causes, and no research can investigate all of these at the same time. Thus among the causes which make heart disease more likely for some people are their dietary behaviour and their smoking behaviour and the poverty or the affluence of their mothers and themselves immediately before birth and in their early years. These are all topics which have been investigated by social and psychological research as applied to medicine. Framing 'the problem' of heart disease around each of these bits of the causal network points in the direction of different kinds of 'solution'. But, in turn, each of these tacks might itself be framed in different ways. Thus dietary and smoking behaviour might be conceptualised as behaviour chosen by the people concerned, perhaps under conditions of imperfect knowledge of the consequences of what they are doing to their health. This constructs them as morally responsible for their health, and predicates some kind of health education intervention as a solution. Alternatively their dietary and smoking behaviour might be attributed not to individual choices but to the blandishments of the food processing and tobacco industries. This points towards some solution in terms of the state regulation of industry and advertising. Or, in the case of smoking, the researcher might draw attention to the socially structured stresses and strains of life for which people find smoking a relief, to the fact that poorer people seem to suffer these more, and to a solution in terms of some redistribution of incomes or advantages.

Note what is happening here. Different framings construct different people as the 'goodies' and 'baddies' in the situation, and carry different implications as to who is to blame for the problem and different implications for who should change their ways. Reframing the problem around the idea of poverty in the early years of life has different moral and political implications again. Now it appears that the current pattern of heart disease was in large part determined by social conditions 50–90 years ago. No one living can be held responsible for doing anything about that. But this framing has implications for the present day. It directs attention to current patterns of socio-economic inequality as they impact on maternity and infancy and to whatever it is that governments should be doing in the here and now to prevent heart disease and other health problems in the future.

The above was written as if problems were framed in such a way as to lead to proposals for solutions. But it is equally apposite to suggest that the way problems are framed *follows from* the kinds of solutions people would prefer. Thus it is understandable that health educators prefer research which points towards a solution lying in health education interventions, drug companies in research which suggest pharmaceuticals as the solution, tobacco companies prefer research which will show that people freely choose to smoke and that advertising influences only which brand they choose. Governments prefer research which attributes problems to individual behaviour rather than failures of government policy, while opposition parties, of whatever political persuasion, often take the opposite view. Socialists prefer framings of problems which have socialist solutions, feminists framings which have feminist solutions and so on. The advancement of occupations and of political groups relies on finding problems for the solutions they have on offer, as much as it does on finding solutions for problems (Spector and Kitsuse 1987).

Social science research which gets tied to particular occupational groups tends to incorporate the values and interests of the occupational group in ways that are not always immediately apparent. Nurses, for example, have developed their own genre of research and have called it 'nursing research'. It is not surprising that it tends to portray nursing as an important occupation and doctors as less important than people believe they are. Although not always the case, it is common in nursing research for the term 'the role of the nurse' to mean 'the role nurses think nurses *ought* to play'. This **prescriptive** rather than **descriptive** use of terms, then allows states of affairs to be described in a slanted way, as descriptions of how things deviate from what nurses would prefer. Partly to avoid such problems, sociologists have asserted their independence from occupational groups of practitioners or from the state. Criminology became the sociology of deviance (for sociologists, at least). Medical sociology became first the sociology of medicine and then the sociology of health and illness. Educational sociology became the sociology of education. These all represent attempts to move towards framing topics for research as puzzles rather than as problems. There has been a counter-movement with practitioners trying to seize back control of research in their fields with various 'practitioner–researcher' movements (section 12.5).

'Cause' in social affairs is often taken to mean 'blame' so, whatever a researcher says, it is likely that someone will claim that the research is wrong if the blame seems to fall on them. The claim may be that it is wrong in a factual sense. But the motivation for the complaint is likely to be that the research has the wrong moral and political implications, those which the complainant does not like. In an often-cited paper called 'Whose side are we on?', the sociologist Howard Becker drew attention to what is an occupational problem for sociologists: that whatever sociologists say it is likely to be complained about as being biased in someone else's favour (Becker 1967). You have now seen why this is an occupational problem. Becker's paper is often misquoted as an argument in favour of researchers siding with 'underdogs' as against the 'establishment'. But, as Becker himself has made clear, he takes a Weberian line on values and social research and prescribes that research should be value relevant and value neutral (Becker 1971; Hammersley 2000a). Becker's own approach to the sociology of deviance is instructive here (1963). He attempts as far as possible to approach deviance as a sociological puzzle, rather than as a social problem. His central question is not 'Why do people commit deviant acts and how can we stop them?' but 'Why is it that some people find the activities of some other people so objectionable that they attempt to stop them acting thus?' Becker's framing of the issue for research is much more threatening to 'respectable and right-minded people' than it is to the groups labelled as 'deviant'. But subverting respectability and improving the reputations of deviant groups was a side effect rather than a central objective of Becker's approach. Becker's own answer to his question 'Whose side are we on?' is that sociologists shouldn't be on anybody's side, but they will always be accused of siding with someone and against someone else.

The researcher's moral expertise and political mandate

Becker's position also represents another part of the rationale for attempting a value-neutral approach when investigating value-relevant issues. In order, knowingly, to allow his or her own values to influence the research, a researcher must assume some special skill in deciding moral or ethical issues. To do research in an attempt to change the world for the better, researchers have to assume both that they have a superior grasp of what is 'for the better' and that they have some kind of mandate to use research to change the lives of other people. Researchers who adopt the value-relevant, value-neutral position, argue that what researchers are particularly good at is doing research. That should include following the moral codes designed to minimise the chances of harm coming to those involved in the research (Chapter 13). Their personal morality should decide what research topics they select and what kinds of sponsorship they will accept. But otherwise, it is argued, researchers have no special expertise in deciding moral issues such as who should have an obligation for what with regard to whom, or whether this state of affairs is fair or unfair. Similarly, so the argument goes, no one has given researchers, as researchers, any mandate to prescribe social morality or political action. This doesn't mean that as individuals they are disbarred from philanthropy or political activism, but that that is in their role as citizen, or town councillor, or university dean: Max Weber himself was heavily involved in the German politics of his time. The mandate for influencing political affairs is what is held by duly elected governments, duly appointed administrators, or people playing their role as active citizens. It is noticeable, for example, how in writing articles about global warming or the loss of bio-diversity, natural scientists often take pains to separate out what they are saying as scientists and what they are saying as concerned citizens (Halliday and Martin 1993). Value-neutral social researchers often adopt the same literary convention (see also Chapter 11, section 11.6).

Looked at in this way, for a researcher to do research deliberately to provide a persuasive case for or against some public policy would be to act without a mandate, and to abuse a privileged position. The argument is buttressed by the assumption that to design research so that it would have the maximum political impact would almost inevitably distort the truth of the findings.

Section 12.4 will explain why those researchers who engage in value-led or partisan research find this rationale unsatisfactory. But in the next section I want to deal with the way in which researchers who do highly value-relevant 'evaluation research' manage the values embedded in the topics they study.

12.3 Evaluation studies and evaluation criteria

Evaluation studies are one of the most common kind of applied social research. Some of them remain unpublished because they are primarily of interest to the future planning of a particular agency, and some because their findings are embarrassing for those who commissioned the research. They are frequently commissioned by government departments, social services departments, education authorities or health authorities to investigate the success or failure of a policy or a project.

Here there is no clear boundary between social scientific research and other kinds of investigations with similar purposes, such as inspections by one of the many official inspectorates such as OfStEd for schools, or the prison inspectorate, by bodies such as the Audit Commission and its Scottish counterpart, official inquiries, judicial reviews, performance indicator measurement, internal agency reviews, clinical audit and such like. Many such exercises rely more on the expert judgements of those conducting them than on rigorous use of social scientific methodologies. Where such methodologies are used they range from experimental and quasi-experimental designs (see Chapter 2 and Chapter 3, section 3.4) to surveys of consumer satisfaction (see Chapters 4 and 7) to interview studies (see Chapter 8) and naturalistic observation (for example see Chapter 10, section 10.6, though this was not a commissioned evaluation study).

Value pluralism and evaluation criteria

The methods used in evaluation studies are diverse and discussed in other chapters. Here I want to focus on something they have in common, which is the need to define **evaluation criteria**. Evaluation studies always ask questions such as 'Is it as good as it could be?' or 'Does doing this have better outcomes than doing something else?'. In order to answer such questions it is necessary to have criteria for defining 'good' or 'better'. What it is that an agency or a policy ought to achieve is nearly always subject to some disagreement. For example, ideas about what a welfare benefits system ought to be achieving are likely to be quite different according to the view of the Treasury, the Department for Social Security (DSS), people thinking of themselves as tax payers, or various benefits recipients. Even where there is less radical disagreement, no agency can coherently pursue more than a few goals and the goals it prioritises must be chosen from many others it might otherwise pursue. No agency can ever satisfy all of the people all of the time. Similarly no evaluation study can ever measure performance against more than a limited number of standards.

Thus evaluation researchers face a problem of **value-pluralism**, which raises questions about:

- Whose values, desires, preferences and so on, should inform the criteria for evaluation?
- Which among the many matters which might be evaluated should be featured in an evaluation study?

Sometimes evaluation researchers are employed to do research which leads to the formulation of evaluation criteria. For example, on the assumption that what is 'good' is what is approved of by a clientèle, they might be commissioned to conduct a survey, or run some focus groups to discover what clients want most from an agency, or what the public wants most from a policy, thus providing information for setting criteria. Then the evaluation is conducted in terms of client satisfaction according these goals. As you saw from Chapter 8, the results of such research are likely to depend on what questions people are asked and how they are asked them. The sample surveys of consumer satisfaction now conducted annually with reference to the British National Health Service (NHS), define evaluation criteria by the questions asked. For example:

> Thinking generally about your experience in hospital last year, please tell us whether you agree or disagree with the statements below:
>
> - You were encouraged to ask questions about your treatment
>   Agree Disagree Don't Know
>
> (Cohen, Forbes and Garraway 1994)

And the responses given are taken to indicate the extent to which these criteria have been met. In this case, what percentage of patients felt they were encouraged to ask questions about their treatment is a measure of success or failure, or of greater or lesser success comparing area with area, and or of progress or regress comparing the same area in succeeding years.

Sometimes evaluation researchers have only limited choice about the criteria to use. Much evaluation research is commissioned by bodies who already have fairly clear ideas what they mean by 'good', 'bad' or 'better': that, for example, in a neighbourhood watch scheme, 'good' means reducing property crime by 10 per cent over a 5-year period. For a hired-hand researcher, accepting these notions of 'good' and 'better' may come with accepting the contract to do the research.

Turning a value statement into a factual standard

It is an expression of values to say:

> This agency should be offering a service to all clients irrespective of their ethnicity, but according to their need for the service and capacity to benefit from it.

But it can be made a matter of fact as to whether the agency is actually doing this. In this example there would be some tricky decisions to make as to how to define 'need' and 'capacity to benefit' in identifiable ways; how to *operationalise* these terms. In principle to turn value statements into standards for judging matters of fact is the same as making decisions as to what questions to ask to elicit information about alcohol consumption, or where to draw the line between 'often' and 'rarely'. But it is important not to forget, first, that the criterion did originate from a value judgement; second, that this was *someone's* value judgement, about which others might disagree; and, third, that in judging performance against some criteria the researcher will not be judging the performance against others which might be more highly valued by someone else.

Pluralistic evaluation

Evaluation researchers may start with a more open-ended brief. Then they often agonise over the question of whose values should inform an evaluation, among the many 'stake holder' groups associated with the service. One response among evaluators to this problem of value pluralism is **pluralistic evaluation,** which goes under a wide range of other names as well, such as Fourth Generation evaluation (Guba and Lincoln 1989). This approach accepts that different kinds of people want different kinds of outcomes from an agency or policy, and frames the evaluator's task as clarifying these diverse wants and discovering who has and who has not had their requirements satisfied. Smith and Cantley's (1985) study of a Scottish, psycho-geriatric day hospital provides an illustration of this. Smith and Cantley did not themselves take a value position of what would count as 'success' and 'failure' in the hospital. Instead, they investigated the ways in which different groups defined 'success' and whether they were satisfied: each in terms of their own notion of 'success'. For example, everyone agreed that 'patient flow' should be properly managed, but there were disagreements as to the proper management of patient flow.

As Box 12.1 suggests Smith and Cantley have made the decision that as researchers they have no particular expertise or mandate to decide what a day hospital ought to be achieving or how it ought to do it. What they do in their research is to make the value positions of various different groups 'objective' by bringing them into the open, without themselves taking sides.

The result of a pluralistic evaluation is to produce information which reflects back to an agency or service the diversity of view points of different stake holder groups, so that these can be reconciled, or not, as the case may be. Some evaluation researchers themselves go so far as to conduct debates and negotiations in order to produce consensus within agencies they have evaluated (Dukes 1996). But it could be argued that in doing this they have gone beyond a researcher role, and have taken on the mantle of an organisational development consultant. Indeed, much of what is described as 'evaluation research' is better described as organisational development, when the object is for members of the organisation to discuss issues, learn

---

BOX 12.1 Pluralistic evaluation: different notions of 'success' in a psychogeriatric day hospital

---

Everyone agreed that admissions and discharges – patient flow – should be properly managed, but with disagreements as to what proper management would be:

- *Consultants* judged patient flow in terms of 'not silting up' hospital beds and favoured an active discharge policy to keep on creating spaces in the hospital. Their view on the intake policy was that there should always be room to admit the patients they wanted admitted.
- *Day hospital staff* also favoured an active discharge policy, but also a selective intake policy operated by them: hence there were disagreements with the consultants.
- *GPs* were most interested in patient flow as a means of getting admission for their patients, but were less enthusiastic about discharges for their own patients, unless to long-term residential care.
- *Social workers* were in favour of discharges home to the care of relatives, but slowed down discharges in order to create suitable arrangements at home.
- *Relatives*, on the whole, were opposed to discharges, seeing these as a withdrawal of a valued service and creating an additional burden for them.
- *Patients* looked at matters in an entirely individual way: those who wanted to continue coming to the day hospital were unhappy about their own discharge; those who wanted to stop coming wanted to be discharged.

Sources: Smith, Cantley and Ritman (1983); Smith and Cantley (1984, 1985).

---

from them and plan better ways of doing things for the future. The kinds of *group facilitation techniques* used in the brokering of mutual understanding and consensus are not 'research methods' in the usual sense of the term and are therefore beyond the subject matter of this book.

Sympathetic bias in evaluation research

Often an evaluator's report will have important consequences in the form of the renewal or non-renewal of funding for a project. There is a temptation not to blight the chances of a group who the evaluator may have grown to like and respect. While not often written about, there is much anecdotal evidence that evaluator-researchers sometimes omit some criticisms from their written reports and give them verbally and confidentially to project teams and management. I will admit to having done this myself. This means that published reports are often more complimentary than the project deserves, which may cause problems for someone trying to emulate a 'successful' project elsewhere on the basis of a published report alone. Pluralistic evaluation demands that researchers take everyone's views into consideration and deal with them in an even-handed way. But some groups will always be much easier to relate to than others.

So far in this chapter I have dealt with those researchers who attempt to maintain some value neutrality with regard to their research, whether the research is of the kind designed to produce general knowledge, or evaluation research designed to judge the value of some practice, or the success of some agency or policy. However some researchers reject the idea of value neutrality.

12.4 Critical and emancipatory research

The term 'critical' used to mean 'objective', 'rational' and 'disinterested' as in the subtitle for this book. But these days in social science it often means '*socially* critical' and 'critique' means complaining about something from a particular point of view. The field of critical research includes marxist (Lather 1986), feminist (Mies 1991), anti-racist (Ben-Tovim *et al.*1986) and disability rights researchers (Barnes and Mercer 1997) among others, although each of these fields is internally very diverse. The term 'critical' is sometimes very narrowly used to refer to the writings of the Frankfurt School, and even more narrowly to the writings of Jurgen Habermas, one of its members (Cuff, Sharrock and Francis 1990 Chapter 4). But I shall use the term more broadly to encompass a wide range of socially critical positions.

Partisanship

Unlike researchers who attempt value neutrality, these researchers believe that, as researchers, they do have a particular expertise in making moral judgements about social arrangements and attempting to change them. They usually draw their mandate for this from representing themselves as researching on behalf of a constituency of oppressed people such as women, black people, working class people, gays, disabled people and so on, who deserve to have their concerns articulated by a researcher – another moral judgement here. Sometimes they are members of such a category themselves (see also Chapter 11, section 11.6).

Writing of feminist research Mies says that research must be subordinated to the political aims of the women's movement, and that research: 'is not just the study but the overcoming of women's oppression and exploitation' (1991: 61).

Similar manifesto statements can be found from critical thinkers who align themselves with other social groups. The best known of these is that from Marx to the effect that the object of philosophy is not to understand society but to change it, meaning to change it for the better. The philosopher Martin Heidegger's insistence that scholarship should primarily be directed towards helping the German people to fulfil their historic destiny is a similar mission statement (Sluga 1993). Thus whether the orientation is feminist, marxist or fascist, the research it proposes is value-led and evaluative. The mission of each establishes a 'regime of truth', which determines what will count as relevant and credible knowledge. This will be different according to values leading the research. Although most such theories make some claims to be aiming to change society for the better for nearly everyone, there is usually some group whose interests are prioritised. Thus this kind of research is sectarian and it is often termed **partisan research**.

A value-neutral researcher such as Becker (section 12.2) would be particularly interested in the political processes through which 'private troubles' are converted into 'public issues' (Mills 1959). The interest would be in this as a sociological topic: some puzzles to solve. By contrast, critical researchers are interested in taking an active part in putting 'private troubles' on the public agenda: that is, in drawing attention to what they define as 'social evils' which ought to be remedied. There is a huge quantity of sociological research which is 'issue-raising' in this way, in fields such as poverty research, educational inequality, domestic violence, gender and ethnic inequality, and various kinds of discriminatory behaviour by employers, the police, the courts and other public agencies. The feminist Carol Erhlich (Stanley and Wise 1983: 24–38), approvingly calls this 'muck-raking research'.

Inequality as a moral category

Writers of this kind very frequently present what are matters of moral judgement as if they were matters of fact. This is particularly the case with the idea of inequality. The term inequality sits rather unhappily between the straightforward and factual 'difference', and the much more problematic and morally loaded 'unfair' or 'inequitable'. In much social research differences are treated as evidence of inequity without researchers justifying the moral judgement they make to convert a difference into an inequity. They routinely commit the naturalistic fallacy (see above).

Ethnographic studies in the sociology of education provide many examples where differences in treatment of pupils by teachers are treated as inequalities, and these inequalities as inequities, as if researchers could observe unfairness without making a moral judgement to do so. To use the idea of unfairness or inequity means dividing people into categories of similar deservingness and judging whether all those in the same category are treated the same. Arguments in this field have a scissors–paper–stone quality where each ethical proposition about who deserves what can be countered by another which, to someone at least, will seem more persuasive (Western 1990). For example, in deciding whether different pupils deserve 'the same treatment' should we regard or disregard the fact that some try harder than others? If a teacher gave the same marks to two pupils turning in work of different quality on the grounds that each had invested the same amount of effort, there would be a complaint that the pupil whose work was best was being unfairly treated. But if two different marks were given, then there might be an argument that the pupil who achieved least, achieved least because circumstances prevented her from investing as much effort as her more fortunate colleague, and that therefore the marking was unfair to her. These are very difficult, and probably irresolvable moral issues which teachers have to grapple with. Many researchers who have carried out ethnographic studies of schools seem to solve them at a stroke, by simply assuming that however teachers treat pupils differently it is unfair.

Among the kinds of teacher behaviour which have attracted most attention are disciplinary actions. Contrasts are usually drawn between the treatment of black pupils as opposed to white, working-class as opposed to middle-class, girls as opposed to boys. Sometimes it is the girls and sometimes it is the boys who are depicted as the disadvantaged group. In critical studies of the classroom there are two versions of what constitutes 'unfair' behaviour in the field of discipline. One is that some disadvantaged group of pupils is subjected to *too much* control by teachers (Clarricoates 1980; Gillborn 1990; Wright 1992). Evidence is cited of allegedly 'the same' naughtiness or inattention being disciplined if committed by the disadvantaged group and ignored among the favoured group. The other is that it is the favoured group who are 'kept on task' while the disfavoured group is ignored: that the disfavoured group receives *too little* control (Sharp and Green 1975; Stanworth 1983). Thus in one study we will read that the educational needs of girls are neglected because teachers spend too much time controlling boys (Spender 1982; Stanworth 1983; Licht and Dweck 1987) and in another that when girls step out of line this is heavily checked, while similar behaviour for boys is ignored as natural male high spirits (Clarricoates 1980). In one study it is a scandal that African-Caribbean boys are subjected to heavy control (Wright 1986) and in another it is a scandal that teachers don't know how to control them and they are allowed to waste valuable learning time (Green 1983).

In addition, not only do such studies issue complaints when teachers treat different kinds of pupils differently when they should treat them the same, they also complain when teachers treat different kinds of pupils the same when they should treat them differently; hence critiques of teaching which is 'colour-blind' or 'gender-blind' or where teachers do not take into consideration that pupils come from different social classes. Where teachers are supposed both to treat everyone the same and everyone differently it is extremely easy to describe whatever they do as wrong. These moral judgements are made in the context of an argument that it is these unfair actions by teachers which cause differences in educational achievement. As noted in Chapter 10 observational studies of these kinds have no way of linking observations in a classroom to educational outcomes (Foster, Gomm and Hammersley 1996: Chapter 5; Foster, Gomm and Hammersley 2000). As you saw from Chapter 5, section 5.3, the effects of social class or gender on educational achievement cannot be seen directly by looking in a classroom.

To issue judgements of this kind, a critical researcher has to assume that he or she knows what the teacher ought to do, and is better able than the teacher to make the everyday moral decisions that teaching entails. It is worth remembering the remarks made in Chapter 10 about the necessarily selective nature of ethnographic observation. If researchers start out with the intention to find unfairness, then they will easily find examples. This is an expectancy effect on a grand scale (Chapter 2, section 2.6). The position taken on such research by those of a value-neutral persuasion is not that unfairness towards a gender, or a social class or an ethnic group is a figment of the critical researcher's imagination. Rather it is that such research rarely provides sound evidence *one way or the other*.

Political impact

Some research has been politically influential, particularly the early poverty surveys of Booth (1902) and Rowntree (1901), the national birth cohort studies (Chapter 6, section 6.3) and studies such as Peter Townsend's *Last Refuge* (1962) which was an exposé of institutional care for older people. Up until the 1960s the mass media tended to be rather deferential to the establishment and there was a greater role for sociological studies to put issues on the public agenda, or to present sympathetic pictures of stigmatised groups. But nowadays it seems that at least one new social issue is placed on the agenda per week by journalists, and each week's television and radio contains a rich diet of personal accounts of what it is like to be black, or gay, or a victim of domestic abuse or child abuse, to be mentally ill or to have learning difficulties and so on. Doing social research these days does not seem to be such an effective way of influencing the political process as does doing journalism. Of course, there is no sharp boundary between the two. Social concern documentary makers employ researchers, and social researchers from academia are sometimes interviewed on screen. But the principles of putting together a piece of social research, and those of constructing a 'hard-hitting' social documentary, are rather different: audience impact and entertainment, rather than truth, are the principal concerns of the latter.

Partisanship versus pluralism

Box 12.1 is useful in distinguishing value-neutral and critical approaches. Smith and Cantley (1985) lay out the viewpoints of the majority of people in each category. They try to be even-handed between them. No doubt they fail in some regards, under-representing minority views within each category, perhaps. Probably it was easier for them to elicit accurate information from some kinds of people compared with others. By contrast, critical researchers would make a moral judgement as to which of all the stake holders was the most deserving. They would probably choose the elderly patients and concentrate almost entirely on the way in which the hospital failed to satisfy their interests. The views of other participants might then be displayed as 'misunderstanding' the 'needs' of the patients and as evidence of an ideology. 'Ageism' would be the most likely ideology referred to here (Blytheway and Johnson 1990).

Of course, Smith and Cantley's decision to be even-handed is as much a moral and political decision as is the critical researcher's judgement to be partisan. Each follows from a different view as to proper conduct for researchers. They also follow from different views as to the implications of being even-handed or of taking sides. From the value-neutral position, taking sides seems likely to produce a partial and distorted view of the truth, favouring one set of views or interests as against others. For a partisan researcher, current knowledge is viewed as already biased against certain kinds of people: say, older people with mental health problems. Therefore being even-handed simply perpetuates this bias. What is needed, it is argued, is research which strongly advocates for the interest of disadvantaged groups and strongly expresses their point of view to redress the balance.

This idea of redressing the balance is often expressed in terms of research having a function of 'giving voice' to people who otherwise would not be heard, or who are so stigmatised that few people would otherwise believe what they say. Research here is being thought of in terms of making a contribution to the democratic process so that minority viewpoints can be broadcast. There is a logical relationship between this and the notion that the object of social research is to foster mutual understanding by enabling different kinds of people to understand things from each other's point of view (Chapter 8, section 8.5). In this regard researchers act as if public relations consultants to various groups of people, choosing the group to advocate for according to the researcher's own political and moral predilections; feminists for groups of women they regard as silenced and oppressed, anti-racists for minority ethnic groups similarly regarded, researchers employed by the Institute of Directors on behalf of those 'misunderstood' to be undeserving 'fat cats', and researchers employed on behalf of the Tory party to correct 'media distortion' of Tory party policy. There is virtually no group in society which does not believe that it is seriously misunderstood by others: quite rightly, too, if being 'misunderstood' means that other people's views about them are other than they would prefer.

12.5 Participative research, action research and practitioner research

Participative research

Feminist and disability rights researchers, in particular, are inclined to regard the traditional distinction between researcher and researched as elitist and exploitative. One of the arguments made in favour of focus group research (for example, Wilkinson 1999) is that it reduces the power of the researcher over those researched, because the researcher is confronted by the power of the group. This may sometimes be so. But power is not necessarily a matter of numbers. In therapeutic and educational contexts it is sometimes argued to the contrary that a skilled group worker can harness the power of the group to give her more persuasive power than she would have in one-to-one encounters. This is why group work is so highly favoured in health promotion, drug rehabilitation or anger management programmes.

However, the terms *'collaborative'* or *'participative research'* usually mean something more than allowing those researched to participate in group discussions facilitated by a researcher. They usually mean research where those who are the subjects of the research become co-researchers.

In social work and health this might also be called **user-led** or **user-controlled** research (Beresford and Evans 1999). The terms **emancipatory** and **empowering** are often used in this respect. There are published evaluation studies of this kind, for example involving people with learning difficulties (Whittaker, Gardner and Kershaw 1990), with mental health problems (Nettle 1996) and other disadvantaging characteristics (Barnes and Mercer 1997). Sometimes collaborations of this kind take the form of group dialogues in which participants share their feelings and experiences; there are no 'findings' as such and the object is to *raise the consciousness* of those participating. 'Raising consciousness' refers to enabling people to come to understand themselves in terms of some given framework of ideas, such as marxism, feminism or anti-racist theory.

Helping members of oppressed groups to articulate their view of the world, or express their political demands more forcefully, is another kind of enterprise. A particularly vigorous area of this kind of work has been that of anthropologists assisting in the advocacy of the tribal land claims of indigenous peoples in Australasia, Canada and South America (Maddock 1998). One of the major programmes of the Joseph Rowntree foundation is its *Voice* programme. Projects funded thus have the aim of helping otherwise inarticulate groups to clarify their concerns and make cases on their own behalf: for example, Deborah Marks' work with school excludees (1995). Again, helping women to write their own autobiographies is regarded as a feminist research strategy (Stanley 1992).

The major interest in the activities above is in having an immediate and benign effect rather than in producing general knowledge. The effects sought might be:

- *Therapeutic* – in improving some group's image of themselves and their morale through doing the research
- *Educative* – in improving the knowledge and skills of those doing the research
- *Political* – in improving the public image of a group, or building them into a cohesive political force, or in helping them win some political battle.

Many of these activities are primarily of interest to those immediately involved rather than to other people. Since the kinds of people likely to participate in participative research are likely to be rather unusual kinds of people, it is doubtful if generalisations could be based on this kind of research anyway. Published success stories, however, are important in building a movement, and published stories of failure important in reminding members of the movement how powerful are the forces they have to strive against.

The practices and skills centrally involved in this kind of research are those such as counselling, group therapy, education (particularly political education), organisational development and political activism. This raises questions as whether it is apposite to call these kinds of activities 'research' at all, and why anyone should want to do so, for often exactly the same activities are carried out without being called 'research'. Some writers, such as Hammersley (2000b) would deny the term 'research' to this kind of activity on the grounds that the term should be restricted to investigations directed towards producing knowledge with some reasonable claim to being generally applicable. But no one has the monopoly on the term 'research', and if people want to use it for other kinds of activities they will. So why would people want to represent what might otherwise be called political activism, or group therapy, as being 'research'? There seem to be two kinds of reason for this.

Action research

The first is on the basis that this is an extension of experimental method. This is the argument most likely to be made when these activities are called *action research*. Then reference will probably be made to the psychologist Kurt Lewin who in the 1930s allegedly coined that term (Lewin 1997). He clearly saw the difficulties of generalising from highly controlled experiments as discussed in Chapter 2, section 2.10 and Chapter 3. His picture of action research is as a way of doing experiments under natural conditions. Lewin reports only one such 'change experiment' (1997:148) which involved dividing delegates to a congress on race relations into groups who received different kinds of support after the congress, and seeing which groups were more successful in fostering good race relations on their return to their home areas. The fact that Lewin desired to make a particular change didn't stop him setting up one comparison group who received no support at all, because had he not done this he would have been unable to discern whether offering post-congress support had any effect. And, except for the way in which 'field experiments' have to differ from controlled ones (Chapter 3, section 3.2) Lewin otherwise followed an orthodox experimental approach.

Like Lewin, some people who say they are practising action research model their practice on experimental methods, building in controls where possible, taking care to define the situation prior to the action and to describe it accurately after the action (for example, Barker 1992; Titchen and Binnie 1994). They see their main objective as contributing to a general stock of knowledge about what interventions are likely to have what consequences under what circumstances, and adopting their interpretation of action research as a means of getting round the problem of the artificiality of experimental situations (see Chapter 3).

By contrast, there is much of what is called 'action research' which seems much more interested in making an immediate and local change, where the only aspect of 'experimentalism' is that of doing something and seeing what happens. There may be no controls, little attempt to produce an accurate picture of the situation before the action and the situation after it, and hence great difficulty in knowing what effects the action taken actually had. Typically, the evidence presented will be in the form of personal testimonies by those involved. Many of the articles published in the journal *Educational Action Research* take this form. 'Educational' in this title does not mean that the research is conducted in educational institutions, but that its main purpose is to provide opportunities for people to learn from doing the research. What people are supposed to learn from doing the research is not how to do research, but about themselves and their situations.

In some circles at least, the term 'research' is prestigious. This may be a second reason why people want to label what would otherwise be called 'practice' as 'research'. This may go with the notion that making a distinction between researchers and others is indefensibly elitist. In these terms participative research in which, say, the tenants of a council estate become co-researchers, represents a democratisation of research: a kind of 'people's research'. To be interesting to them the 'research' has to address their immediate concerns and to have some tangible pay-offs: for example, winning a campaign against damp housing (Hunt 1993). Thus again 'research' becomes more like 'practice'. Nonetheless, writing about the research continues to be published in academic journals in very difficult theoretical terms, which most members of disadvantaged groups would find very difficult to understand.

Practitioner research

In its more orthodox forms, research not only divides researchers from research subjects, but also divides researchers from practitioners. Applying the term 'research' to what otherwise would be called social work, or nursing, or community work, or teaching, turns what practitioners would ordinarily do as practice into research. There have been strong movements for *practitioner research* in education (Elliott 1991; Middlewood, Coleman and Lumby 1999), health (Nichols 1997) and social work (Fuller and Petch 1995), all favouring action research. Doctors continue to control 'medical research' and nurses, 'nursing research'. The need for practitioners to do the research is argued on the grounds that it is practitioners who really know what research needs to be done to provide the knowledge which will be useful in their field. This usually turns out to be research which looks very much like practitioners doing their thing and studying it at the same time. Practitioner research also has the advantage of 'cutting out the middle-man' so that there is an immediate feedback of results from the practitioner as researcher, to the (same) practitioner as practitioner. Very often the desired results are in terms of learning for professional development (Middlewood, Coleman and Lumby 1999; Blenkin, Kelly and Rose 2001) and/or improvement in the organisation where the research was conducted (Coghlan and Brannick 2000), rather than the production of findings for widespread dissemination. However, another advantage of re-labelling 'practice' as 'research' is that it enables a nurse, a teacher, or a social worker to gain a research degree by submitting a study of their own practice.

Action researchers also vary so much in what they set out to achieve and who they are trying to benefit that it is difficult to find any common set of standards to judge them by. However, these kinds of research are claimed to produce effects, such as greater community cohesion, enhanced self-images, better political understanding, more empathetic relationships between practitioners and clients, or furthering the cause of women's liberation. To this extent, then, they should be amenable to appraisal in terms of whether the methods used did indeed produce the effects claimed. As noted in Chapter 3, section 3.4 and in Chapters 5 and 6, the only way to bring off a convincing claim that doing something had a particular effect is by using a research design which includes devices for controlling variables. However, with few exceptions, these kinds of research tend to reject the idea of control, so many such studies in action research (participative or practitioner) fail to produce convincing accounts that the 'action' taken had the effects claimed for it.

ACTIVITY 12.1 Appraising a performance indicator

Performance indicators are increasingly used to evaluate the performance of public services. There are well over 400 performance indicators for the NHS (Appleby and Mulligan 2000), about 200 for social services. For education, scores on Standard Achievement Tests (SATs) and in national examinations are used to judge the relative performance of schools. Many of the common performance indicators are poorly designed for their use. The Department for Education and Skills now publishes the GCSE results for schools in a way that shows the relationship between pupils' SATs scores in earlier years and their 16+ examination results (DfES 2003). This 'value added' approach makes it possible to see whether schools with intakes of a similar ability, measured by SATs, achieve better or worse 16+ examination results than each other. It provides a measure of the differences in progress between similar pupils in different schools. Understandably, schools which rated badly on this measure tended to regard it as unfair and misleading.

   Table 12.1 lays out some questions which need to be asked in order to appraise any performance indicator. The fourth cell has been emboldened since, above all, what performance indicators ought to indicate is performance. For this activity:

a)   Re-read Chapter 5, section 5.3.
b)   Visit the DfES web site, look at the secondary school league tables and read the explanation given there, http://www.desf.gov.uk.
c)   Use the questions in Table 12.1 to appraise the use of 16+ examination results as data for performance indication:
   (i)   in comparing the performance of schools one with another, both without and with reference to previous SATs scores;
   (ii) in comparing the performance of the same school year on year, both without and with reference to previous SATs scores.

TABLE 12.1	Questions to ask about performance indicators

1 *Values* On what, and on whose values is performance measurement based? Who decides what measures and by what justification? What performance indicators (PIs) would be appropriate to other values held by other people?	7 *Even-handedness* Is there provision for judging performance according to what it is feasible for practitioners/agencies to achieve in their different circumstances?
2 *Costs* Is the cost of collecting and processing the data justified by the benefits of having them, and where do the costs and the benefits fall?	8 *Validity* Does the PI measure what it purports to measure? (See also 4)
3 *Incentives* Does the measurement provide incentives to improve performance? What is counted as 'improvement' and by whom? (See 1) Or does it divert effort into achieving less worthwhile objectives (according to someone's judgement)?	9 *Reliability* Are the same means of measurement used in the same way by different people/agencies? (See also 5 and 7)
4 *Performance* Are changes on the PI clearly attributable to the actions of those whose performance it is supposed to evaluate, and are they able to respond effectively to what the PI shows?	10 *Sensivity and robustness* Are changes in performance speedily and attributably reflected in changes in the indicator and is the indicator unaffected by irrelevant factors? (See also 4)
5 *Independence* Is the production of performance indicator data protected from the influence of interested parties: can the data be massaged or rigged?	11 *Transparency*: Is the method through which the PI data are produced transparent and open to inspection?
6 *Simplicity* Is the meaning of the PI easily understood by whosoever is the audience for the information?	12 *Timeliness and availability*: are the PI data available at a time when they are needed to the people who are supposed to respond to them?

12.6 Summary

This chapter has been about values and research. But it was also about a struggle over who should be able to apply the term 'research' to what kinds of activities, and who should be able to appraise research, and by what criteria.

The more orthodox position is that research should be about the production of high-quality knowledge about matters of fact. It is argued here that it is the community of professional researchers which is in the best position to ensure quality control. Though in practice there are impediments of social class, ethnicity and gender to becoming a member of the research community, the aspiration is that the community should be open to anyone willing to abide by some ground rules for researchers:

1. All findings are subjected to communal assessment in which there is an effort to resolve disagreements by seeking common grounds of agreement and trying to work back to a resolution of the dispute relying only on what is accepted as valid by all disputants. This rules out the dismissal of arguments on the basis of the personal and social characteristics of the person advancing them. Thus, for example, it is not legitimate to reject an argument on the grounds that it has been advanced by a male, or to accept an argument on the grounds that it is advanced by a female, or vice versa.
2. Scientists are willing to change their views if such arguments from common ground suggest those views to be false. They are to assume and behave as if other scientists have the same attitude.
3. The scientific community is open to participation by anyone able and willing to operate on the basis of the first two rules. (Hammersley 1990: 62–3)

In this view it is essential for the production of high-quality knowledge that research should be insulated to some extent from politics and commerce. This means both from the interests of governments and big business and from the interests of oppositional groups such as marxists and feminists. Researchers of this view separate off their personal political and moral views from those they adopt as researchers. Research designs include various devices to prevent values thought to be irrelevant from influencing the outcomes of research, as described earlier. Making the research process accountable to the research community is seen as the most important way in which the biasing influence of values can be detected. No one who adopts this view believes that research can ever be entirely 'value neutral'. But for them there is no conceivably better alternative than doing as much as possible to achieve this.

Since they conceptualise the world as being divided into groups with opposing interests, socially critical researchers represents the orthodox position as something that perpetuates the views and interests of people who are already powerful and as marginalising those of others. In this world-view there is no position which researchers can adopt which is not favourable to one side or the other. Since research produced by the orthodox route is already biased against the poor, or women, black people or gays, what is needed is research which is biased in the opposite direction, and ideas can be rejected or accepted according to the personal and social characteristics of those who advocate them. Partisan and value-led research sometimes takes the form of raising issues in an attempt to put them on the political agenda. Here researchers sometimes do not talk of 'producing findings' but of 'making contributions to a political debate'. Or the research might not be designed to produce findings, but to produce personal change among the participants or some improvement in the circumstances of their lives. Such researchers tend to argue that researchers should be accountable not to a research community but to those who are involved in the research, and to others who share their oppression (Lather 1986).

Various other interests also claim the right to determine what research should be conducted and what counts as 'good research'. These include governments and companies. Both tend to view research in terms of providing information for the solution of practical problems as they define them – and, of course, their favoured solutions might not be those favoured by others. They also include various occupational groups. For the social sciences the important occupational groups are the problem-solving occupations of health care, education, social work and the criminal justice system. It is understandable that all of these are likely to believe that if they controlled social science research then it would focus on the important problems as they define them, and generate the kind of knowledge they believe is necessary for their resolution. In all these fields there are vigorous 'practitioner researcher' movements.

All of this brings us back to the idea of *value pluralism*. Given that different groups in society have different ideas as to what is of value, it is understandable that there should be dissensus as to what research should be for, what it should be like and what criteria should be used to judge its results.

Further reading

Hammersley (2000b) is a book of essays on various aspects of values and social research, advocating value neutrality. Partisan or value-led research is marked by vigorous disputes about ethics, politics and research strategy so that it is difficult to find works which adequately represent even the feminist, anti-racist and disability versions. However, Lather (1986) is a widely cited essay advocating value-led research from a marxist, or marxist–feminist point of view. Stanley and Wise (1983, 1993) are arguments for partisan feminist research, Ben-Tovim *et al.* (1986) for partisan research of the anti-racist kind and Barnes and Mercer (1997) for disability research.

Reason (1994) puts the case for participative research. Hart and Bond (1995) is a good introduction to action research by enthusiasts for this approach.

13 Research ethics

By the end of this chapter, you will:

- Understand the way different ethical prescriptions for research follow from adopting value-neutral or value-led approaches to research (see Chapter 12)
- Have considered some of the ways in which harm might come to the subjects of social research and ways of avoiding this
- Have considered some of the ethical dilemmas faced by researchers
- Have acquired one of the codes of research ethics in use in social research and used it to appraise the ethicality of a piece of research.

And know the meaning of the following terms:
accountability ■ anonymisation ■ randomised controlled experiments ■ research ethics ■ sympathetic bias.

13.1 Introduction

'**Research ethics**' refer to rules of morally good conduct for researchers. Just as research cannot tell us what is the good life, research itself cannot tell us what is morally good research. Thus research ethics are grounded in moral and political beliefs which are external to research itself.

Research ethics are not first and foremost a matter of individual morality. Rather they are a communal discipline upheld by communities of researchers, who police each other's conduct. Individual researchers thus have to commit themselves to communal ethics, or suffer censure from their colleagues. There are communities within the community (Chapter 12). Different groups of researchers subscribe to different values. Nonetheless, there is enough common agreement, or enough social pressure, for most to sign up to professional codes of conduct such as those issued by the British Sociological Association (BSA), or the British Psychological Society (BPS), or the British Society for Criminology (BSC). To practise as a doctor, nurse or lawyer, clinical or educational psychologist requires registration with a professional body and breaches of professional codes can result in de-registration. There is no such ultimate sanction for research misconduct, with the partial exception of the registration of people who are licensed to conduct psychometric tests. Despite their codes it can hardly be said that the BSA, BPS or BSC function as powerful disciplinary bodies: their codes are offered as 'guidelines' rather than as by-laws with sanctions for misconduct.

Other agencies also play a role in regulating research. For example, researchers are subject to the Data Protection Act and its regulations about the extraction, curation, confidentiality and use of data about individuals (Backhouse 2002). Applications for research grants are usually vetted for their ethicality. Accepting a research grant is accepting a contractual obligation to follow ethical guidelines. Grants given by the Economic and Social Research Council, the main funding body for social research in the UK, require researchers both to follow ethical guidelines and to place their unpublished data in central archives to improve its availability for peer review. Grants managed by universities are subject to the universities' research ethics committees. Therefore for university-based researchers, following ethical guidelines becomes part of their contract of employment and breaches could be a dismissable matter. Research conducted within the NHS, and sometimes within social services and education, has to be approved by local research ethics committees (Department of Health 1991, 1997; Parker 1994). Irrespective of who does it, all research in the NHS falls under the research ethics code for medical research (Smith 1999). Thus the rather weak codes of practice are strengthened by being drawn in as parts of more binding contracts. Researchers who are also members of professional associations such as doctors or nurses are bound by the codes of conduct of their profession while they are doing research.

Access to many research locations involves the negotiation of local agreements about the conduct of the research. Breaching such agreements may lead to permissions being withdrawn. And, then, there is the criminal law and the civil law on tort, privacy, confidentiality, defamation, slander and copyright, and intellectual property rights, within the bounds of which researchers are supposed to stay. The Nuremberg code, passed in the aftermath of the revelations about Nazi atrocities in research, and the Helsinki code adopted by the World Health Organisation (WHO) both cover social research in medical settings (Nicholson 1997; Eby 2000), and the European Declaration of Human Rights which is incorporated into British law as the British Human Rights Act is also relevant (Sprumont 1999).

13.2 The ethic of producing truthful and transparent research

Researchers may disagree as to what the 'truth' is and how to get at it, but they are all subject to a moral requirement to do research truthfully. Knowingly falsifying research is an important form of deviance for all researchers. It may be very difficult for others to know whether researchers have intentionally falsified research, or have inadvertently allowed expectancy effects (Chapter 2, section 2.6) or other sources of bias to flaw their judgements.

Researchers require each other to take 'all reasonable precautions' to prevent the production of misleading results, just as health and safety law lays a duty on employers to take all reasonable precautions to keep their workforce safe. Different kinds of researchers would interpret this in different ways. Among quantitative researchers there is an array of devices used as preventatives against inadvertent bias and against error arising from slipshod methods: for example, blinding in experiments (Chapter 2, section 2.6) and the blind selection of subjects in experiments and surveys (Chapter 2, section 2.3; Chapter 4, section 4.4); the independent scrutiny of data and its protection from post-hoc revision, inter-rater reliability tests (Chapter 2, section 2.9) and so on. Many qualitative researchers regard all this as interfering with their capacity to get at the truth. They ask others to trust them to get it right without the aid of all these disciplinary mechanisms. From the viewpoint of a researcher committed to controlled experiments, this sounds rather like the company boss who says 'we don't need a health and safety policy here; it would destroy our happy family atmosphere'. But there is no doubt that for some research topics over-regulation may grossly distort whatever it is that the researcher is trying to study. This relates to the debate between the merits of control as against the merits of naturalism running though most of the chapters in this book (see particularly Chapter 10, section 10.1).

The most important disciplinary mechanism in research is making the research available for scrutiny by others (Chapter 1, section 1.7). The kinds of methods used by quantitative researchers lend themselves relatively easily to accountability. Apart from ethnomethodological studies and others of a similar kind, the methods used by qualitative researchers can be more difficult to give accounts of, and hence more difficult to audit by others (see Chapter 10). Though it probably isn't, much ethnographic research could be pure invention and no third party would be in a position to detect this. Again, then, qualitative researchers ask for more trust from their readers than do quantitative researchers. A great deal hinges here on the relationship between what is claimed and the account given to support the claim. It makes a difference whether a researcher says 'it seems to me that ...' or 'this is definitely so'.

There are always temptations for researchers to 'lose' data which goes against their main conclusions, or to push data further than it will go. But it is worth noting that falsified and biased research does not necessarily lead to false conclusions. Gregor Mendel who was the first to work out the mechanism of genetic inheritance (Stern and Sherwood 1966: 173–5), and Isaac Newton who established the subject of optics and discerned the mechanics of planetary motion and the role of gravity (Westfall 1973), both invented or massaged their data to make it fit their theories. Their conclusions were correct but did not follow from their data. So their conclusions were really speculations, and had no right to be regarded as any more than that, until properly supported by evidence. Cyril Burt's false data (Chapter 5, section 5.2) supported conclusions which subsequent research has modified considerably. But it still seems true that genes determine something about intelligence and personality, if not as much as hereditarians once believed. Kinsey's biased interviewing procedures (Chapter 7, section 7.4) produced a very inaccurate account of child sexual abuse in the USA, but may well have produced an accurate picture of the extent of sex with animals.

Thus falsifying data, or skewing the analysis, doesn't necessarily lead to error, just as the police planting evidence doesn't necessarily lead to the conviction of the wrong person. There is a difference between convicting the wrong person and wrongful conviction. The latter implies a 'due process' which is a general-purpose set of procedures, not necessarily successful in every case, but adopted in an attempt to ensure fair and accurate disposals in the majority of cases. In the same way, the commitment to the 'due procedures' of bias control and peer accountability may inhibit the discovery of the truth in particular cases, but there are dangers in making exceptions for particular cases or for particular kinds of research. What once was the exception may drift into becoming the norm.

Temptations to make special cases, and to 'fit up' the opposition as it were, are experienced by those researchers who commit their research to the furtherance of a political cause. Consider this example from Back and Solomos (1993), committed anti-racist researchers:

> [while] we are rejecting a 'value free' perspective we still have to show why our account is a plausible explanation of processes and events. While we recognize that accounts provided by research are partial, this does not absolve us of the need to provide an analysis which is persuasive.
>
> (Back and Solomos 1993: 196; cited in Hammersley 2000b: 10)

On this Hammersley comments:

> by using the terms 'plausible' and 'persuasive' in place of 'valid', they seem to imply that what is required is simply that research findings be convincing enough to have the correct political effect. At the same time, these authors expect lay people to treat their research as objective.
>
> (Hammersley 2000b: 10)

In the famous words of the otherwise unknown Senator Hiram Johnson in 1917, 'the first casualty when war comes is truth' (Knightley 1975: Preface). Hammersley's point is that in 'declaring war' on social evils, partisan researchers such as Back and Solomos are tempted to compromise a commitment to the truth with a commitment to win the war. The literature of critical research is indeed rich with militaristic metaphors about struggles and battles and forces and sides (see Chapter 11, section 11.6). And things do look different from the partisan viewpoint. For them the war started long ago. The opposition have already produced huge quantities of false knowledge; truth is already a 'casualty', and what is needed to secure the truth is counter-propaganda. A metaphor alternative to warfare here is that of the adversarial justice systems of Britain or the USA. Counsels for the prosecution and counsels for the defence each put a spin on the facts and this is justified for each because each is doing the same. The truth is supposed to emerge by the juxtaposition of two not entirely false, but highly partial accounts. But in the last resort the truth is supposed to be decided by judge and jury in a *disinterested* way.

With regard to their accountability, researchers divide. The more orthodox position associated with the idea of value neutrality (see Chapter 12, section 12.2 and 12.6) is that researchers should first and foremost be accountable to the research community, and only secondarily to other social groups. This makes sense as an expediential strategy on two kinds of grounds. The first is the argument that researchers need to be free of other influences in order to see the truth; hence the proscriptions against getting too emotionally evolved with research subjects in order to avoid **sympathetic bias** (Chapter 10, section 10.2) and the demand not to be regulated by companies or politicians whose interests might bias the research (Chapter 12, section 12.2). The second is that being accountable to the research community is being accountable to the group who have the expertise to discern good research from bad, truth from error. In the metaphor of adversarial legal systems the research community are supposed to play the role of the distinterested jury. In practice they will often be far from disinterested. Some will prefer some findings rather than others, because these support or undermine their own line of thought. It is in medicine that this problem of 'jury bias' has been most seriously addressed, with specially commissioned independent reviews of research on particular treatments, most notably those of the Cochrane Collaboration network and the National Institute for Clinical Excellence or NICE (Needham 2000: 146–8).

By contrast, feminist, anti-racist and disability researchers take the position that they should make themselves accountable first to the oppressed group among whom they do research, and only secondarily to the research community (Lather 1986; Romm 1997). This stance makes sense on the assumption first, that research should be about improving the circumstances of the oppressed, rather than accumulating knowledge in academia, and second that it is the oppressed who really know the truth and are in the best position to evaluate the research: no disinterested jury here. In practice however, since such researchers publish in academic journals and make their careers that way, they do make themselves significantly accountable to that part of the research community which reads their work, and in publishing in academic journals they certainly don't make themselves directly accountable to many people suffering from oppression.

Associated with this division is another about the proper conduct of researchers towards those whom they research. The more orthodox position is that researchers should behave so as to do subjects *no harm,* while critical researchers prescribe that researchers should behave so as to *do some good* to favoured categories of people.

13.3 Doing no harm and doing some good while doing research

Table 13.1 gives a synopsis of the more important possibilities for doing harm and doing good, *while* doing the research. Section 13.8 looks at the possibilities for doing harm or good in publishing the results.

In what follows it is worth keeping in mind that the vast majority of social research does none of the subjects any significant harm or good. The fact that most social research has no benign effects for those researched is sometimes elevated into a serious sin. This is based on the assumption that social researchers, as researchers, could actually do some good to people.

The last column of Table 13.1 suggests that deciding on ethical conduct involves balancing harms and benefits. Ethical considerations usually throw up *ethical dilemmas*. General principles and codes of practice may provide steps on the way to resolving these, but in the last resort most ethical dilemmas have to be dealt with in an ad hoc, best-of-the-worst kind of way. The conflicts here may be between:

- One ethical principle and another: for example, maintaining confidentiality towards one person, as against preventing harm coming to another; telling the whole truth as against protecting someone's interests
- Serving the interests of one group of people as against serving the interests of another
- The researcher's desire to find something out and the researcher's obligations to inform the subjects fully: for example, much psychological research would be impossible without deception.

13.4 The ethics of the lottery: randomised controlled experiments

Randomised controlled experiments (see Chapter 2) are widely used in psychology. As randomised controlled *trials* (RCTs) they are regarded as the 'gold standard method' in testing the effectiveness of treatments in medicine. As the demand for 'evidence-based practice' grows in social work, criminal justice interventions, counselling and education, it is likely that RCTs will be used more widely in these contexts in the future (Oakley 2000). When used in studies of effectiveness, the interest is in some intervention which is designed to do people good: to cure their illness, for example. And there is often a suspicion that there is a risk that the intervention might do some harm: drug side effects for example. Such trials, then, ask research subjects to give their 'informed consent' to be entered into a lottery with various hazards.

The first aspect of the lottery is that if researchers already knew who, if anyone, would benefit, and who, if anyone, would be harmed and in what kinds of ways, precisely, there would be no need for the research. Thus researchers are not fully in a position to facilitate *fully* informed consent by

TABLE 13.1 Doing good and harm to subjects in doing research

Possibilities	Possible harm	Possible good	Trade-offs
Physical harm and good	Outside the field of health research, social research rarely presents any particular risks to the physical health and safety of subjects	Only in health research is doing the research likely to have any benign effects on the physical health and safety of subjects	In randomised controlled trials used in testing treatments in medical research (Chapter 2) members of one group are more likely to experience improvement or deterioration of their health than the other (Section 2.4), but which may be unknown in advance
Psychological harm and good	The risks of emotional harm are greatest where subjects are vulnerable and the research involves close, emotionally charged relationships between researcher and subjects and/or between research subjects High-risk situations include some psychological experiments (section 13.6) qualitative interviews or focus groups on sensitive topics, participative research and action research (section 13.7) High-risk groups include children, people with mental health problems and victims of abuse	The possibility of improving people's emotional state while doing the research depends on the kinds of relationship it is possible for researchers to make with subjects, and research subjects with each other There are greater opportunities in clinical trials of psychotherapeutic treatments, in-depth interviews, focus groups, participative and action research (section 13.7)	The situations with the greatest risks of doing emotional harm to people are similar to those in which there are the greatest opportunities to do emotional good to them In some situations it is possible that some subjects will improve their emotional state at the expense of some other subjects: for example in a focus group or a consciousness raising group
Educative effects	In most social research participants have little opportunity to learn much of significance to them, but harm might come via the emotionally charged relationships of some participative research, or in a poorly managed focus group	In participative research and action research, it may be the prime objective of the research to improve the knowledge and skills of the participants (Chapter 10, section 10.5)	What people learn about themselves as research subjects may not be congenial to them (see section 10.5). This may be true in action research where the action fails to have the desired results

Self-determination	The right to self-determination for subjects of research is a common item in codes of research practice, usually phrased in terms of the need to obtain the subject's 'informed consent to participate'. However, much research simply would not work if subjects were fully informed about the details of the research beforehand (sections 13.5 and 13.6). Hence this is a right which is often breached in research, though rarely with any tangible harm arising	In participative and action research (Chapter 10, section 10.5) it may be among the primary objectives of the research to enhance the participants' ability to take charge of their own lives	Much research, particularly in psychology, relies on deceit. Hence there is a conflict between the subject's rights to self-determination and the researcher's need to mislead them. In overt participant observation research constantly reminding people as to the fact that they are being researched will increase any Hawthorne effect (Chapter 9, section 9.4). Covert observation research is a direct breach of the right to self-determination (section 9.5). In participative/action research with political aims, the gains of the subjects may be at the expense of someone else (Chapter 10, section 10.5)
Privacy and confidentiality	While people's right to privacy is an important right, breaching it does little tangible harm without an accompanying breach of confidentiality. Breaches of confidentiality may have serious consequences if the information falls into the wrong hands	Breaches of confidentiality may forewarn other people of dangers to themselves or may give them an edge in some conflict in which they are engaged where the researcher supports their cause	Conflicts between: the rights of subjects not to have their privacy breached and the researcher's need to study people unbeknown to them; the researcher's obligations to prevent harm coming to other people and the rights of the subjects to confidentiality
Material, political and reputational gains and losses	Research may influence policy or practice against the subjects' interests or consolidate a stereotyped view of them	Research may influence policy or practice in the research subjects' favour or improve their public reputation. In participative research may inaugurate a research career	Gains for the subjects may be at the expense of someone else

the subjects, except in the sense that subjects can be informed that they will face risks of unknown kinds and magnitude. Properly conducted RCTs do involve a risk assessment, but however well this is done there will be a residuum of risk unknowable in advance. All RCTs include a provision to 'withdraw' subjects who seem to be in distress, but this will not protect against harmful effects which show only in the long term.

The second aspect of the lottery is that subjects will not know to which comparison group they will be allocated. With a control group and a treatment group those in the control group may be deprived of a treatment which would improve their health, but be protected from any adverse side-effects of the treatment, while those in treatment group might receive a treatment beneficial to them, and/or might experience unpleasant or occasionally even fatal side-effects.

People's attitudes to the ethics of RCTs as lotteries tend to polarise between those who feel that any element of lottery is unfair and unethical, and those who feel that in situations of uncertainty some blind and disinterested decision-making is fairer than choosing people according to their known characteristics when various biases and prejudices might play a part (Elander 1991; Featherstone and Donovan 1998). But apart from gut feelings of this kind, it is important to view RCTs in a broader context and consider the implications of <u>not</u> proceeding in this way. Here the question is whether the risks and deprivations suffered by the losers in the lottery are justified by the benefits gained for much larger groups of people. No one would argue these days, surely, that medical treatments should be implemented without prior research to establish their benefits and risks. And increasingly people are asking why social workers, counsellors and educationalists should be allowed to launch into what are ad hoc uncontrolled experiments on their clients and pupils as a routine aspect of their work, without some prior research evidence about the future effects of what they are doing (Oakley and Fullerton 1996). Some legitimate doubts can be framed about the appropriateness of RCTs in these other fields because of the complexity of the interventions concerned (Chapter 2, section 2.4). But there is no doubt that the RCT is the best design for judging the effects of many interventions. Randomisation in RCTs is not adopted because it is the *fairest* way of allocating risks between research subjects. It is adopted because it is the most *efficient* way of controlling out prior subject variables, and hence essential for producing less ambiguous results (Chapter 2, section 2.3 and Table 3.4). If an effect were so large and so unambiguous that it was not necessary to use randomisation in the research to detect it, then the research would probably be unnecessary: no one has to conduct RCTs to discover that heavy blows to the head with large hammers do a lot of damage, for example.

Thus the argument here is that if a large number of people in the future are to benefit from practitioners' knowledge about the effectiveness and risks of particular treatments, then RCTs are the best way of producing such knowledge and the risks to the experimental subjects are justified, so long as they are willing to play the role of public benefactors and are fully appraised of the fact that an RCT will be a risky business for them (see Box 13.1)

I have used the example of medical trials because here there are the highest risks. But the same might apply with regard to a particular method of teaching. It might be argued that if a method of teaching was particularly effective it would be an unfairness to the controls to deprive them of this. But if it proved otherwise, then the unfairness might be to the experimental group. Trying to solve this by treating all the same actually makes the problem worse. For if the method is used and is ineffectual everybody suffers; and if the method is not adopted but would have been an improvement, then everyone loses too. The gamble is on the unknown effectiveness of the method, which is what the research is supposed to clarify.

BOX 13.1 Informed consent

In codes of ethics for social researchers informed consent is among the most important principle. Put crudely, participants to research need to be told what they are letting themselves in for, before they make a decision to co-operate. For informed consent the social researcher should:

> Explain as fully as possible, and in terms meaningful to participants, what the research is about, who is undertaking it and financing it, why it is being undertaken, and how it is to be disseminated [and] not as a once-and-for-all prior event, but as a process, subject to re-negotiation over time.
>
> (British Sociological Association 2002)

Ideally, informed consent would be part of a contracting process with a written agreement between the researcher and each subject, laying out the terms and conditions of the research (for examples, see Hart and Bond 1995: 199–201). There are particular difficulties about deciding whether consent has indeed been 'informed' with subjects who are very distressed, have mental health problems or learning disabilities, or those for whom informed consent is made by others on their behalf, such as children.

In practice, providing for informed consent depends on researchers having some idea of the trajectory and outcomes of the research, on the possibilities of subjects understanding the purposes of the research, on the feasibility of doing the research in the full knowledge by the participants of what is going on and/or of constantly being reminded that they are being researched and, in much ethnographic research, on decisions about who among the many people who float into view are to be regarded as research subjects with a right to be informed.

Justifications for not gaining informed consent rest on the practical issues above and on the estimation either that no harm will come to the participants in the absence of their consent, or that any such harm is more than compensated by some good done to other people.

As used in psychology, randomised controlled experiments have less dire ethical implications, unless of course there is also some risk of harm to research subjects (see section 13.6).

The remarks about RCTs in medicine above assumed that they were properly conducted. In practice many medical trials are rather badly done, with poor briefings of the subjects and negligible support for them while they are research subjects (Bosley 1999). But there is a difference between the ethics of a particular research strategy competently used and those of using the method without due care and attention.

13.5 Privacy, confidentiality and covert research

The canonical case for discussing the ethics of covert research is Laud Humphreys' (1975) *Tearoom Trade*: his study by naturalistic observation of male homosexual liaisons in public toilets. It is inconceivable that this research could have been done by observation other than covertly. At the time at which it was conducted, homosexuality was in the United States illegal and highly stigmatised. It is unlikely that Humphreys could have conducted an interview study instead. Reiss (1964) is an interview study, but of a group of what we would now call 'rent boys', while Humphreys was interested in the engagement of otherwise 'respectable' people in homosexual acts. How else, in the 1970s, could he find them except by going to the places where such acts were committed and disguising his intentions for doing so?

So if the research was to be done, it had to be covertly. The research is not a straight forward breach of the subjects' privacy, for they were knowingly and consentingly observed. But the consent was gained under false pretences. They did not give fully informed consent, since they did not know Humphreys' purposes for observing them. Apart from observing homosexual acts, Humphreys also collected the men's car registrations. From these he traced their addresses, and then arranged interviews with them not about their homosexuality but about other aspects of their lives. They remained unaware of the linkage between the being observed and being interviewed. Thus they did not give fully informed consent to the way in which Humphreys used the interview data either. In addition, by having a list of names and addresses Humphreys put his subjects at risk of being investigated and prosecuted by the police should the addresses have fallen into the wrong hands. Though this did not happen, it is this risk of a breach of confidentiality that Humphreys most regretted in retrospect.

So far then, Humphreys' research looks entirely unjustifiable in an ethical sense, and it would certainly breach today's research ethics codes of practice. But it looks less unjustifiable when we consider the following. Humphreys was an ordained minister and an active civil libertarian who had spent times in gaol for his political activities in supporting civil rights. He was deeply committed to liberalising the law on homosexuality and in removing the stigma attached to it. The purpose of his research was to provide evidence that male homosexuals were not derelicts and vicious perverts but often 'family men' and pillars of their local communities. The evidence he collected showed just that, and the *Tearoom Trade* probably did have some influence in the subsequent liberalisation of the law in the USA, though homosexuality still remains illegal in some states of the union.

This case raises a host of ethical dilemmas. First, should we judge the ethicality of research by reference to the motivations of the researchers? Probably the answer to this is 'yes, up to a point'. Second, in judging the ethicality of research how much weight should we place on the conduct and how much on the outcomes? In this respect the Humphreys' case has a format very familiar in fiction. Think of all those cop movies where 'our hero' disregards the constraints of ethical policing, but by so doing rids the streets of hoodlums and serial killers. On these lines we might perhaps judge research which was unethical in its commission as nonetheless ethical because of its outcomes.

Anne Other's research cited in Chapter 9, section 9.6, is a similar case. She was refused permission to conduct her research on hygiene behaviour in a hospital by a local research ethics committee, who decreed that she should gain informed consent not only from the staff, but also from all the patients or, in the case of their incapacity from their next of kin. Other regarded the latter requirement as a 'wrecking' strategy to make quite sure her research was not carried out. She is not the first researcher to suspect that NHS research ethics committees, dominated as they are by doctors and nurses, are sometimes used as a way of preventing researchers prying into their affairs. And it would have wrecked her research to have announced the fact and the purpose of her research to the staff. Thus she conducted her research covertly and 'unethically'. Having done the research without ethical clearance, as a nurse she is vulnerable to disciplinary action by the disciplinary committee of her profession, and might well be struck off and prevented from earning her living as a nurse. Anne Other is not her real name.

Even where observational research is overtly engaged in, it may be difficult and impractical to secure and maintain the subjects' informed consent (see Box 13.1). Much ethnographic research is open-ended (Chaper 10, section 10.6). If researchers do not know where it will lead, then how can they forewarn the subjects adequately? And if they are forever reminding subjects that research is going on then this will influence the way people behave, when the object of most ethnographic research is to observe 'things as usual'. It is sometimes very difficult for researchers to explain the concept of the research adequately to the subjects. Like many anthropologists I found it very difficult to explain the idea of anthropological research to the people I studied in Kenya. We settled in the end on the understanding that I was studying history, a concept they did understand, but this was hardly true. And then, many settings for ethnographic research are full of people coming and going: a village, a market place, a hospital ward. Do they all have a right to know that research is being conducted in the setting? If they do, then much research by naturalistic observation must of necessity breach these rights since it would simply be impracticable to uphold them.

Anne Other's main defence against a charge of research deviance would be in terms of 'public interest'. After all, hospital-acquired infections are a major source of death and unnecessary suffering in hospital (Plowman, Fraves and Roberts 1997). She could claim that only by studying hygiene behaviour covertly could the causes of the problem be adequately investigated. The public interest defence is widely used, or over-used, by journalists for breaches of privacy and confidentiality. Other's own position is stronger these days than it would have been in the past with the passing of legislation to protect whistle-blowers from recriminations from those they blow the whistle on (HMSO 1998). Thus with both the case of Humphreys and that of Other, we are forced to balance the rights of people studied to their privacy and to the confidentiality of their affairs as against the value of the findings made in breach of these rights.

Of course any value the findings might have may not be to the benefit of the people studied. And this is not a straightforward balance.

First, we rarely regard everybody as having equal rights to privacy and confidentiality. These days, no doubt, most readers of this book would say that homosexuals in public toilets should have their privacy respected. But in the climate in which Humphreys was working a very large constituency would argue that they had no such rights since what they were doing was evil and illegal. Similarly, there is relatively little controversy today about researchers who breach the rights of privacy and self-determination of people stealing from their employers (Ditton 1977) or people engaged in racially discriminatory behaviour (Bowler 1993). In her study of prostitution Julia O'Connell Davidson felt that it was necessary to inform the prostitutes of her research intentions, but not their clients (O'Connell Davidson and Layder 1994).

Second, rights of self-determination, privacy and confidentiality do not mean much unless we specify the degree of harm which follows from their breach. In fact, very little harm follows from breaches of privacy alone. It is never entirely clear what rights to privacy people have or should be granted. For example, as the current law stands, there is an obligation to inform people that their image may be captured via a security camera but there are no procedures for them to give or withhold permission for this, nor to arbitrate how the information is used, though that is circumscribed by the Data Protection Act. Rights to privacy always seem to relate to the social role someone is playing, the ownership of the space they are occupying, or of the documents on which details of themselves are inscribed, and the legality of their activities. Thus pedestrians in public spaces seem to have little in the way of rights to privacy, people in their homes have many, but people in their homes may have their privacy legally invaded if there is a reasonable suspicion that they are engaged in illegal activities. Researchers' behaviour seems roughly to mirror the legal situation, though they have no legal right to bug phones, use secret cameras, or demand entry to private places.

Breaches of privacy are relatively trivial if they are not accompanied by breaches of confidentiality. Nearly all published research is anonymised as to place and persons with some exceptions. I shall deal with these in relation to the ethics of publication in section 13.8. Some researchers take care to use pseudonyms or code numbers to anonymise people in their research notes. Although there has been no legal case to date it remains a possibility that a court might subpoena a researcher's notes. Similarly, breaching a subjects' rights to self-determination has serious consequences only where this may lead them into actions which will do them harm. In all these regards, then, no tangible harm came to research subjects from Humphreys' or Other's research in their breaching of the subjects' rights to privacy and self-determination, mainly because no confidentiality was actually breached.

However, there is also a public interest defence for breaching the subjects' rights to confidentiality. This is one which researchers rarely use, and where others might regard them as being unethical in not doing so. Particularly in the field of deviancy studies, researchers get to know and sometimes to observe criminal acts and other acts of harm done by their research subjects. In English and Scottish law there is no legal requirement to inform the police that a crime has been committed, but it might be argued that, as good citizens, researchers should do just this. At a sub-legal level even feminist and anti-racist researchers will often allow racist and sexist language to be used in their presence and for apparently discriminatory acts to take place without challenging these (for example Bowler 1993). Other stood by while zillions of MRSA bacteria were transmitted from patient to patient and did nothing to prevent this happening. There is an issue here of *when* to be ethical. To act immediately would be to jeopardise the research. In the case of covert research this might sometimes lead to personal danger, as in Fielding's study of the National Front (1981). Most researchers prefer to be ethical in their publications rather than on the spot, for being ethical on the spot may mean that there is no publication.

13.6 Psychological harm, self-determination and deceit

If the Humphreys study is the canonical case for discussing the ethics of covert research, then it is Stanley Milgram's studies in obedience (1963, 1974, 1992) which constitute the canonical case for considering psychological harm arising from research. Milgram's research involved a suite of experiments all with a similar structure. Subjects were told that they would be participating in an experiment to investigate whether pain would improve the way people learned. From the subjects' point of view the experiments seemed to consist of a random selection between two subjects: one to be a 'learner', and one to be a 'teacher'. In fact the learner was a confederate of the experimenter, a stooge. The only subject in each case was the 'teacher'. The subject was shown the learner being strapped into an apparatus which would deliver an electric shock and then taken into another room (in most versions of the experiment) and seated at the consol of an impressive 'electric shock machine' with calibrated shock levels, the higher levels being marked 'Danger: do not use'. The subject as teacher was asked to read lists of words over a microphone, allegedly to the stooge as learner in another room, and then to test him on his accuracy of recall. In the event of an error, or a silence, the subject was to administer an electric shock, stronger for each successive error. In most versions of the experiment the learner's apparent responses were supplied on a light-up screen, with pre-recorded protests and sounds of distress relayed over a loudspeaker to standardise the stimulus for all subjects. Pre-recorded responses were arranged so that if the subjects followed their instructions they would continue until they reached the highest shock level – '450 volts', despite the learner's requests to stop, his reports of having a heart condition, his refusal to continue and eventually ominous silence. Variations on this basic design included the presence or the absence of the experimenter in the same room as the learner stooge, and the venue of the experiment in a prestigious university building or in a shabby down-town office. A more radical departure required the subject directly to apply shocks to the 'learner' by pressing his hand on an electrode; the learner acting out the pain of the experience.

The whole suite of experiments included 900 subjects, but in the basic experiment, 26 out of 40 subjects continued to the highest shock level, while 14 refused to go any further than between '300' and '375' volts, after the learner complained about the pain and refused to supply any more answers.

All this is impressive as an experimental design in its control of variables. Despite their staged nature, the experiments do achieve some degree of naturalism if compared with the circumstances of the 'death' laboratories of Nazi Germany or Stalinist Russia. Milgram's findings carried a valuable lesson for understanding atrocities committed by the Nazis, or by American servicemen in Korea and Vietnam; for example see Browning's (1993) study of a Nazi death squad in wartime Poland. They made it impossible to attribute such behaviour to deranged psychopaths, to the stresses of war, or to the power to punish in dictatorial regimes. They showed that ordinary men, under rather minimal conditions of compulsion, would follow instructions to inflict pain on harmless strangers. These were findings which were widely regarded as valuable. But the way they were obtained is ethically very dubious.

Most psychologists would not raise ethical objections to the experiment simply on the grounds that it involved trickery (but see Baumrind 1964 on Milgram's experiments and Milgram's replies 1964, 1992). A very large amount of psychological research could not be done without directly misleading subjects as to the purpose of the research, or by allowing them to misinterpret what was going on by withholding important information. Almost all of the psychology of perception, for example, involves tricking the senses.

In Milgram's experiments the major ethical problems are associated with the obvious psychological distress caused to the subjects. They displayed this at the time as perspiration, hysterical laughter and nervous tics. More importantly, however, those subjects who complied, learned something unpleasant about themselves. The experiment showed them that they did not have the moral fibre to resist the instructions of someone else, despite the fact that the experimenter had no serious sanctions he could use to enforce compliance. And it showed them that they were the kinds of people who would inflict pain and maybe death on a fellow human being who had done them no harm. It might be argued that what they learned about themselves was true, but whether it is always beneficial for people to know the truth about themselves, and who has a right to tell it to them, are difficult questions to answer.

In provoking an ethical controversy the Milgram experiments led to a revision of the code of practice for American psychologists (Harris 1988), mirrored in the British code, requiring experimenters to 'debrief' their subjects. This means both to explain to them how they had been misled, and to provide such care and counsel needed for their psychological welfare. In fact Milgram did debrief his subjects immediately after the experiments but he did not provide any follow-up. Milgram notes that 80 per cent per cent of the subjects said that they were glad to have been involved in the experiment (1992:130–3), but this in turn might be regarded as another 'obedient' response. And there remains a question as to whether the value of the findings of the research justified the infliction of distress on the subjects.

It is unlikely that Milgram's experiments would gain ethical approval today. But that is from the wisdom of hindsight, to which Milgram's experiments contributed. Milgram himself expected most subjects to refuse to continue at a much earlier stage. He might, however have aborted the series before completion, as Philip Zimbardo did with his prison simulation experiment (Haney, Banks and Zimbardo 1981). This involved no deception but the allocation at random of students to the roles of 'prisoners' or 'guards' in a simulated live-in gaol. Within a few days prison 'guards' were behaving with considerable cruelty towards the 'prisoners'. As with the Milgram experiments, it was the perpetrators of cruelty who were the most psychologically disturbed by the experience. Zimbardo and his colleagues provided a counselling service for the experimental subjects. Like Milgram they had not expected the results they produced and were not therefore able to put subjects in a position where they could exercise *informed* consent.

The ethical problem in these two experiments is about causing psychological harm to people who do not deserve it. But Diana Scully considered that she faced the opposite problem of doing psychological good to people who did not deserve that benefit. Her study involved conducting loosely structured interviews with men who had been convicted of rape:

> The type of information sought in this research required a supportive, non judgemental neutral façade – one that I did not always genuinely

feel. Frankly, some of the men were personally repulsive ... additionally the stories they told were horrible and a few of the men were not overtly co-operative. Indeed, some of the interviews require immense effort to remain neutral. But the fact is that no one tells his or her secrets to a visibly hostile and disapproving person.
(Scully 1990:18, cited in O'Connell Davidson and Layder 1994:141)

Apart from these issues of practicality, Scully 'worried that some of these men might interpret neutrality as a signal of agreement or approval' (1990:19) – that they would feel better about themselves as a result of the interviews, and that the interviews might reinforce their propensity towards violent sexuality.

Avoiding doing research subjects psychological harm, or good when they don't deserve it, requires some percipience. Researchers have to be able to guess what people will find upsetting or supportive. To some extent this can be taken as given by the topic and the subjects of the research. Much interview research is done about sensitive topics, such as victimisation or bereavement, or with subjects who have a mental illness problem. Here it is a reasonable assumption that the interviews will need to be handled with care, subjects pre-briefed as to their rights to discontinue, and interviewers willing to switch from extracting information to offering support. But any interview about any topic can trigger distress occasionally. Handling distress in an interview context is rarely a skill taught in research methods courses. It is not something which can simply be accomplished by making a befriending relationship with subjects. Our friends and other intimates are usually those who hurt us most.

Some feminists (Grumet 1991; Stacey 1991), against the grain in feminist research, have suggested that befriending relationships can lead to a sense of false intimacy and hence are unethically exploitative and create a false promise of a future relationship which the researcher will not fulfil. The literature on counselling suggests that what some might see as supportive, educative and empowering relationships, are seen by others as manipulative and indoctrinating (Masson 1988).

In their study of dual career families (Chapter 7, section 7.5) the Rapoports (1976) interviewed couples several times. It is likely that these interviews themselves became important components of marital dynamics, having some effect on how the couples viewed themselves and each other. It seems highly likely that the way the interviews twisted and turned sometimes favoured one of a couple rather than the other. Something like this seems inevitable. But the difficulty here is knowing what effect the interviews did have. Only if researchers know this can they actually address this as an ethical problem, and do something practical about it. Discovering the effects of the researchers' actions on the subjects in this case would be a much more challenging research topic than the research the Rapoports actually conducted. Much the same is true of most research with regard to the retrospective estimation of the effects of the researcher on the morale, self-images and social relations of the subjects. It is true of almost all research with regard to knowing this in advance.

13.7 Doing good while doing research

Researchers who believe that research should be designed to do those researched some good usually have in mind benefits such as improved self-image, improved competences and knowledge, greater understanding of their social and political situation, more cohesive communities, or some tangible improvement in their situation. As you might guess from Scully's feminist research on rapists, such benefits are supposed to be supplied only to those whom the researcher believes deserves them, and what counts as greater social or political insight depends on what beliefs the researcher subscribes to.

This ethical position is usually accompanied by the idea that it is unethical for researchers to take the commanding role in directing the research. The ethical grounds for this are nicely captured by Heron (1981):

> For persons, as autonomous beings, have a moral right to participate in decisions that claim to generate knowledge about them. Such a right ... protects them ... from being managed and manipulated ... the moral principle of respect for persons is most fully honored when power is shared not only in the application ... but also in the generation of knowledge ... doing research on persons involves an important educational commitment: to provide conditions under which subjects can enhance their capacity for self-determination in acquiring knowledge about the human condition.
>
> Heron (1981: 34–5)

This then, is the kind of ethical argument advanced for participative or collaborative research where the 'subjects' are both co-researchers and principal beneficiaries.

It is worth noting that following this ethic would rule out the acquisition of a great deal of 'knowledge about the human condition', particularly in psychology with its reliance on deceit, and also in sociological studies of crime, racial and sexual discrimination, many of which have been done covertly. But then being morally good always has costs, and it has to be decided whether the good which would come from following these principles is worth the cost in general or in particular cases. I shall restrict my remarks to some of the difficulties of putting these principles into operation.

Here is a prescription for doing good, by the researcher *not* being in control.

> The study of an oppressive reality is not carried out by experts but by the objects of the oppression. People who before were objects of the

research become subjects of their own research and action. This implies that scientists who participate in this study of the conditions of the oppression must give their research tools to the people.

(Mies 1983:126)

There are two problematic aspects of this. First, most such research is open-ended. No one will be able to predict where it will end up. Open-ended research is always a high-risk enterprise. Where the research is designed to effect political change, or to change people, then the risks are that much higher. Any book on counselling or group work practice issues warnings about this. This raises problems of informed consent. If the future cannot be predicted, then no one can be adequately informed. Involvement in the kind of political activism associated with community action research (Hunt 1993) can be a bruising experience, and involvement in the kind of consciousness raising associated with some feminist research (Patai and Koertge 1994) even more so.

However, second, if the researcher devolves control and responsibility to the subjects of the research as co-researchers, then what is there to ensure that *they* will behave in an ethical way? Enthusiasts for this approach write of the need to establish ethical ground rules to which all will subscribe (Romm 1997). But if the participants won't follow the rules, then apart from persuasion, the only sanction the 'professional' researcher has is to say 'goodbye'. I found myself in this position when doing participatory action research on claimants' unions in the 1970s. Because of the vicious infighting between members I eventually withdrew. As they told me in no uncertain terms, I had no right to tell them how to behave, and this was actually written into the agreement I made to ensure their 'informed consent' (see Box 13.1). Again, in evaluating a piece of 'user-controlled' consultation research which had been conducted to inform the planning for the closure of a mental hospital, I was forced to the conclusion that the group of inmates doing the research had wrongly represented their own ideas for community care as those desired by all the inmates. The latter illustrates a violation of Heron's prescription that 'persons ... have a moral right to participate in decisions that claim to generate knowledge about them'. But, as always, talk about 'rights' is idle if there are no mechanisms to ensure that one group of people accepts another's rights as their obligations.

The idea of participatory research sits rather awkwardly with the idea of the professional regulation of research ethics, for participatory research is a deprofessionalised practice. Nonetheless professional researchers who engage in it do publish their work in the professional journals and are thereby vulnerable to judgement according to professional codes of practice. This is even more so if they receive research grants from most of the major funders. It might be argued that to regard the professional researcher as the one ethically responsible for the research would be patronising and demeaning of their non-professional co-researcher subjects. But equally other people might say: 'You're the professional researcher; the buck stops with you.'

Of course, some participatory research achieves its objectives fairly well. There must often be some doubt about this because the notion that accountability is primarily to the subjects makes them, as both subjects and researchers, advocate, judge and jury in their own case. In this kind of research the most usual evidence of success is in the form of the personal testimonies of those still involved at the end of the research. Publication of these angles the reader into a moral bind. Any independent ethical judgement by the reader is an impertinence committed by an outsider who has no right to make it and, as someone who is not oppressed, as having insufficient understanding to make it. Hence the only moral response allowable for a reader is to agree with the ethical appraisal of the writer(s). However, this is not a bind that readers have to accept.

As with the ethical consideration of all kinds of research, it is important to judge the risks and the harms of such research against the benefits of its outcomes. Participatory research is usually research which is designed to bring a direct benefit to a small group of people, and only secondarily to generate knowledge for use by others.

13.8 The ethics of publication

The fate of the vast majority of published research is to sit on library shelves unread. In this, research is no different from any other kind of publication. However, researchers might be said to have some moral obligations to manage the effects of what they publish. This includes the decision not to publish at all.

The most obvious obligation is that of publishing truthful research, and of publishing, or otherwise making available, sufficient information to allow for scrutiny by others (Chapter 1, section 1.7). Beyond this it is worth distinguishing between the effects of publication on those from whom the information was derived, and the effect on practices, policies and public opinion which might affect much larger groups of people.

Effects of publication on the people researched

With regard to the researchers' obligations to those from whom the information was derived, the most obvious harmful effects are avoided through anonymising persons. This is automatic in most quantitative research where information is expressed in numbers. It is a more important concern in qualitative research where accounts have to be written to ensure anonymity, as is usual. In addition, in published qualitative accounts which do not require individual case studies, what is said by one person is often presented under several different names. Where there are case studies of people, sometimes minor details about them are changed to disguise identity further (Dingwall 1977). Anonymity might not be adopted in specially commissioned evaluation studies where the performance of identifiable individuals is subjected to judgement (these are rarely published, however), in performance indicator (PI) and other studies where the purpose is to make agencies publicly accountable and in other research concerning well-known institutions or events: thus Eileen Barker's (1984) study is published as a study of the 'Moonies' and not of an unnamed religious cult. Barry Turner's studies of disasters (for example, 1994) identifies the disasters in question and John Wakeford's study of public schools (1969) names the schools to which the data apply.

The naming of institutions becomes more necessary the more the researcher derives from documents. Without the naming, the sources cannot be cited and no one can check the author's interpretations of these. Nor can an agency be located in terms of larger data sets if the geographical location of the agency is disguised. In the same vein the accountability of case studies is undermined by the anonymisation of the site. For example, the Commission for Racial Equality (CRE) study *Set to Fail* (CRE 1992; see also Troyna 1991) charges an anonymous school as discriminating against South Asian pupils in the way it divided pupils into sets and entered them for examinations. But the analysis of the data was biased towards this finding and ultimately the verity or otherwise of the charge rests on data which was missing from the published study (Gomm 1993b). Since the school was anonymous it is impossible for another researcher to remedy this. The anonymity of the school protected it from public censure, but it also prevented anything being done about its private shame if that were undeserved.

As noted in Chapter 12 (section 12.3) evaluation researchers sometimes tone down their criticisms if the people evaluated may suffer career setbacks from adverse comments in the report, in return for their undertaking to do better in the future. I would not identify the name of the mental hospital of the user-led consultation referred to earlier, because I have no wish to harm the reputations of those who conducted it. But, in my keeping this secret, you have no way of knowing that I didn't invent the whole thing. As you can see, there is a conflict between anonymisation and accountability.

Some researchers agree in advance to allow those they study to amend and veto publication, on the grounds that they have the right to control the publication of information derived from themselves. This is particularly the case with research commissioned by organisations and governments, though there the veto is usually with the funder rather than with the people studied. In their study of dual-career families (1976) the Rapoports allowed their subjects a veto, with the result that subjects vetoed the publication of some of the most enlightening data. Without actually making such an agreement with the police he studied, Lidz (1989: 51) felt it would be a betrayal of their trust to publish information about false arrests, perjury, planting evidence, racism and brutality.

There are two different issues here. One is the expediental one of eliciting co-operation. The other is the ethical one about the subjects' rights to determine what is published about them. Participatory research always implies some such control over what is published. On the assumption that people really truly know the truth about themselves, such practices might be defended as improving the truth value of the research. But on the assumption that people are likely to use their veto to foster benign images of themselves there is a conflict here between the researcher's obligation to tell the truth and the subjects' rights to be represented as they would prefer to be. Leaning too far in the direction of saying what respondents want said about them, respondents may put the researcher in the position of perpetrating their lies through publishing them (Ozga and Gerwirtz 1994; Sikes 2000).

Effects of publication on policies, practices and public perceptions

It is not at all clear what effect social research has on policies, practices and public thinking. It is rarely the case that policy-makers draw on psychological or social research to formulate policies in a rational way (Bulmer 1982b; Davies 2000). The main exceptions here are evaluation studies (Chapter 3, section 3.4; Chapter 12, section 12.3). But even here, policy decisions are usually made with an eye to political expediency and budgetary possibilities. Nor is there any close relationship between the practices of practitioners in human services and a knowledge base accumulated via research (for example Lomas 1994; Hargreaves 1996; MacDonald 1999). One reason for this is that social research tends to generate contradictory indications. If practitioners draw on it they can pick and mix at will. This was also the situation in medicine until the 1990s. At that point in time, the disjuncture between medical research and medical practice was defined as an important problem. Various measures and institutions were introduced to bring medical practice into line with research evidence (*Effective Health Care* 1999; Needham 2000). But elsewhere in the human services such linkages are weak.

Nor is it clear how social science research influences public thinking. Little of it is reported in the mass media. That which is, may be treated in a hostile or garbled way (Haslam and Bryman 1994; Fenton et al.1998; Hammersley 2000.) Perhaps the best model of the influence of social science research on public thinking is one of a haphazard process of percolation, rather like rumour dissemination, with fragments of social science entering through school sociology and social studies mixing with television 'social concern' documentaries, and being remembered by people in ways that are modified by their other beliefs and experiences (Chapter 6, Box 6.1). It is extremely difficult for researchers to know what effects their publications will have. For example, it is doubtful as to whether Margaret Mead (1948) could have predicted that what was received in America as a sympathetic picture of the Samoan people, would be regarded by Samoan opinion leaders 50 years later as highly offensive (Freeman 1983).

This preamble is to indicate that it is difficult for social researchers to predict what kinds of effects publishing their research might have on wider society, though the best odds are on 'none at all'. This is not necessarily a matter of great concern to researchers who adopt a value-neutral stance. For most of them the primary purpose of social research is to produce high-quality knowledge about the social world. It is someone else's business as to how this knowledge might be used. For critical researchers, however, the primary purpose of doing research is to improve the world, and to do it as quickly as possible. For them then, publication can seem a way of publicising how unfair social arrangements are, and how they might be improved. If the world is an evil place, then the only ethical publications are those which attack it. The problem with this strategy is that hardly anyone, except other social researchers, read such publications, and among social researchers socially critical research is mainly read by those who are already committed to the particular cause.

Much critical research is published as a corrective to ideas and images which critical researchers believe to be supporting the *status quo*. For researchers of these persuasions an important ethical question is whether anything they are about to publish might be taken to support some state of affairs or way of thinking of which they disapprove. Again much is invested in designing publications to give 'voice' to the views and concerns of groups of people whose ideas are rarely heard and in the promotion of positive images of groups who are misunderstood and stigmatised in order to challenge stereotypes which are alleged to exist about them. Sometimes doing both leads to some rather vicious stereotypes of other kinds of people, for example of teachers (for example, Carrington 1983), or of health service personnel (Bowler 1993), or police officers and judges (for example Young 1971). Dingwall, attacking such publications from the value-neutral position suggests that an important ethical consideration in judging research should be that:

> it displays its adherence to an ethic of fair dealing ... does it convey as much understanding of its villains as its heroes? Are the privileged treated as having something serious to say, or simply dismissed as evil, corrupt or greedy without further inquiry?
>
> (Dingwall 1992: 172)

Here there are directly contradictory ethical prescriptions among researchers. And they are predictable ones given the different assumptions about the purpose of research. For Dingwall research is primarily about presenting evidence and argument and allowing readers to decide whether to believe this or not. For him, producing stereotypes of 'baddies' is not just unethical, it is misleading. Sculley's feminist research on rapists was primarily designed on the grounds that rapists could not be understood via the stereotypical picture usually conveyed of them. Milgram's research undermines the stereotype of those who commit atrocities; Humphreys' was designed to dissolve the contemporary stereotype of homosexuals. All these manage to do this while adhering to an ethic of 'fair dealing'. Much critical research, by contrast, is designed as a foray in an ongoing battle, where stereotyping the opposition is fair game and rhetorical tricks are fair play in eliciting the reader's belief. Here, to paraphrase Karl Marx, the object of social research is not to understand the world but to change it for the better. How to do this remains unclear, but it is certainly not by producing socially critical work for low-circulation academic publications.

ACTIVITY 13.1 Ethically appraising research

Ideally for this activity you should download or otherwise obtain one of the following codes of research practice, according to your own sphere of interests.

British Sociological Association: <http://www.britsoc.org.uk>
British Psychological Society <http://www.bps.or.uk>
British Society of Criminology
<http://www.lboro.ac.uk/departments/ss/bsc/council/CODEETH.HMT>

If you can't obtain one of these then use Table 13.1 and Box 13.1 as a framework for the activity.

1 Either:
  (a) design a piece of research which you might conduct given the time and resources to do so

  or

  (b) find a published research article.

In either case review the research in terms of what ethical issues doing it and publishing the results raises, and how you might, or the author did, resolve these issues. Use either a published code of practice or Table 13.1 as a framework for doing this.

13.9 Summary

This chapter has been about morally good conduct for researchers, or research ethics as this is usually called. It followed closely from Chapter 12, because the difference between researchers adopting a value-neutral policy towards research and those who adopt a politically committed position underlies important differences in interpretations of what is ethical conduct for researchers. Despite these differences all researchers are required by their peers to commit themselves to producing truthful research, though they don't necessarily agree as to the truth, and there is a disagreement as to who is in a position to judge it. Hence for value-neutral researchers, researchers should be first and foremost accountable to the research community, for both their truthfulness and other moral matters, while for critical researchers the more important accountability is to the various disadvantaged groups for whom they advocate. It is worth noting here the close relationship between the idea of 'accountability', and the idea of 'ethicality'. Unless people make themselves accountable it is impossible to judge their conduct as morally good or bad, or to praise or condemn them, and hence impossible to enforce ethical conduct.

The chapter looked at various ethical dilemmas as presented by research and the way in which their resolution is usually necessarily ad hoc and often contentious, though research codes do offer some guidance. The dilemmas included examples of balancing the requirement to be truthful and accountable with the requirement to protect the confidentiality of sources, and examples of dilemmas about how to balance the value of research findings against any harm done to people in obtaining them. A further distinction between researchers, still on the value-neutral/value-led divide, is that the former may be satisfied that research is ethical if it does no one any harm, while the latter often demand that for research to be ethical it must do some tangible good to the people researched. This latter position is often associated with participative research where those who would otherwise be subjects become co-researchers. It was noted that this alters the ethical framework within which research is conducted. While it serves ethical principles of self-determination and human dignity to elevate subjects to researchers, it also dilutes ethical responsibility, so that it becomes unclear as to who is morally responsible for the research, and it may place a professional researcher in a position where he or she is unable either to prevent harm or to promote good.

Further reading

If you are going to conduct research you must be familiar with one of the codes of ethics available as shown in the chapter activity. Bulmer's *Social Research Ethics* (1982b) is a sound text written from the value-neutral position. The ethics section of May (1993) discusses research ethics in relation to more recent philosophical debates. Williams (1995) discusses the ethics of action research when conducted by practitioners. Value-led researchers tend not to separate their discussions of research ethics from their discussions of research in general, so any research text of this kind will contain ethical discussion, though Reason (1994) addresses ethics directly. Feminists often write about having an ethical epistemology: an ethical theory of knowledge, contrasting this with the objective theory of knowledge adopted by value-neutral researchers. For discussions of this kind see Addleson (1993, 1994), Stanley and Wise (1993: 200–3) and Walker (1989).

References

Addelson, K. (1993) 'Knowers/doers and their moral problems' in Alcoff, L. and Potter, E.(eds), *Feminist Epistemologies*, New York, Routledge: 265–94.

Addelson, K. (1994) *Moral Passages: Towards a Collectivist Moral Theory*, New York, Routledge.

Alrek, P. and Settle, R. (1995) *The Survey Research Handbook* (2nd edn), Burr Ridge, Irwin.

Andersen, M. (1993) 'Studying across difference: race, class and gender in qualitative research', in Stanfield, J. and Dennis, R. (eds), *Race and Ethnicity in Research Methods*, London, Sage: 39–53.

Appleby, J. and Mulligan, J.-A. (2000) *How well is the NHS performing?* London, King's Fund.

Arksey, H. and Knight, P. (1999) *Interviewing for Social Scientists*, London, Sage.

Armstrong, D., Gosling, A., Weinman, J. and Matineu, T. (1997) 'The place of inter-rater reliability in qualitative research: an empirical study', *Sociology* 31(3): 597–606.

Atkinson, J. M. (1978) *Discovering Suicide: Studies in the Organisation of Sudden Death*, Basingstoke, Macmillan.

Atkinson, J. M. and Heritage, J. (eds) (1984) *Structures of Social Action*, Cambridge, Cambridge University Press.

Atkinson, M. W., Kessell, N. and Dalgaard, J. (1975) 'The comparability of suicide rates', *British Journal of Psychiatry*, 127: 427–56.

Atkinson, P. (1990) *The Ethnographic Imagination: Textual Constructions of Reality*, London, Routledge.

Austin, J. (1962) *How to do Things with Words*, Oxford, Clarendon (Oxford University Press edns, 1975 and 1980).

Ayer, A. J. (1956) *The Problem of Knowledge*, Harmondsworth, Penguin.

Babbie, E. and Halley, F. (1994) *Adventures in Social Research: Data Analysis Using SPSS*, Thousand Oaks, CA, Pine Forge Press.

Back, L. and Solomos, J. (1993) 'Doing research, writing politics; the dilemmas of political intervention in research on racism', *Economy and Society*, 22(2): 178–99.

Backhouse, G. (2002) 'How preserving confidentiality in health research can be compatible with preserving data for future use', *Medical Sociology News*, 28(3): 32–35.

Barber, T. and Silver, M. (1968) 'Fact, fiction and the experimenter bias effect', *Psychological Bulletin Monograph Supplement*, 70:6(2): 1–29.

Barbour, R. and Kitzinger, J. (1999) *Developing Focus Group Research: Politics, Theory and Practice*, London, Sage.

Barker, E. (1984) *The Making of a Moonie: Brainwashing or Choice?*, Oxford, Blackwell.

Barker, W. (1992) 'Health visiting: action research in a controlled environment', *International Journal of Nursing Studies*, 29(3): 251–9.

Barnard, H. (1994) *Research Methods in Anthropology: Qualitative and Quantitative Approaches*, London, Sage.

Barnes, C. and Mercer, G. (1997) *Doing Disability Research*, Leeds, The Disability Press.

Barrett, R. (1996) *The Psychiatric Team and the Social Definition of Schizophrenia: An Anthropological Study of Person and Illness*, Cambridge, Cambridge University Press.

Bateson, G. (1972) *Steps Towards an Ecology of Mind*, Harmondsworth, Allen Lane.

Baumrind, D. (1964) 'Some thoughts on ethics of research: after reading Milgram's "Behavioural Study of Obedience" ', *American Psychologist*, 19: 421–23.

Bazeley, P. and Richards, L. (2000) *The NVivo Qualitative Project Book*, London, Sage.

Beck, A. (1970) *Depression: Causes and Treatment*, Philadelphia, University of Philadelphia Press.

Becker, H. (1952) 'Social class variations in teacher–pupil relationships', *Journal of Educational Sociology*, 52: 451–65.

Becker, H. (1963) *Outsiders: Studies in the Sociology of Deviance*, New York, Free Press.

Becker, H. (1967) 'Whose side are we on?', *Social Problems*, 14: 239–47.

Becker, H. (1971) 'Reply to Riley's "Partisanship and objectivity" ', *American Sociologist*, 6: 13.

Benzeval, M., Judge, K. and Whitehead, M. (eds) (1995) *Tackling Inequalities in Health: An Agenda for Action*, London, King's Fund.

Ben-Tovim, G., Gabriel, J., Law, I. and Stredder, K.(1986) *The Local Politics of Race*, London, Macmillan.

Beresford, P. and Evans, C. (1999) 'Research note: research and empowerment', *British Journal of Social Work*, 29: 671–7.

Berg, B. (1995) *Qualitative Research Methods for the Social Sciences*, 2nd edn, Boston, Allyn & Bacon.

Berger, A. (2000) *Media and Communication Research: An Introduction to Qualitative and Quantitative Approaches*, London, Sage.

Berlak, A., Berlak, H., Bagenstos, N. and Mikel, E. (1975) 'Teaching and learning in English primary schools', *School Review*, 83(2): 215–43.

Best, G., Dennis, J. and Draper, P. (1977) *Health, the Mass Media and the National Health Service*, London, Unit for the Study of Health Policy, Guy's Hospital Medical School.

Blair, P., Fleming, P., Benskey, D., Smith, I., Bacon, C., Taylor, E., Berry, J., Golding, J. and Tripp, J. (1996) 'Smoking and sudden infant death syndrome: results from 1993–95 case-control study for confidential inquiry into still births and deaths in infancy', *British Medical Journal*, 313: 195–8.

Blenkin, G., Kelly, A. and Rose, J. (2001) *Action Research for Professional Development: An Early Years' Perspective*, London, Paul Chapman.

Bloor, M. (1991) 'A minor office: the variable and socially constructed character of death certification in a Scottish city', *Journal of Health and Social Behaviour*, 32: 273–87.

Bloor, M. (1994) 'On the conceptualisation of routine medical decision-making. Death certification as an habitual activity', in M. Bloor and P. Taroborrelli (eds), *Qualitative Studies in Health and Medicine*, Aldershot, Avebury: 96–109.

Bloor, M., Samphire, M. and Prior, L. (1987) 'Artefact explanations of inequalities in health: an assessment of the evidence', *Sociology of Health and Illness*, 9(3): 231–64.

Bloor, M., Venters, G. and Samphire, M. (1978) 'Geographical variations in the incidence of operations on the tonsils and adenoids: an epidemiological and sociological investigation: parts 1 and 2, *Journal of Laryngology and Otology*, 96: 791–801, 833–95.

Bloor, M., Frankland, J., Thomas, M. and Robson, K. (2000) *Focus Groups in Social Research*, London, Sage.

Blumstein, P. (1991) 'The production of selves in personal relationships', in J. Howard and P. Callero (eds), *Self-Society Dynamic: Cognition, Emotion and Action*, Cambridge, Cambridge University Press: 305–22.

Blytheway, B. and Johnson, J. (1990) 'On defining ageism', *Critical Social Policy*, 29: 27–39.

Booth, C. (1902) *Life and Labour of People in London*, 18 vols, London, Macmillan.

Boreham, R. and Shaw, A. (eds), (2001) *Smoking, Drinking and Drug Use among Young People in England in 2000*, London, Office of National Statistics, Stationery Office.

Bosely, S. (1999) 'Trial and error puts patient's at risk', *Guardian*, 27 July: 1, 7, and 8.

Bosanquet, N. and Zarzecka, A. (1995) 'Attitudes to health services 1983 to 1993', in A. Harrison and S. Bruscini (eds), *Health Care UK 1994/95*, London, King's Fund Policy Institute: 88–94.

Bottomley, K. and Pease, K. (1986) *Crime and Punishment: Interpreting the Data*, Milton Keynes, Open University Press.

Bowler, I. (1993) '"They're not the same as us": midwives' stereotypes of South Asian descent maternity patients', *Sociology of Health and Illness*, 15(2): 157–78.

Boydell, D. and Jasman, A. (1983) *The Pupil and Teacher Record: A Manual For Observers*, Leicester, Leicester University Press.

Bridgewood, A., Lilly, R., Thomas, M., Bacon, O., Sykes, W. and Morris, S. (2000) *Living in Britain: Results from the 1998 General Household Survey*, London, HMSO.

British Medical Journal (1998) 'Dealing with research misconduct in the United Kingdom', Special Section, 316: 1726–33.

British Sociological Association (2002) *Statement of Ethnical Practice*, Durham, BSA <http://www.britsoc.org.uk>

Broad, W. and Wade, N. (1982) *Betrayers of the Truth: Fraud and Deceit in the Halls of Science*, London, Century Publishing.

Brown, C. and Gay, P. (1985) *Racial Discrimination: 17 years after the Act*, London, Policy Studies Institute.

Brown, G. and Yule, G. (1983) *Discourse Analysis*, Cambridge, Cambridge University Press.

Browning, C. (1993) *Ordinary Men: Police Battalion 101 and the Final Solution in Poland*, New York, Harper Perennial.

Bruun, H. (1972) *Science, Values and Politics in Max Weber's Methodology*, Copenhagen, Munksgaard.

Bryman, A. (1988) *Quality and Quantity in Social Research*, London, Unwin Hyman.

Bryman, A. and Burgess, R. (1994) 'Developments in qualitative data analysis', in A. Bryman and R. Burgess (eds), *The Analysis of Qualitative Data*, London, Routledge: 1–17.

Bryne, D. (1998) *Complexity Theory and the Social Sciences*, London, Routledge & Kegan Paul.

Bucke, R. (1997) *Ethnicity and Contacts with the Police: Latest Findings from the British Crime Survey*, London, Home Office Research Findings, 59, London, Home Office.

Bulmer, M. (1982a) *The Uses of Social Research: Social Investigation in Public Policy-Making*, London, Allen & Unwin.

Bulmer, M. (1982b) *Social Research Ethics*, London, Macmillan.

Bulmer, M. (2002) *Questionnaires* (4 vols), London, Sage.

Butler, N., Haslam, M., Barker, W. and Morris, A. (1982) *Child Health and Education Study: First Report to the Department of Education and Science on Ten-Year Follow-Up*, Bristol, Department of Child Health, University of Bristol.

Burgess, R. (ed.) (1982) *Field Research: A Sourcebook and Field Manual*, London, Unwin Hyman.

Burke, K. (1966) *Language as Symbolic Interaction: Essays on Life, Literature and Method*, Los Angeles, University of California Press.

Burns, T. (1992) *Erving Goffman*, London, Routledge.

Buttney, R. (1993) *Social Accountability in Communication*, London, Sage.

Byrd, D. (1981) *Organizational Constraints on Psychiatric Treatment: The Outpatient Clinic*, Greenwich, Connecticut, JAI Press.

Campbell, M. (1991) 'Children at risk: how different are children on the child abuse registers?', *British Journal of Social Work*, 21: 259–75.

Campbell, T. and Stanley, J. (1996) *Experimental and Quasi-experimental Designs for Research*, Chicago, Rand MacNally.

Carrington, B. (1983) 'Sport as a sidetrack: an analysis of West Indian involvement in extra-curricular sport', in L. Barton and S. Walker (eds), *Race, Class and Education*, London, Croom Helm: 40–65.

Charleton, J., Kelly, S., Dunnell, K., Evans, B., Jenkins, R. and Wallis, R. (1992) 'Trends in suicide deaths in England and Wales', *Population Trends*, 69: 10–16.

Chisnall, P. (1986) *Marketing Research*, 3rd edn, London, McGraw-Hill.

Chiu, L.-F. and Knight, D. (1999) 'How useful are focus groups for obtaining the views of minority groups?', in Barbour, R. and Kitzinger, J. (eds) *Developing Focus Group Research: Politics, Theory and Practice*, London, Sage: 99–112.

Cicourel, A. (1982) 'Interviews, surveys and the problem of ecological validity', *American Sociologist*, 17(1): 11–20.

Cicourel, A. and Kitsuse, J. (1963) *The Educational Decision-Makers*, Indianapolis, Bobbs-Merrill.

Clarricoates, K. (1980) 'The importance of being Ernest . . . Emma . . . Tom . . . Jane: the perception and categorisation of gender conformity and gender deviation in primary schools', in R. Deem (ed), *Schooling for Women's Work*, London, Routledge: 26–41.

Cochrane, A. (1972) *Effectiveness and Efficiency*, Oxford, Nuffield Provincial Hospitals Trust.

Coghlan, D. and Brannick, T. (2000) *Doing Action Research in your own Organization*, London, Sage.

Cohen, G., Forbes, F. and Garraway, M. (1994) *Lothian Health Survey – Summary of Initial Findings*, Edinburgh, University Department of Public Health Sciences.

Cohen, G., Forbes, J. and Garraway, M. (1996) 'Can different patient satisfaction surveys yield consistent results? A comparison of three surveys', *British Medical Journal*, 313(7061): 841–4.

Collins, H. (1985) *Changing Order: Replication and Induction in Scientific Practice*, London, Sage.

Collins, P. H. (1990) *Black Feminist Thought*, London, Unwin Hyman.

Commission for Racial Equality (CRE) (1992) *Set to Fail: Setting and Banding in Secondary Schools*, London, Commission for Racial Equality.

Cook, D. and Allen, C. (1983) 'Self-reported alcohol consumption and dissimulation in a Scottish urban sample', *Journal of Studies on Alcohol*, 44: 617–29.

Coolican, H. (1994) *Research Methods and Statistics in Psychology*, 2nd edn, London, Hodder & Stoughton.

Coulthard, M. and Montgomery, M. (1981) 'Originating a description', in M. Coulthard and M. Montgomery (eds), *Studies in Discourse Analysis*, London, Routledge & Kegan Paul: 1–12.

Crawford, A. (1987) 'Bias in a survey of drinking habits', *Alcohol and Alcoholism*, 22(2): 167–79.

Cuff, E., Sharrock, W. and Francis, D. (1990) *Perspectives in Sociology*, 3rd edn, London, Unwin Hyman.

Dale, A. (1992) 'The OPCS Longitudinal Study', in A. Dale and C. Marsh (eds), *The 1991 Census User's Guide*, London, HMSO.

Dale, A., Arber, S. and Proctor, M. (1988) *Doing Secondary Analysis*, London, Unwin Hyman.

Daston, L. (1992) 'Objectivity and the escape from perspective', *Social Studies of Science*, 22(4);597–618.

Davie, N. (1999) 'Revealed: how the police fiddle crime figures', *Guardian*, 18 March.

Davie, R. (1993) 'The impact of the National Child Development Study', *Children and Society*, 7(1): 20–36.

Davies, C. (2000) 'Understanding the policy process', in A. Brechin, H. Brown and M. Eby (eds), *Critical Practice in Health and Social Care*, Milton Keynes and London, Open University/Sage: 211–30.

Davies, J. (1997a) *The Myth of Addiction*, Amsterdam, Harwood Academic.

Davies, J. (1997b) *Drugspeak: The Analysis of Drug Discourse*, Amsterdam, Harwood Academic.

de Heer, W., de Leeuw, E. and van der Zouwen, J. (1999) 'Methodological issues in survey research', *Bulettin de Méthodologie Sociologique*, 64: 25–48.

de Leeuw, W. (1999) 'Item non-response: prevention is better than cure', *Survey Methods Newsletter*, 19(2): 4–8.

Demark, S., Drew, D. and Grimsley, M. (2000) 'Minding the gap: ethnic, gender and social class differences in attainment at 16, 1988–95', *Race Ethnicity and Education*, 3(2): 117–43.

Dennett, D. (1995) *Darwin's Dangerous Idea: Evolution and the Meanings of Life*, Harmondsworth, Allen Lane/Penguin.

Department for Education and Skills (DfES) (2003) *Secondary Schools Performance Table 2002*, London, DfES <httpe://www.dfes.gov.uk/index.htm

Department of Health (1991) *Guidelines to Local Research Ethics Committees*, London, Department of Health.

Department of Health (1997) *Briefing Pack for Research Ethics Committees*, London, Department of Health.

de Vaus, D. (1995) *Surveys in Social Research*, 4th edn, London, Allen & Unwin.

Dingwall, R. (1977) *The Social Organisation of Health Visitor Training*, Beckenham, Croom Helm.

Dingwall, R. (1992) 'Don't mind him – he's from Barcelona: qualitative methods in health studies', in J. Daly, I. McDonald and E. Willis (eds), *Researching Health Care: Designs, Dilemmas, Disciplines*, London, Routledge: 161–75.

Dingwall, R. and Murray, T. (1983) 'Categorisation in accident departments: "good" patients, "bad" patients and children', *Sociology of Health and Illness*, 5(12): 121–48.

Dingwall, R., Eekelaar, J. and Murray, T. (1983) *The Protection of Children*, Oxford, Blackwell.

Ditton, J. (1977) *Part-Time Crime: An Ethnography of Fiddling and Pilferage*, London, Macmillan.

Docherty, T. (ed.) (1993) *Postmodernism: A Reader*, London, Harvester Wheatsheaf.

Doll, R. and Hill, A. (1964) 'Mortality in relation to smoking: ten years' observation of British doctors', *British Medical Journal*, June, 1399–1410, 1460–7.

Doll, R., Peto, R. Wheatley, K., Gray, R. and Sutherland, I. (1994) 'Mortality in relation to smoking: 40 years' observations on male British Doctors', British Medical Journal, 309: 901–11.

Douglas, J. (1964) *The Home and the School: A Study of Ability and Attainment in the Primary School*, London, McGibbon & Kee (Panther edn 1967).

Douglas, M. (1966) *Purity and Danger: An Analysis of the Concepts of Pollution and Taboo*, Harmondsworth, Penguin.

Douglas, M. (1987) *How Institutions Think*, London, Routledge & Kegan Paul.

Drever, F., Whitehead, M. and Roden, M. (1996) 'Current patterns and trends in male mortality by social class (based on occupation), *Population Trends*, 86: 15–20.

Drew, P. and Gray, J. (1990) 'The fifth-year examination achievements of black young people in England and Wales', *Education Research*, 32(2): 107–17.

Dukes, E. (1996) *Resolving Public Conflict: Transforming Community and Governance*, Manchester, Manchester University Press.

Durkheim, E. (1952) *Suicide: A Study in Sociology*, trans. F. Spalding and G. Simpson, London, Routledge (original French edn 1897).

Dwyer, T. and Ponsonby, A.-L. (1996) 'Sudden infant death syndrome: after the "back to sleep" campaign', *British Medical Journal*, 313: 180–1.

Eby, M. (2000) 'Producing evidence ethically', in R. Gomm and C. Davies (eds), *Using Evidence in Health and Social Care*, London, Sage: 108–28.

Edmundson, R. (1984) *Rhetoric in Sociology*, Basingstoke, Macmillan.

Effective Health Care (1998) 'Cholesterol and coronary heart disease: screening and treatment', *Effective Health Care*, 4(1): 1–18.

Effective Health Care (1999) 'Getting evidence into practice', *Effective Health Care*, 5(1): 1 16.

Elander, G. (1991) 'Ethical conflicts in placebo treatments', *Journal of Advanced Nursing*, 16: 947–51.

Elliott, J. (1991) *Action Research for Educational Change*, Buckingham, Open University Press.

Farquhar, C. and Das, R. (1999) 'Are focus groups suitable for "sensitive topics"?', in Barbour R. and Kitzinger, J. (eds), *Developing Focus Group Research: Politics, Theory and Practice*, London. Sage: 47–63.

Featherstone, J. and Donovan, J. (1998) 'Random allocation or allocation at random? Patients' perspectives in a randomised controlled trial', *British Medical Journal*, 317: 1117–80.

Fenton, N., Bryaman, A., Deacon, D. and Birmingham, P. (1998) *Mediating Social Science*, London, Sage.

Field, A. (2000) *Discovering Statistics: Using SPSS for Windows*, London, Sage.

Fielding, J. (1993) 'Coding and managing data', in N. Gilbert (ed.), *Researching Social Life*, London, Sage: 218–38.

Fielding, N. (1981) *The National Front*, London, Routledge & Kegan Paul.

Fielding, N. (2003) *Interviewing* (Four Volumes) London, Sage.

Ferguson, M. (1983) *Forever Feminine: Women's Magazines and the Cult of Femininity*, London, Heinemann.

Fink, A. (1998) *How to Conduct Surveys: A Step by Step Guide*, London, Sage.

Finkel, S., Guerbock, T. and Borg, M. (1991) 'Race-of-interviewer effects in a pre-election poll: Virginia 1989', *Public Opinion Quarterly*, 55: 313–30.

Fishman, M. (1981) 'Crime waves as ideology', in S. Cohen and J. Young (eds), *The Manufacture of News: Social Problems and the Mass Media*, London, Constable: 98–117.

Fiske, J. (1989) *Reading the Popular*, London, Unwin Hyman.

FitzGerald, M. and Hale, C. (1996) *Ethnic Minorities, Victimisation and Racial Harassment*, London, Home Office Research Study, http://www.houroffice. gov. uk.rds/.

Flick, U. (1998) *An Introduction to Qualitative Research*, London, Sage.

Foster, J. (2000) *Data Analysis using SPSS for Windows Versions 8.10–10.0*, London, Sage.

Foster, P., Gomm, R. and Hammersley, M. (1996) *Constructing Educational Inequality*, Lewes, Falmer.

Foster, P., Gomm, R. and Hammersley, M. (2000) 'Case studies as spurious evaluation: the example of research on educational inequalities', *British Journal of Educational Studies*, 48(3): 115–30.

Foucault, M. (1967) *Madness and Civilization: A History of Insanity in the Age of Reason*, London, Tavistock.

Foucault, M. (1973) *The Birth of the Clinic: An Archaeology of Medical Perception*, London, Tavistock.

Foucault, M. (1977) *Discipline and Punish: The Birth of the Prison*, London, Allen Lane.

Foucault, M. (1979) *The History of Sexuality: Volume 1: An Introduction*, London, Allen Lane.

Fowler, F. (1993) *Survey Research Methods*, London, Sage.

Franke, R. and Kaul, J. (1978) 'The Hawthorne Experiments: first statistical interpretation', *American Sociological Review*, 43(5): 623–43.

Freeman, D. (1983) *Margaret Mead and Samoa: The Making and Unmaking of an Anthropological Myth*, Cambridge, MA, Harvard University Press.

Fuller, M. (1982) 'Young, female and black', in E. Cashmore and B. Troyna (eds), *Black Youth in Crisis*, London, George Allen & Unwin: 87–99.

Fuller, R. and Petch, A. (1995) *Practitioner Research: The Reflexive Social Worker*, Buckingham, Open University Press.

Galtung, J. and Ruge, M. (1965) 'The structure of foreign news: the presentation of the Congo, Cuba and Cyprus crises in four foreign newspapers', *Journal of International Peace Research*, 1: 64–90.

Galtung, J. and Ruge, M. (1981) 'Structuring and selecting news', in S. Cohen and

J. Young (eds), *The Manufacture of News: Deviance, Social Problems and the Mass Media*, London, Constable: 52–63.

Garfinkel, H. (1967) *Studies in Ethnomethodology*, Englewood Cliffs, Prentice-Hall.

Geertz, C. (1973) 'Thick description: towards an interpretive theory of culture', in *The Interpretation of Cultures: Selected Essays of Clifford Geertz*, London, Hutchinson: 3–30.

Geertz, C. (1988) *Works and Lives: The Anthropologist as Author*, Stanford, Stanford University Press.

Gilbert, N. (ed.) (1993) *Researching Social Life*, London, Sage.

Gilbourn, D. (1990) *Racism and Anti-Racism in Real Schools*, Buckingham, Open University Press.

Gillespie, R. (1988) 'The Hawthorne experiments and the politics of experimentation', in J. Morowski (ed.), *The Rise of Experimentation in American Psychology*, London, Yale University Press: 114–37.

Glaser, B. and Strauss, A. (1964) *Awareness of Dying*, Chicago, Aldine.

Goffman, E. (1959) *The Presentation of Self in Everyday Life*, Harmondsworth, Penguin (Anchor Books edn 1956).

Goffman, E. (1968) *Asylums: Essays on the Social Situation of Mental Patients and other Inmates*, Harmondsworth, Penguin.

Goldberg, D. and Huxley, P. (1992) *Common Mental Disorders*, London, Routledge.

Goldblatt, P. (ed.) (1990) *Longitudinal Study: Mortality and Social Organisation 1971–1981* OPCS series LS, 6, London, HMSO.

Goldblatt, P. and Whitehead, M. (2000) 'Inequalities in health: development and change', *Population Trends*, 100: 14–19.

Goldthorpe, J. and Payne, C. (1986) 'Trends in inter-generational mobility in England and Wales 1979–83, *Sociology*, 20: 1–24.

Goldthorpe, J., Lockwood, D., Bechofer, F. and Platt, J. (1968a) *The Affluent Worker: Industrial Attitudes and Behaviour*, Cambridge, Cambridge University Press.

Goldthorpe, J., Lockwood, D., Bechofer, F. and Platt, J. (1968b) *The Affluent Worker: Political Attitudes and Behaviour*, Cambridge, Cambridge University Press.

Goldthorpe, J., Lockwood, D., Bechofer, F. and Platt, J. (1969) *The Affluent Worker in the Class Structure*, Cambridge, Cambridge University Press.

Goldstein, H. (1987) *Multilevel Models in Education and Social Research*, Oxford, Clarendon.

Gomm, R. (1975) 'Bargaining from weakness: spirit possession among the coastal Digo', *Man(n.s.)*, 10: 530–43.

Gomm, R. (1976) 'Discovering anthropology', *Cambridge Anthropologist*, 3(1): 27–41.

Gomm, R. (1986) *Normal Results: An Ethnographic Study of Health Visitor Student Assessment*, Milton Keynes, PhD thesis presented to the Open University.

Gomm, R. (1993a) 'Issues of power in health and welfare', in J. Walmsley, J. Reynolds, P. Shakespeare and R. Woolfe (eds), *Health, Welfare and Practice: Reflecting on Roles and Relationships*, London, Open University/Sage: 131–8.

Gomm, R. (1993b) 'Figuring out ethnic equity: a response to Troyna', in R. Gomm and P. Woods (eds), *Educational Research in Action*, London, Open University/Paul Chapman: 199–215 (also in *British Educational Research Journal*, 19(2): 147–63).

Gomm. R. (2000a) 'The basics of experimental design' in R. Gomm, G. Needham and A. Bullman (eds) *Evaluating Research in Health and Social Care*, London, Sage: 47–70.

Gomm, R. (2000b) 'Research instruments in experimental design', in R. Gomm, G. Needham and A. Bullman (eds), *Evaluating Research in Health and Social Care*, London, Sage: 71–85.

Gomm, R. (2000c) 'Reading the results of experimental research', in R. Gomm, G. Needham and A. Bullman (eds), *Evaluating Research in Health and Social Care*, London, Sage: 86–105.

Gomm, R. (2000d) 'Uncertain minds or uncertain times? Expressions of uncertainty in professional discourse', in R. Gomm, G. Needham and A. Bullman (eds), *Evaluating Research in Health and Social Care*, London, Sage: 230–8.

Gomm, R. (2000e) 'Controlling for age and socio-economic circumstances', in R. Gomm, G. Needham and A. Bullman (eds), *Evaluating Research in Health and Social Care*, London, Sage: 170–195.

Gomm, R. (2000f) 'Understanding experimental design', in R. Gomm and C. Davies (eds), *Using Evidence in Health and Social Care*, London, Sage: 46–64.

Gomm, R. and Davies, C. (eds) (2000) *Using Evidence in Health and Social Care*, London, Sage.

Gomm, R., Hammersley, M. and Foster, P. (eds) (2000) *Case Study Method: Key Issues, Key Texts*, London, Sage.

Gomm, R., Needham, G. and Bullman, A. (eds) (2000) *Evaluating Research in Health and Social Care*, London, Sage.

Gould, S. J. (1992) 'The case of the creeping fox terrier clone', in *Bully for Brontosaurus*, Harmondsworth, Penguin: 155–67.

Gray, J. (1993) 'Publish and be damned? The problem of comparing examination results in two Inner London Schools', in R. Gomm and P. Woods (eds), *Educational Research in Action*, London, Paul Chapman: 99–108 (previously in *Educational Analysis*, 4(3) (1982): 47–56).

Gray, J., Goldstein, H. and Jesson, D. (1996) 'Changes and improvements in schools' effectiveness: trends over five years', *Research Papers in Education*, 11(1): 35–51.

Gray, J., Jesson, D. and Sime, N. (1993) 'Estimating differences in the examination performances of secondary schools in six LEAs: a multilevel approach to school effectiveness', in R. Gomm and P. Woods (eds), *Educational Research in Action*, London, Paul Chapman: 118–40.

Green, J. and Hart, L. (1999) 'The impact of context on data', in R. Barbour and J. Kitzinger (eds), *Developing Focus Group Research: Politics, Theory and Practice*, London, Sage: 21–35.

Green, P. (1983) 'Teachers' influence on the self-concept of pupils of different ethnic origins', PhD thesis, University of Durham.

Griffiths, L. (1997) 'Accomplishing team: teamwork and categorisation in two community mental health teams', *Sociological Review*, 45: 59–78.

Groves, R. (1989) *Survey Error and Survey Costs*, New York, John Wiley.

Grumet, M. (1991) 'The politics of personal knowledge', in C. Withering and N. Noddings (eds), *Stories Lives Tell: Narrative and Dialogue in Education*, New York, Teachers' College Press: 67–78.

Guba, Y. and Lincoln, E. (1989) *Fourth Generation Evaluation*, London, Sage.

Gunter, B. (1999) *Media Research Methods, Measuring Audiences, Reactions and Impact*, London, Sage.

Hage, J. and Meeker, B. (1988) *Social Causality*, London, Unwin Hyman.

Hakim, K. (1987) *Research Design: Strategies and Choices in the Design of Social Research*, London, Allen & Unwin.

Hall, S., Critcher, C., Jefferson, T., Clarke, J. and Roberts, B. (1978) *Policing the Crisis: Mugging, the State and Law and Order*, Basingstoke, Macmillan.

Halliday, M. and Martin, J. (1993) *Writing Science: Literacy and Discursive Power*, Lewes, Falmer.

Hammersley, M. (1990) *Reading Ethnographic Research: A Critical Guide*, London, Longman.

Hammersley, M. (1992) *What's Wrong with Ethnography?*, London, Routledge.

Hammersley, M. (1997) 'Qualitative data archiving: some reflections on its prospects and problems', *Sociology*, 37(1): 131–142.

Hammersley, M. (1998) *Reading Ethnographic Research: A Critical Guide*, 2nd edn, London, Longman.

Hammersley, M. (2000a) 'Whose side was Becker on ?', in M. Hammersley, *Taking Sides in Social Research: Essays on Partisanship and Bias*, London, Routledge: 60–89.

Hammersley, M. (2000b) *Taking Sides in Social Research: Essays on Partisanship and Bias*, London, Routledge.

Hammersley, M. (2000c) 'Media representation of social and educational research: the case of a review of ethnic minority education', paper presented to British Educational Research Association conference, Cardiff University, September.

Hammersley, M. and Atkinson, P. (1995) *Ethnography: Principles in Practice*, 2nd edn, London, Routledge.

Hammersley, M. and Gomm, R. (2000) 'Bias in social research', in M. Hammersley, *Taking Sides in Social Research: Essays on Partisanship and Bias*, London, Routledge: 151–66.

Hammersley, M. and Scarth, J. (1986) 'The impact of examinations on secondary school teaching', unpublished report.

Haney, C., Banks, C. and Zimbardo, P, (1981) 'A study of prisoners and guards in a simulated prison', in D. Potter, J. Anderson, J. Clark, P. Coombes, S. Hall, L. Harris, C. Holloway and T. Walton (eds), *Society and the Social Sciences: an Introduction*, London, Open University/Routledge & Kegan Paul: 226–39.

Harding, S. (1995) 'Social class differentials in men: recent evidence from the OPCS longitudinal study', *Population Trends*, 80: 31–7.

Hargreaves, D. (1967) *Social Relations in a Secondary School*, London, Routledge & Kegan Paul.

Hargreaves, D. (1996). *Teaching as a Research-Based Profession: Possibilities and Prospects*, London, Teacher Training Agency.

Harris, B. (1988) 'Key words: a history of debriefing in social psychology', in J. Morawski (ed.), *The Rise of Experimentation in American Psychology*, London, Yale University Press: 188–212.

Harris, J. and Grace, S. (1999) *A Question of Evidence? Investigating and Prosecuting Rape in the 1990s*, Home Office Research Studies 196, London, Home Office, http://www.homeoffice.gov.uk/rds/.

Hart, E. and Bond, M. (1995) *Action Research for Health and Social Care: A Guide to Practice*, Buckingham, Open University Press.

Hartman, P. and Husband, P. (1981) 'The mass media and racial conflict', in S. Cohen and J. Young (eds), *The Manufacture of News: Deviance, Social Problems and the Media*, London, Constable: 288–302.

Haskey, J. (1996) 'The ethnic minority populations of Great Britain: their estimated sizes and age profiles', *Population Trends*, 84: 33–9.

Haslam, C. and Bryman, A. (eds) (1994) *Social Scientists Meet the Media*, London, Routledge.

Heath, A. (1981) *Social Mobility*, Glasgow, Fontana.

Heath, C. and Luff, P. (1993) 'Explicating face-to-face interaction', in N. Gilbert (ed.), *Researching Social Life*, London, Sage: 306–26.

Heider, K. (1988) 'The Rashomon effect: when ethnographers disagree', *American Anthropologist*, 90: 73–80.

Hemminki, E., Topo, P. and Kangas, I. (1995) 'Experience and opinions of climacterium by Finnish women', *European Journal of Obstetrics Gynecology and Reproductive Biology*, 62: 81–97.

Heritage, J. (1984) *Garfinkel and Ethnomethodology*, Cambridge, Polity Press.

Heritage, J. (1985) 'Analyzing news interviews: aspects of the production of talk for an "over-hearing" audience', in T. van Dijk (ed.), *Handbook of Discourse Analysis*, London, Academic Press.

Her Majesty's Stationery Office (HMSO) (1998) *Public Interest Disclosure Act 1998*, London, HMSO.

Heron, J. (1981) 'Experimental research methods', in P. Reason and J. Rowan (eds), *Human Inquiry*, New York, Wiley: 153–66.

Herzlich, C. and Pierret, J. (1985) 'The social construction of the patient: patients and illnesses in other ages', *Social Science and Medicine*, 20(2): 145–57.

Hoey, M. (1983) *On the Surface of Discourse*, London, George Allen & Unwin.

Holloway, W. and Jefferson, T. (2000) *Doing Qualitative Research Differently: Free Association, Narrative and the Interview Method*, London, Sage.

Humphreys, L. (1975) *Tearoom Trade: Impersonal Sex in Public Places*, Chicago, Aldine.

Hunt, S. (1993) 'The relationship between research and policy: translating knowledge into action', in J. Davies and M. Kelly (eds), *Healthy Cities: Research and Practice*, London, Routledge & Kegan Paul: 71–82.

Hurry, J. and Lloyd, C. (1997) *A Follow-Up Evaluation of Project Charlie: A Life Skills Drug Education Programme for Primary Schools*, London, Paper 16, Drug Prevention Advisory Service, Home Office.

Hutchby, I. and Wooffitt, R. (1998) *Conversation Analysis*, Cambridge, Polity Press.

Irvine, J., Miles, I. and Evans, J. (eds) (1979) *Demystifying Social Statistics*, London, Pluto.

Jenkins, R., Smeeton, N., Markiner, M. and Shepherd, S. (1985) 'A study of the classification of mental ill-health in general practice', *Psychological Medicine*, 15: 403–9.

Jenkinson, C. (ed.), (1994) *Measuring Health and Medical Outcomes*, London, UCL Press.

Jesson, D., Gray, J. and Tranmer, M. (1992) *GCSE Performance in Nottinghamshire: Pupil and School Factors*, Nottinghamshire County Council, Education Advisory and Inspection Service.

Jones, P. (1993) *Studying Society: Sociological Theories and Research Practices*, London, Collins Educational.

Journal of Contemporary Ethnography (1992) (Special Issue) 'Street Corner Society Revisited', 21: 3–132.

Kalton, G. (2000) 'Developments in survey research in the past 25 years', *Survey Methodology*, 26(1): 3–10.

Kamin, L. (1974) *The Science and Politics of IQ*, Potomac, Erlbaum.

Kamin, L. (1981) 'Separated identical twins', in H. Eysenck and L. Kamin, *Intelligence: The Battle for the Mind: H. K. Eysenck versus Leon Kamin*, London, Pan: 106–13.

Kaplan, A. (1964) *The Conduct of Inquiry: Methodology for Behavioural Science*, San Francisco, Chandler.

Kelly, G. (1955) *The Psychology of Personal Constructs*, New York, Norton.

Kellett, J. (1996) 'An ethical dilemma: a nurse is suspended', *British Medical Journal*, 313(7067): 1249–50.

Kelley, H. and Michela, J. (1980) 'Attribution theory and research', *Annual Review of Psychology*, 31: 457–503.

Kertzer, D. and Arel, D. (eds) (2002) *Census and Identity: The Politics of Race, Ethnicity and Language in National Censuses*, Cambridge, Cambridge University Press.

Kish, L. (1965) *Survey Sampling*, London, Wiley.

Kitzinger, J. and Farquhar, C. (1999) 'The analytical potential of "sensitive moments" in focus group research', in Barbour, R. and Kitzinger, J. (eds) *Developing Focus Group Research: Politics, Theory and Practice*, London, Sage: 156–73.

Knightley, P. (1975) *The First Casualty*, London, Purnell.

Korovessis, C. (2001) 'Sampling minority ethnic groups in the UK population', *Survey Methods Newsletter*, 21(1): 12–19.

Krejcie, R. and Morgan, D. (1970) 'Determining sample size for research activities', *Educational and Psychological Measurement*, 30: 607–10.

Krippendorff, K. (1980) *Content Analysis: An Introduction to its Methodology*, London, Sage.

Kruger, R. (1994) *Focus Group Research: A Practical Guide to Applied Research*, 2nd edn, London, Sage.

Kunz, R. and Oxman, A. (1998) 'The unpredictability paradox: review of empirical comparisons of randomised and non-randomised clinical trials', *British Medical Journal*, 317: 1185–90.

Labov, W. (1973) 'The linguistic consequences of being a lame', *Language in Society*, 2(1): 81–115.

Lacey, C. (1975) *Hightown Grammar*, Manchester, Manchester University Press.

Lather, P. (1986) 'Research as praxis', *Harvard Educational Review*, 56(3): 257–77.

Laycock, G. (1985) *Property Marking: A Deterrent to Domestic Burglary? Crime Prevention Paper*, 3, London, Home Office.

Lepper, G. (2000) *Categories in Text and Talk: A Practical Introduction to Categorization Analysis*, London, Sage.

Levinson, S. (1983) *Pragmatics*, Cambridge, Cambridge University Press.

Lewin, K. (1997) 'Action research and minority problems', in G. Lewin, *Resolving Social Conflicts: Selected Papers on Group Dynamic and Field Theory by Kurt Lewin*, Washington, DC, American Psychological Association: 143–152 (1948 Harper Brothers edn).

Licht, B. and Dweck, V. C. (1987) 'Sex differences in achievement orientations', in M. Arnot and G. Weiner (eds), *Gender and the Politics of Schooling*, London, Hitchinson: 95–107.

Lidz, C. (1989) '"Objectivity" and rapport', in B. Glassner and J. Moreno (eds), *The Qualitative–Quantitative Distinction in the Social Sciences*, Boston, Kluwer Academic: 43–56.

Lipsey, M. (1995) 'What do we learn from 400 research studies on the effectiveness of treatment with juvenile delinquents?', in J. McGuire (ed.), *What Works? Reducing Re-Offending*, Chichester, John Wiley: 63–78.

Lloyd-Jones, G. (2002) *A multiple case study of the first year student perspective in a medical undergraduate PLB curriculum*, Liverpool, University of Liverpool, unpublished PhD thesis.

Logan, C. (1972) 'Evaluation research in crime and delinquence: a reappraisal', *Journal of Criminal Law, Criminology and Police Science*, 63(3): 378–87.

Lomas, J. (1994) 'Teaching old (and not so old) Docs new tricks: effective ways to implement research findings', in E. Dunn, P. Norton, M. Stewart, F. Tudiver and J. Bass (eds), *Disseminiating Research/Changing Practice*, London, Sage: 1–15.

Lythgoe, P. (1979) 'The social security snowball', *Media Reporter*, 3(1): 21.

Macdonald, G. (1999) 'Social work and its evaluation: a methodological dilemma?', in F. Williams, J. Popay and A. Oakley (eds), *Welfare Research: A Critical Review*, London, UCL Press: 89–103.

Macdonald, G., Sheldon, B. and Gillespie, J. (1992) 'Contemporary studies of the effectiveness of social work', *British Journal of Social Work*, 22(6): 615–43.

Macdonald, K. and Tipton, C. (1993) 'Using documents', in N. Gilbert (ed.), *Researching Social Life*, London, Sage: 187–200.

McGuffin, P. (1999) 'Getting personal', *Medical Research Council News*, 80: 20–3.

McPherson, K., Strong, P. and Epstein, A. (1981) 'Regional variations in the use of common surgical procedures: within and between England and Wales, Canada and the United States of America', *Social Science and Medicine*, 15A: 2773–85.

Maddock, K. (1998) 'The dubious pleasures of commitment', *Anthropology Today*, 14(5): 1–2.

Mant, J. and Jenkinson, C. (1997) 'Case control and cohort studies', in C. Jenkinson (ed.), *Assessment and Evaluation of Health and Medical Care*, Buckingham, Open University Press: 31–46.

Marks, D. (1995) 'Accounting for exclusion: giving a "voice" and producing a subject', *Children and Society*, 9(3): 81–98.

Marmot, M. (1995) 'In sickness and in wealth: social causes of illness', *Medical Research Council News*, 65: 8–12.

Marsh, C. (1988) *Exploring Data. An Introduction to Data Analysis for Social Scientists*, Cambridge, Polity Press.

Marshall, G., Rose, F. D., Newby, H. and Volger, C. (1988) *Social Class in Modern Britain*, London, Unwin Hyman.

Mason, J. (1996) *Qualitative Researching*, London, Sage.

Masson, J. (1988) *Against Therapy: Emotional Tyranny and the Myth of Psychological Healing*, London, Fontana.

Martin, J. (1999) 'An overview of imputation methods and their application to survey data', *Survey Methods Newsletter*, 19(2): 9–11.

May, T. (1993) *Social Research: Issues, Methods and Process*, Buckingham, Open University Press.

Mayhew, P., Elliot, D. and Dowds, L. (1989) *The 1988 British Crime Survey*, London, HMSO.

Maynard, D. (1989) 'On the ethnography and analysis of discourse in institutional settings', *Perspectives on Social Problems*, 1: 127–46.

Mead, M. (1948) *Coming of Age in Samoa*, Harmondsworth, Penguin (first published 1928).

Meadows, K. and Wisher, S. (2000) 'Establishing cross-cultural validity in health surveys', *Survey Methods Newsletter*, 20(2): 16–22.

Meltzer, H. (1985) *Dementia: Epidemiology Based Needs Assessment: Report 5*, London, Department of Health.

Meltzer, H., Gill, B., Petticrew, M. and Hinds, K. (1995) *The Prevalence of Psychiatric Morbidity among Adults living in Private Households in Great Britain*, OPCS Surveys of Psychiatric Morbidity in Great Britain, Report 2, London, HMSO.

Middleton, D. and Edwards, D. (1990) 'Conversational remembering: a social psychological approach', in D. Middleton, and D. Edwards (eds), *Collective Remembering*, London, Sage: 23–45.

Middlewood, D., Coleman, M. and Lumby, J. (1999) *Practitioner Research in Education: Making a Difference*, London, Paul Chapman.

Mies, M. (1983) 'Towards a methodology of feminist research', in G. Bowles and R. Klien (eds), *Theories of Women's Studies*, London, Routledge & Kegan Paul.

Mies, M. (1991) 'Women's research or feminist research? The debate surrounding feminist research and methodology', in M. Fonow and J. Cook (eds), *Beyond Methodology: Feminist Scholarship and Lived Research*, Bloomington, Indiana University Press: 60–84.

Miles, M. and Huberman, A. (1994) *Qualitative Data Analysis: An Expanded Sourcebook*, London, Sage.

Milgram S. (1963) 'Behavioural study of obedience', *Journal of Abnormal and Social Psychology*, 67(4): 317–78.

Milgram, S. (1964) 'Issues in the study of obedience: a reply to Baumrind', *American Psychologist*, 19: 849–50.

Milgram, S. (1974) *Obedience to Authority*, New York, Harper & Row.

Milgram, S. (1992) *The Individual in a Social World: Essays and Experiments*, 2nd edn (edited by J. Sabini), New York, McGraw-Hill.

Miller, G. and Stiff, J. (1993) *Deceptive Communication*, London, Sage.

Miller, S. (1953). 'The participant observer and "over-rapport"', *American Sociological Review*, 18: 97–99.

Mills, C. W. (1959) *The Sociological Imagination*, New York, Oxford University Press.

Mirrlees-Black, C. (1998) *Domestic Violence: Findings from the BCS Self-Completion Questionnaire*, London, Home Office Research Studies, 86. http://www.houroffice.gov.uk.rds/.

Mirrlees-Black, C., Budd, T., Partridge, S. and Mayhew, P. (1998) 'The 1998 British Crime Survey', *Home Office Statistical Bulletin*, 21/98, London, HMSO.

Moerman, D. (2002) *Meaning, Medicine and the 'Placebo Effect'*, Cambridge, Cambridge University Press.

Morgan, D. (1988) *Focus Groups as Qualitative Research*, London, Sage.

Mortimore, P., Sammons, P., Stoll, L., Lewis, D. and Ecob, R. (1988) *School Matters: The Junior Years*, Wells, Open Books.

Mortimore, R. and Atkinson, S. (2000) 'Political polling in Britain: the history', *Poll Digest*, 15 December, http://www.mori.com/digest/c001215.htm.

Mumby, D. (ed.) (1993) *Narrative and Social Control: Critical Perspectives*, London, Sage.

Muncie, J. and McLaughlin, E. (2001) *The Problem of Crime*, London, Sage.

Munck, R. and Rolston, W. (1987) *Belfast in the '30s: An Oral History*, Belfast, Blackstaff Press.

Nathanson, C. (1978) 'Sex roles as variables in the interpretation of morbidity data: a methodological critique', *International Journal of Epidemiology*, 7(3): 253–62.

Nazroo, J. (1997) *Mental Health and Ethnicity: Findings from a National Community Study*, London, Policy Studies Institute.

Needham, G. (2000) 'Research and practice: making a difference', in R. Gomm and C. Davies (eds), *Using Evidence in Health and Social Care*, London, Sage: 131–51.

Nettle, M. (1996) 'Listening in the asylum', in J. Read and J. Reynolds (eds), *Speaking Our Minds: An Anthology*, Basingstoke, Macmillan: 202–6.

Neunendorf, K. (2002) *The Content Analysis Guidebook*, London, Sage.

Newell, R. (1993) 'Questionnaires', in N. Gilbert (ed.), *Researching Social Life*, London, Sage: 94–115.

Nichols, R. (1997) 'Action research in health care: the collaborative action research network health care group', *Educational Action Research*, 5(2): 185–92.

Nicholson, R. (1997) 'Helsinki declaration revising continues', *Bulletin of Medical Ethics*, 146, March: 3–5.

Oakley, A. (1981) 'Interviewing women: a contradiction in terms', in H. Roberts (ed.), *Doing Feminist Research*, London, Routledge & Kegan Paul: 30–61.

Oakley, A. (1989) 'Who's afraid of the randomised controlled trial? Some dilemmas of the scientific method and good research practice', *Women and Health*, 15: 25–59.

Oakley, A. (1993) 'Telling stories: auto/biography and the sociology of health and illness', *Sociology of Health and Illness*, 15(3): 414–18.

Oakley, A. (2000) *Experiments in Knowing: Gender and Method in the Social Sciences*, Cambridge, Polity Press.

Oakley, A. and Fullerton, D. (1996) 'The lamp-post of research: support or illumination?', in A. Oakley and H. Roberts (eds), *Evaluating Social Interventions*, Essex, Barnados: 4–38.

Oakley, A., Rajan, L. and Robertson, P. (1990) 'A comparison of different sources of information about pregnancy and childbirth', *Journal of Biosocial Science*, 22: 477–87.

O'Connell Davidson, J. and Layder, D. (1994) *Methods, Sex and Madness*, London, Routledge.

O'Donoghue, C., Thomas, S., Goldstein, H. and Knight, T. (1997) '1996 DfEE study of value-added for 18 years olds in England', *DfEE Research Series*, March, London, DfEE.

OPCS (1994) *Undercoverage in Great Britain 1991: Census User Guide no. 58*, London, OPCS.

Other, A. (1999) 'Above infection: status and hygiene behaviour in a hospital setting', unpublished paper.

Owusu-Bempah, J. (1994) 'Race, self-identity and social work', *British Journal of Social Work*, 24, 123–36.

Ozga, J. and Gerwirtz, S. (1994) 'Sex, lies and audiotape: interviewing the education policy elite', in D. Halpin and B. Troyna (eds), *Researching Education Policy: Ethical and Methodological Issues*, Lewes, Falmer, 34–59.

Padfield, M. and Proctor, I. (1996) 'The effect of interviewer's gender on the interviewing process: a comparative study', *Sociology*, 30(2): 355–66.

Parker, B. (1994) 'Research ethics committees', in V. Tschudin (ed.), *Ethics, Education and Research*, Harrow, Scutari: 72–112.

Patai, D. and Koertge, N. (1994) *Professing Feminism: Cautionary Tales from the Strange World of Women's Studies*, New York, Basic Books.

Patrick, J. (1973) *A Glasgow Gang Observed*, London, Eyre Methuen.

Pawson, R. and Tilley, N. (1997) *Realistic Evaluation*, London, Sage.

Payne, N. and Saul, C. (1997) 'Variations in the use of cardiology services in a health authority: comparison of artery revascularisation rates with the prevalence of angina and coronary mortality', *British Medical Journal*, 314: 257–61 (reprinted in R. Gomm, G. Needham and A. Bullman (eds), *Evaluating Research in Health and Social Care*, London, Sage, 2000).

Pearson, G. (1983) *Hooligan: A History of Respectable Fears*, Basingstoke, Macmillan.

Peneff, J. (1990) 'Myth in life stories', in R. Samuel and P. Thompson (eds), *The Myths We Live By*, London, Routledge: 36–48.

Pett, M. (1997) *Non-Parametric Statistics for Health Care Research: Statistics for Small Samples and Unusual Distributions*, London, Sage.

Philo, G. (1990) *Seeing and Believing: The Influence of Television*, London, Routledge.

Philo, G., Secker, J., Platt, S., McLaughlin, G. and Burnside, J. (1994) 'The impact of the mass media on public images of mental illness: media content and audience belief', *Health Education Journal*, 53: 271–81.

Pinch, T. and Clark, C. (1986) 'The hard sell: "patter merchanting" and the strategic (re)production and local management of economic reasoning in the sales routines of market pitchers', *Sociology*, 20(2): 169–91.

Platt, J. (1981) 'Evidence and proof in documentary research', *Sociological Review*, 29(1): 31–66.

Plowman, R., Graves, N. and Roberts, J. (1997) *Hospital Acquired Infection*, London, Office of Health Economics.

Plummer, K. (1983) *Documents of Life: An Introduction to the Problems and Literature of a Humanistic Method*, London, George Allen & Unwin.

Plummer, K. (2000) *Documents of Life 2: An Invitation to Critical Humanism*, London, Sage.

Potter, J. and Wetherell, M. (1987) *Discourse and Social Psychology*, London, Sage.

Prior, L. (1989) *The Social Organization of Death: Medical Discourse and Social Practices in Belfast*, London, Macmillan.

Prior, L. (1993) *The Social Organization of Mental Illness*, London, Sage.

Proctor, M. (1993a) 'Analysing survey data', in N. Gilbert (ed.), *Researching Social Life*, London, Sage: 239–54.

Proctor, M. (1993b) 'Measuring attitudes', in N. Gilbert (ed.), *Researching Social Life*, London, Sage: 116–34.

Radley, A. (1990) 'Artefacts, memory and a sense of the past', in D. Middleton and D. Edwards (eds), *Collective Remembering*, London, Sage. 46–59.

Ramsay, M., Barker, P., Goulden, C., Sharp, C. and Sondhi, A. (2001) *Drug Misuse Declared in 2000: Results from the British Crime Survey*, Home Office Research Study 224, London, Home Office, http://www.homeoffice.gov.uk.rds/.

Rapoport, R. and Rapoport, R. (1971) *Dual Career Families*, Harmondsworth, Penguin.

Rapoport, R. and Rapoport, R. (1976) *Dual Career Families Re-Examined*, London, Martin Robertson.

Reason, P. (ed.), (1994) *Participation in Human Inquiry*, London, Sage.

Reid, D. (1977) *Social Class Differences in Britain: A Source Book*, London, Open Books.

Reiss, A. (1964) 'The social integration of peers and queers', in H. Becker (ed.), *The Other Side: Perspectives on Deviance*, New York, Free Press: 181–210.

Rex, J. and Moore, M. (1967) *Race, Community and Conflict*, London, Oxford University Press.

Reynolds, D., Creemers, B., Nesselrodt, P., Schaffer, E., Stringfield, S. and Teddlie, C. (eds) (1994) *Advances in School Effectiveness Research and Practice*, Oxford, Elsevier Science.

Richards, L. and Richards, T. (1991) 'The transformation of qualitative method: computational paradigms and research processes', in N. Fielding and R. Lee (eds), *Using Computers in Qualitative Research*, London, Sage.

Riessman, C. (1993) *Narrative Analysis: Qualitative Research Methods Series 30*, London, Sage.

Roeslisberger, F. and Dickson, W. (1939) *Management and the Worker*, Cambridge, MA, Harvard University Press.

Rogers, A., Pilgrim, D. and Lacey, R. (1993) *Experiencing Psychiatry: Users' Views of Services*, Basingstoke, Mind/Macmillan.

Romm, N. (1997) 'Becoming more accountable: a comment on Hammersley and Gomm', *Sociological Research Online*, 2(3) http://www.socresonline.org.uk/socresonline/2/3/2.html.

Rose, D. (ed.) (1988) *Social Stratification and Economic Change*, London, Hutchinson.

Rose, G. (1982) *Deciphering Sociological Research*, Basingstoke, Macmillan.

Rose, G. (2001) *Visual Methodologies: An Introduction to the Interpretation of Visual Materials*, London, Sage.

Rose, G., McCartney, P. and Reid, D. (1977) 'Self-administration of a questionnaire on chest pain and intermittent claudication', *British Journal of Preventative Social Medicine*, 31: 42–8.

Rosenhan, D. (1973) 'On being sane in insane places', *Science*, 179: 250–8.

Rosenhan, D. (1996) 'On being sane in insane places', in T. Heller, J. Reynolds, R. Gomm, R. Muston and S. Pattison (eds), *Mental Health Matters: A Reader*, Basingstoke, Mind/Macmillan: 70–8.

Rosenthal, R. (1966) *Experimenter Effects in Behavioral Research*, New York, Appleton-Century-Croft.

Rosenthal, R. and Fode, L. (1963) 'The effects of experimenter bias on the performance of the albino rat', *Behavioural Science*, 8: 183–9.

Rosenthal, R. and Rosnow, R. (eds) (1969) *Artifact in Behavioral Research*, New York, Academic Press.

Rosenthal, R. and Rubin, D. (1978) 'Interpersonal expectancy effects: the first 345 studies', *The Behavioural and Brain Sciences*, 3: 377–413.

Roth, J. (1963) *Timetables*, Indianapolis, Bobbs-Merrill.

Roth, J. (1974) 'Turning adversity to account', *Urban Life and Culture*, 3(3): 347–59.

Rowbotham, S. (1973) *Woman's Consciousness, Man's World*, Harmondsworth, Penguin.

Rowntree, B. (1901) *Poverty: A Study of Town Life*, London, Macmillan.

Rutter, M. (1999) 'Natural experiments to study psychosocial risks', *Medical Research Council News*, 80: 24–7.

Sackett, D., Haynes, R., Guyatt, G. and Tugwell, P. (1991) *Clinical Epidemiology: A Basic Science for Clinical Medicine*, London, Little, Brown & Co.

Sacks, H. (1992a) *Lectures on Conversation*, ed. G. Jefferson, vol 1, Oxford, Blackwell.

Sacks, H. (1992b) *Lectures on Conversation*, ed. by G. Jefferson, vol 2, Oxford, Blackwell.

Sacks, H., Schegloff, H. E. and Jefferson, G. (1974) 'A simplest systematics for the organization of turn-taking in conversation', *Language*, 50(4): 696–735.

Sadler, R. (1981) 'Intuitive data processing as a potential source of bias in naturalistic observation, *Educational Evaluation and Policy Analysis*, July–August: 25–31.

Sapsford, R. (1999) *Survey Research*, London, Sage.

Scarth, J. and Hammersley, M. (1993) 'Questioning ORACLE: an assessment of ORACLE's analysis of teachers' questions', in R. Gomm and P. Woods (eds), *Educational Research in Action*, London, Paul Chapman: 184–98.

Schagan, I. (1993) 'Beyond league tables. How modern statistical methods can give a truer picture of the effects of schools', in R. Gomm and P. Woods (eds), *Educational Research in Action*, London, Paul Chapman: 109–17 (previously in *Educational Research*, 33(3), 1991: 216–28).

Schegloff, E. and Sacks, H. (1973) 'Opening up closings', in R. Turner (ed.), *Ethnomethodology*, Harmondsworth, Penguin: 233–64.

Schultz, K., Chalmers, I., Hayes, R. and Altman, D. (1995) 'Empirical evidence of bias: dimensions of methodic quality associated with estimates of treatment effects in controlled trials', *Journal of the American Medical Association*, 273: 408–12.

Schuman, J. (1999) 'The ethnic minority populations of Great Britain: latest estimates', *Population Trends*, 96: 33–42.

Schutz, A. (1964) *Studies in Social Theory: Collected Papers II*, ed. A. Brodersen, The Hague, Martinus Nijhoff: 91–105.

Scolari (2000) *Sphinx Survey*, London, Scolari/Sage.

Scully, D. (1990) *Understanding Sexual Violence*, London, HarperCollins.

Sharp, C., Hutchinson, D. and Whetton, C. (1994) 'Children's attainment at key stage 1', *Educational Research*, 36(2): 107–19.

Sharp, R. and Green, A. (1975) *Education and Social Control*, London, Routledge.

Shepherd, P. (1985) *The National Child Development Study: An Introduction to the Background to the Study and the Methods of Data Collection*, National Child Development User Support Group Working Paper, 1, London, Social Statistics Unit, City University.

Shipman, M. (1988) *The Limitations of Social Research*, 3rd edn, London, Longman.

Shields, J. (1965) *Monozygotic Twins Brought up Apart and Brought up Together*, London, Oxford University Press.

Shotter, J. (1990) 'The social construction of remembering and forgetting', in D. Middleton and D. Edwards (eds), *Collective Remembering*, London, Sage: 120–38.

Sikes, P. (2000) ' "Truth" and "Lies" Revisited', *British Educational Research Journal*, 26(2): 257–70.

Silverman, D. (1993) *Interpreting Qualitative Data: Methods for Analysing Talk, Text and Interaction*, London, Sage.

Silverman, D. (ed.) (1997) *Qualitative Research: Theory, Method and Practice*, London, Sage.

Sluga, H. (1993) *Heidegger's Crisis: Philosophy and Politics in Nazi Germany*, Cambridge, MA, Harvard University Press.

Smaje, C. (1995) *Health, 'Race' and Ethnicity: Making Sense of the Evidence*, London, Share/King's Fund Institute.

Smith, D. and Tomlinson, S. (1989) *The School Effect: A Study of Multi-Racial Comprehensives*, London, Policy Studies Institute.

Smith, G. and Cantley, C. (1984) 'Pluralistic evaluation', in J. Lishman (ed.), *Evaluation Highlights in Social Work Research*, 8, Aberdeen, University of Aberdeen: 140–162 (Jessica Kingsley edn: 118–36).

Smith, G. and Cantley, C. (1985) *Assessing Health Care: A Study in Organisational Evaluation*, Buckingham, Open University Press.

Smith, G., Cantley, C. and Ritman, V. (1983) 'Patient turn-over in a new psychogeriatric day hospital: pluralistic evaluation', *Aging and Society*, 13(3): 325–56.

Smith, T. (1999) *Ethics in Medical Research*, Cambridge, Cambridge University Press.

Snyder, C. and Higgins, R. (1990) 'Reality negotiation and excuse-making: President Reagan's 4 March 1987 Iran arms scandal speech and other literature', in M. Cody and M. McLaughlin (eds), *The Psychology of Tactical Communication*, Clevedon, PA, Multilingual Matters Ltd: 207–28.

Spender, D. (1980) *Man-Made Language*, London, Routledge & Kegan Paul.

Spender, D. (1982) *Invisible Women: The Schooling Scandal*, London, Writers and Readers Publishing Cooperative.

Sprumont, D. (1999) 'Legal protection of human research subjects in Europe', *European Journal of Health Law*, 6(1): 25–43.

Stacey, J. (1991) 'Can there be a feminist ethnography?', in S. Gluck and D. Patai (eds), *Women's Words: The Feminist Practice of Oral History*, London, Routledge: 111–20.

Stake, R. (1994) 'Case studies', in N. Denzin and Y. Lincoln (eds), *Handbook of Qualitative Research*, Thousand Oaks, CA, Sage.

Stanley, L. (1992) *The Autobiographical I: The Theory and Practice of Feminist Auto/Biography*, Manchester, Manchester University Press.

Stanley, L. and Wise, S. (1983) *Breaking Out: Feminist Consciousness and Feminist Research*, London, Routledge & Kegan Paul.

Stanley, L. and Wise, S. (1993) *Breaking Out Again: Feminist Ontology and Epistemology*, London, Routledge.

Stanworth, M. (1983) *Gender and Schooling: A Study of Sexual Divisions in the Classroom'*, London, Hutchinson.

Stern, C. and Sherwood, E. (1966) *The Origin of Genetics: A Mendel Source Book*, San Francisco, W. H. Freeman.

Stimson, G. (1972) *The Drug Takers*, London, Tavistock.

Strauss, A. (1990) *Qualitative Analysis for Social Scientists*, Cambridge, Cambridge University Press.

Spector, M. and Kitsuse, J. (1987) *Constructing Social Problems*, New York, Aldine & Gruyter.

Strauss, A. and Corbin, J. (1998) *Basics of Qualitative Research: Techniques and Procedures for Developing Grounded Theory*, 2nd edn, London, Sage.

Stubbs, M. (1983) *Discourse Analysis: The Sociolinguistic Analysis of Natural Language*, Oxford, Blackwell.

Suchman, L. and Jordan, B. (1990) 'Interactional troubles in face-to-face survey interviews', *Journal of the American Statistical Association*, 85(409): 232–41.

Suls, J. and Rostow, R. (1988) 'Artifacts in psychological experiments', in J. Morowski (ed.), *The Rise of Experimentation in American Psychology*, London, Yale University Press: 163–87.

Swan, S., Shaw, G. and Schulman, J. (1992) 'Reporting and selection bias in case control studies of congenital malformations', *Epidemiology*, 3: 356–63.

Taris, T. (2000) *A Primer in Longitudinal Data Analysis*, London, Sage.

Taylor, H. (1980) *The IQ Game: A Methodological Inquiry into the Heredity–Environment Controversy*, Brighton, Harvester Press.

Taylor, S. (1982) *Durkheim and the Study of Suicide*, Basingstoke, Macmillan.

Teague, A. (1993) 'Ethnic groups: first results from the 1991 census', *Population Trends*, 72: 12–17.

Thines, G. (1987) 'Phenomenology', in R. Gregory (ed.), *The Oxford Companion to the Mind*, Oxford, Oxford University Press: 614–16.

Thomas, S. (1999) *Designing Surveys that Work*, London, Sage.

Thompson, L. (1961) *Towards a Science of Mankind*, New York, McGraw-Hill.

Titchen, A. and Binnie, A. (1994) 'Action research: a strategy for theory generation and testing', *International Journal of Nursing Studies*, 31(1): 1–12.

Titscher, S., Meyer, M., Wodak, R. and Vetter, E. (2000) *Methods of Text and Discourse Analysis*, London, Sage.

Townsend, P. (1962) *Last Refuge: A Survey of Residential Institutions and Homes for the Aged in England and Wales*, London, Routledge & Kegan Paul.

Troyna, B. (1991) 'Underachievers or underrated? The experience of pupils of South Asian origin in a secondary school', *British Educational Research Journal*, 17: 361–76.

Tudor Hart, J. (1993) 'Hypertension guidelines: other diseases complicate management', *British Medical Journal*, 306: 1337.

Tudor Smith, C., Nutbeam, D., Moore, L. and Catford, J. (1998) 'Effects of Heart-beat Wales programme over five years on behavioural risks for cardio-vascular disease: quasi-experimental comparison of results from Wales and a matched reference area', *British Medical Journal*, 316: 818–22.

Turner, B. (1994) 'Patterns of crisis behaviour: a qualitative inquiry', in A. Bryman and R. Burgess (eds), *Analyzing Qualitative Data*, London, Routledge: 173–94.

Tzamourani, P. (2000) 'An experiment with a promised contribution to charity as a respondent incentive on a face-to-face survey', *Survey Methods Newsletter*, 20(2): 13–15.

Tzamourani, P. and Lynn, P. (2000) 'Do respondent incentives affect data quality? Evidence from an experiment', *Survey Methods Newsletter*, 20(2): 3–7.

van Dijk, T. (1991) *Racism and the Press*, London, Routledge.

van Dijk, T. (1993) 'Principles of critical discourse analysis', *Discourse and Society*, 4(2): 249–83.

van Leeuwen, T. and Jewitt, C. (eds) (2000) *The Handbook of Visual Analysis*, London, Sage.

van Maanen, J. (1988) *Tales of the Field: On Writing Ethnography*, Chicago, University of Chicago Press.

Vass, A. (1986) *AIDS: A Plague in Us – A Social Perspective*, St Ives, Venus Academica.

Wadsworth, M. (1996a) 'The survey that shocked the nation', *Medical Research Council News*, Winter: 28–32.

Wadsworth, M. (1996b) *The Imprint of Time: Childhood History and Adult Life*, Oxford, Oxford University Press.

Walker, M. (1989) 'Moral understanding: an alternative "epistemology" for a feminist ethics', *Hypatica* 4(1): 15–28.

Wall, W. and Williams, H. (1970) *Longitudinal Studies and Social Science*, London, Social Science Research Council/Heinemann.

Wakeford, J. (1969) *The Cloistered Elite: A Sociological Analysis of English Public Boarding Schools*, London, Macmillan.

Warren, C. (1988) *Gender Issues in Field Research*, London, Sage.

Weber, M. (1949) *The Methodology of the Social Sciences*, New York, Free Press.

Wertsch, J. (1987) 'Collective memory: issues from a socio-historical perspective', *Quarterly Newsletter of the Laboratory of Comparative Human Cognition*, 9(1): 19–22.

West, D. and Farrington, D. (1973) *Who Becomes Delinquent*, London, Hutchinson.

Western, P. (1990) *Speaking of Equality: An Analysis of the Rhetorical Force of 'Equality' in Moral and Legal Discourse*, Princetown, Princetown University Press.

Westfall, R. (1973) 'Newton and the fudge factor', *Science*, 179: 751–8.

Whittaker, A., Gardner, S. and Kershaw, J. (1990) *Service Evaluation by People with Learning Difficulties*, London, King's Fund.

Whyte, W. F. (1981) *Street Corner Society: The Social Structure of an Italian Slum*, 3rd edn, Chicago, University of Chicago Press (1st edn 1935).

Wilkinson, S. (1999) 'How useful are focus groups in feminist research?', in Barbour, R. and Kitzinger, J. (eds), *Developing Focus Group Research: Politics, Theory and Practice*, London, Sage: 64–78.

Williams, A. (1995) 'Ethics and action research', *Nurse Researcher*, 2(3): 49–59.

Willis, P. (1977) *Learning to Labour: How Working Class Kids get Working Class Jobs*, Farnborough, Saxon House.

Wilson, P and Elliot, D. (1987) 'An evaluation of the postcode address files and its use within the OPCS', *Journal of the Royal Statistical Society*, Series A, 150(3): 230–40.

Wright, C. (1986) 'School processes: an ethnographic study', in J. Eggleston, D. Dunn and M. Anjali (eds), *Education for Some: The Educational and Vocational Experiences of 15–18 Year Old Members of Minority Ethnic Groups*, Stoke on Trent, Trentham Books: 127–80.

Wright, C. (1992) *Race Relations in the Primary School*, London, David Foulton.

Wodak, R. and Meyer, M. (eds) (2001) *Methods of Critical Discourse Analysis*, London, Sage.

Woolgar, S. (ed.) (1982) *Laboratory Studies*, Theme issue of *Social Studies in Science*, 11(3).

Yablonsky, L. (1967) *The Violent Gang*, Harmondsworth, Penguin.

Young, J. (1971) 'The role of the police as amplifiers of deviancy: negotiators of reality and translators of fantasy; some consequences of our present system of drug control as seen in Nottinghill', in S. Cohen (ed.), *Images of Deviance*, Harmondsworth, Penguin: 27–61.

Index

Note: where there are several entries the more important ones are **emboldened**.